FORTRAN

A STRUCTURED, DISCIPLINED STYLE

BASED ON 1977 AMERICAN NATIONAL STANDARD FORTRAN AND COMPATIBLE WITH
WATFOR, WATFIV, WATFIV-S, AND MNF FORTRAN COMPILERS

Gordon B. Davis
Thomas R. Hoffmann

University of Minnesota

McGraw-Hill Book Company

New York St. Louis San Francisco Auckland Bogotá Düsseldorf
Johannesburg London Madrid Mexico Montreal New Delhi
Panama Paris São Paulo Singapore Sydney Tokyo Toronto

FORTRAN: A STRUCTURED, DISCIPLINED STYLE
Based on 1977 American National Standard FORTRAN
and Compatible with WATFOR, WATFIV, WATFIV-S,
and MNF FORTRAN Compilers

567890 EBEB 783210

This book was set in Times Roman by Cobb/Dunlop Publisher Services
Incorporated. The editor was Charles E. Stewart; the cover was
designed by Scott Chelius; the production supervisor
was Milton J. Heiberg.
Edwards Brothers Incorporated was printer and binder.

Library of Congress Cataloging in Publication Data

Davis, Gordon Bitter.
    FORTRAN.

    Includes index.
    1. FORTRAN (Computer program language) I. Hoffmann,
Thomas Russell, date   joint author. II. Title.
QA76.73.F25D385   001.6'424   77-28603
ISBN 0-07-015901-7

CONTENTS

PREFACE

Why another FORTRAN book? This text was written for three reasons:

1 The 1977 changes in the American National Standard FORTRAN made existing FORTRAN texts obsolete.

2 Recent developments in programming style and programming discipline made most existing FORTRAN texts inappropriate.

3 In the past, the teaching of FORTRAN has generally emphasized individual statements; we feel a better method is to teach students to write complete programs in a disciplined, clear style.

The text has been class-tested with students having a variety of backgrounds—undergraduate, graduate, and nondegree students. The response from this diverse group of students to the approach and content of the text has been very encouraging.

The text adheres to the 1977 American National Standard (ANS) FORTRAN. Most of the newer FORTRAN compilers will meet this standard, but many small computers will implement only a simplified version of the 1977 Standard FORTRAN called Subset FORTRAN. The full 1977 FORTRAN is presented in the text, but features not included in the 1977 Subset FORTRAN are noted in the chapters and summarized in Appendix C.

During the period from 1966 when FORTRAN was first standardized and 1977 when the revised FORTRAN standard was adopted, there were important changes in FORTRAN compilers for student use. The most significant development was a student-oriented FORTRAN in three versions called WATFOR, WATFIV, and WATFIV-S. Intended primarily for use on IBM computers, these versions added a number of useful features to FORTRAN that were not part of the 1966 standard. MNF was a similar student-oriented FORTRAN for users of large-scale Control Data computers. The revised 1977 FORTRAN standard incorporates almost all of the WATFOR, WATFIV, and MNF innovations. The 1977 FORTRAN also adds other features not included in the 1966 standard, but makes almost no changes in the 1966 features. In other words, programs written in 1966 FORTRAN will generally work under the new standard.

Although this text is based on the 1977 American National Standard FORTRAN, users of older versions of FORTRAN may employ the text very effectively keeping in mind the fact that the text covers fundamental features of FORTRAN in Chapters 1–5, file processing in Chapter 6, and character manipulation and other features in Chapter 7. Since the major changes and additions to the language in the 1977 standard are in connection with file processing and character manipulation, most differences affecting the use of the new standard are found in the two advanced features chapters. In general, students may use older versions of FORTRAN with this text as follows:

WATFOR/WATFIV version   The material in Chapters 1 through 5 is compatible, with minor exceptions that are presented in Appendix C. Sequential file processing (Chapter 6) and most features of Chapter 7 (such as character processing) are also the same in WATFOR/WATFIV as the 1977 Standard FORTRAN.

WATFIV-S version   Of the six structured programming instructions introduced by WATFIV-S, only the block IF instruction is implemented by the 1977 Standard FORTRAN; otherwise, WATFIV-S has the same compatibility as WATFIV.

MNF version   All of the features presented in Chapters 1 through 5 are allowed by the latest version of MNF.

1966 Standard FORTRAN version   The major problem affecting the use of Chapters 1 and 2 is the lack of the list-directed (free format) input and output with the 1966 version. A FORMAT statement must be used. A short section at the end of Chapter 1 explains how to introduce the needed FORMAT statement without changing the flow of instruction. Other differences are explained in Appendix C.

Other versions of FORTRAN   The major compatibility question is the existence of list-directed input and output. Some versions have it; others do not. If not included, a FORMAT statement can be introduced with Chapter 1 as explained above.

Sequential file processing instructions in Chapter 6 do not represent significant changes over past standards; however, there are major changes for direct-access processing. The student who is doing file processing with direct-access files will therefore need to have the reference manual for the compiler being used. New character instructions in Chapter 7 may not be implemented, so this area again requires careful scrutiny of the reference manual for the FORTRAN implementation being used.

The text explanations generally refer to programs and data punched in cards (and Appendix A describes how to use a card punch), but there are, of course, significant numbers of students programming from terminals. Appendix B describes the procedures for programming of FORTRAN from a terminal.

The philosophy of the text is that students should, from the beginning, learn to write programs in a disciplined style using a well-developed program structure. Programming that is done in a structured, disciplined manner is more productive and results in programs that have fewer errors, are simpler to debug, and are more easily maintained (altered and updated) than programs written without this approach. This text does not simply teach the rules for FORTRAN; it teaches by explanation and by example how to apply the rules of the FORTRAN language to write clear, structured programs.

Many students are able to learn a programming language with little assistance; others require lectures to reinforce the langugage text. Recognizing the need for both instructional approaches, this text was written so that it may be used in a self-instructional mode without lectures. This also makes it suitable for in-company training. When the lecture method is preferred, the text is still well suited because the organization of each topic chapter into an A and B part facilitates lecture presentation. Part A presents language features. An instructor can amplify and illustrate these features in an accompanying lecture. Part B contains two sample programs and the programming exercises, one of which will normally be assigned. An instructor may wish to use the sample program as the subject of a lecture, adding comments on style and usage.

FORTRAN courses (and students taking courses) have differing learning objectives. These range from "getting a feel for this important language" to learning to be a good FORTRAN programmer. The text is suitable for a wide range of objectives by selective use of part or all of the material. An objective of introducing students to the elements of the FORTRAN language and the structure of FORTRAN programs can be achieved by Chapters 1–4 (and perhaps 5). Students needing to understand the entire range of capabilities for the language will also use Chapters 5, 6, and 7. The text may be used alone if the objective is only to learn FORTRAN; it may be used as the language text for a course that also introduces students to computer science or computer data processing. For the latter type of course, a compatible companion text to this FORTRAN is by Gordon Davis, *Computers and Information Processing,* McGraw-Hill, 1978.

A large number of students have provided feedback that has been incorporated in the text. Graduate teaching assistants have provided ideas and pointed out sections needing improvement. Timothy Hoffman reviewed the manuscript and validated the problems by writing solution programs. Alison Davis reviewed the manuscript. Janice DeGross did an outstanding job of typing the manuscript.

The features of this text that we feel are especially useful in teaching and learning FORTRAN are:

1 The division of each chapter into Part A, a language explanation, and Part B, complete programs and accompanying documentation to illustrate features in Part A.

2 An emphasis on programming style with an example of a recommended style being used throughout.

3 Reference material easily accessible—list of functions on inside front cover and list of features following the index.

4 A method for recording and easily referencing the specifications for the FORTRAN compiler being used (inside back cover).

5 The use of list-directed (free format) input and output for the first two chapters. This allows a student to write programs without learning the FORMAT statement.

6 Where alternative FORTRAN features exist, emphasis on the use of features that are less error-prone, such as apostrophe editing and logical IF.

7 A large number of problems suited to different disciplines. At the end of each chapter, there are 15 problems divided into five different categories. This allows the text to be used for students with different backgrounds and interests. Solutions have been written for all of the problems. These solutions are available in an Instructors Guide.

8 An explanation of keypunching in Appendix A and terminal entry in Appendix B.

We appreciate receiving suggestions for corrections or changes and ideas for additional exercises from readers. Comments may be sent to Gordon B. Davis or Thomas R. Hoffmann, Department of Management Sciences, College of Business Administration, University of Minnesota, Minneapolis, Minnesota 55455.

Gordon B. Davis
Thomas R. Hoffmann

CHAPTER

1A

PROGRAMMING DISCIPLINE, THE FORTRAN LANGUAGE, AND FORTRAN STATEMENTS TO WRITE A SIMPLE PROGRAM

This chapter introduces the concept of a programming language, and explains the value of programming discipline. The chapter describes the FORTRAN language, explains general procedures for preparing a FORTRAN program, and introduces five FORTRAN statements needed to code a simple FORTRAN program. Two complete FORTRAN programs are contained in Chapter 1B. Using these example programs as guides, you will be able to code, keypunch, and submit a simple FORTRAN program for processing. Chapter 1A thus provides concepts necessary for understanding the nature of FORTRAN programming and Chapter 1B provides an introductory experience in preparing a FORTRAN program. The program written as the assignment for Chapter 1B is also used to provide experience in following the procedures by which a FORTRAN program is submitted to the computer center and processed.

Instructing a Computer

Before starting the explanation of the FORTRAN language, it may be helpful to review how a computer is instructed. A computer system requires both hardware and software. The *hardware* consists of all of the equipment; the *software* includes the programs of instructions which direct the operations of the computer equipment.

Hardware and Software

A hardware computer system as shown in Figure 1-1 has input units (such as card reader), a central processing unit or CPU, and output units (such as printer). It also has external storage devices such as magnetic disks or magnetic-tape units (also called secondary or auxiliary storage). In a typical processing job, data comes from the input unit (and perhaps from external

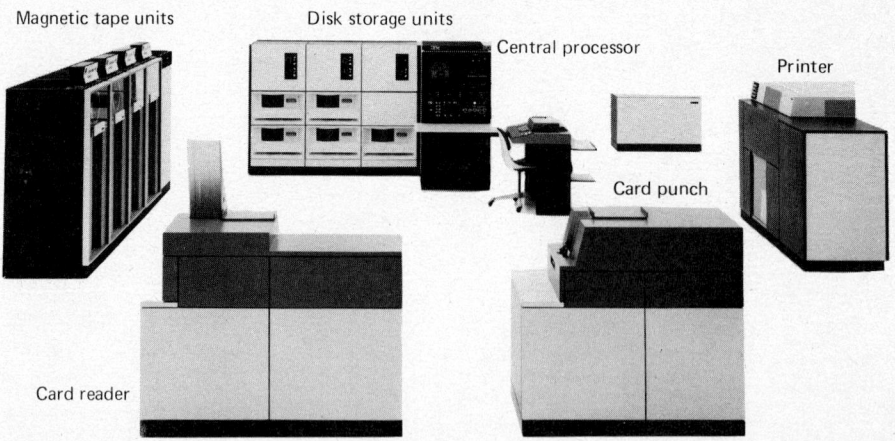

FIGURE 1-1   Hardware in a computer system. Illustrations from IBM System/370 equipment. (*Courtesy of International Business Machines Corporation.*)

storage) into the central processor where computation and other processing is performed. After processing, the results are sent to the output device (say a printer) or to a secondary storage device to be held for later output or further processing.

The hardware can perform operations such as read, write, add, etc., but the sequence in which these operations are to be performed and the specific input and output units to be used are specified by a set of instructions stored in the computer memory. The general term applied to these computer processing instructions is *software*. The instructions are organized into sets called routines and programs. A *routine* refers to a set of instructions which directs the performance of a specific task such as calculating the square root of a quantity or producing an error message when an error is encountered in input data. A *program* consists of one or more routines which direct the solution of a complete problem.

There are several major types of software. Three types especially relevant to the study of FORTRAN are application programs, compilers, and operating systems.

1 *Application programs* Programs which direct the processing for an application of computers such as calculating a rate of return for a proposed project, calculating stress factors for a building structure, etc. The FORTRAN examples in this text are application programs. Application programs may be written by personnel in organizations needing them, or they may be purchased from software vendors who prepare and sell programs for frequently encountered applications.

2 *Compilers* Programs which prepare machine-language instructions from instructions written in a high-level language such as FORTRAN.

3 *Operating system* A set of routines which directs and manages the operations of the computer. The operating system supports and directs the running of application programs. For example, if an application program has an instruction to read a card from the card reader but the card reader is not operable, the operating system sends a suitable message to the computer operator.

Operating systems and compilers are generally obtained from the hardware vendor, but independent software vendors are also a source. Programs which are being executed are stored in the internal (main or primary) storage or memory, which is part of the central processing unit (CPU). Programs not currently being executed but which need to be available are stored in external storage. Some parts of the operating system remain in main storage all of the time. Based on job control instructions to be described later, these operating system routines bring into internal memory the routines and programs to be executed and direct their execution. The programs to be run may be compilers, application programs, or other software.

Machine-level Languages

A program in main memory must be in machine language to be executed. A machine language instruction is represented as a string of binary digits called bits (represented by 1s and 0s) which identify the operations to be performed and the data, etc., to be used. For example, a typical addition instruction for the IBM System/370 has the following form (with 1 standing for a 1-bit and 0 for a 0-bit in storage):

0 1 0 1 1 0 1 0 0 0 1 1 0 0 0 0 1 0 1 1 1 0 1 0 0 1 0 0 0 0 0 0

Even though the internal machine representation is in this form, it would be very difficult and could lead to error if a programmer were required to deal with such instructions. In cases when machine instructions are printed for operator or programmer use, a condensed notation is employed. For example, the preceding instruction would be printed out for operator/programmer inspection as: 5A30BA40

Although more usable than the machine representation, this condensed notation is still difficult to use. Therefore, if a program is to be written in machine-level instructions, the programmer generally uses a symbolic assembly language. Symbolic assembly languages as a class are often referred to as low-level languages. These languages are machine-oriented because each symbolic assembly instruction is converted into one machine-language instruction. The preceding machine-language instruction coded in symbolic assembly language might be: A   3,PAY where, for example, A means "add." The computer cannot directly execute the symbolic instructions, so these must be translated into machine-language instructions. This is done by a program called a *symbolic assembly system* which converts each symbolic instruction into an equivalent machine-level code instruction. Machine-oriented programming is very useful for some applications because instruction coding can be very machine-sensitive and thus obtain very efficient use of the computer. However, an assembly language program is relatively difficult to code, and logic errors are difficult to find. It is also difficult and time-consuming to change. A program in a low-level, machine-oriented language also has limited transferability (portability) from one computer to another.

High-level Languages

A high-level language is oriented to problem solution or processing procedures rather than to the machine-level instructions of a particular computer. The instruction statements use words, phrases and symbols that are similar to those commonly used to describe solution or processing procedures. Another major difference between a high-level instruction and a symbolic assembly instruction is that one high-level instruction is translated into many machine-language instructions.

There are a number of different high-level languages for different types of problems. Each of these languages consists of a grammar (set of rules) and predefined words for writing instructions. A compiler is used to translate the program written in the high-level language (the source program) into machine-level instructions (the object program) for the computer on which the program is to be run. The compiler is a computer program, and therefore there must be a unique compiler for each computer for which a high-level language program is to be translated.

There are two important advantages of high-level languages over symbolic assembly languages: They are machine-independent in the sense that programs written in a high-level language can be compiled and run on any computer (for which there is a compiler) with few or no changes, and they are relatively easy to learn. Today, these languages are generally so powerful and efficient that they have virtually eliminated the need for symbolic assembly language coding except for a few specialized applications. It is also relatively easy to standardize methods of programming with high-level languages. Organizations having a concern with program accuracy and a desire for programming discipline have strongly influenced the trend toward use of high-level languages.

The two most common high-level languages are FORTRAN and COBOL. FORTRAN is best suited for formula-type mathematical problems while COBOL is the dominant language in business data processing.

The FORTRAN Language

FORTRAN (an acronym for FORmula TRANslator) is the most widely used of a class of high-level languages called scientific or algebraic language and is available for use on almost all computers. Although not limited to mathematical problems, it is especially useful for problems which can be stated in terms of formulas or arithmetic procedures. This covers a wide range of problems. For example, FORTRAN is suitable for such diverse problems as analysis of sales statistics in a business and analysis of structural stress for designing a building.

Development of FORTRAN

FORTRAN was developed in 1957 by IBM in conjunction with some major users, but it is now used by all computer vendors. FORTRAN has changed and evolved. This evolutionary process resulted, during the development period, in several FORTRANs of increasing complexity. Major versions were called FORTRAN, FORTRAN II, and FORTRAN IV. Each new version made a few changes in the basic instructions and included additional features. In 1966, a voluntary FORTRAN standard, American National Standard (ANS) FORTRAN, was adopted. The International Standards Organization (ISO) also defined standard FORTRAN.

A revised American National Standard (ANS) FORTRAN was adopted in 1977. This 1977 standard adds features to the previous 1966 standard FORTRAN, clarifies some ambiguities, and makes a few minor changes. The new standard also defines two different levels for FORTRAN implementation: Subset FORTRAN and full FORTRAN. Subset FORTRAN is a compatible subset of the higher-level full FORTRAN. This text is based on the 1977 standard, although differences between the 1977 standard and the 1966 standard will be noted because many compilers may not accept the added 1977 features. The text concentrates on the most-used features of FORTRAN; some advanced or little-used features will be summarized in less detail in Chapter 7.

Concurrent with the development of standard FORTRAN has been the development of special teaching-oriented FORTRAN compilers. The best known of these, developed at the University of Waterloo (Waterloo, Ontario), are termed WATFOR and WATFIV. A similar compiler for large Control Data computers is MNF. WATFIV-S is a version of WATFIV containing six special structured programming instructions (see Appendix C). These compilers were designed to provide excellent error-diagnostic messages for students, do fast execution of small student programs, and relax some error-prone features of FORTRAN. The new 1977 FORTRAN standard adopted the most significant features of WATFOR, WATFIV, and MNF, so the American National Standard FORTRAN is recommended as the basis for all FORTRAN programming, by students as well as professional programmers.

How to Study FORTRAN Using This Text

FORTRAN is a machine-independent language for instructing a computer. In other words, the programmer writing FORTRAN does not need to know the details of how the computer operates. The language is procedure-oriented—designed for instructing the computer in a problem-solving procedure. The language consists of a vocabulary of symbols and words and a grammar of rules for writing procedural instructions. The symbols, words, and rules utilize many common mathematical and English-language conventions so that the language is fairly easy to learn and to understand. The rules are, however, precise and must be followed with care. In other words, learning FORTRAN is like learning a special-purpose language. There are rules of construction and vocabulary to learn, and one becomes proficient by doing rather than by much reading.

The objective of the text is to assist you in learning to write clear, understandable, error-free FORTRAN programs. To achieve this objective you need to do each of the following:

1 Learn the instructions and other elements of the language.

2 Learn how to apply the language rules and to use the FORTRAN instructions to compose a clear, understandable program.

3 Learn how to submit a program to be compiled and executed (using the computer that is available to you).

The first objective is met by part A of each chapter. There is a description of instructions or rules and illustrations of their use are provided. To assist in learning, there are self-testing exercises after every major unit in each chapter. At each self-testing exercise, answer the questions and check your responses against the answers at the end of the chapter.

The second objective is achieved by part B of each chapter, which contains complete programs with documentation. You should study the example programs, noting the style, the error-control features included in the program, and the documentation supporting the programs. These examples of good programming style provide a pattern to follow in writing your programs.

The third objective requires the programming of a problem, carrying out the procedures to keypunch the program (or enter it at a terminal), submitting the program to be run, and removing errors. A variety of different programming problems are provided with each chapter. In carrying out the writing, coding, running, etc., of a program, the text provides the following aids:

1 A reference list of all FORTRAN language features (List of 1977 American National Standard FORTRAN Statements and Specifications, follows index).

2 A reference list of specifications and features you need to know about the computer you will use. On the inside of the back cover, the features on the checklist and specifications list related to a chapter should be filled in from material furnished to you by the instructor or obtained by consulting the FORTRAN reference manual for your computer.

3 A reference list of all FORTRAN intrinsic functions on the inside of the front cover (front endpaper). Check off those functions that are available to you (you can wait to do this until after completing Chapter 2).

4 An appendix (Appendix A) describing how to use the keypunch to punch instructions and data. Also, Appendix B describes procedures for programming in FORTRAN from a terminal.

The text is based on the latest 1977 American National Standard FORTRAN, but because the fundamental features of all versions of FORTRAN are the same or nearly the same, it is possible to use this text with FORTRAN versions that are based on the older 1966 standard and on WATFOR, WATFIV, WATFIV-S and MNF implementations of FORTRAN. Appendix C assists in understanding differences in these versions of FORTRAN. Before proceeding, scan the front and back endpapers, the three appendices, and the List of 1977 ANS FORTRAN Statements and Specifications (follows index).

A Structured, Disciplined Style in FORTRAN Programming

Mention has been made of a structured, disciplined style in writing FORTRAN programs. Since the text follows this approach, it will be useful to understand the reasons for the approach and the basic methods to implement it.

Computer programs frequently do not meet user requirements, are not produced on time, cost considerably more than estimated, contain errors, and are difficult to maintain (to correct or change to meet new requirements). These difficulties have been observed with such frequency that many organizations have attempted to change the practice of programming in order to improve performance. The revised approach can be termed *programming discipline—* well-defined practices, procedures, and development control processes. A student should not merely learn to code FORTRAN statements. It is equally important to learn how these statements are combined into a high-quality program—one which is easy to understand and change if necessary and which uses computer resources efficiently.

Objectives of a Disciplined Approach to Programming

Because programming discipline is an underlying philosophy for this text and because of the importance of programming discipline to industry, it will be useful to summarize the major objectives of this approach to programming:

1 *Meet user needs* A program has a purpose, such as to produce an analysis or to compute a set of statistics. An assignment to prepare a program is a failure if the program is not used because the potential users of the application find it too complex or too difficult. A disciplined approach to program design includes a careful analysis of user requirements before programming.

2 *Development on-time within budget*   Estimates of time and cost for writing computer programs have frequently been substantially in error. By using a more structured, disciplined approach, installations have achieved dramatic improvements in productivity and have improved their ability to estimate time to complete.

3 *Error-free set of instructions*   It is generally considered that all large-scale computer programs contain errors, and it may be impossible to remove every single error from a large set of programs. However, using a disciplined, structured approach, programs may be designed and developed in a manner which minimizes the likelihood of errors and which facilitates detection and correction of errors in testing. The result is virtually error-free programming.

4 *Error-resistant operation*   A program may produce erroneous results, due either to program errors or to incorrect input. The program should be designed so that errors will, whenever possible, be detected by the program itself during execution. The design features to assist in detecting errors are:
(*a*)   Input validation
(*b*)   Tests of correctness during processing
Input validation is a process of testing all input data items to determine whether or not they meet the criteria set for them. For example, data input may be tested for:

Existence of necessary input data items

Data item values within acceptable range

Illogical relationships among input items

Incorrect class of data (e.g., alphabetic characters in a data item which should be numeric)

Tests of correctness during processing generally take the form of tests for reasonableness of results and checks of logical relationships among different results.

5 *Maintainable programs*   Computer programs change, especially when first placed into use. Programs should be written with the maintenance activity in mind. The program documentation and the style in which a program is written should allow another programmer to understand the logic of the program and to make a change in one part of the program without unknowingly introducing an error in another part of the same program.

6 *Portable programs*   A tested program, written in FORTRAN, should be transferable without substantial change to another computer having a FORTRAN compiler. This means that programming which takes advantage of FORTRAN features unique to one computer or compiler should be avoided, as should all nonstandard FORTRAN instructions. Straightforward, well-documented instructions which follow a disciplined, structured approach are portable with little difficulty; programs with intricate or poorly documented logic are not.

Modular Design of Programs

One of the key concepts in the application of programming discipline is the design of a program as a set of units referred to as *blocks* or *modules*. A program module is defined as the part of a program which performs a separate function such as input, input validation, processing one type of input, etc. A program module may be quite large (in terms of logic and instructions required), so that it may be further divided into logical submodules. The process of subdivision continues until all modules are of manageable size in terms of complexity of logic and numbers of instructions. In practice, a FORTRAN module that is more than 60 statements (takes more than one page to list) is too large.

Although computer programs differ greatly in purpose and processing, it is possible to identify types of functions which are commonly needed in programs. Programs can be logically separated into functional modules.

Functional module	Description
Initialization	Establishes initial values for some variables, prints headings, messages, etc. may not be necessary
Input	Performs input of data required by the program
Input data validation	Performs validation of input data to detect errors or omissions
Processing	Performs computation or data manipulation
Output	Performs output of data to be provided by the program
Error handling	Performs analysis of error condition and outputs error messages. For small programs, error handling may be included in other modules
Closing procedure	Performs procedures to end the execution of the program

The processing proceeds logically with input, input validation, various processing modules, and output. Error handling may be required during execution of any of the modules and may be incorporated in these modules. At the conclusion of processing, the closing procedures to complete the program are performed. Although all of the functions are normally found in well-written programs, they are not always defined as separate program modules; they may be combined or rearranged to suit the flow of a particular program.

Structured Programming

One method of achieving the objective of accurate, error-resistant, maintainable programs is to code (write the program) in a simple, easily understood format.

All computer programs can be coded by using only three logic structures (patterns) or combinations of these structures:

1 Simple sequence

2 Selection

3 Repetition

The three structures are useful in a disciplined approach to programming because:

1 The program is simplified. Only the three building blocks are used. There is a single point of entry into the structure as well as a single point of exit.

2 The three coding structures allow a program to be read from top to bottom, making the logic of the program more visible for checking and for maintenance.

The simple sequence structure consists of one action followed by another. In other words, the flow of control is to first perform operation A (Figure 1-2) then perform operation B.

The selection structure consists of a test for a condition followed by two alternative paths for the program to follow. The program selects one of the program-control paths depending on the test of the condition. After performing one of the two paths, the program control returns to a single point. This pattern can be termed IF . . . ELSE because the logic can be stated (for condition P and operations C and D): IF P (is true) perform C ELSE (otherwise) perform D (Figure 1-2).

The repetition structure can also be called a *loop*. In a loop, an operation (or set of operations) is repeated while some condition is satisfied. The basic form of repetition is termed DO WHILE (Figure 1-3) in the literature of structured programming. Using FORTRAN terminology to be explained in Chapter 4, it might be termed a DO loop. In the DO WHILE pattern, the program logic

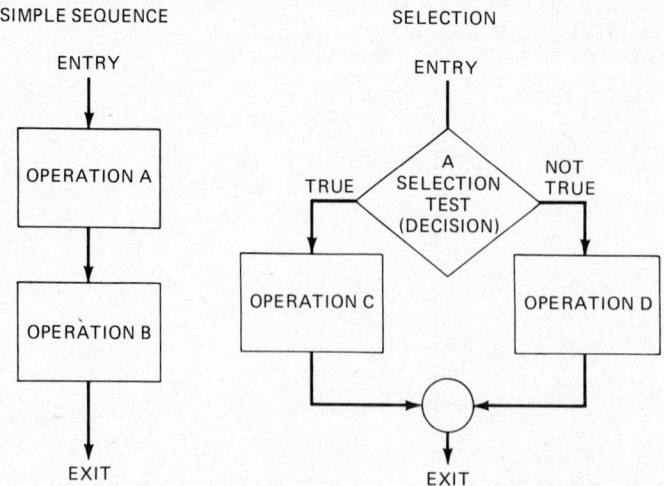

FIGURE 1-2   Simple sequence and selection program structures.

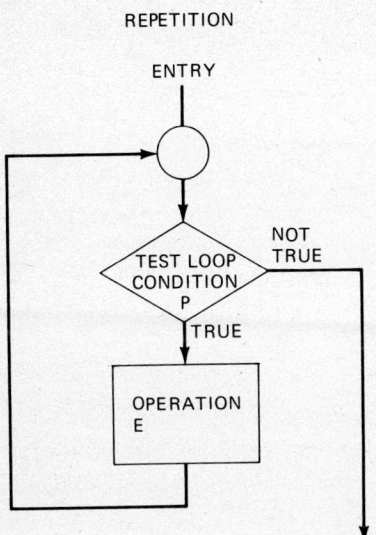

REPETITION

FIGURE 1-3   The DO WHILE repetition structure.

tests a condition governing the continued operation of the loop; if it is true, the program executes the operation (called E in Figure 1-3) and loops back for another test. If the condition is not true, the repetition ceases. In other words, DO the loop repetition WHILE (as long as) the loop repetition condition is true.

One of the objectives in using the three basic structures is to make programs more understandable to those concerned with design, review, and maintenance. It is possible to combine the three simple structures to produce more

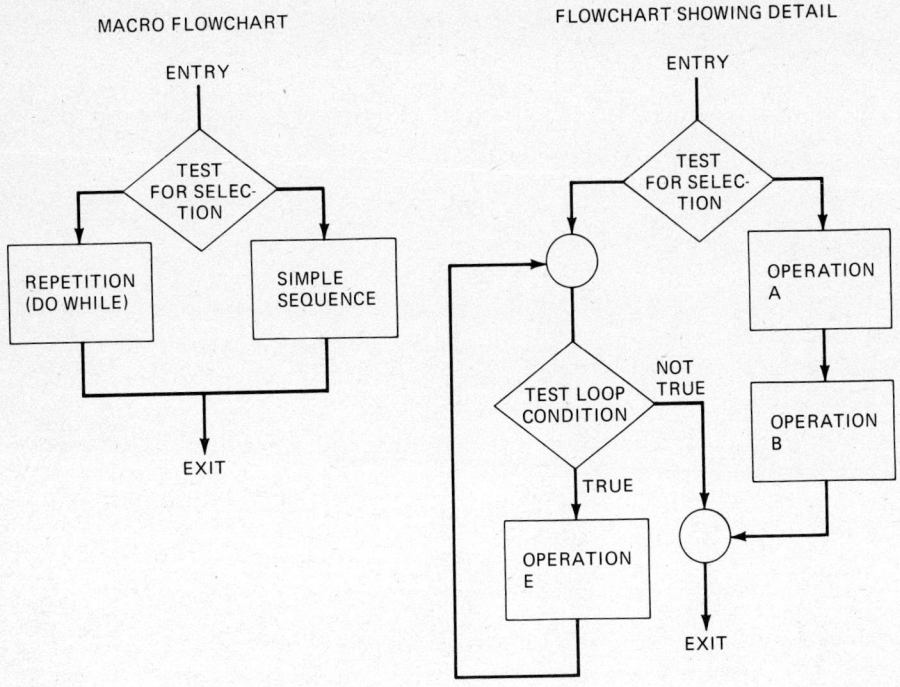

FIGURE 1-4   Nesting of coding structures.

complex coding while maintaining the simplicity inherent in the three patterns. For example, the logic of the program may involve a selection between two program paths. If one path is chosen, there should be a repetition loop; if the other is selected, there is a simple sequence. The combination of the structures is illustrated in Figure 1-4. Note that there is still a single entry/single exit for the entire structure.

The FORTRAN language was not designed for structured programming, but it is possible to follow the ideas reasonably well. Rules for doing this will be explained in the text as they become relevant.

Planning a FORTRAN Program

A FORTRAN program needs to be planned before it is coded. Some tools and techniques for planning the program are pseudocodes, flowcharts, and layouts. Pseudocode and flowcharts are explained in this chapter; layouts are explained in Chapter 3.

Prior to planning the program, there will have been problem recognition and definition of what the program is to accomplish. This problem definition is followed by the selection of a solution procedure (algorithm) and definition of the data to be used. The overall structure of the program is established by defining the major modules in the program. The logic of the program can then be defined by pseudocode and/or program flowcharts.

Pseudocode in Program Planning

The pseudocode approach consists of a series of abbreviated statements which specify the procedures the program is to perform. The statements are independent of the FORTRAN language but tend to recognize the features of the language. For example, a program to read input data from punched cards, compute the sum of the two input values, and print the input values plus their sum might read as follows:

READ values for x and y from card

Compute sum $= x + y$

PRINT x, y, and sum

STOP

In this simple case, each line of pseudocode results in one line of FORTRAN, but in other cases, a single line of pseudocode may require many lines of FORTRAN. Pseudocode tends to be quite useful in planning the general flow of a program.

There are no standard rules of pseudocode; the main objective is an understandable description of the program logic. A useful approach to pseudocode will be illustrated in the descriptions of sample programs in part B of each chapter.

Program Flowchart in Program Planning and Documentation

FORTRAN is well suited to the use of flowcharts in planning and documenting programs because the language is oriented toward procedural logic. Some programmers find flowcharts very useful; others do not use them. We find flowcharts are less useful than pseudocode for planning the general flow of a program but are more useful in planning and documenting detailed logic. In any case, flowcharts are found frequently enough that a FORTRAN programmer should be familiar with them. Therefore, we recommend their use in the problems in this text.

Flowcharts are a means of symbolically depicting the (1) logic and procedures of programs and (2) the elements and flows of systems. The American National Standards Institute has defined standard flowcharting symbols and their use in data processing.[1] The following are the most common symbols used in flowcharting FORTRAN programs:

FORTRAN PROGRAMS

Symbol	Represents
INPUT/ OUTPUT	The input or output of data to or from the computer. The input or output medium is unspecified
DOCUMENT	Input or output using a document such as a printed output
PUNCHED CARD	Input or output using punched cards
PROCESS	Any manipulation or processing of data within the computer
PROCESS USING SUBPROGRAM	Perform processing using a separate subprogram unit
TERMINAL	The beginning or end of a program module
DECISION	The taking of alternative actions based upon presence or absence of some condition. Often called a decision symbol
ANNOTATION	Annotation. Used for added comments. Connected to flowchart where helpful to provide additional information
◯	Connector. Used to connect flowlines and to identify flowlines going to or coming from another place on the same page or another page.

Additional, supplementary symbols not included here may also be used.

[1] American National Standards Institute, X3.5-1970, ''Flowchart Symbols and Their Usage in Information Processing.''

The symbols are connected with flowlines in order to indicate the direction or sequence of processing. Flowcharts are written to be read from top to bottom and from left to right. If the flow is right to left or bottom to top, arrowheads must be used on the flowlines to indicate direction of flow. Otherwise arrowheads are optional but recommended. The flowchart symbols were used in Figures 1-2, 1-3, and 1-4 to describe basic program structures. Review these figures as examples of how the symbols are put together. The design of flowcharts for FORTRAN programs will be explained in the text by example and by explanations associated with programming exercises.

Self-testing Exercise 1-1

There will be frequent self-testing exercises to help you test your comprehension of the material just explained. The answers are at the end of the chapter.

1 Distinguish between hardware and software.
2 What is the difference between machine language and symbolic assembly language?
3 What are the advantages of high-level languages over symbolic assembly languages?
4 FORTRAN stands for _____ .
5 What has been the role of the American National Standards Institute (ANSI) in the development of FORTRAN?
6 Name six objectives of a disciplined approach to program design.
7 Name the functional modules in a program.
8 Name and describe the three basic program structures.
9 Match the flowchart symbol with its definition.

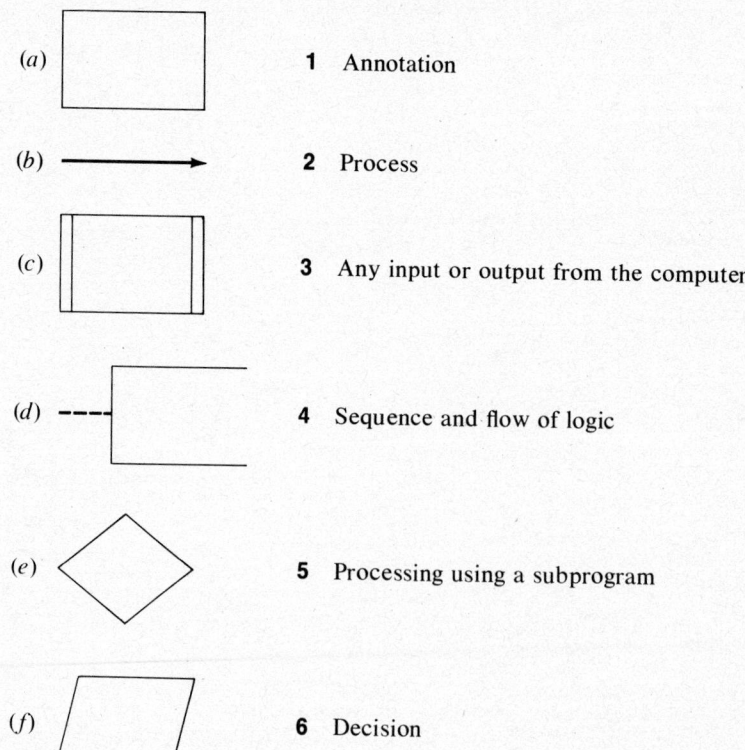

(a)   1 Annotation

(b)   2 Process

(c)   3 Any input or output from the computer

(d)   4 Sequence and flow of logic

(e)   5 Processing using a subprogram

(f)   6 Decision

10 If a program is transferable to another computer having a compiler for that language, without substantial change, the program is _____ .

11 The most common tools for planning the logic for a FORTRAN program are _____ and/or _____ .

Coding a FORTRAN Program

When the program flowchart and/or pseudocode statements have been prepared, the next step is to code the FORTRAN statements, using FORTRAN coding paper. The coding form defines 80 columns for writing program statements (Figure 1-5). The coding form is designed especially for programs to be punched into cards. Other conventions may apply to statements entered via a terminal. The columns on the coding sheet are used as follows:

Column	How used
1	Comments and special options. An asterisk (*) or the letter C in column 1 (or C only in older versions) indicates that what follows on the line is not translated by the FORTRAN compiler. The line is printed as part of the program listing and is therefore used for explanatory comments in the program listing
1–5	Statement reference number. Can be written anywhere in the five columns (spaces are ignored), but it is usually right-justified (extra spaces to left). In other words, reference number 349 is usually written as bb349 instead of 349bb (where b stands for a blank)
6	If a FORTRAN statement is too long for one line, it may be continued on succeeding lines by putting a nonzero character (say 1, 2, etc.) in column 6 of each continuation line. The initial line which is to be continued may have a blank or a 0 in column 6. Clarity of coding is enhanced if the FORTRAN statements on the continuation lines are indented to, for example, column 11
7–72	FORTRAN statement. The statement can begin anywhere from 7 to 72. Indentation and spacing may be used to improve readability
73–80	When the statements of a program are punched into cards, each statement will be punched onto one 80-column card utilizing only columns 1 to 72. The last eight columns of the program statement cards either are not used or are used for identification. They are not translated. (Note, however, that all 80 columns of a data card can be used for data.)

In coding FORTRAN statements, certain conventions will reduce the possibility of error when the lines of coding are punched into cards or entered at a terminal:

1 Use the FORTRAN coding paper. Each space on the coding form corresponds to a column on a punched card, so that one character is written in each space. This reduces errors in keypunching.

2 Code only in printed capital letters because the printed capitals are easier to read.

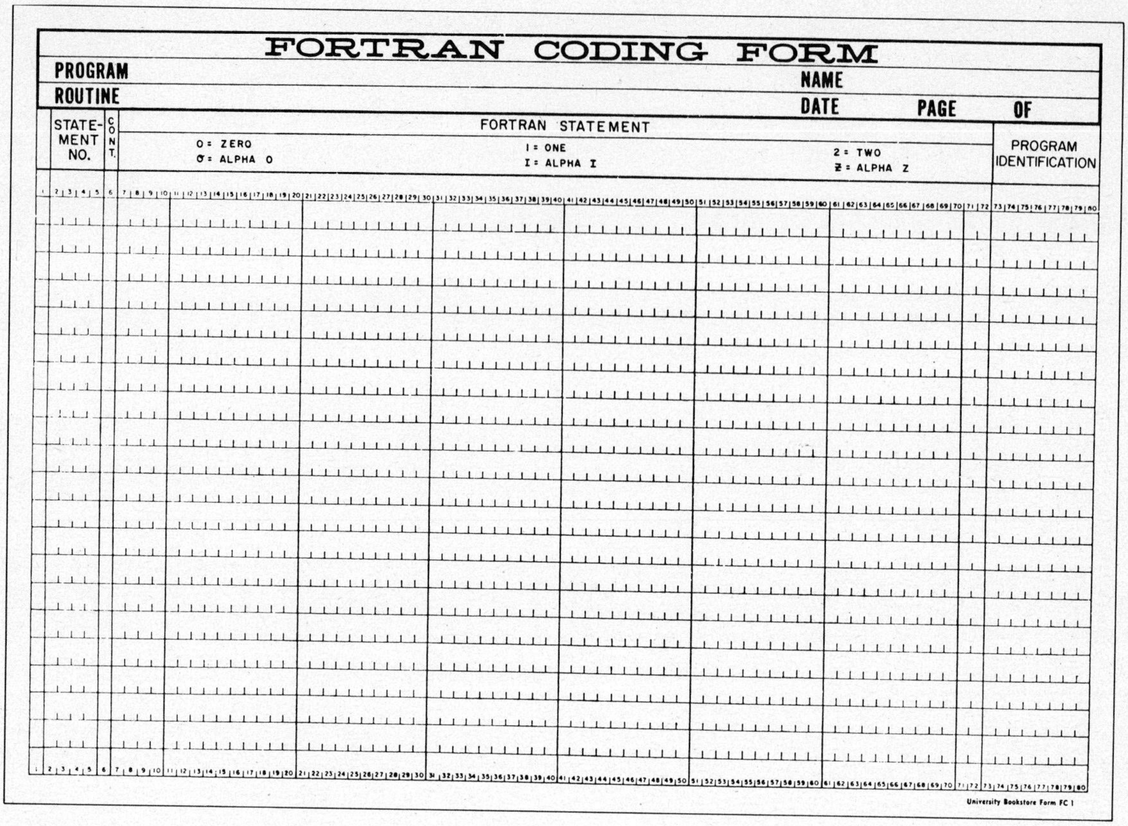

FIGURE 1-5 FORTRAN coding form.

3 Clearly differentiate between numbers and letters which are similar. The letter O and the zero are the biggest problems, but S and 5, Z and 2, and I and 1 are often confused. Various methods are used for differentiating, such as underlining or slashing either the letter or the number. It is very common for FORTRAN programmers to slash the alphabetic O. The American National Standard coding convention (shown below) is to put a line through the letter Z and to add a loop to O, leaving the related numbers as they are usually written.

Letter	Number
O̶	0
Z̶	2
I	1
S	5

4 FORTRAN statements may be punched on any standard card punch (see Appendix A).

FORTRAN is available on most time-sharing services in which the user enters a program from a terminal. However, the most common practice is to punch the program into cards, and this procedure is assumed in the text explanations. Appendix B contains a description of terminal entry and time-shared running of FORTRAN programs.

Five FORTRAN Statements for Writing a Simple Program

In order to get started, five FORTRAN statements will be explained. These are sufficient to write a simple but complete FORTRAN program.

1 List-directed input (free format READ)

2 List-directed output (PRINT in preset format)

3 Arithmetic assignment statement

4 STOP

5 END

In using these instructions, it will be necessary to refer to data items. Data items can be constants, which have the same value throughout the program, or variables, which can assume different values. Therefore, before explaining the five statements, the FORTRAN rules for writing and referencing data items will be discussed.

Variables and Constants

Constants and variables are used in FORTRAN in the same sense as in mathematical notation. A quantity which is not known or which can vary in different problems is a *variable* and is assigned a variable name. The name refers to a computer storage location where the data is stored. This name may be a single symbol, such as A, X, or Y, or it may be a descriptive name, such as ALPHA, BETA, or RATE. If, however, the quantity in the mathematical expression is constant and does not change, then the number itself may be written. In FORTRAN, a number written in an arithmetic expression is called a *constant*. Thus, if a variable is used in formulating a problem-solving procedure, a variable name is used in FORTRAN; if a constant is used in the solution procedure, a constant is written in the corresponding FORTRAN statement. At this point, there is a direct correspondence between the symbol used in the formula to denote a variable and the variable name in FORTRAN and also between the constant used in the formula and the constant in FORTRAN. In certain instances in FORTRAN, it is necessary to be more precise than the mathematical notation. In hand computation, many things are understood and do not need to be expressed, but a computer program proceeds *exactly* as instructed without judgment about whether the computation is meaningful. For example, in many computations, it is understood that certain values can only be integers while other values can be numbers with fractional parts. These are referred to as integer and real numbers. In FORTRAN, there are two different types of variables and constants to distinguish between integer data and real data. These allow the FORTRAN program to be precise as to type of data. The integer and real types of data are the most used in FORTRAN, but there are other types to be explained in Chapter 7.

An *integer quantity* (sometimes called a *fixed point quantity*) is one which has no fractional parts. It contains only whole numbers. The numbers 3, 19, and 475 are integer quantities. Integer variables and integer constants are especially useful in certain cases where the quantity cannot assume a fractional value. For example, a set of statements can be executed only an integer number of times; in a list of numbers, the position in the list must be a whole number. The use of a number with a fractional part would not make sense in cases such as these.

Most computations can result in an answer having a fractional part. *Real quantities* can have, but do not require, a nonzero fractional part. The numbers 7.1, 3.1417, 99.01, 0.32, and 81.0 are real quantities (also called *floating point quantities*). In order to clearly identify the decimal point location, it is good programming practice to write a zero following the point for real quantities without a fractional part (4.0 instead of 4.) and a zero in front of the decimal point for numbers less than 1 (0.2 instead of .2). It is also good practice to code zero as 0.0 instead of 0 alone in order to reduce keying errors.

FORTRAN has specific rules for differentiating between names for real variables and names for integer variables and between real constants and integer constants.

RULES FOR SYMBOLIC VARIABLE NAMES

Purpose of variable name
To associate a symbolic name with a value which is not known or can vary

Rules for forming
1 First character must be alphabetic

2 No special characters are allowed (i.e., the names can contain only letters and numbers, not &, $, #, etc.). Blank spaces in a name are ignored

3 The total number of characters must not exceed 6

Integer variable names
Starts with one of the letters I, J, K, L, M, or N. (*HINT:* The first two letters in the word INTEGER are the bounds for the integer variable names which are from I through N.)

Real variable names
Starts with one of the letters other than I, J, K, L, M, or N. In other words, names starting with A through H and O through Z are real variable names

EXAMPLES

Variable name	Valid or not valid	If valid, integer or real	If not valid, why
X	Valid	Real	
X123	Valid	Real	
XY	Valid	Real	
ALPHA	Valid	Real	
BETA-3	Not valid		(-) is special character
$134	Not valid		$ is special character
X19.1	Not valid		(.) is special character
NUTS	Valid	Integer	
MOTHERS	Not valid		Too many characters
MOM	Valid	Integer	
RATE	Valid	Real	
1455A	Not valid		Does not start with alphabetic character
PAY DAY	Valid	(equivalent to PAYDAY since blanks are ignored)	

Before describing the rules for writing constants, the use of exponent notation in FORTRAN will be explained. The use of exponent notation is common in mathematics. For example, 315 billion (315,000,000,000) can be written as 315×10^9. The exponent notation is used whenever very large or very small numbers are to be written, but not all digits need be represented. In FORTRAN, the letter E as a separator between the number and the exponent ($\pm$nn) is used instead of 10. In other words, 315 billion may be written in FORTRAN as 315.0E + 09. The zero following the decimal and the zero in front of the 9 are optional, e.g., 315.E + 9 is also correct. In writing a quantity in E format, the significant digits of the number (sometimes referred to as the fraction or characteristic) can have any scaling desired; but the exponent ($\pm$nn) must reflect the scaling. For example, the following are identical in value.

    3 1 . 5E+ 1 0

    3 . 1 5E+ 1 1

    . 3 1 5E+ 1 2

A negative 315 billion would have the sign in front ($-315.0E + 9$). To interpret any E form, multiply the fraction by the power of 10 ($\pm$nn) following E. This is the same as moving the decimal point nn places to the right for a positive exponent and nn places to the left for a negative exponent. The plus sign on the exponent is optional, but we recommend it be used for clarity.

Number in E format	Stated in mathematical form	Quantity being represented
1 . 3 1 7 5 6E+ 1 0	1.31756×10^{10}	13175600000.
1 . 3 1 7 5 6E− 5	1.31756×10^{-5}	.0000131756

RULES FOR CONSTANTS

Purpose of constant
To write a specific number in the program. Two types are used—integer (fixed point) and real (floating point)

General rules for forming constants
1 The decimal digits 0 through 9 are used to form a constant

2 The minus sign must be used for a negative constant; an unsigned constant is considered positive; a plus sign is optional

3 The size of a constant is limited to either a maximum number of digits or a maximum magnitude. There is a considerable range in allowable sizes for different computers.

4 Spaces within a constant are allowed, but their use is discouraged because it can be error prone

Rules for forming an integer constant
1 A constant *without* a decimal point

2 Size limit ranging from 6 to about 10 digits. All processors accept at least six digits and most allow more

Rules for forming a real constant
1 A constant *with* a decimal point

2 All processors accept real constants with up to eight digits. Most processors accept more digits

Rules for exponent form of real constant
If the quantity to be represented is larger or smaller than the maximum number of digits can represent, a special exponent form is used. The form consists of a number with a decimal point in it followed by the letter E and a signed integer exponent. A positive exponent means the actual decimal point should be moved the number of places to the right specified by the integer. A minus exponent moves the decimal point to the left. This corresponds to scientific exponent notation. The limits of the exponent vary with different computers, but all accept E forms with a magnitude between 10^{38} and 10^{-38} and most allow much larger exponents

EXAMPLES

Constant	Valid or not valid	If valid, integer (I) or real (R) or if not valid, why
123	Valid	I
123.	Valid	R
123.0	Valid	R
12 3	Valid, but blank not recommended (and may be invalid in some versions)	
123.E+13	Valid	R (exponent form)
123.E−13	Valid	R (exponent form)
3.141769984376432	Uncertain	May have too many digits
987.4E+299	Uncertain	Exponent may be too large

As indicated by the rules for constants and variables, different FORTRAN processors may have different limits for the number of characters in a constant, the size of the exponent in the exponent form, etc. If a program is to be written for running on only one processor, the limits of that processor can be followed. Otherwise, using the minimum specifications will ensure compatibility with other FORTRAN compilers. The inside of the back cover of this text provides a place to record the specifications and limits for the FORTRAN compiler you are using.

Self-testing Exercise 1-2

1 What is the purpose of a C or * in column 1 of the FORTRAN coding form?
2 What is the purpose of the variable name in FORTRAN and what is the difference between a variable and a constant?
3 What are the rules for naming a real variable?
4 What is the purpose of the E format for expressing quantities in FORTRAN?
5 In mathematical notation, ab means $a \times b$. What does AB stand for in FORTRAN?
6 Fill in the following table for constants and variables. If a form is invalid for most implementations but may be valid for some, note this difference.

	Valid or not valid	If valid, constant or variable	Integer or real type	If invalid, why
(a) FATHERS				
(b) DAD-O				
(c) FICA				
(d) INTR				
(e) F145				
(f) ABLE				
(g) X-14				
(h) 19E25				
(i) 18.47				
(j) 19876.45110				
(k) 98				
(l) 19875694315				

List-directed Input Statement

The basic format of the list-directed READ statement (also called free format READ) is shown in the box.

> LIST-DIRECTED INPUT STATEMENT
>
> READ *, v_1, v_2, . . . , v_n
> where v_1 = variable name which references first input data item, v_2 the second input data item, etc. The input data items must be separated by a comma or spaces. Integer values should have no decimal point; real values should have a decimal point. Large values may be input in E exponent form.
>
> In some pre-1977 implementations, the asterisk is not used. The statement is READ, v_1, v_2, . . . , v_n. In some limited versions of FORTRAN, list-directed input may not be implemented. (If not available to you, see section at end of this chapter.)

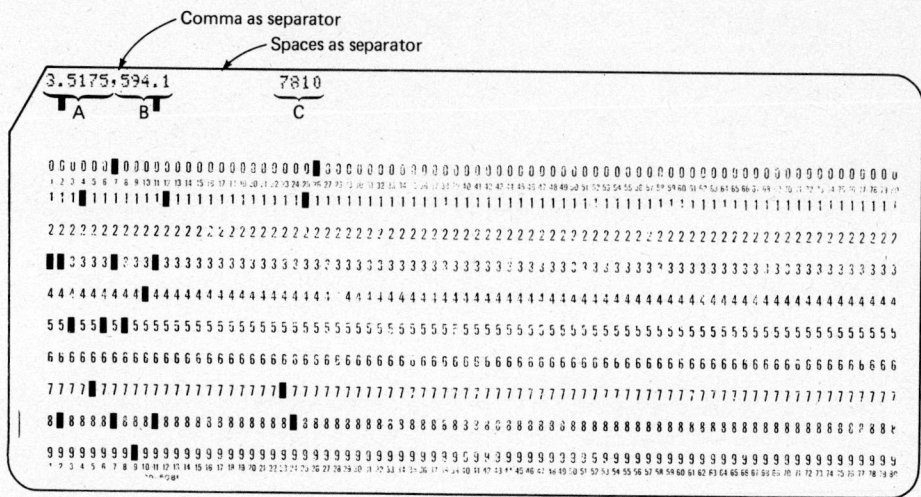

FIGURE 1-6   Punched card with three data items to be read by list-directed READ.

If a program is to read three data items from a punched card, the three items are each assigned a variable name, say A, B, and C. The data items are punched into a punched card with either a comma or one or more spaces between them (Figure 1-6). Decimal points are also punched for real quantities as are minus signs in front of negative quantities. Leading zeros and/or plus signs may be used in front of the first digit (but are not required). Large numbers may be input in exponent form. The statement to read the data in Figure 1-6 is:

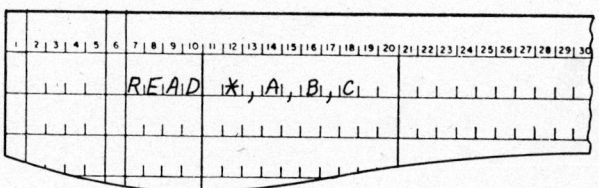

The statement reads three values from the punched card, stores them in the computer, and associates them with the variable names A, B, and C. The order of the variable names in the READ statement must correspond with the order in which the data appear in the data card.

List-directed Output Statement

List-directed output prints out the values associated with a list of variables. The values are printed in a standard preformatted way—generally in preset positions on the printer paper. Decimal points and minus signs will be printed where necessary. The basic form of the list-directed output is shown in the box.

LIST-DIRECTED OUTPUT

PRINT *, v_1, v_2, . . . , v_n

where v = a variable name associated with a stored quantity or is a set of characters enclosed in apostrophes. The values are printed in preset areas on the output line. A preset number of digits is printed. Trailing zeros may be printed to make the preset number of digits. Exponent (E) form is used to represent values too large or too small for the output area. Standard E format provided with list-directed output is $\pm$ X.XXX . . . XE $\pm$ ee with number of digits in the fraction dependent on the implementor. The first column on each print line is left blank.

In some pre-1977 implementations, the asterisk is not used.

In some limited versions of FORTRAN, list-directed output may not be included. (If not available to you, see section at end of this chapter.)

Since the print positions available for output of a quantity are preset, a large number requiring more digits for output is represented by the E format in which the symbol E is used to indicate a powers of 10 exponent notation. As explained earlier, the digits following E, if positive, mean the decimal should be moved to the right that many places; if negative, to the left.

In the list-directed output instruction, the names of the quantities to be printed are listed in the order they are to be output. A heading or label is printed by including it in the list, preceded and followed by an apostrophe. For example, PRINT *, A, B will print as follows if A = 13.17 and B = 1.09.

13.1700   1.09000

The statement PRINT *, A, 'SUM', B will print:

13.1700   SUM   1.09000

Although list-directed output is preset and the form is not under programmer control, the form of list-directed output is somewhat dependent on the compiler being used. In general, each compiler has a preset value for the maximum number of digits that will be printed for each value. If the number to be printed exceeds this limit on digits, it will automatically be printed in E format, but the fraction will have only the maximum number of digits (rounded). For example, if the computer prints up to six digits for each value, it will probably allocate 13 spaces (called a field size) for each value and the numbers will be printed as follows:

1 Integers up to six digits printed to right (right-justified) with no decimal point and spaces to left.

2 Real quantities up to six digits printed as blank, blank or minus, six digits with a decimal point, and then four blank spaces. If necessary, trailing zeros will be used to fill the six digits, e.g., 5.0 prints as 5.00000.

3 Exponent form for integer or real quantities larger than six digits is printed as blank, blank or minus sign, six-digit number with decimal point in the form X.XXXXX, letter E, plus or minus sign, and a two-digit exponent.

As an example of a preset maximum of six significant digits and a preset field size of 13 spaces, the following statement causes printing in columns as shown (assuming IX = 57, X = −19.7764, and Y = 6.87580E+06):

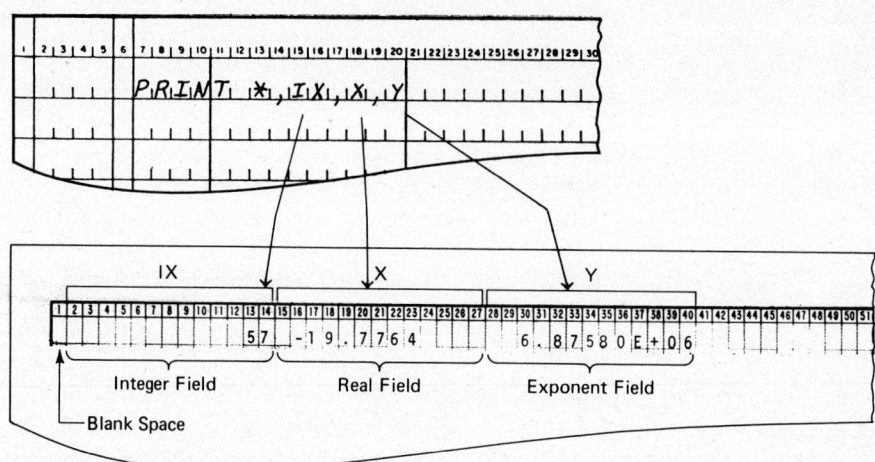

Arithmetic Assignment Statements

An arithmetic assignment statement is of the general form:

$v = e$

where v stands for a variable name and e stands for an arithmetic expression. The expression consists of one or more variable names and/or constants connected by operation symbols.

EXAMPLES

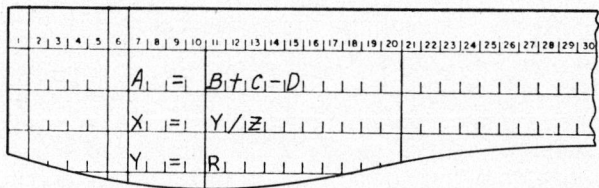

While X = X + 1.0 is not a legitimate mathematical statement, it is correct FORTRAN because the form $v = e$ does not necessarily mean that v is equal to e. It directs the computer to replace the previous value of the variable on the left side of the equals sign with the results of the expression on the right. Or, in other words, it assigns the value of the expression on the right to the variable name on the left of the equals sign. Thus, a statement X = X + 1.0 means that the value of X is increased by the constant 1.0, and this new value is assigned to (stored at) X. If X is referred to later in the program, the new value is the one made available. Because the computer executes the expression on the right side of the equals sign and then stores the result at the location of the variable on the left, having anything but a variable name to the left of the equals sign is illegal.

The operation symbols are those normally used in mathematics except for multiplication and exponentiation, which make use of the asterisk.

OPERATION SYMBOLS

Symbol	Stands for	Example
+	Addition	A + B
−	Subtraction or negation	A − B −A
/	Division	A/B
*	Multiplication	A∗B
**	Exponentiation	A∗∗B

The compiler ignores spaces before or after operation symbols and before or after the variable names and other operands. Thus, K = A + B + C is equivalent to K = A + B + C. The use of spaces may add clarity for the reader. The multiplication operator must be used; it cannot be implied as is often done in mathematical notation, e.g., ab meaning $a \times b$ must be written in FORTRAN as A∗B.

In a mathematical expression, there is an accepted notational form which specifies the order in which the operations are to be performed. For example, $X + \dfrac{Y}{Z}$ is not the same as $\dfrac{X + Y}{Z}$. In the first instance, Y is divided by Z, and the result is added to X; in the second, X is added to Y, and the result is divided by Z. In some cases, the order of operation is not important because operations are commutative. Thus, $X = A + B + C - D$ can be performed in any order, and the results will be identical. The most common mathematical notation uses parentheses to specify the order of computation.

FORTRAN uses both a precedence rule and a parentheses rule to specify the way an arithmetic expression is to be handled. The *precedence rule* is that all exponentiation will be performed first, all multiplication and division next, and all addition and subtraction last. Where the precedence of operations is the same, such as multiplication and division, the operations will be performed in order from left to right.

The *parentheses rule* is that operations will be performed in the innermost set of parentheses first (using the precedence rule where appropriate) and then in the next set, etc., until all operations inside parentheses have been performed. Then the remaining operations in the expression are carried out according to the precedence rule.

Parentheses should be used freely. If redundant, they do no harm, and they improve the readability and maintainability of the program. It is better to be explicit by using parentheses than to rely on the precedence rule. Parentheses are also used in order to avoid having two operation symbols together. It is illegal to write A∗ − B where the minus sign is a sign relating to B. Using parentheses to separate the two operation symbols makes the expression valid: A∗(−B). Parentheses are always used in pairs. A common error in writing FORTRAN is to forget the closing side of the pair.

EXAMPLES

FORTRAN	Formula
X = A + B / C − D * * 2	$x = a + \dfrac{b}{c} - d^2$
X = (A + B) / (C + D)	$x = \dfrac{a + b}{c + d}$
X = (A + B) / C + D	$x = \dfrac{a + b}{c} + d$
X = A * B * C + 1 . 5	$x = abc + 1.5$
X = (A * B * C) + 1 . 5	$x = abc + 1.5$
X = (A * B) * (C + 1 . 5)	$x = (ab)(c + 1.5)$
X = A * * Z + 1 . 0	$x = a^z + 1.0$
X = A * * (Z + 1 . 0)	$x = a^{z+1}$

The rules for forming arithmetic expressions and statements can now be summarized. The student should pay particular attention to the precedence rules.

RULES FOR FORMING ARITHMETIC STATEMENTS

1 The general form of an arithmetic statement is $v = e$, where v stands for any variable name and e stands for an arithmetic expression

2 The portion of the arithmetic statement to the left of the equals sign is a variable name. It must not be a constant nor contain arithmetic operations

3 The equals sign means "assign as the value of the variable on the left the result of the expression on the right." It is not an equality sign in the mathematical sense

4 Two operation symbols may not be used next to each other (except for two asterisks, which mean exponentiation)

5 Spaces may be used whenever desired to improve readability. The compiler ignores them

6 Parentheses are used to specify order of operation and to avoid the two-operation symbol restriction. Operations inside parentheses are performed first. Parentheses must always be used in pairs

7 In the absence of parentheses, the precedence rule for performing arithmetic operations specifies the order. Within one of the precedence levels, the operations are performed from left to right. The precedence rule is:

First—exponentiation

Second—multiplication and division

Third—addition, subtraction, or negation

As explained earlier, real type variables or constants may have a fractional part; an integer variable or integer constant cannot have a fractional part. In arithmetic operations involving integer data, the result cannot have a fractional part. This will receive further explanation in Chapter 2, but it suggests that mixing data of different types must be done with caution. For this chapter, the student should avoid possible problems in writing the assigned program by not using any integer variables or integer constants in arithmetic assignment statements. Make all variables and all constants real constants. An exception may be made in the case of exponents which are whole numbers. In other words, X**2 or X**N can be used but write X**0.2 instead of X**(1/5). There are no restrictions on integer data used for identification purposes and not included in an arithmetic expression.

STOP and END Statements

The STOP statement is used to specify that the program execution is to be terminated. In a large program, there may be more than one possible stopping point, each having a separate STOP instruction. If a program has more than one STOP statement, the different STOP commands can be identified by coding the word STOP followed by 1 to 5 digits. The digits will print out when the STOP is executed.

The END statement is the last statement in the program. It signals the end of the program unit. It consists only of the word END.

The difference between STOP and END is that STOP is an instruction to stop the program when it is being executed, whereas END is an instruction to the compiler that there are no more statements in the program unit.

In a simple program the next to last statement will be STOP, the last statement will be END.

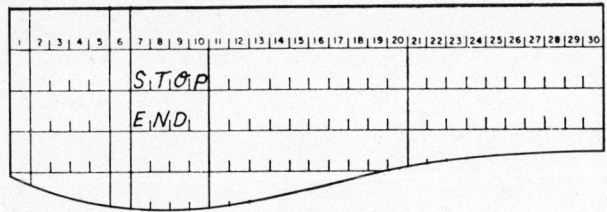

STOP and END STATEMENTS	
STOP or STOP n	Where n is from one to five digits. If n is used, n will be printed out when the program executes the STOP
END	The last statement in a program

Blank Spaces in FORTRAN Statements and Data

The use of blanks or spaces in writing FORTRAN is sometimes confusing to beginning programmers. Rules and recommended practices are therefore summarized for review.

BLANKS IN FORTRAN

Blanks are ignored in the following situations:

1 Blanks imbedded in a constant

X = 3.1751   and   X = 3.1   751

are interpreted the same, but for clarity of programming, do not imbed blanks

2 Blanks in a statement number field (columns 1–5)

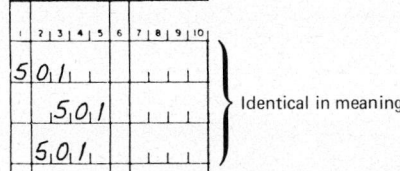

Identical in meaning

Recommended form is right-justified (blanks to left)

3 Blanks before or after FORTRAN words, parentheses, and symbols. Use or omit blanks to improve readability. The following pairs are identical to FORTRAN

Blanks	No blanks
X = Y / Z	X = Y/Z
P R I N T * , X , Y	PRINT * , X , Y

4 Blanks imbedded in a variable name are ignored, but we recommend they not be used.

Blanks are important in the following cases:

1 For list-directed input, one or more blanks (or a comma) are used to separate data items. The following are identical input data:

9 3 . 1 7 , 4 5
9 3 . 1 7   4 5

2 For input, blanks cannot be imbedded in a data item. The value 93.176 cannot be input as 93.1   76

3 For character input or output, blanks are treated the same as other characters. For example, in the following statement, the blanks inside the apostrophes are characters the same as N, O, etc.

PRINT * ,   'NOW IS THE TIME'

Self-testing Exercise 1-3

1 Write FORTRAN statements for each of the following formulas, using sufficient parentheses to make the statement execution precedence very clear.

(a) $x = \dfrac{a}{b} + c$

(b) $x = \dfrac{3y^2}{z^2}$

$(c)\ x = a^b + \dfrac{d}{e}$

$(d)\ x = \left(\dfrac{a}{b}\right) cd$

$(e)\ x = \dfrac{a+b}{c+d}$

2 Write the following FORTRAN statements, eliminating redundant parentheses used for clarity:

Formula	FORTRAN
$(a)\ x = \dfrac{a+b}{ef}$	X = (A + B) / (E * F)
$(b)\ x = abc + 1$	X = (A * B * C)+ 1 . 0
$(c)\ x = \left(\dfrac{ab}{c}\right) d$	X = ((A * B) /C) * D

3 Write FORTRAN statements to perform the following:
  (a) Read the values for A, B, and D from a punched card.
  (b) Print the values for A, B, and D but in the order B, A, D.
  (c) Print the value for A plus the words IS ALL.
  (d) Stop the program.
  (e) Identify the end of the program.
  (f) Read values for C and D from an input data card. Print the inputs for visual inspection along with a label C before the value of C and a label D before the value of D.

Compiling and Executing a FORTRAN Program

The five statements that have been explained are sufficient to write a simple program. The writing (coding) of the FORTRAN program (called the source program) is only one step in the process by which the computer is used in solving a problem. The entire process is summarized as the following steps (assuming punched cards are used for the program and the data input):

1 Problem recognition and definition

2 Selection of solution procedures (algorithms) and definition of data

3 Specification of program structure and logic (by flowcharts and/or pseudocode)

4 Coding of FORTRAN statements

5 Source deck preparation
  (a) Punching of FORTRAN statements into punched cards— one line of coding into one card to produce the source program deck
  (b) Preparation of input data by punching into punched cards
  (c) Preparation of job control instructions and punching into cards

6 Compilation and debugging
   (*a*) Submission of job (the job consists of job control cards, source program deck, and data deck)
   (*b*) Detection and removal of errors (called debugging). The compilation listing from the computer is useful in this process

7 Execution (after all errors have been removed)

8 Completion of documentation

Step 5*c* needs some explanation. Every job to be run on the computer from punched cards must have job control instructions along with it. These instructions, punched into cards, provide specifications for the operating system (the set of programs which manage the compilation and execution of the program). For example, one of the job control instruction cards will specify that the job is a FORTRAN program to be compiled. The operating system will interpret the job control card and bring the FORTRAN compiler into the main storage of the computer. The operating system then turns control over to the compiler program which reads and translates the FORTRAN program statements, etc. The job control cards are different for each computer. A job control manual for the computer being used provides the programmer with the necessary specifications and instructions. For the common case of compilation and immediate execution, a complete source deck is composed of:

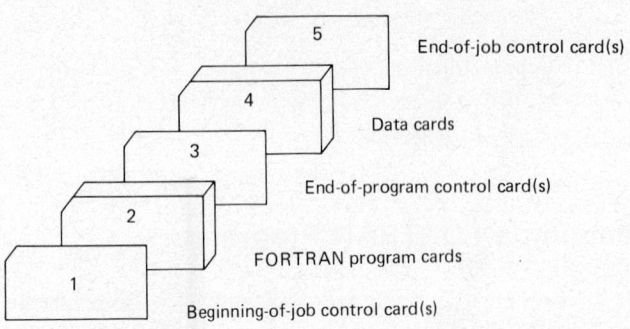

Computer centers running student jobs normally prepare a short description of the job control cards usually required for student programs. The inside of the back cover of this text provides a space for you to summarize these requirements.

The output from compilation of a FORTRAN program will vary depending on (1) whether or not the job ran successfully to completion or was aborted because of an error and (2) what output options have been selected by the job control cards. The output from compilation may have a first or top sheet with data required for returning the job (job number, name of programmer, etc.) plus summary job statistics and an end-of-job message. Following this output, there is a listing of the FORTRAN program along with error messages, if any. The last output will be the results from the execution of the program, if any. Optional output elements include label tables, linkage editing, cross-reference tables, core storage maps, and the object listing. These optional elements are used by advanced programmers as aids in debugging program errors which may not have been detected by the compiler. Since most errors made by beginning programmers are detectable by the compiler, the beginning programmer can generally rely on messages which are generated during attempted compilation and ignore the optional debugging output.

Compilers will detect most errors made by student programmers because most student errors are errors in program statement syntax—errors in punctuation, spelling, spacing, and omission of necessary elements. Two methods of indicating the location of error entries are used: (1) the compiler numbers each source program line and generates at the end of the program a list of the numbered lines which have errors, with related error messages, or (2) as errors are detected, the diagnostic messages or codes are printed close to the source program lines. Many compilers also print warning messages which alert the programmer to possible errors.

A program may be compiled without error diagnostics and yet not be correct; it may still have incomplete or incorrect program logic. Completion of the program requires testing of program logic and removing errors. Documentation of the program also needs to be completed. Testing and documentation will be explained in subsequent chapters.

Self-testing Exercise 1-4

1 Every job run on the computer must have job control instructions (cards) which provide specifications for the _____
_____ .

2 For a common computer program job of compilation and immediate execution, what is the order of the following elements of the job deck (assuming input via punched cards)?
   (*a*) Data cards
   (*b*) End-of-job control cards
   (*c*) FORTRAN program cards
   (*d*) Beginning-of-job cards
   (*e*) End-of-program control cards
3 Compilers will detect most errors made by student programmers because most errors they make are _____ (punctuation, spelling, etc.) rather than program logic errors.

Summary

FORTRAN is one of the most-used high-level languages for programming a computer. It is used primarily for formula-type problems such as mathematical solutions, engineering analysis, statistical processing, and economic analysis. In designing and writing FORTRAN programs, the result will generally be improved if a disciplined style of design and coding is used. This will include the division of the program into logical modules and following coding rules which emphasize the program structure. The program will generally contain logical modules to perform input, input validation, processing, normal output, error output, and termination procedures.

The design of a FORTRAN program can usually make effective use of a program flowchart and/or pseudocode. Special coding paper is recommended for use in writing FORTRAN statements and it is recommended that standard conventions for handprinting be followed.

Five FORTRAN statements were explained in the chapter: list-directed input, list-directed output, arithmetic assignment, STOP, and END. These five statements are sufficient for writing simple but complete FORTRAN programs. In order to compile and execute a FORTRAN program, it will be necessary to obtain the job control cards to place with the program and data. If programming is done via a terminal, special terminal instructions must be followed.

Answers to Self-testing Exercises

Exercise 1-1

1 Hardware is the computer equipment; software consists of the operating system, compilers, application programs, and other sets of computer routines to direct the operation of the equipment.

2 A program exists in primary storage in machine language. This is the language the computer actually uses. A symbolic assembly language is a language for symbolically describing the parts of a machine-language instruction. The symbolic assembly language is easier to code and to read than machine language and is directly translatable into machine-language instructions by the symbolic assembly system (generally one symbolic assembly instruction is translated into one machine-language instruction).

3 Compared to symbolic assembly languages, high-level languages such as FOR-TRAN are machine-independent (in the sense that they can be compiled and run with little or no changes on any computer having a compiler for the language); they are relatively easy to learn because they use formula-like instructions, require fewer instructions, provide more understandable documentation, and are easier to test and debug.

4 FORmula TRANslator.

5 ANSI has established a standard language set for FORTRAN, divided into two different levels of implementation.

6 (a) Meet user needs
   (b) Development on-time within budget
   (c) Error-free set of instructions
   (d) Error-resistant operation
   (e) Maintainable programs
   (f) Portable programs

7 (a) Input
   (b) Input data validation
   (c) Processing
   (d) Output
   (e) Error handling
   (f) Closing procedure

8 (a) Sequence. One action followed by another.
   (b) Selection. Test for a condition followed by two alternative program paths.
   (c) Repetition. A set of operations is repeated while some condition continues to be true.

9 (a) 2   (b) 4   (c) 5   (d) 1   (e) 6   (f) 3

10 Portable

11 Flowcharts and/or pseudocode

Exercise 1-2

1 The character C or * in column 1 means the line is a comment line.

2 The variable name is used to specify a value which can change with each execution

of the program. The variable name identifies the storage location where the value is stored. Whereas a variable represents a quantity which is unknown or which may change in value during the program, a constant is used to write a specific, unchanging value in the program.

3 The name begins with the letter A to H and O to Z and may contain up to six alphabetic characters and numeric digits.

4 The E format is used to represent very large and very small numbers.

5 AB is a FORTRAN variable name for a real variable.

6

	Valid or not valid	If valid, constant or variable	Integer or real type	If not valid, why
(a)	Not valid	——	——	Too many characters
(b)	Not valid	——	——	Special character not allowed
(c)	Valid	Variable	Real	
(d)	Valid	Variable	Integer	
(e)	Valid	Variable	Real	
(f)	Valid	Variable	Real	
(g)	Not valid			Special character (-) not allowed
(h)	Not valid (May be allowed in some FORTRAN implementations but not standard)			Decimal point missing. Exponent should be signed. Correct is 19.E+25.
(i)	Valid	Constant	Real	
(j)	Not valid (For most implementations)			Too large
(k)	Valid	Constant	Integer	
(l)	Not valid (For most implementations)			Too large

Exercise 1-3

1 (a) X = A/B + C

(b) X = 3.0*Y**2/Z**2 but better as (3.0*(Y**2))/(Z**2)

(c) X = A**B + D/E or X = A**B+(D/E)

(d) X = A/B*C*D but better as X = (A/B)*C*D

(e) X = (A+B)/(C+D)

2 (a) All are necessary   (b) A*B*C+1.0   (c) A*B/C*D

3 (a) READ *,A,B,D

(b) PRINT *,B,A,D

(c) PRINT *,A, 'IS ALL'

(d) STOP

(e) END

(f) READ *,C,D

PRINT *, 'C', C, 'D', D

If C has a value of 12.1 and D has a value of 98.13, the output will be:

C   12.1000   D   98.1300

Exercise 1-4

1 Operating System

2 d, c, e, a, b

3 Syntactical (or syntax)

Questions and Problems

1 Define the following terms:
 (a) application program
 (b) compiler
 (c) flowchart
 (d) hardware
 (e) high-level language
 (f) job control cards
 (g) machine-oriented language
 (h) object program
 (i) program module
 (j) pseudocode
 (k) routine
 (l) software
 (m) source program
 (n) structured program
 (o) symbolic assembly system

2 What are the hardware elements of a computer system?

3 What is the main difference between a machine-oriented language and a high-level language?

4 List and describe the main steps in developing a FORTRAN program.

5 Fill in the following table.

	Valid or not valid	Constant or variable	Integer or real type	If not valid, why
(a) MAN				
(b) WOMAN				
(c) X − 19				
(d) RATE				
(e) I				
(f) OUTPUT				
(g) 9FOUR				
(h) DOLL				
(i) 18.97				
(j) BETA				
(k) J19				
(l) 134.1E19				
(m) 1.9E−20				

6 Assume three variables A, B, C. Indicate whether each of the following statements is valid. If not valid, explain.

 (a) READ *,A,B,C
 (b) PRINT ABC
 (c) READ A,B,C
 (d) PRINT *,A, TOTAL IS, B
 (e) PRINT 'THE SUM IS', A

7 Rewrite the following as FORTRAN statements. Use sufficient parentheses to make the order of operations clear.

(a) $x = \dfrac{a + b}{c}$

(b) $x = \dfrac{c + d}{f + g}$

(c) $x = (a^c)(d + f)$

(d) $x = (a^c)(b^d)$

(e) $x = a + b - c$

Section Only for Those Using FORTRAN Versions Without List-directed Input and Output

Chapters 1 and 2 use only list-directed (free form) input and output because this simplifies the learning of the language. However, many older FORTRAN versions (or restricted versions such as 1977 Standard Subset FORTRAN) do not include the list-directed input and output. For those students using compilers without these list-directed instructions, the problems in Chapters 1B and 2B require a change in the input and output instructions. Each input or output will require a pair of instructions, the first being an input or output instruction in a slightly different form and the second a FORMAT statement. The general form is:

READ(u,fs) list of variables separated by commas
fs FORMAT(list of specifications)

WRITE(u,fs) list of variables separated by commas
fs FORMAT(list of specifications)

where u is a unit number assigned by the installation to the card reader or printer and fs is a statement number.

Since these instructions will be explained fully in Chapter 3, two pairs of general-purpose statements will be given here for use with programs in Chapters 1B and 2B.

1 Statements to be used with problems having no integer variables to input or output:

To read:		READ(5,8001)	list of real variables
	8001	FORMAT(8F10.0)	
To write:		WRITE(6,8002)	list of real variables
	8002	FORMAT(8E16.8)	

To use these statements, the input data must be punched with a decimal point in fields of 10 in the input card, i.e., the first data item is in columns 1 to 10, the second in columns 11 to 20, etc. The unit numbers 5 (for card reader) and 6 (for printer) may be different for different computers (for example, 1 and 3). The instructor will furnish the unit numbers for you to use. Output will all be in E format with no provisions for descriptive labels. These statements apply to all problems in Chapter 1B except 2 and 13, and for all problems except 2 and 6 in Chapter 2B (except that both sets of statements apply to 9, 11, 13, 14, and 15 in Chapter 2B).

2 Statements to be used with input or output of one integer variable as the first variable in the list and the remaining variables as real variables:

To read:	`READ (5, 8003)`	*integer variable, real variables*
	`8003  FORMAT (I10, 7F10.0)`	
To write:	`WRITE (6, 8004)`	*integer variable, real variables*
	`8004  FORMAT (I10, 7E16.8)`	

On input, the first data item must be in columns 1 to 10 without a decimal and with any extra spaces to the left. The remaining variables are in fields of 10 with a decimal point in each data item. The first output item will be an integer variable; the remaining items will be in E format. There is no provision for descriptive labels on the output. These statements apply only to problems with one integer input and one integer output. Since all variables may be given real names and input as real numbers, these statements are optional but fit the nature of the problem for 2 and 13 in Chapter 1B and for 2, 6, 9, 11, 13, 14, and 15 in Chapter 2B.

CHAPTER

EXAMPLE PROGRAMS AND PROGRAMMING EXERCISES TO READ, COMPUTE, AND PRINT

Chapter 1A contained a descriptive and conceptual introduction to programming, programming discipline, and the FORTRAN language. Five FORTRAN instructions were explained. These instructions are sufficient to write simple programs using the sequence programming structure.

Chapter 1B consists of two complete examples of programs (using the features and the five statements explained in Chapter 1A) plus programming exercises. The programming exercises provide a learning experience in following the procedures for writing a FORTRAN program and getting it to run on a specific computer. The student assignment is to design a program using a pseudocode description and a program flowchart, code the instructions, arrange keypunching of the program, prepare data cards and job control instructions, and compile and execute the program (after removing all errors).

The emphasis of Chapter 1B is on learning by examining complete example programs and by doing a complete program. This first programming problem not only provides experience with coding a simple FORTRAN program but also assists the student in learning the specific job control instructions and FORTRAN job submission procedures for the computer to be used. Because the program is a simple one, the student can concentrate on the structure of a well-written program, on the submission procedures, and on interpreting the output without being distracted by complex program logic.

General Comments on the Example Programs

There are two example programs for two somewhat different types of problems:

1 *General Program 1*   Compute an employee paycheck

2 *Statistical Program 1*   Calculate the ordinates of the normal curve for two values of the abscissa

The two programs provide insight into the use of FORTRAN for different types of problems. Also, some students may be more familiar with one problem area than the other; the two examples allow the student to concentrate on the example in which the problem context is best understood.

The example programs are actual listings from compilation of the programs. The listing is exactly the same as the FORTRAN statements punched into the cards used for job submission except for the line numbers along the left side. These were added by the compiler. Not all compilers will add line numbers; however, these line numbers will be useful in the text as references when statements are discussed. Look ahead and note in Figures 1-9 and 1-12 that the line numbers added by the compiler are not placed alongside comment lines; they are used only for statements that can be executed. Do not punch these line numbers in your program cards.

Example Program Structure

Note the structure of the example programs. The structure makes extensive use of comment lines. As explained, a comment line has an asterisk or the letter C in column 1. The ∗ convention is new with 1977 FORTRAN, so some older versions may allow only the C for a comment line.

The structure used in the example programs is recommended for the programs you are to write. This structure is not required by the FORTRAN language; it is recommended as a matter of style in writing clear, understandable, well-documented programs. The style issue becomes more significant as programs become larger and more complex; the style should be followed in even small programs as a learning experience and as a matter of programming discipline. The programs consist of the following blocks of coding:

1 *Program identification*   This block of comments describes the program and identifies the author and the date written. Any special comments regarding the program can be placed here.

2 *Variable identification*   Every variable name used in the program should be listed along with a description. The names should be as descriptive as possible, bearing some resemblance to the quantity being represented. The variable description lines may be written as variables are named in writing the program. This will result in the variable identification list being arranged in order by the first use of a variable. It is also a relatively simple matter to rearrange these cards so as to have the list in alphabetical order. Alphabetical arrangement is optional but useful, especially with long lists. For readability, we have chosen to start names in column 11 and to start the definitions in column 21. The variable identification block is for clear program documentation; it does not affect program execution.

3 *Constant identification*   It is frequently useful to name constants rather than to employ the constants directly in the program. It sometimes makes the program easier to understand. Also, constants which may change (such as tax rates) are more easily changed if the constant value is named. This block may be omitted if no constants are named. The block is for documentation purposes.

4 *Initialization*   If constants are named, the values are set by arithmetic assignment statements before any processing. There will be additional instances where initial values need to be set, such as setting variables to zero. This block may be omitted if no initialization is performed.

5 *Processing blocks*   In the simple program, a single processing block may be sufficient. In later programs there will be several separate blocks such as to read data, validate input data, process, output normal values, output error messages, and terminate the program.

Each block is identified by a name, set off by asterisks.

          *********   PROGRAM IDENTIFICATION   *********

We have chosen to have the title for each block begin in column 21 so that it is somewhat centered and stands out. Blank comment lines to visually separate parts of the program begin in column 1 with an asterisk (or C) and end in column 72 with an asterisk. The end of the block is set off by a solid line of asterisks. Other conventions could be used; these are recommended and will be followed in this text.

Comments should be used freely within the processing modules. In order to differentiate comment lines from executable statements, we have chosen to have each set of one or more comment lines preceded and followed by a blank comment line having only an asterisk (or C) in column 1 and an asterisk in column 72. The comment line(s) have asterisks in columns 1 and 72, plus the comment which begins in column 11. Additional program style conventions will be given in subsequent chapters.

Pseudocode and Program Flowcharts for Example Programs

The documentation for each program includes a pseudocode description of the program and a program flowchart. Since these programs use only the sequence program structure, the pseudocode description and flowchart are simple and perhaps not necessary. However, these forms of documentation in simple situations will provide practice in understanding them and in applying them in more complex programming situations. A programmer would probably not use both a pseudocode description and a program flowchart, although the pseudocode might be used in planning the program and the flowchart in documenting the final result. Both are included to provide experience in using these alternatives. An explanation of the process by which pseudocode and flowcharts are developed as part of program planning is included in the explanation for general example 1.

General Program Example 1—Compute Employee Pay

Problem Description for General Example 1

The program is to compute an employee gross pay, taxes, net pay and average net pay per hour based upon the following factors:

Total hours worked

Wage rate in dollars per hour

Taxes at the rate of 15 percent of gross pay

Pension contribution at the rate of 5 percent of gross pay

Miscellaneous deductions (an input given in dollars)

The input will consist of the employee identification number, hours worked, wage rate, and amount of miscellaneous deductions. The output should show gross pay, taxes, net pay (paycheck), and average rate of net pay per hour. The basic arithmetic operators and list-directed input and output are to be used in this program. Appropriate labels are to be used to identify the outputs. The program is to follow good programming practice for control of input errors. The input is to be checked (validated) by printing out (echoing) the input data for visual inspection.

Program Documentation for General Example 1

Both forms of program planning documentation are given here—a pseudocode program description (Figure 1-7) and a program flowchart (Figure 1-8). The program listing and sample output are given in Figure 1-9. Remember that the

READ, id, hours, wage rate, deductions
PRINT input variables for visual validation
Gross pay = hours × rate
Taxes   = pay × tax rate of 15%
Net pay   = pay − taxes − misc. deductions − pension contribution of 5% of pay
Av. pay   = net pay ÷ hours
PRINT gross pay, taxes, net pay, ave. net pay per hour
STOP

FIGURE 1-7 Pseudocode description for planning general program 1—compute employee pay.

line numbers are not part of the program as written by the programmer; they were added by the compiler used for the example as a statement reference.

Planning Program Logic Using Pseudocode

The pseudocode for general example 1 will be used to illustrate the process of developing pseudocode as part of program planning and design. The resulting

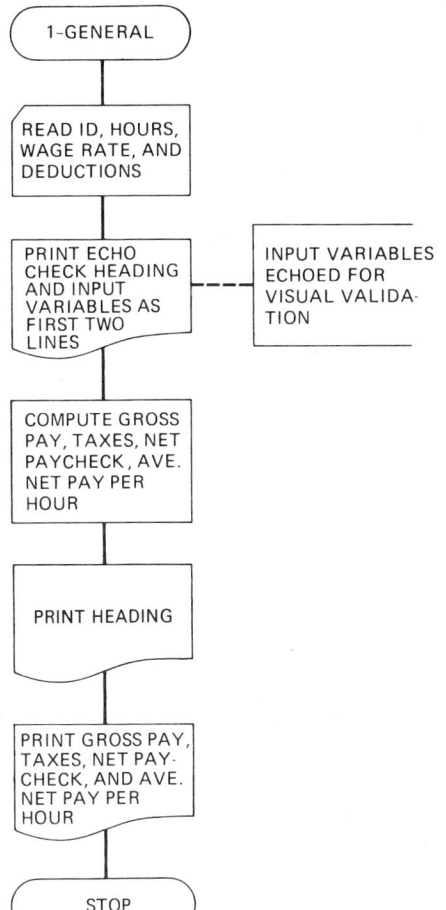

FIGURE 1-8 Flowchart for planning general program 1—compute employee pay.

PROGRAM

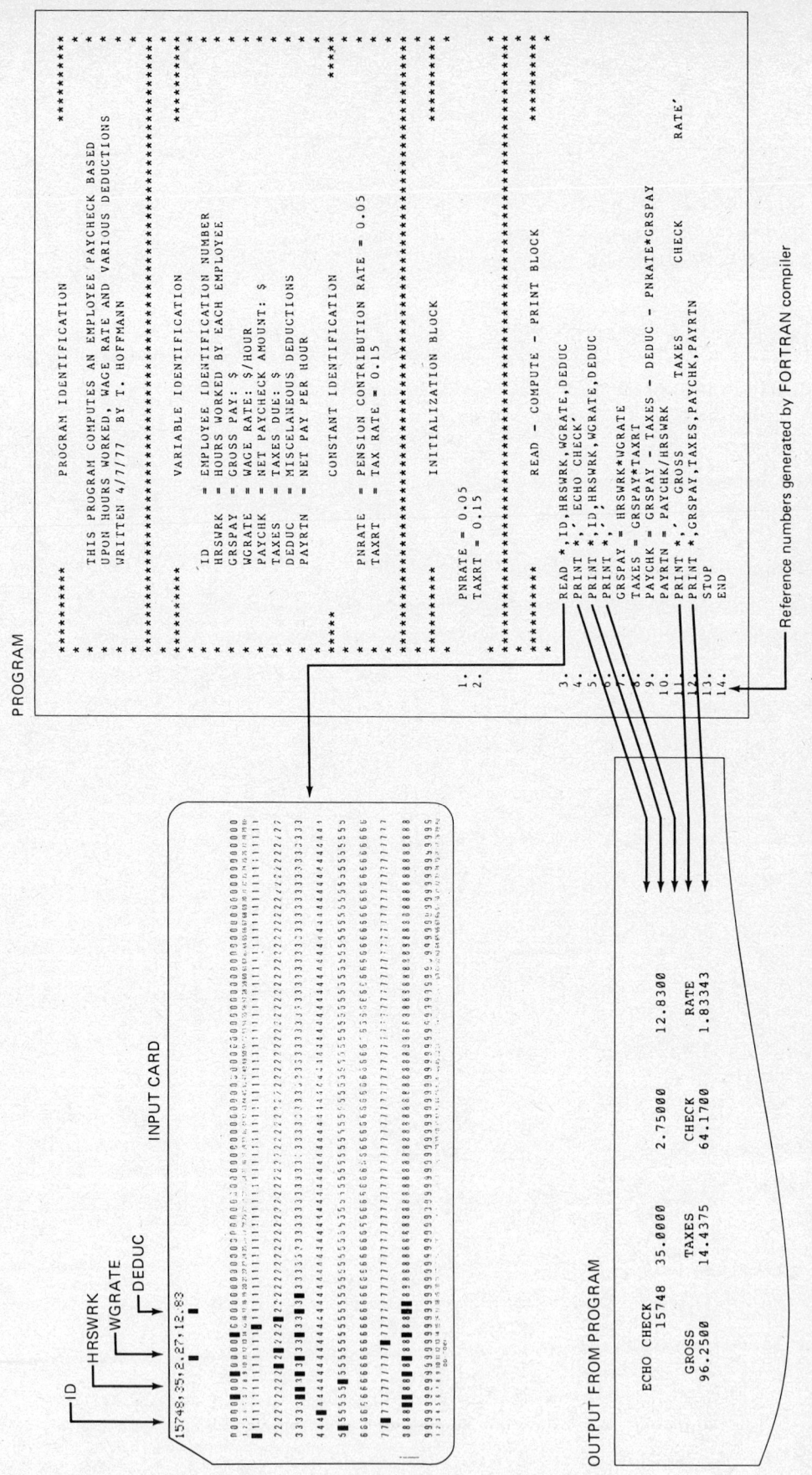

```
********************                PROGRAM IDENTIFICATION                ********************
*                                                                                           *
*        THIS PROGRAM COMPUTES AN EMPLOYEE PAYCHECK BASED                                    *
*        UPON HOURS WORKED, WAGE RATE AND VARIOUS DEDUCTIONS                                 *
*        WRITTEN 4/7/77  BY T. HOFFMANN                                                      *
*                                                                                           *
********************                VARIABLE IDENTIFICATION               ********************
*                                                                                           *
*        ID      =  EMPLOYEE IDENTIFICATION NUMBER                                           *
*        HRSWRK  =  HOURS WORKED BY EACH EMPLOYEE                                            *
*        GRSPAY  =  GROSS PAY: $                                                             *
*        WGRATE  =  WAGE RATE: $/HOUR                                                        *
*        PAYCHK  =  NET PAYCHECK AMOUNT: $                                                   *
*        TAXES   =  TAXES DUE: $                                                             *
*        DEDUC   =  MISCELANEOUS DEDUCTIONS                                                  *
*        PAYRTN  =  NET PAY PER HOUR                                                         *
*                                                                                           *
*****                                CONSTANT IDENTIFICATION                                 *
*                                                                                           *
*        PNRATE  =  PENSION CONTRIBUTION RATE = 0.05                                         *
*        TAXRT   =  TAX RATE = 0.15                                                          *
*                                                                                           *
********************                INITIALIZATION BLOCK                  ********************

 1.         PNRATE = 0.05
 2.         TAXRT = 0.15

********************          READ - COMPUTE - PRINT BLOCK                ********************

 3.         READ *,ID,HRSWRK,WGRATE,DEDUC
 4.         PRINT *,' ECHO CHECK'
 5.         PRINT *,ID,HRSWRK,WGRATE,DEDUC
 6.         PRINT *,' '
 7.         GRSPAY = HRSWRK*WGRATE
 8.         TAXES = GRSPAY*TAXRT
 9.         PAYCHK = GRSPAY - TAXES - DEDUC - PNRATE*GRSPAY
10.         PAYRTN = PAYCHK/HRSWRK
11.         PRINT *,'   GROSS      TAXES     CHECK       RATE'
12.         PRINT *,GRSPAY,TAXES,PAYCHK,PAYRTN
13.         STOP
14.         END
```

Reference numbers generated by FORTRAN compiler

INPUT CARD

ID
HRSWRK
WGRATE
DEDUC

15748;35;2.27;12.83

OUTPUT FROM PROGRAM

```
ECHO CHECK
   15748    35.0000     2.75000    12.8300

   GROSS      TAXES      CHECK       RATE
  96.2500    14.4375    64.1700     1.83343
```

FIGURE 1-9 Program listing, sample input, and resulting output for general program 1—compute employee pay.

pseudocode is also useful as documentation of the program. The planning and design of a program using pseudocode is an iterative process starting with a few general statements and expanding these statements as more program details are planned. When the program planning and design is complete, program coding is begun. The process is illustrated for general example 1.

1 The major steps in the normal flow of processing by the program are described by general pseudocode statements. In other words, the programmer first plans for processing when input data is as expected and there are no exceptions. Four statements are sufficient to describe the general flow of processing for general example 1:

Read input data
Calculate pay amounts
Print pay amounts
Stop

More detail can be added in the pseudocode if desired. For example, the general pseudocode statements describing the flow of processing can be replaced by statements showing more detail or by sets of statements. The relationship between the pseudocode statements and planned FORTRAN coding may be made explicit by using capital letters for pseudocode words that correspond to actual coding instruction words.

General pseudocode statement	Detailed pseudocode
Read input data	*READ id, hours, wage rate, deductions*
Calculate pay amounts	*Gross pay = hours × rate* *Taxes = gross pay × tax rate of 15%* *Net pay = gross pay − taxes − deductions − (pension contribution of 5% of pay)* *Ave. net pay per hour = net pay ÷ hours*
Print pay amounts	*PRINT gross pay, taxes, net pay, ave. net pay per hour*
Stop	*STOP*

2 The pseudocode program plan is expanded to include processing that is required in order to validate input data and to handle errors in input data and other exceptions. In the case of general example 1, the input data is to be printed out to allow visual validation. A pseudocode statement to reflect this requirement is:

PRINT input variables for visual validation

The statement is inserted after the statement to read the input variables. The completed plan for the program, written in pseudocode, is shown in Figure 1-7.

There are no standard rules for pseudocode in planning a FORTRAN program. However, the following suggestions may be useful; they will be followed in the text:

1 Each pseudocode statement describes one or more processing steps to be performed. The line is written in a condensed English-like form that also reflects the FORTRAN coding to be done.

2 Pseudocode statements which refer to a specific FORTRAN instruction word (such as READ or PRINT) can include the FORTRAN word which is then written in all capital letters.

3 A reference to a variable can describe it in words (such as sum or sum of pay amounts) or can use a descriptive name which is to be a program variable name (such as SUM or SUMPAY). The variable name in such cases is written in all capital letters. All other words in the pseudocode statement line are lowercase.

Additional pseudocode notation will be explained in later chapters.

Planning Program Logic Using a Flowchart

The process of planning and designing a program using a flowchart is similar to the process with pseudocode. The major steps and logic of processing can be defined and then expanded. A major difference in using a flowchart compared to pseudocode is that the flow of processing is visually defined by symbols and lines. The symbols may indicate the media or equipment to be used. In more complex programs, flowcharts are especially useful in showing the flow of processing down alternative paths. For the simple processing flow of general example 1, there is little difference between the flowchart and the pseudocode.

The steps in planning a program using a program flowchart are:

1 Define the general flow of the program for normally expected input data using general processing symbols for input, processing, and output. Expand the description to a suitable level of detail.

2 Add processing boxes and processing flow to perform validation of input data and to handle exceptions.

Figure 1-8 shows the flowchart at the end of step 2. The amount of detail to be shown in the boxes should be enough to clearly define what is to be done. The flowchart boxes for reading and printing contain the words READ and PRINT. These words are not necessary because the symbols imply reading from cards or printing on paper; we include them to improve the readability of the flowcharts.

Notes on General Example 1

The variable names for this program illustrate the need to choose names that as clearly as possible identify the quantity they represent. Other names might have been used (e.g., GROSPY for GRSPAY or IDNUM for ID).

Even in a beginning program like this one there are alternative codings possible. For example, each data output could have been printed on a separate line. Note the printing of a space to create a blank line between outputs (line 6 written as PRINT *, ' '). The statement PRINT* without the blank enclosed in apostrophes will also print a blank line. Either method is acceptable.

The program also illustrates a good programming practice. Simple input validation is provided by having a printout (echoing) of all input data. The reader of the output can visually validate the input data. Other forms of input validation will be explained in a later chapter; but echoing of input data and visual input validation should always be considered as part of program design.

Another interesting feature of this program is the naming of the two constants—rates for tax and pension. These are constants and need not be named except that rates such as these are subject to change. By naming them, a single change in the initialization block will change the rate throughout the program.

Statistical Program Example 1—Calculate Ordinates of the Normal Curve

Problem Description for Statistical Example 1

Calculate the ordinates (y values) of the normal curve for two values of the abscissa (x values) and print them out with a simple heading using list-directed input and output. Use approximate values for π and e.

Equation: $\quad y = \dfrac{1}{\sqrt{2\pi}} e^{-(X^2/2)}$

where π is the value for pi and the expression $1/\sqrt{2\pi}$ has an approximate value of 0.3989. e is the base for natural logarithms—a value of 2.7183 can be used for this problem.

Program Documentation for Statistical Example 1

There are a pseudocode description (Figure 1-10), a program flowchart (Figure 1-11), and a program listing (Figure 1-12) with sample output. There are two outputs shown, from two different compilers, to demonstrate how different implementations of FORTRAN may provide different precision (number of digits) for list-directed output. Input data is printed as part of the output of the results rather than having a separate printout of input data for visual validation.

Identify values (from math tables) of e and $1/\sqrt{2\pi}$
READ X1, X2
Compute Y1 and Y2
PRINT heading
PRINT X1, Y1
PRINT X2, Y2
STOP

FIGURE 1-10 Pseudocode description for planning statistical program 1—compute ordinates of normal curve.

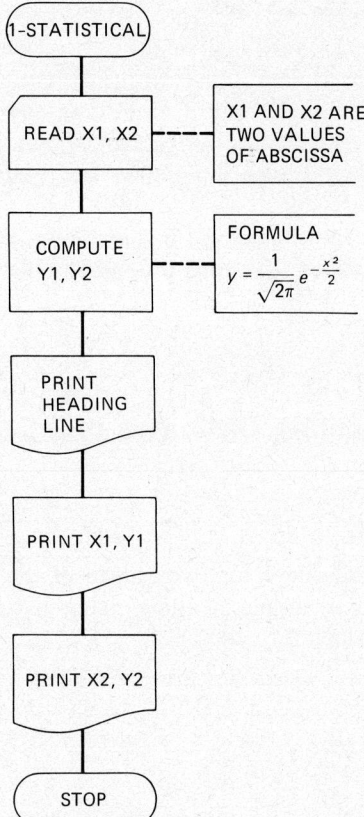

FIGURE 1-11   Program flowchart for planning statistical program 1—compute ordinates of normal curve.

Notes on Statistical Example 1

The names for the values on the ordinates and abscissas could have been more descriptive: for example, ORD1 and ABSC1 might have been used in place of X1 and Y1. However, the equation used X and Y and so those names were selected. The first X was called X1, the second X2. The second variable is called YTWO (whereas the corresponding X variable was called X2. This was done merely to illustrate alternatives in naming variables. Y1 would have been just as good.

There are different ways to write the $e^{-(X^2/2)}$ portion of the equation using only the instructions in Chapter 1A. Four representative ways are shown below; two are used in the example program. Another way, using computer generated values for e instead of 2.7183, will be explained in Chapter 2A.

1   2.7183 ** ((X**2)/(−2.0))

2   2.7183 ** ((−X*X)/2.0)

3   2.7183 ** (−(X**2)/(2.0))

4   1.0/(2.7183 ** ((X**2)/2.0))

In other words, there are different ways to code the equations, all of which are correct. It is generally preferable to use a straightforward, easily understood formulation.

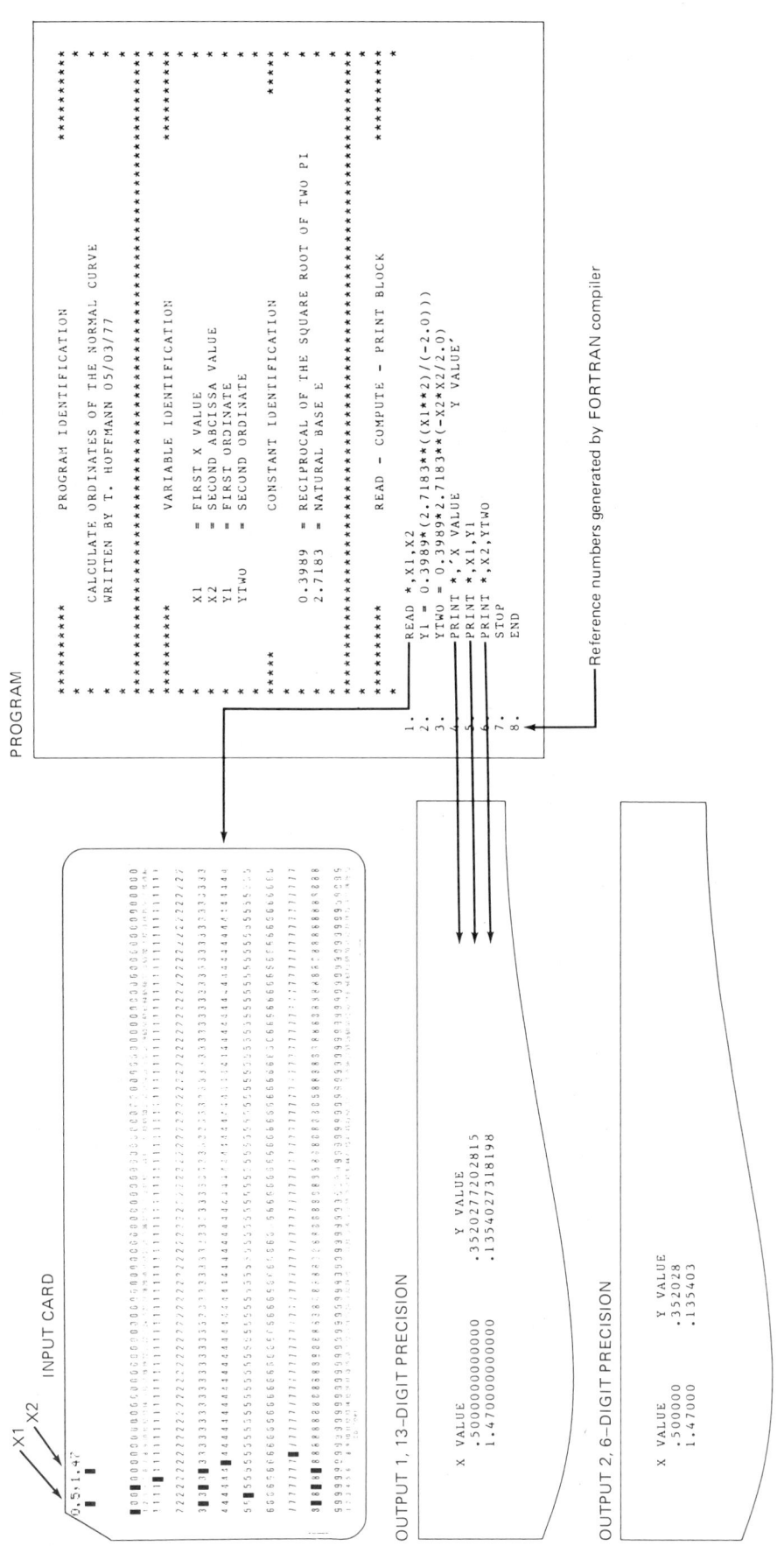

FIGURE 1-12 Program listing, sample input, and resulting outputs for statistical program 1—compute estimates of the normal curve.

47

> **1** Analyze the problem and design the program before beginning to code instructions. If you do not understand the problem and the solution procedure, you cannot tell the computer what to do. Useful design and planning methods are pseudocode and program flowcharts. In planning the program logic, follow a systematic approach:
>
>   (*a*) Plan the general logic of processing for normally expected input data. Expand to desired level of detail.
>
>   (*b*) Add processing logic for input validation and other exceptions.
>
> **2** Use FORTRAN coding paper to aid in writing instructions in proper format.
>
> **3** Use a block structure to divide the program into logical segments. Include an identification block and a list of variables block. The style selected for this text is to have a block name line consisting of 10 asterisks, 10 blanks, name of block starting in column 21, and 10 asterisks starting in column 63.
>
> **4** Use explanatory comments. Use comments freely inside the blocks. Set off each group of one or more comments by a blank comment line before and after the comment lines. In the text style, the comment is indented to column 11.
>
> **5** Use parentheses to avoid ambiguity. Do not rely upon unfamiliar precedence rules.
>
> **6** Consider printout (echo) of input data as a visual check against incorrect input.
>
> **7** Print headings or labels to clearly identify all output values.

FIGURE 1-13 Guidelines for programming style.

Summary of Suggestions for Programming Style

After having reviewed the two example programs, a set of guidelines for programming style may be summarized. Additional guidelines will be added in later chapters. The guidelines are given in Figure 1-13.

Programming Exercises

Description of Assignment

Select one or more problem(s) (or take the problem(s) assigned to you by the instructor). Use only the five statements presented in Chapter 1A. Write the program so that either input value specified in the problem can be used (even though only one input value is to be read and processed). Follow the style guidelines in Chapters 1A and 1B in doing the assignment.

1 Write a pseudocode description of the program you design. Plan for only one set of input data; provide for validation by printing (echoing) the input data.

2 Draw a program flowchart.

3 Code the program. Use only real variables and real constants in assignment statements. Do not use any integer variables or integer constants in computations.

4 Debug and execute with a set of data.

HINT: If a problem requires a value of e (the base for natural logarithms) or π (the ratio of the circumference of a circle to its diameter), use an approximate value of 2.7183 for e and 3.1416 for π. If a square root is required, exponentiate to the 0.5 power (i.e., 1.0/2.0 power). Use only real constants for exponents requiring computations (e.g., 1.0/3.0 instead of ⅓). Feel free to label variables with real names even when the formula gives letters such as n.

Mathematics and Statistics

1 For an input value of r compute the volume of the corresponding sphere.

$$v = \frac{4}{3}\,\pi r^3$$

Use input values for r of 10 or 26.5 inches.

2 A geometric progression is of the following form:

$$a \quad ar \quad ar^2 \quad ar^3 \quad \ldots \quad ar^n$$

The sum of the terms of such a progression is:

$$s = a\,\frac{r^n - 1}{r - 1}$$

Use one of the following two sets of data as input values for a, r, and n and compute the sum.

a	r	n
1	3	6
1	0.5	7

3 The Pythagorean formula can be stated as follows:

$$h = (a^2 + b^2)^{0.5}$$

where h is the hypotenuse and a and b are the sides of a right triangle. Compute h using one of the following two sets of input values for a and b.

a	b
5.0	5.0
3.0	4.0

Business and Economics

4 When interest compounds q times per year at an annual rate of i percent for n years, the principal called p, compounds to an amount a as follows:

$$a = p\left(1 + \frac{i}{q}\right)^{nq}$$

Write a program to compute the compound amount. Use either of the following two sets of input data:

p	i	q	n
1000	0.07	4	7
18.75	0.045	12	5.25

5   Various methods are used in depreciating capital goods; one of these is the declining balance method. The value of the item at the end of year n (v_n) is given by the following relationship:

$$v_n = v_0(1 - r)^n$$

where v_0 is the initial value and r is the depreciation rate. Compute v_n using either set of input data.

n	r	v_0
5	0.2	10,000.00
4	0.275	5,000.00

6   The economic order quantity (EOQ) is a function of annual usage (a), interest rate (i), the costs of setup (s), and the cost of the item itself (c). These are related as follows:

$$EOQ = (2as/ci)^{1/2}$$

Compute the EOQ using either of the following sets of values as input data.

a	s	c	i
8750	1.75	0.55	0.15
4000	1.55	0.45	0.20

Science and Engineering

7   The earth is not a sphere; it is slightly flattened at the poles and is therefore more of an oblate spheroid. The formula for its volume is

$$v = \frac{4}{3} \pi a^2 b$$

Compute the volume of the earth for input values of $a = 7927$ and $b = 7900$ miles or input values of $a = 3963$ and $b = 3950$.

8   An eraser falling out of a window is timed in its fall. Use an input for time to fall of either 5 or 6.4 seconds. Calculate and print the height of the windows in feet and in

meters plus the floor from which the eraser fell (18 feet = 1 floor). The relationship between free-fall distance (d) in feet and time (t) in seconds is

$$d = 16t^2$$

(HINT: 1 foot = 0.3048 meters)

9 An empirical study has shown that the relationship between pressure and volume for superheated steam is

$$p = 1000 \, v^{-1.4}$$

where v = volume.
For an input for v of 1.6 or 2.0, compute the pressure.

Humanities and Social Sciences

10 Empirical studies have shown a relationship between the time to perform a task and its frequency of repetition:

$$t_x = px^{-l}$$

where x = number of repetitions
  t_x = cumulative average task time for x th repetition
  p = time to perform task first time
  l = a learning factor

Compute the cumulative average time. Use one of the following sets of data as input.

x	p	l
100	3.4	0.465
50	3.4	0.93

11 A study was made of different groups of people to determine the number of males, females, orientals, and nonorientals. Use either set of input data. Compute the percentage of each category.

Study number	Male	Female	Oriental
1	256	244	302
2	108	492	413

12 Assuming towns are approximately circular and area equals πr^2, compute the population density of a town. Use either set of input data.

Town	Radius in miles	Population
1	0.6	65
2	1.7	395

General

13 Students are awarded points toward their grades based upon a weighted average of their quizzes, midterm exam, and final exam. The weighting is the average of three quizzes (Q_1, Q_2, Q_3) plus midterm grade (MT) plus twice their final exam grade (F). Compute total weighted points using as input either set of data.

Student ID	Q_1	Q_2	Q_3	MT	F
64358	45	95	87	74	83
17651	50	89	76	71	85

14 Cars can be rented on either a daily or weekly basis. The cost for daily rental is number of days (N_d) times daily rate (R_d) plus miles driven (m) times rate per mile (R_m). The weekly cost is a weekly charge (w) plus cost of buying your own gas. The latter is a function of miles driven (m), gas consumption (miles per gallon, mpg) and the cost of gasoline per gallon (C_g). Compute both the daily and weekly costs for a rental. Use one of the sets of data as input.

Situation	N_d	R_d	m	R_m	w	mpg	C_g
1	5	$10	200	$.10	$50	15	$.59
2	4	$12	150	$.12	$55	12	$.63

15 The relationship between Celsius and Fahrenheit temperatures is given by

$$c = \frac{5}{9}(f - 32)$$

Convert a Fahrenheit temperature to Celsius. Use either 50° or 92° as input data.

CHAPTER

INTRINSIC FUNCTIONS, INTEGER-TYPE DATA, IF SELECTION, DATA VALIDATION, AND INTRODUCTION TO PROGRAM TESTING

This chapter will explain a convenient method of programming common operations using a FORTRAN feature called intrinsic functions. It will explain the use of integer data and how the characteristics of integer data affect FORTRAN statements. Chapter 1A described the coding of a simple sequence of operations; this chapter will explain how to code a selection pattern using the IF statement. The chapter continues the description of good programming practices with a survey of input validation, simple repetition loops, and program testing, concluding with some suggestions for programming.

Basic Intrinsic Functions

The five operations symbols for addition (+), subtraction (−), multiplication (*), division (/), and exponentiation (**) were presented in Chapter 1A. In addition to these five operation symbols, FORTRAN provides prewritten program modules that perform common mathematical functions. These built-in functions are termed *intrinsic functions*. The use of an intrinsic function is specified by writing the function name followed by the expression to be operated upon (the argument) inside a set of parentheses. This is illustrated by four commonly used intrinsic functions:

SQRT   Take square root of the expression

ABS   Take absolute value of the expression

EXP   Exponentiate e to the power represented by the expression

AMAX1   Take largest value from list of real values in the argument

EXAMPLES

Problem	FORTRAN expression
$x = \sqrt{y}$	X = SQRT (Y)
$x = \sqrt{y + b}$	X = SQRT (Y + B)
$x = \lvert y - b \rvert$	X = ABS (Y − B)
$x = e^{y+b}$	X = EXP (Y + B)
$x = \max(a,b,c)$	X = AMAX1 (A , B , C)

The expression for a function can include another function. As an example, X = SQRT(ABS(Y − 7.0)) takes the square root of the absolute value of (Y − 7.0) and assigns it to X.

The FORTRAN standard specifies a generic name for each function plus specific names for use with different data types (integer, real, etc.) in the arguments and results. (The implications of the distinction between the real and integer functions will be made clear in the next section.) If the generic name is used, the compiler examines the type of the arguments and selects the correct function type. In other words, either the generic or type-specific function name

TABLE 2-1 SELECTED FORTRAN INTRINSIC FUNCTIONS

Generic name	Specific name	Type of argument	Type of function result	Function performed on expression
ABS	IABS	Integer	Integer	Take absolute value
	ABS	Real	Real	
MAX	MAX0	Integer	Integer	Take largest value from list of integer values
	AMAX1	Real	Real	Take largest value from list of real values
MIN	MIN0	Integer	Integer	Take smallest value from list of integer values
	AMIN1	Real	Real	Take smallest value from list of real values
SQRT	SQRT	Real	Real	Take square root
EXP	EXP	Real	Real	Exponentiate e to power represented by expression
LOG	ALOG	Real	Real	Take natural log (to base e)
LOG10	ALOG10	Real	Real	Take log to base 10

may be used. In the older 1966 FORTRAN, only the specific names were used. Specific names are more common in older programs and preferred for the sake of FORTRAN portability. In the text, specific names will generally be used. A few commonly used functions are summarized in Table 2-1; additional functions are explained in Chapter 7. A list of all functions for reference purposes is on the inside of the front cover. There are boxes to check off the functions available to you on the computer being used.

There is a set of trigonometric functions (Table 2-2) to calculate the sine, cosine, etc., of angles. The argument for a simple trigonometric function is stated in radians of an angle, and can have a fractional part (which means it is real-type data); the result of the use of the function is also a real quantity.

TABLE 2-2 TRIGONOMETRIC FUNCTIONS IN FORTRAN*

Simple trigonometric		Arc functions		Hyperbolic functions	
Name	Function	Name	Function	Name	Function
SIN	Sine	ASIN	Arcsine	SINH	Hyperbolic sine
COS	Cosine	ACOS	Arccosine	COSH	Hyperbolic cosine
TAN	Tangent	ATAN	Arctangent	TANH	Hyperbolic tangent

* Generic and real argument names are the same; integer arguments are not allowed.

Self-testing Exercise 2-1

1 Write the FORTRAN statements for the following formulas:

   (a) $X = \sqrt{a + b}$

   (b) $X = \sqrt[3]{\dfrac{a}{b} + 2}$

   (c) $Y = e^{x}$

   (d) $X = \sqrt{|y + 5|}$

   (e) $Y = \log_e x$

   (f) $r^2 = x^2 + y^2$ (find r)

   (g) $X = \max(x^2, y^2)$

2 Write the formulas for the following FORTRAN statements:

   (a) X = A L O G (Y + Z)

   (b) Y = S I N (A B S (A))

   (c) D I S C R = A B S (B * * 2 – 4 . 0 * A * C)

   (d) Y = E X P (– (X * * 2))

   (e) R H O = A * C O S (T H E T A)

   (f) X = S Q R T   (A + B / C * * D * E * F + 1 . 0)

3 Rewrite a FORTRAN statement making use of intrinsic EXP function for the formula used in statistical problem example 1 (see page 46).

Use of Integer-type Data and Mixed-type Arithmetic

In Chapter 1A, two types of variables and constants were identified—real constants and variables, which can have a fractional part, and integer constants and variables which cannot have a fractional part. Real constants, for example, always have a decimal point (4.0, 3.1, 39.) even if the fractional part is zero. Integer constants have no decimal point (4, 7, 39). The distinction between these two types was very important to pre-1977 versions of FORTRAN and rules for using them were very precise and, unfortunately, very error-prone. Current compilers relax most of the older restrictions, but the basic concept of real and integer data types remains in the language because the difference is useful in many programming situations.

The major points to remember in using integer-type data are:

1 On input, no fractional part will be accepted.

2 In processing, no fractional part is saved, so on output, no fractional part and no decimal point will be printed.

3 When real-type data is converted to integer-type data, the fractional part is dropped; there is no rounding prior to this truncation. For example, the real quantity 7.8 would be expressed by an equivalent integer quantity of 7 with no decimal point.

4 When division is performed with integer-type data and there is a fractional part in the answer, the fractional part is dropped. For example, the result of $7 \div 4$ when both 7 and 4 are integers is 1 and the result from $1 \div 3$ is 0.

There are programming situations where it is desirable to convert a real variable to an integer variable and an integer variable to a real variable. This can be done in two ways: across the equals sign and using an intrinsic function.

TABLE 2-3 INTRINSIC FUNCTIONS TO CONVERT DATA TYPES

Generic name	Specific name	Type of argument	Type of function result	Function performed on expression
REAL	FLOAT	Integer	Real	Convert from integer- to real-type
INT	IFIX	Real	Integer	Convert from real to integer (truncating the fractional part)

In the first method, data types are converted across the equals sign. If the types are different, the result of the expression on the right is converted to the type of the expression on the left of the equals sign. Thus, $I = X + Y$ will convert the sum of X and Y to an integer result called I. Any fractional part from $X + Y$ is lost.

EXAMPLES

Statement	Result
I = 3.1417	I contains 3
R = 75	R contains 75.0
JIX = X * PRICE	JIX contains 3
where X = 3.5 and PRICE = 1.1	because result of X * PRICE = 3.85

The function method (Table 2-3) specifies conversion by the use of an intrinsic function: REAL or FLOAT to convert from integer to real and INT or IFIX to convert from real to integer. REAL and INT are generic names; FLOAT and IFIX are specific names for the conversion functions.

EXAMPLES

Statement		Result
	I = I F I X (3 . 1 4 1 7)	I = 3
or	I = I N T (3 . 1 4 1 7)	
	R = F L O A T (7 5)	R = 75.0
or	R = R E A L (7 5)	
	J I X = I F I X (X * P R I CE)	JIX = 3
or	J I X = I N T (X * P R I CE)	

The FORTRAN programmer should be careful in using integer division because the fractional result is lost (truncated, not rounded), as illustrated by the following examples:

Arithmetic statement	Result
J = 7/3	J = 2
If M = 4, N = 5 then: X = N/M	X = 1.0 because 5/4 was truncated to 1 and then converted to a floating point 1.0
JIX = M/N	JIX = 0 because 4/5 will result in no whole numbers

Since the integer and real data types have different characteristics with respect to a fractional part, there are restrictions on mixing them in an expression. If the expression has only integer-type variables and constants, the expression is integer and integer arithmetic will be used. If only real variables are used, real arithmetic will be applied. Exponents do not change the type of an expression; thus a real expression may have an integer exponent without mixing the types. However, an integer variable with a real exponent is mixed type.

It is often convenient in programming to use both integer and real variables in the same expression. Most modern FORTRAN compilers will perform the conversion of mixed-type expressions automatically, but it is generally not a good idea to rely on this feature. Since conversion of real to integer results in the loss of the fractional part, the programmer may not perceive the consequences of a mixed-type expression. If the program explicitly codes the conversion, the logic is clearer to the programmer when debugging as well as to those who read or revise the program.

Desired expression	Coded as
X = A + K	X = A + FLOAT (K) or X = A + REAL (K)
I = K + A	I = K + IFIX (A) or I = K + INT (A)
X = I**A	X = FLOAT (I) ** A or X = REAL (I) ** A

The FORTRAN programmer should also be aware that an integer number generally has an exact representation in the computer, whereas a real number may have a representation that is very close but not exact. In the computer, data is represented by the two states of computer storage devices. For example, the number 75 is represented as 1001011 with 1 and 0 referring to the two states (say open or closed for a semiconductor switch or two directions of magnetization for a magnetic core). The computer represents data and processes it using the binary number system in which there are only two values rather than the decimal system which has ten values (0 to 9). The conversions between binary and decimal are done automatically. However, an exact binary equivalent cannot be obtained for some decimal fractions. The problem is similar to the inexact decimal representation of some common fractions ($4/3$ cannot be represented exactly but only reasonably closely as 1.333. . .).

The slightly inexact representation of some real fractions does not normally cause an error except when conversions from real to integer are involved. For example, assume KMONT = 12 in the following expression:

IDAY = INT (2 . 6 * FLOAT (KMONT) – 0 . 2)

The answer should be 31 but may be 30. The result of 2.6 $*$ 12.0 $-$ 0.2 is represented in the computer (in binary) as 30.99999. . . . If the result were to be printed out, it would be 31 because the program would make the small rounding adjustment required before printing. However, in internal processing, the truncation function is performed before any rounding adjustment; it merely drops the fractional part. Such difficulties as the above happen *very seldom* in programming, but the student should be aware of the possibility. The program can, in such cases, be written to include a small rounding factor.

RULES FOR INTEGER AND REAL TYPES IN EXPRESSIONS

1 If integer and real data types are mixed in an expression, integer variables or constants will be converted by floating. Good programming practice is to explicitly code these conversions

2 In the statement $a = b$, if a is of a different type than b, the results of b will be converted to the type of a. If the conversion is from real to integer, the fractional part of the expression result will be truncated and discarded

3 Fractional parts from division of integer variables are truncated

4 The allowable combinations of types in exponentiation are:
(a) Integer expression with integer exponent
(b) Real expression with real exponent
(c) Real expression with integer exponent
The exponent may be any arithmetic expression meeting these type restrictions

5 An integer expression to a real exponent is a mixed-type expression. If used, the integer expression will be automatically converted to a real expression. Some older compilers will reject this form.

It may now be helpful to review the list of intrinsic functions in Table 2-1. Note the generic name that can be used with either a real or integer argument and the specific name which applies only to a given data type in the argument.

Self-testing Exercise 2-2

1 Complete the following table

Expression or statement	Valid or not valid. Note if mixed type	If not valid, why. If mixed type, how converted
(a) A $*$ $*$ 2+ 1		
(b) A $*$ $*$ (2+ 1)		
(c) A $*$ $*$ (B+C /D)		
(d) A /B+D / 3		
(e) I X + JX+ 4		
(f) KX =A+B I		
(g) FUN = SQRT (A+AXEL /BETA)		
(h) X = (A+B) / ((C+D)$*$E $*$ I X)		
(i) X+Y =Z $*$ ALPHA		
(j) JX = I X $*$ $*$ A		
(k) X =A $*$ $*$ I		

2 If A = 3.0, B = 2.5, IX = 3, and JX = 2, what will be the result of the following statements?
(*a*) X = A/B
(*b*) K = IX/JX
(*c*) KIX = JX/IX
(*d*) NIX = IX + 2/JX
3 Write statements using both intrinsic functions: generic and type-specific.
(*a*) Take absolute value of integer value KDATA.
(*b*) Find the minimum for values of I, J, and K.
4 Convert the following, by using first the generic intrinsic function, next the specific intrinsic functions, and finally by coding a new variable name across the equals sign.
(*a*) JIX to a real variable
(*b*) DATA1 to an integer variable
5 Remove mixed mode by using explicit coding of conversion.
(*a*) X = I*B**I
(*b*) X = B+(C/J)+K**D

Selection among Alternative Processing Paths Using the IF Statement

As explained in Chapter 1A, program logic is simplified by using only three program-coding structures:

1 Simple sequence

2 Selection

3 Repetition

Simple sequence was explained and used in Chapter 1; selection and simple repetition will be explained in this chapter; and repetition will be described more completely in Chapter 4.

The Selection Programming Structure

As explained in Chapter 1A, the selection structure consists of a test for a condition followed by two alternative paths for the program to follow. The program selects one of the program-control paths, depending on the test of the condition. After performing one of the two paths, the program control returns to a single point. This coding pattern can be termed IF . . . ELSE because the logic can be stated (for condition P and operations C and D): IF P (is true), perform C; ELSE perform D (Figure 2-1). A flowchart for the selection structure consists of a decision symbol followed by two paths, each with a process symbol, coming together following the operation symbols. An allowable variation is for no processing in one of the branches.

Statement Numbers in FORTRAN

FORTRAN statements may have a statement label, a number written in columns 1 to 5 on the coding sheet. The statement label number may be from one to five numeric digits. If there are less than five digits, it is customary to

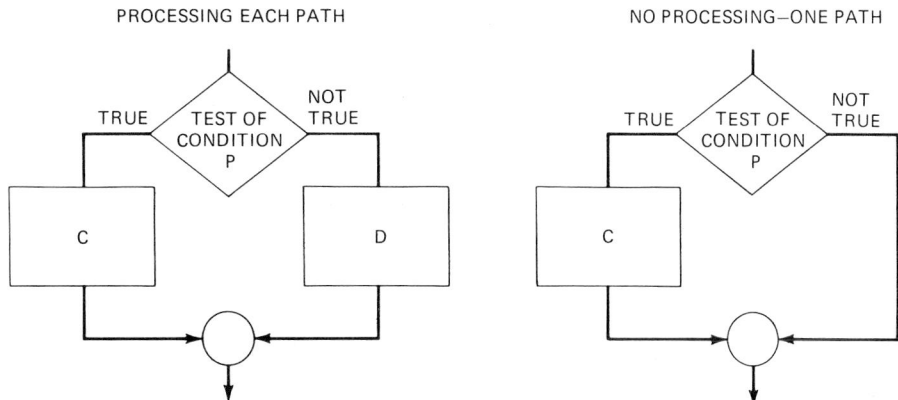

FIGURE 2-1   Flowchart of selection program structure.

right justify them (leave the blanks at the left). The statement label numbers are coded by the programmer and used by the program; there is no connection with the line reference numbers added to the program listing by many compilers.

Any FORTRAN statement may be numbered, but only those statements that are referenced by another program statement *must* be numbered. For example, in Chapter 1B, none of the statements were numbered. A good practice is to use statement numbers only when they are needed for reference or documentation because excess statement numbers make it more difficult to locate a statement number being referenced. The rules of the language allow the statement numbers to be in any order, and they need not be sequential. In other words, the statement numbers are identifying labels, not sequencing numbers. However, having statement numbers in sequence or approximate sequence makes it easier to locate a referenced statement number.

As explained, a disciplined style for a FORTRAN program will divide the program into logical blocks of code. A useful approach to numbering is to have each block of code start a new set of numbers. For example, the first block will be labeled with numbers in the 100s. In fact, it is often useful to number the first statement in the block with 101. The second block will use 200s, with the first statement being labeled with 201, etc. This has the advantage that whenever a statement is referenced, its location in the program and the logical block to which it belongs are also identified. This is illustrated in Figure 2-2.

GOTO Statement

The GOTO statement (also written as GO TO) is used to branch around one or more statements. The branching is unconditional; i.e., it does not depend on any test or condition.

GOTO STATEMENT

GOTO s (or GO TO s)

where s is a statement label

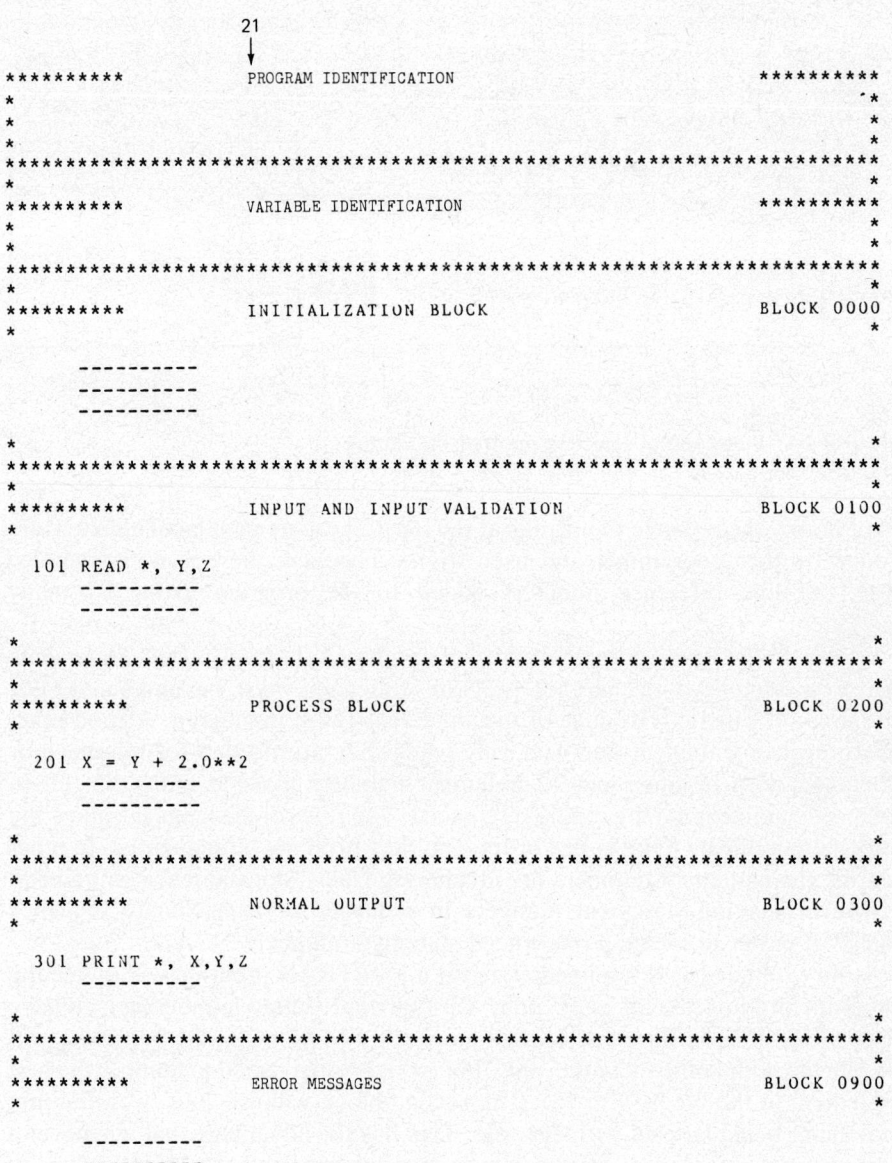

```
                              21
                              ↓
*********            PROGRAM IDENTIFICATION                        **********
*                                                                        `*
*                                                                         *
*                                                                         *
***************************************************************************
*                                                                         *
*********            VARIABLE IDENTIFICATION                       **********
*                                                                         *
*                                                                         *
***************************************************************************
*                                                                         *
*********            INITIALIZATION BLOCK                      BLOCK 0000
*                                                                         *

         ----------
         ----------
         ----------

*                                                                         *
***************************************************************************
*                                                                         *
*********            INPUT AND INPUT VALIDATION                BLOCK 0100
*                                                                         *

   101 READ *, Y,Z
         ----------
         ----------

*                                                                         *
***************************************************************************
*                                                                         *
*********            PROCESS BLOCK                             BLOCK 0200
*                                                                         *

   201 X = Y + 2.0**2
         ----------
         ----------

*                                                                         *
***************************************************************************
*                                                                         *
*********            NORMAL OUTPUT                             BLOCK 0300
*                                                                         *

   301 PRINT *, X,Y,Z
         ----------

*                                                                         *
***************************************************************************
*                                                                         *
*********            ERROR MESSAGES                            BLOCK 0900
*                                                                         *

         ----------
         ----------
```

FIGURE 2-2 Outline of program form with block numbering.

When a GOTO is encountered, the next statement to be executed will be the one numbered by s. After statement s is executed, control continues with the statements following s. Because use of GOTOs may make a program difficult to debug and maintain, they should be used with care. To aid in understanding the logic of a program, we have chosen to place a set of comments before most GOTOs explaining the nature of the branching as shown by the following example:

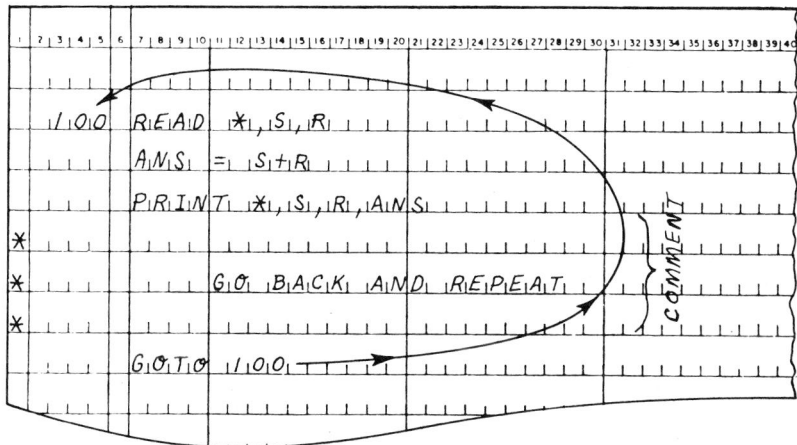

Logical IF Statement

The selection structure is coded by an IF statement. There are two forms of the IF statements: the logical or relational IF statement and the arithmetic IF statement (explained later in this chapter). For clarity of programming, the logical IF is always preferred even in cases where two logical IF statements are required to do the same test as a single arithmetic IF. The 1977 FORTRAN standard contains FORTRAN features that enhance the basic IF statement. These enhancements (block IF) are explained in the next section.

LOGICAL IF STATEMENT

IF (e) st

where e = a logical (relational) expression and st is almost any executable statement. If the relation is true, execute the statement; else do not execute the statement and continue with the statement following the IF statement.

In a simple case, the logical expression in an IF statement consists of two arithmetic expressions (which may be only variable names) separated by a relational operator. The relational operators are shown below.

RELATIONAL OPERATORS

Operator	Representing
.LT.	Less than
.LE.	Less than or equal to
.EQ.	Equal to
.NE.	Not equal to
.GT.	Greater than
.GE.	Greater than or equal to

Note that a period precedes and follows the operators to differentiate them from variable names. Examples of logical IF statements are:

```
IF (A .GT. B) GO TO 300
IF (SQRT (X) .LE. 5.0) JS=1
```

If control is to go to 150 if A is negative, 160 if A is zero, and 140 if A is positive, two logical IF statements are required:

```
    IF (A .LT. 0.0) GOTO 150
    IF (A .EQ. 0.0) GOTO 160
140 (A is positive)
```

If two or more relational expressions are to be compared, the logical operators .AND. and .OR. may be used. The basic logical operators are .AND., .OR., and .NOT.; additional logical operators are explained in Chapter 7.

BASIC LOGICAL OPERATORS	
Operator	Expression is true when
.AND.	Both relations are true
.OR.	One or both relations are true
.NOT.	Opposite is true

A statement with the operator .AND. is true only if both relations connected by .AND. are true; a statement with the operator .OR. is true if either or both of the relations connected by .OR. are true. True means that the relationship is satisfied, e.g., X .GT. Y is true if X is greater than Y. The operator .NOT. is used to indicate negation (opposite) of the relation. Statements can contain a number of relations connected by more than one logical operator. When more than one .AND. and .OR. are used in the same expression, the parenthesis rule (inside parentheses first) and a precedence rule can be applied. In the absence of parentheses, the following precedences are applied:

1   Arithmetic operations (using the precedence rule for them)

2   .NOT.

3   .AND.

4   .OR.

Operations having the same precedence are executed from left to right. For a clear program style, parentheses should be placed around the portions of the expressions connected by .AND. and .OR. even though they are not required.

    The use of the simple logical IF statement in coding selection is illustrated by examples of coding to find the largest of two real quantities A and B and to assign the largest value to BIG. Note the need for the GO TO in the first example because only a single statement can follow the simple IF test.

EXAMPLES

I F   ((P A Y   . G T .   4 5 . 0)   . A N D .   (A G E   . L E .   1 7 . 0))   T A L L Y = T A L L Y + 1 . 0

Add 1 to TALLY only if PAY .GT. 45 and also AGE .LE. 17 (both are true)

I F   ((H R S   . G E .   6 0 . 0)   . O R .   (O T   . E Q .   1 0))   G O T O   1 0

Transfer control to statement 10 if either of the relational statements is true

I F   ((H R S . L E . 6 0 . 0) . A N D . (H R S . G T . 0 . 0) . O R . (K O D E . E Q . 1)) G O T O   2 0 0

Transfer to 200 if HRS are less than or equal to 60 and are greater than zero or if KODE = 1

I F   (. N O T .   (K O D E   . E Q .   1))   G O T O   3 0 0

Transfer to 300 if KODE is not equal to 1. This could have been coded more simply as

I F   (K O D E   . N E .   1)   G O T O   3 0 0

Flowcharts	Coding

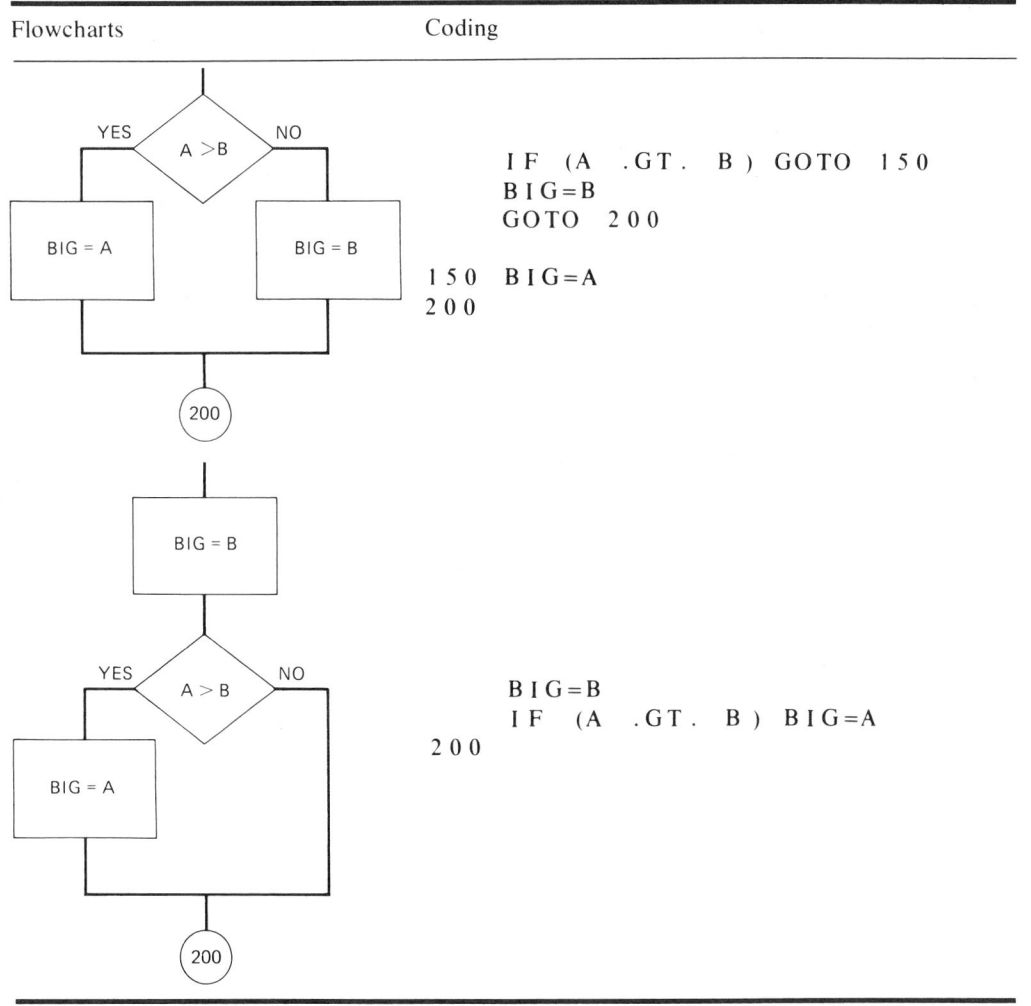

```
       IF  (A  .GT.  B )  GOTO  150
       BIG=B
       GOTO  200

150    BIG=A
200
```

```
       BIG=B
       IF  (A  .GT.  B )  BIG=A
200
```

In the first example, there are two alternative processing statements for the two branches; in the second example, there is only one action for the one branch and no action with the other branch. The first example requires GOTOs; the second does not. In using the basic logical IF, it should be kept in mind that unless the action of the IF is to transfer control (GOTO), the statement following the IF will be executed in both cases, i.e., as part of both selection paths. It is easy to overlook this IF feature and program incorrect logic. For example, an incorrect coding for the above problem is the following:

```
IF  (A  .GT.  B )  BIG=A
BIG=B
```

The program makes BIG = A if A is greater than B and then passes control to the next statement which makes BIG = B. In other words, BIG always equals B. In terms of a flowchart, the programmer has written:

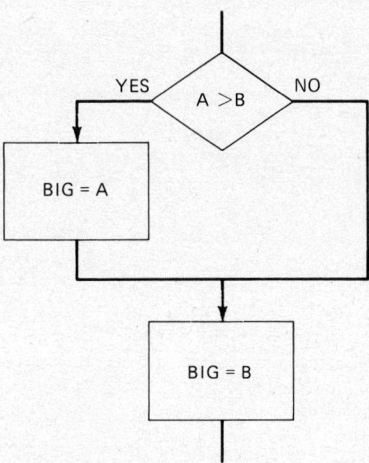

Block IF Statement

The preceding examples illustrate a limitation of the simple logical IF. If two sets of statements can be selected by the IF statements, it is necessary to use GOTOs to branch around the two sets of statements because the IF specifies only what is to be performed if the condition is true and only one statement may be used. In the 1977 FORTRAN, a new feature, the block IF or IF THEN ELSE statement, eliminates these restrictions and makes clearer coding without GOTOs. Check to make sure the feature is available to you before using it. Essentially, the block IF statement provides the capability to execute one of two groups of statements.

To visually show the group of statements in the IF block, statements following the IF are indented (say 4 spaces). The ELSE must be alone on a line and the statements following the ELSE are indented. The ENDIF is alone on a line and aligned with the IF to which it belongs.

BLOCK IF STATEMENT

IF (condition) THEN statements for IF block ELSE statements for ELSE block	All statements between the condition and the ELSE are executed if the condition is true; statements between ELSE and ENDIF are executed if the condition is not true
ENDIF (or END IF)	The ELSE should be the only word on the line. The ELSE and ELSE block statements are optional and may be omitted
	Each IF . . . THEN . . . [ELSE] must end with an ENDIF
ELSEIF (condition) THEN statements for ELSEIF block	Used prior to ELSE if false condition is to be followed by another test of a condition. ELSEIF (or ELSE IF) is part of the IF . . . THEN . . . ELSE block and does not use a separate ENDIF

PAGE 70

The block IF can be best explained by illustration. In the first example, RPAY (for regular pay) is computed at $4.10 per hour for up to and including 40 hours per week; for hours over 40, the OTPAY (for overtime pay) is 1.5 times the $4.10 rate.

Flowchart	Program

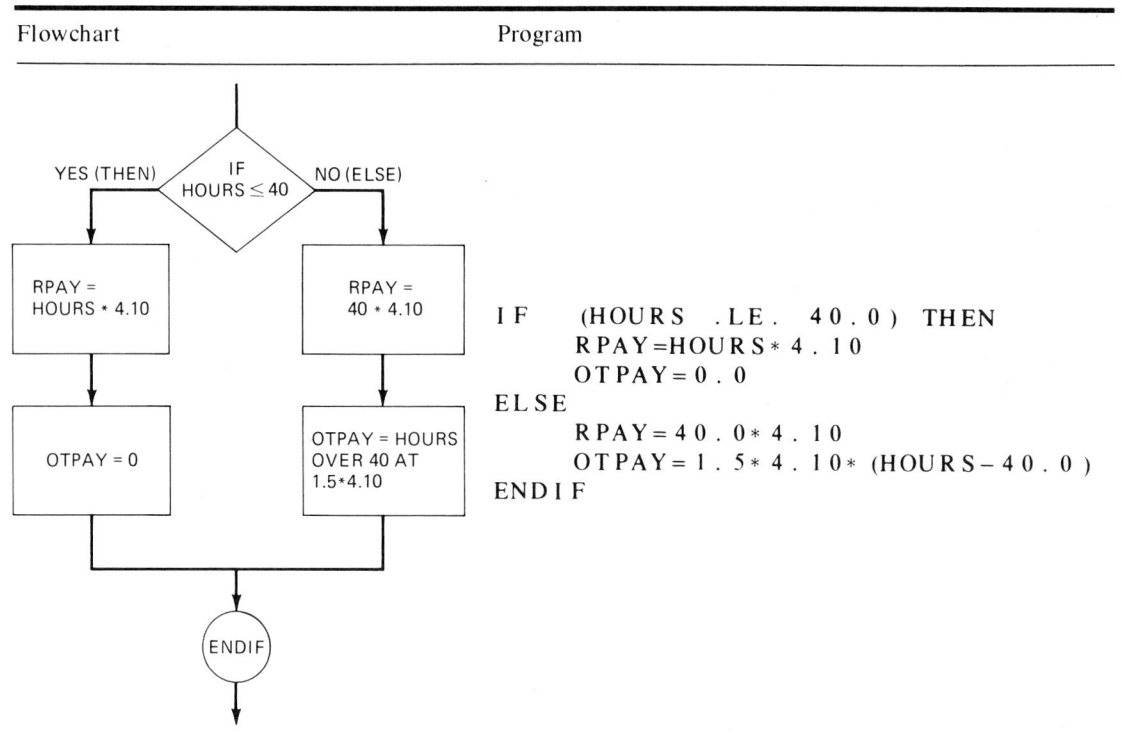

```
IF      (HOURS .LE.  40.0)  THEN
        RPAY=HOURS*4.10
        OTPAY=0.0
ELSE
        RPAY=40.0*4.10
        OTPAY=1.5*4.10*(HOURS-40.0)
ENDIF
```

Block IFs may be nested with each block of IF . . . THEN . . . ELSE ending with an ENDIF. As an example, if the shift code is greater than 1.0 (for other than day shift), the pay for every day or night is $6.00 per hour. For the day shift, the rate is $4.15 per hour, but if the day is Sunday (DAY = 7.0), there is a special premium of $3.00 per hour.

Flowchart   Program

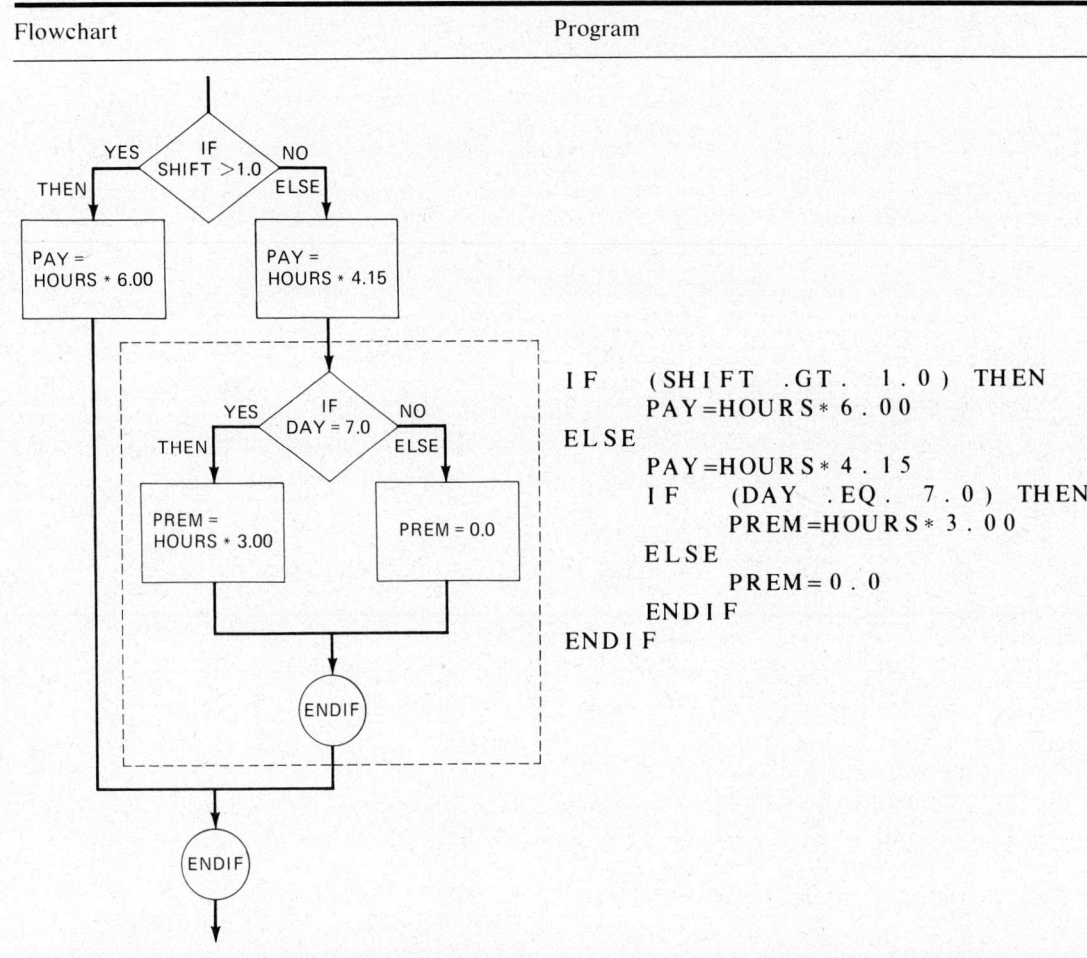

```
IF     (SHIFT .GT. 1.0) THEN
       PAY=HOURS*6.00
ELSE
       PAY=HOURS*4.15
       IF    (DAY .EQ. 7.0) THEN
             PREM=HOURS*3.00
       ELSE
             PREM=0.0
       ENDIF
ENDIF
```

As a style comment, the first test of (SHIFT .GT. 1.0) is satisfactory except when SHIFT is in error (say SHIFT = 6.0 even though there is no shift greater than 4). It is wise to test for a value being within valid limits before making a test in which all other values are assumed to be valid. The test in this case might be IF (SHIFT .LE. 0.0 .OR. SHIFT .GT. 4.0) GOTO error handling statement.

The ELSEIF . . . THEN is used to code another test prior to the coding of the ELSE result. The ELSEIF is part of the IF THEN block and does not use a separate ENDIF. The ELSEIF statement may be repeated. It is useful in programming a series of tests in which testing need not continue if a test passes so that a THEN result is achieved. For example, a program segment is to print student grades based on test scores:

90 to 100	A
80 to 89	B
70 to 79	C
Below 70	See instructor

Note that once a score is identified as being in a range, the remaining tests are not used.

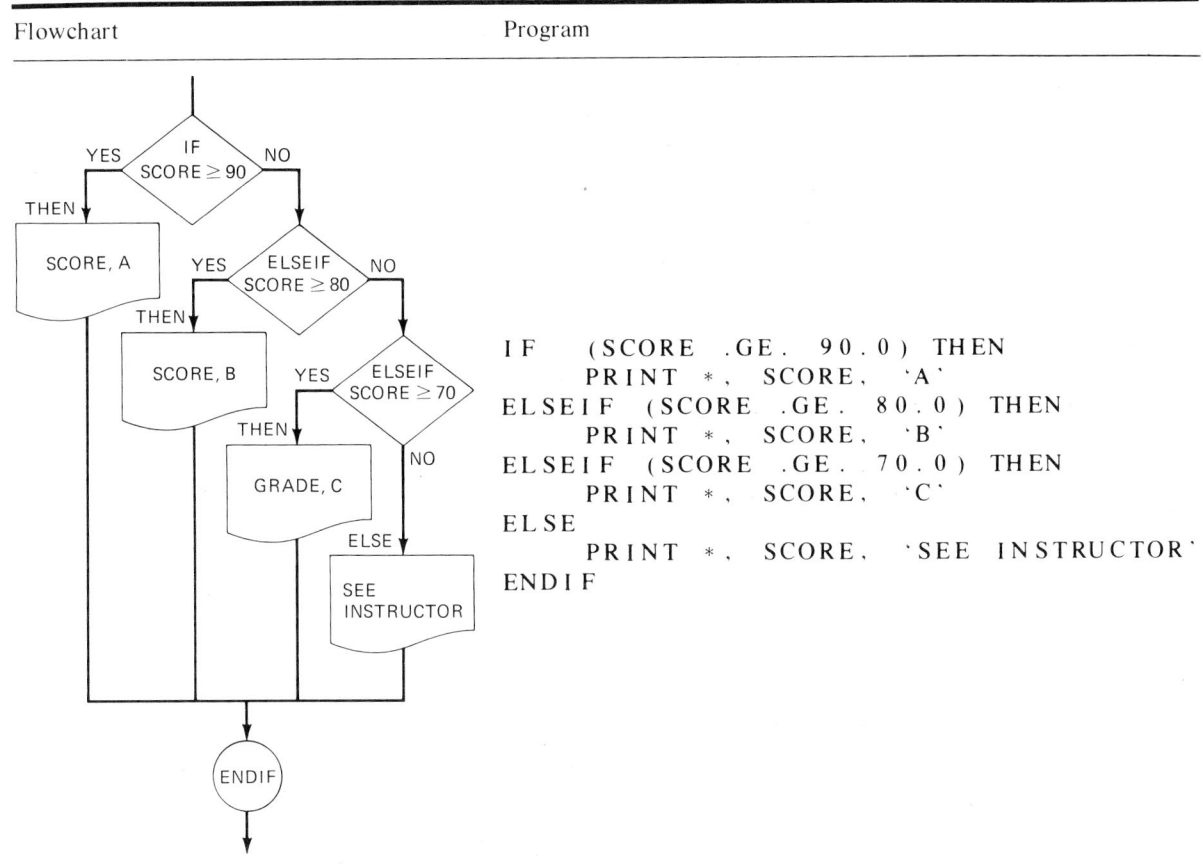

Flowchart   Program

```
IF    (SCORE .GE.  90.0) THEN
      PRINT *, SCORE, 'A'
ELSEIF (SCORE .GE.  80.0) THEN
      PRINT *, SCORE, 'B'
ELSEIF (SCORE .GE.  70.0) THEN
      PRINT *, SCORE, 'C'
ELSE
      PRINT *, SCORE, 'SEE INSTRUCTOR'
ENDIF
```

By way of style comment, the tests of scores were written to test only greater than or equal since previous tests had logically eliminated the upper limit. But a good procedure would be to test explicitly for a score greater than 100.0 (an error). The other tests could also have been written to test for the entire range, as for example, IF (SCORE .GE. 80 .AND. .LE. 89) THEN . . . The test following the .AND. is redundant, but the program logic is made clearer. Unless efficiency is an important consideration, the full coding is preferred.

Arithmetic IF Statement

The arithmetic IF is not recommended because it tends to be error-prone. It is never necessary because the logical IF can be used. However, it was frequently used in older FORTRAN programs. Therefore, it will be explained so that FORTRAN programs written by those employing the feature can be understood.

ARITHMETIC IF STATEMENT

IF (expression) s_1, s_2, s_3

where the expression may be a variable name or arithmetic expression. If the expression, when evaluated, is negative, i.e., less than zero, control goes to the first statement label listed; if zero, to the second statement number; and if positive, to the third. The statement labels are separated by commas.

Two examples illustrate the arithmetic IF:

Condition	IF statement
IF X = 1.0 GO TO 100; IF 2.0, GO TO 200; IF more than 2.0, GO TO 400.	IF (X − 2.0) 100, 200, 400 (Note that subtracting 2.0 from X created a negative condition for X = 1.0, a zero condition for X = 2.0 and positive condition for X > 2.0)
IF X ≤ 6 GO TO 112; IF X > 6 GO TO 210.	IF (X − 6.0) 113, 113, 210

Self-testing Exercise 2-3

Write program segments to perform the operations indicated using a logical IF but not a block IF except as specified.

1 If the square root of $X^2 + Y^2$ is less than 100.0, the answer (ANSWR) is to be 12.0∗X. If greater than or equal to 100.0, the value of ANSWR is to be X^2. Print the answer.

2 Find the largest quantity represented by three variables: ALPHA, BETA, and GAMMA. Call the largest quantity BIG. If two are equal, either value may be used. (a) First write statements without using the AMAX1 (or MAX) function. (b) Then write statements using the AMAX1 function.

3 Two variables, NIX and KIX, should be unequal. Find the largest in absolute value (without regard to sign). Print out the largest. If they are equal, stop the program.

4 Find out if $-550 \leq X \leq 1000$. If X falls within these limits (between −550 and +1000), print out YES. If not, print out NO. Then halt the computer.

5 Write logical IF statements to test whether A is greater than B and greater than C or if A is less than D and equal to E. If so, transfer control to statement 210. If false, go to statement 310.

6 Write a program segment with block IF for question 4.

7 Write a program segment with block IF for a problem in which, if a code number is equal to 1 or 2, pay is computed as 3.75 times regular hours and overtime is set to zero. If the code is 3, pay is 4.15 times regular hours and overtime is 1.5 times 4.15 times overtime hours. If code is more than 3, CODE ERROR and its value are printed.

Validating Input Data

The selection structure programmed by the IF statements allows the coding of an important program block: validation of input data. Perhaps the most error-prone part of the use of a computer program is the preparation of the input data. Good program design suggests, therefore, that a program include features which are useful in detecting erroneous or incomplete input data. Two techniques should be employed where feasible.

1 Print out (echo) the input data for visual review. This printout may be especially for validation purposes or the input data may be printed as part of the final output. This was followed in the example programs in Chapter 1B.

2 Test the input data to check for data items that do not meet the criteria for valid data.

The testing for valid data is based on the fact that it is possible, in many cases, to specify criteria for input data. For example, the data for hours worked might be specified as not negative or zero and not greater than 65.0. A test for validity could consist of three separate tests or a single, composite test, such as:

```
IF  ( (HOURS .LE. 0.0) .OR. (HOURS .GT. 65.0))
    PRINT*,HOURS, 'HOURS ERROR'
```

During processing, it is sometimes desirable to program a test to avoid possible division by zero. For example, a computation of a bonus as a percentage of pay would, if bonus were zero, produce a machine execution error and abort the job. Coding to prevent this execution error might read:

```
    IF  (BONUS .EQ. 0.0) GOTO 500 (an error message)
    RATE=PAY/BONUS

500 PRINT  *, 'ERROR—BONUS IS ZERO'
```

Self-testing Exercise 2-4

1 Write a combined input and input validation block to test input data and reject (with a message) a negative or zero rate (RATE) or a rate greater than 15 percent and stop processing. Write without block IF.
2 Rewrite problem 1 with block IF.

Processing More than One Set of Input Data

The sequence program structure used in Chapter 1 works well for a single set of input data, but it is very cumbersome if more than one data card is to be read and processed. Since each READ statement reads only one card (using the statements explained so far), processing 10 different sets of input data on 10 different cards requires 10 sets of processing statements each with a READ statement, and each set of data has unique variable names. A more efficient program design is to write the program so that the READ statement and its related processing statement are used over again for each set of input data. This method is called *repetition or looping,* a fundamental technique in programming. Repetition will be explained in more detail in Chapter 4; the repetition procedure described in this chapter is a simple IF loop.

A Simple IF Loop

Assume a program segment that is to read values called X and Y from a card, compute the sum (called Z) and print the values assigned to X, Y, and Z. This is to be repeated for several sets of X and Y inputs. The repetition could be programmed with a GOTO statement to transfer control back to the first statement in the set as follows:

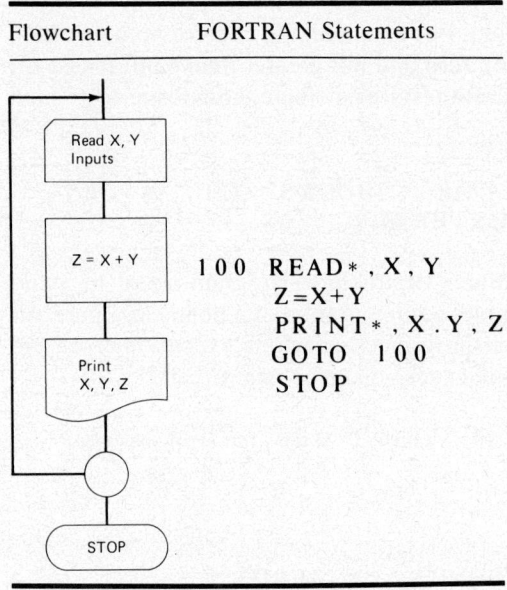

Flowchart	FORTRAN Statements

```
100   READ*, X , Y
      Z = X + Y
      PRINT*, X . Y , Z
      GOTO   100
      STOP
```

The above logic repeats the processing over and over using a new input card for each execution. The difficulty is that the repetition never terminates—it is an endless loop because there is no logic to cause it to stop looping. A program written in this way will eventually be abnormally terminated by the operating system, but this is not a satisfactory way to come to a stop.

A simple method for coding the end of a repetition is to use an IF statement to test whether or not the set of statements has been executed the appropriate number of times. Two methods of coding the test for termination when reading input data illustrate the concept.

1   Use a unique termination value for the input data item following the last set of data to be processed. Examples of such values are a negative value (if no regular value will be negative) or 999 (if no regular input would have this value). The coding and flowchart for a negative value are:

Flowchart	FORTRAN

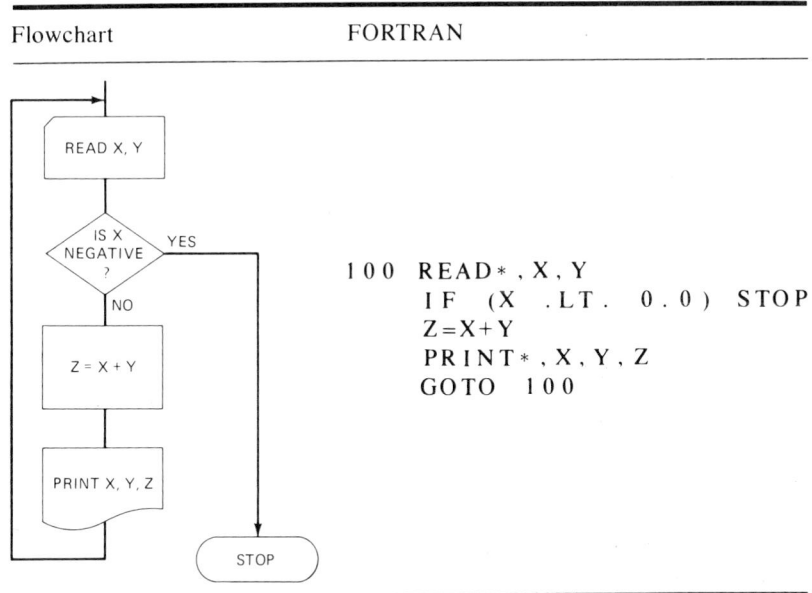

```
100   READ*,X,Y
      IF  (X  .LT.  0.0)  STOP
      Z=X+Y
      PRINT*,X,Y,Z
      GOTO  100
```

2 Establish a counter for input items. Keep track of how many are read and terminate when the required number have been processed. For example, if the input data card counter is called ICOUNT and 10 items are to be processed, the flowchart and coding could be as follows:

Flowchart	FORTRAN

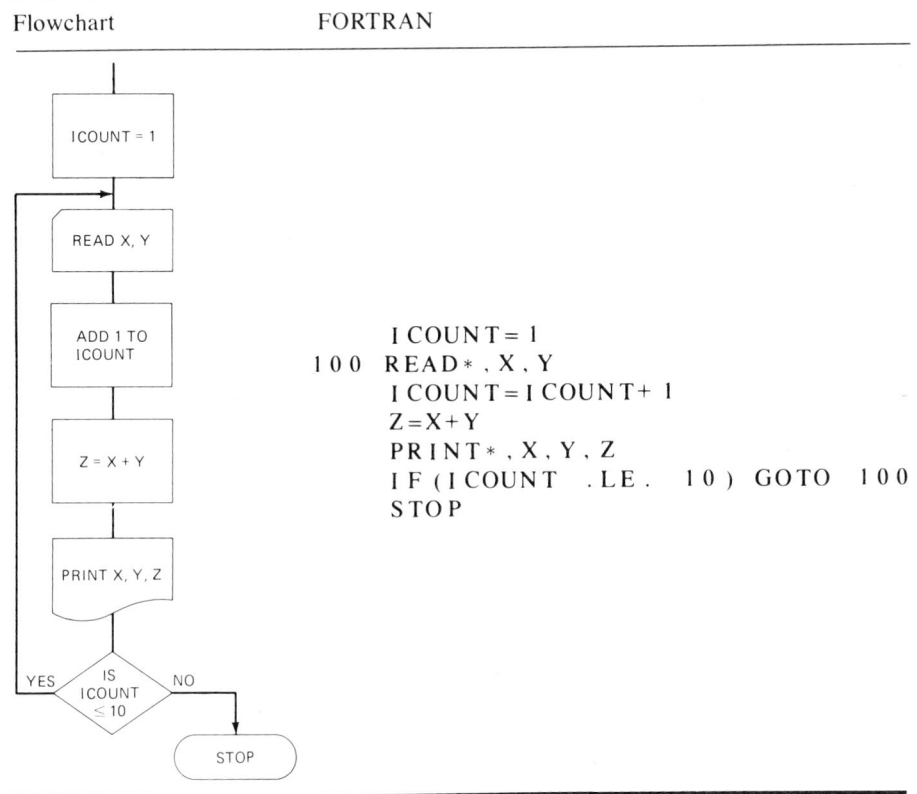

```
      ICOUNT=1
100   READ*,X,Y
      ICOUNT=ICOUNT+1
      Z=X+Y
      PRINT*,X,Y,Z
      IF(ICOUNT  .LE.  10)  GOTO  100
      STOP
```

First- and Last-Time-Through Logic

These two methods are illustrated in the example programs in Chapter 2B—a counter is used in general example 2 and a negative value test is used in statistical example 2. There are many variations on loop design. In the preceding use of a counter, the test for termination was placed at the end of the loop; it can also be placed at the beginning of the loop as will be explained in Chapter 4.

In coding of both simple loops and more complex repetitions to be explained in Chapter 4, a major source of program logic errors occurs in the processing of the first data item through a block of code that will be used repeatedly and in handling of the last data item.

The "first-time-through" errors generally result from failing to initialize properly. Logic which works perfectly once started will not give correct results if begun incorrectly. Two programming situations illustrate the need for first-time-through logic.

1 *Obtaining the largest value so far* If, as each data item is processed, the program tests it to determine if it is the largest value so far and stores the largest value, the instructions might read:

PLARGE = AMAX1 (DATA, PLARGE)

This instruction stores the larger of DATA and the previous PLARGE in PLARGE (which is then the largest so far). But what is PLARGE the first time the comparison is made? To ensure that the test will work properly at the first comparison, PLARGE must be initialized so that the first data item will be larger. This can be done by initializing PLARGE with a value such as $-1.0E10$ that is less than any possible value of DATA.

2 *Adding to previous sum* In many programs, a sum is accumulated by a statement of the form:

SUM = SUM + DATA

In essence, this statement is to add the current value of DATA to the previous value of SUM. In order for the logic to work properly, SUM must be zero the first time through. If the first data amount is 5.0 then the SUM after the first execution will be 5.0 (but only if SUM is zero the first time through). Some (but not all) compilers set all storage to zero before the programming execution, but do not depend on it.

These two situations reflect a large class of first-time situations. They are usually relatively simple to analyze and program if the programmer is alert to the first-time problem.

The last-time problem is at termination when the last data item may not be processed or may be processed incorrectly. For example, assume a termination test based on a card count of 5 and a count (ICOUNT) that started at 1. If the test and increment read

IF (ICOUNT .GE. 5) GOTO termination statement

ICOUNT = ICOUNT + 1

then the fifth card will not be processed past this point. If there is no further processing on data card 5 after these instructions, the last-time-through logic is correct; if there is more processing to be performed, the logic is probably incorrect. As with first-time-through logic, the problem is easily solved if recognized.

Planning and Design of a Program with Multiple Cases and Exceptions

In Chapter 1B, the explanation of the use of pseudocode and a program flowchart in program planning described a two-step planning and design process based on a single case (a single set of input data). In this chapter, statements have been introduced which allow the program to repeat the processing using more than one set of input data (multiple cases); the statements also allow more computer input validation and more complete handling of exceptions. The logic of program planning and design is therefore expanded as follows to include these more complex problem situations.

1 Plan the general logic of processing for one case (one set of normally expected data) to the level of detail useful for the specific problem.

2 Add logic to handle multiple cases (multiple sets of input). Include logic required for first-time-through and last-time-through processing.

3 Add logic for input validation and handling of input errors.

4 Add logic for handling exceptions and unusual cases. Review cases in which data may be zero or negative.

This expanded program planning and design procedure is illustrated in Chapter 2B in connection with the pseudocode for general example 2.

Introduction to Testing and Quality Assurance for a Program

Having written a program, the programmer (and user) needs assurance that the program is correct and performs as expected. Testing and quality assurance of programs can use a variety of techniques. This section will describe the nature of the testing and quality-assurance process, explain the development and use of a set of test data—data designed specifically to test the program—and introduce debugging during compilation.

The Testing and Quality-Assurance Process

With a very simple FORTRAN program, testing is quite simple, but for larger and more complex FORTRAN programs, there is a need for a process of testing and quality assurance that proceeds concurrently with the program design, programming, and debugging.

Programming	Testing and Quality-Assurance Process
1 Problem recognition and algorithm selection	**1** Check literature for existence of tested algorithm. Use a tested algorithm, if available.
2 Program design (e.g., flowcharting and/or pseudocode)	**2** Development of testing strategy and design of initial set of test data
3 Program coding	**3** (*a*) Desk checking. The programmer manually traces a few data items through the program (at the desk prior to compilation) (*b*) Program reading (peer review). It is frequently helpful to have other programmers (or fellow students who are programming) read a program to check for errors in logic, lack of good style, etc.
4 Compilation	**4** Use of compiler diagnostics to identify coding errors
5 Debugging and testing	**5** Use of test data to identify logic errors and provide assurance that program is correct

The Development and Use of Test Data

Data to test a program should be designed to test all paths through the program. If a program consists of a simple sequence (such as the programs in Chapter 1B), a single set of data will test the program. In a program with selection structures, a separate set of test data needs to be provided for each path through the program. For example, assume a program with the following structure (shown in Figure 2-3). With one selection structure, there are two paths through the program. If these two paths are two processing paths for a payroll program that has one computational procedure for less than or equal to 40 hours and another procedure for over 40 hours, one set of test data should test for 40 hours and a second set of test data for over 40 hours. Two sets of test data would be satisfactory except that a frequent source of error in programs is at the breakpoint specified in the decision block; in the example, the breakpoint is 40. It might be quite easy for the programmer to code IF (HOURS .LT. 40.0) rather than IF (HOURS .LE. 40.0). If the breakpoint itself is not tested, this easily made error would not be detected. For this reason, it is recommended that test data include data at the breakpoint, the breakpoint minus one, and the breakpoint plus one. In the simple example, this will require three sets of test data with hours data of 39, 40, and 41.

The testing of all processing logic includes the use of invalid data to test the data validation logic. In other words, a complete set of test data will include:

1 Normal case testing of all breakpoints and breakpoints plus 1 and minus 1.

2 Abnormal or invalid cases.

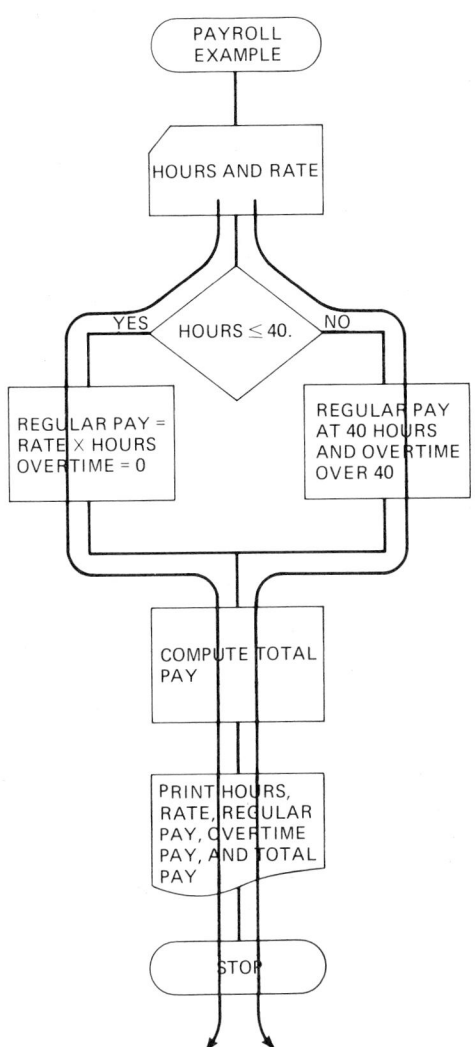

FIGURE 2-3 Paths through a simple payroll program for testing the program.

PATH 1   PATH 2

Debugging of Programs During Compilation

The output from compilation is useful in removing coding-type errors (and keypunching errors that may not have been noticed in checking the FORTRAN deck before submission). The errors that can be detected by the compiler are language-use errors.

Precision and Accuracy in Computing

Accuracy has to do with measurement. For example, suppose we wish to measure a large wooden table. Using three methods of measurement, we arrive at different accuracy.

Method of measurement	Accuracy
By eye	Within 1 foot
By using a hand span as a measure	Within 3 inches
By using a measuring tape	Within $1/16$ inch

Precision refers to the way the result is recorded: how many digits can be recorded. If the common fraction 4/3 is to be recorded as a decimal, there is no limit to the trailing 3s; the limit imposed by the recorder (or by the computer structure) is the precision:

1.3	2-digit precision
1.333	4-digit precision
1.33333	6-digit precision

To understand the nature of precision, assume that only a fixed number of places is available for hand computation. Use both three and six places for the problem $1/16 + 30$. The decimal point will be allowed to float in the example (shown by $\wedge$) and there will be rounding before digits are dropped.

Three-place precision	Six-place precision
1/6 =	1	6	7		1	6	6	6	6	7
30 + 1/6 =	3	0	2		3	0	1	6	6	7

In hand computation, the person doing the computing will usually vary the precision from problem to problem, but a computer is generally designed to operate with a fixed precision. High-level language compilers generally reflect the precision of the computer for which they are written. The precision can and does vary among computers. FORTRAN programs which can benefit from large precision will often have different results when compiled and executed on a computer with smaller precision. For example, Peter Minuit in 1626 paid $24.00 for Manhattan Island. If the Indians had invested the $24 at 6 percent compounded quarterly (6.0/4.0 percent per quarter), what would the Indians have had in 1976 after 350 years? The FORTRAN statement is:

        AMT = 24.0 * (1.0 + (.06 / 4.0)) ** (350.0 * 4.0)

or   AMT = 24.0 * (1.015 ** 1400.0)

Exponentiation to the 1400 power is done by logarithms, but the result is so large that it is very much affected by the precision used by the computer. The results obtained from two different computers illustrates the concept.

Computer	Result
IBM 370/158 (medium precision)	27,058,163,712
CDC CYBER 74 (high precision)	27,081,355,025

The IBM 370/158 result was rerun with a larger double precision specified (explained in Chapter 7); the result was 27,081,351,168, which is closer to the precision obtained on the large CDC computer.

This example should not be a cause for alarm. There are only a few problems where precision will be a significant factor. But the FORTRAN programmer should be aware of precision for those cases in which it is important.

The maximum precision obtainable inside the computer is not necessarily the precision obtained at output. In the case of list-directed output, the output precision is defined by the compiler writer; the programmer has no control over it. As noted in Chapter 1, the precision of list-directed output will vary for different implementations of standard FORTRAN.

Suggestions for the FORTRAN Programmer

Because so much emphasis is placed in the text on good programming style, it may be useful to review the concept of a good program. Writing a good program is not merely writing language statements in correct form. The statements need to code a suitable solution procedure (a computing algorithm) that has been carefully designed. The coding should be done in a clear manner following a disciplined style. The statements need to be coded correctly, i.e., use the language correctly. These three important requirements can be understood by two analogies:

Analogy 1   A term paper on ''Privacy and the Computer'' has (assuming appropriate knowledge of the subject has been acquired by the student writer) three elements that affect the result:

1   The planning of an organization for the paper. This should have logical parts, each part with an objective, and able to fit into the overall structure of the paper. This design is reflected in a clear outline of the topics to be included. This phase is similar to the development of a computer solution procedure which meets the needs posed by the problem.

2   The organization of the paper into paragraphs with headings, subheadings, indentation, underlining, etc. This is similar in concept to computer programming style.

3   The writing of sentences in correct grammatical form. This is the same as coding of correct statements in the program.

Analogy 2   A student is to develop a computer solution procedure for finding the square root of a number. The three steps in the process are:

1   Find or develop a solution procedure. The student finds that the Newton-Raphson algorithm is already known and well defined. This method can be described for this problem in a flowchart or in pseudocode. Organize the solution procedure for program clarity.

2 The program for the Newton-Raphson method can be divided into logically separate functions. For example, the separate activities in the solution procedure might be identified as:

   (a) Read input value and validate, i.e., test for invalid values such as negative or zero.
   (b) Initialize all values for the computational procedure.
   (c) Perform the iterative procedures to find the square root.
   (d) Print out the input value and the square root.

3 The algorithm is coded in correct FORTRAN statements.

The programming style suggestions from Chapters 1 and 2 are listed below. The first seven suggestions are a summary of guidelines described in Chapter 1 which should be reviewed; the remainder summarize good practice explained in this chapter.

1 Analyze the problem and design the program before beginning to code instructions. If you do not understand the problem and the solution procedure, you cannot tell the computer what to do. Useful design and planning methods are pseudocode and program flowcharts. A suggested four-step process in planning and designing a program is:

   (a) Plan the general logic of processing for one normal case to the level of detail useful for the problem.
   (b) Add logic to handle multiple cases. Include logic required for first-time-through and last-time-through processing.
   (c) Add logic for input validation and handling of input errors.
   (d) Add logic for handling exceptions and unusual cases including negative or zero data.

2 Use FORTRAN coding paper to aid in writing instructions in proper form.

3 Use a block structure to divide the program into logical segments. Include an identification block and a list-of-variables block. The style selected for this text is to have a block name line consisting of 10 asterisks, 10 blanks, name of block starting in column 21, and number of block (BLOCK nnnn) starting in column 63. To be manageable, blocks should be less than 60 statements.

4 Use explanatory comments at the beginning of each logical block. Use comments freely inside the blocks. Following the text style, set off each group of one or more inside-block comment lines by a blank comment line before and after. The inside-block comment lines are indented to column 11.

5 Use parentheses to avoid ambiguity. Do not rely upon unfamiliar precedence rules.

6 Consider printout (echo) of input data as a visual check against incorrect input.

7 Print labels to clearly identify all output values.

8 Validate input data to make sure it falls within the limits assumed for the program. Provide suitable error messages and correct or reject bad data.

9 Use the logical IF. Avoid the arithmetic IF. If available, use the block IF whenever appropriate.

10 Check for incorrect logic following a basic logical IF. Remember that unless the action of the IF is to transfer control, the statement following the IF will be executed for both selection paths.

11 When coding tests of conditions, do not assume a value for any remaining condition. Make an explicit test.

12 Provide explicit error stops or error messages for instances when conditions which should never occur actually do occur.

13 Code for clarity, not minimum number of coding lines.

14 Explicitly initialize variables where needed for first-time-through processing.

15 A program should be checked out by running it with comprehensive test data for which the results are known. Test carefully the first-time-through and last-time-through logic, logic at and around breakpoints, input validation, and handling of exceptions.

Summary

The basic intrinsic functions were explained. These reduce coding requirements for common operations. The intrinsic functions have a generic name plus specific names that identify the type of data being produced (such as integer or real). Integer data is important in FORTRAN because there are situations where integer data is needed and because the characteristics of integer arithmetic are often useful. Modern FORTRAN compilers allow mixed types in an expression but good programming style is to code the conversions with conversion functions rather than to rely upon automatic conversion.

The selection structure is coded by the IF statement. The logical IF is preferred but many programs, especially older programs, make use of an arithmetic IF. The comparison in the logical IF statement can include combinations of conditions linked together with ANDs and ORs. A new but very useful form of IF is the block IF that allows blocks of code to follow each of the two condition results.

The IF statement provides the basis for understanding data validation. This should normally be included in well-written programs. A simple IF loop can be used to perform repetitive processing. When loops are used, it is important to carefully code the logic so the program will work correctly the first time through and the last time through. The program should be tested using desk checking and test data. The concepts of precision and accuracy in computing are explained and contrasted. Style guidelines for Chapters 1 and 2 are summarized.

Answers to Self-testing Exercises

Exercise 2-1

1 (a) X = SQRT (A + B)

(b) X = (A / B + 2 . 0) * * (1 . 0 / 3 . 0)

Exponentiating to the ⅓ power is the same as taking the cube root. As was explained more fully in the chapter, the exponent must be real or it would turn out to be zero. The parentheses around the exponent are necessary. Why?

(c) Y = EXP (X)

(d) X = SQRT (ABS (Y + 5 . 0))

(e) Y = ALOG (X)

(f) R = SQRT (X * * 2 + Y * * 2)

Note that the square root of the right side was taken, since no expression is allowed on the left side.

(g) X = AMAX 1 (X * * 2 , Y * * 2)

2 (a) $X = \log_e (Y + Z)$

(b) $Y = \sin |a|$

(c) $d = |b^2 - 4ac|$

(d) $y = e^{-x^2}$

(e) $p = A \cos \theta$

(f) $x = \sqrt{a + \dfrac{b}{c^d} ef + 1.0}$

3 Y = 0 . 3989 * EXP ((–X * * 2) / 2 . 0)

Exercise 2-2

1

Valid or not valid. Note if mixed type	If not valid, why. If mixed type, how converted
(a) Valid. Mixed	Will be converted to A**2 + 1.0
(b) Valid (integer arithmetic for integer exponent is valid)	
(c) Valid real type	
(d) Valid. Mixed	Converts to A/B + D/3.0
(e) Valid integer type	
(f) Valid. Mixed	Result is converted to integer type
(g) Valid real type	
(h) Valid. Mixed	Better to code as X = (A + B) / ((C + D) * E * FLOAT (IX))
(i) Not valid	Expression (X + Y) to left of equals sign not allowed
(j) Mixed	Integer may not have real exponent, so compiler will convert to JX = FLOAT (IX) * * A (or some older compilers will reject it)
(k) Valid (Integer exponent is allowed)	

2 (a) 1.2   (b) 1   (c) 0   (d) 4

3 (a) J = ABS (KDATA)

J = I ABS (KDATA)

(b) M = MIN (I , J , K)
    M = MIN0 (I , J , K)

4 (a) REAL (JIX)
    FLOAT (JIX)
    AJIX = JIX
(b) INT (DATA1)
    IFIX (DATA1)
    IDATA1 = DATA1

5 (a) X = FLOAT (I) * B * * I   or   X = REAL (I) * B * * I
(I in exponent need not be made real because an integer exponent does not cause a mixed-type expression.)
(b) X = B + (C / FLOAT (J)) + FLOAT (K) * * D or
    X = B + (C / REAL (J)) + REAL (K) * * D

Exercise 2-3

1 IF (SQRT (X * * 2 + Y * * 2) . LT . 100 . 0) ANSWR = 12 . 0 * X
IF (SQRT (X * * 2 + Y * * 2) . GE . 100 . 0) ANSWR = X * * 2
PRINT * , ANSWR

2 (a) BIG = ALPHA
    IF (BETA . GE . BIG) BIG = BETA
    IF (GAMMA . GE . BIG) BIG = GAMMA
(b) BIG = AMAX1 (ALPHA , BETA , GAMMA) or
    BIG = MAX (ALPHA , BETA , GAMMA)

3 IF (NIX . EQ . KIX) STOP
LARGE = NIX
IF (ABS (KIX) . GT . ABS (LARGE)) LARGE = KIX
PRINT * , LARGE
STOP

4 IF ((X . GE . - 550 . 0) . OR . (X . LE . 1000 . 0)) PRINT * , `YES`
IF ((X . LT . - 550 . 0) . OR . (X . GT . 1000 . 0) PRINT * , `NO`
STOP
or alternatively,
        IF ((X . GE . - 550 . 0) . AND . (X . LE . 1000 . 0)) GOTO 110
        PRINT * , `NO `
        GOTO 120
110 PRINT * , `YES`
120 STOP

5 IF (((A . GT . B) . AND . (A . GT . C)) . OR . (((A . LT . D)
    . AND . (A . EQ . E))) GOTO 210
GOTO 310

6 IF   ((X . GE . - 550 . 0) . AND . (X . LE . 1000 . 0)) THEN
        PRINT * , `YES`
ELSE
        PRINT * , `NO`
ENDIF
STOP

7

```
IF(ICODE.EQ.1.OR.ICODE.EQ.2) THEN

    RPAY=3.75*RHRS

    OTPAY=0.0                                          IF
                                                      BLOCK
ELSEIF (ICODE.EQ.3) THEN

    RPAY=4.15*RHRS                                            IF...
                                                             ELSE
    OTPAY=1.5*4.15* OHRS                                     with
                                                             ENDIF
ELSE

    PRINT*, 'CODE ERROR', ICODE                       ELSE
                                                      BLOCK
    STOP

ENDIF
```

Exercise 2-4

1 Without block IF
```
        READ*,RATE
        IF ((RATE.LE.0.0).OR.(RATE.GT.0.15)) GOTO 150
120     normal input processing
        GOTO 200 (to skip around next statements)
150     PRINT*,RATE, 'RATE NEG,ZERO,OR LARGE'
        STOP
200     continue with normal processing
```
2 With block IF
```
READ*,RATE
IF ((RATE.LE.0.0).OR.(RATE.GT.0.15)) THEN
    PRINT*,RATE,  'RATE NEG,ZERO,OR LARGE'
    STOP
ELSE (normal input processing)
```

Questions and Problems

    1 Define the following terms:
       (*a*) compilation
       (*b*) desk checking
       (*c*) input validation
       (*d*) intrinsic function
       (*e*) program reading
    2 Describe two methods of input validation.
    3 Describe the testing and quality assurance procedures that accompany the development of a FORTRAN program.
    4 A program is coded with one simple selection. How many sets of data are necessary

to fully test the program? How many are necessary if the program has two simple selections?

5 Write the FORTRAN expressions for the following:

(a) X^a

(b) X^i

(c) X^{i-1}

(d) e^x

(e) $X^{1/3}$

(f) X^{-4}

(g) $X^{i/j}$

(h) $\dfrac{1}{X^2}$

6 What is the result of each of the following statements, given the stated values for the variables?

(a) $X = Y + Z/A$
(b) $IX = Y + Z/A$ $\Big\}$ Y = 3.0, Z = 4.5, A = 2.0

(c) $I = J/K$
(d) $I = L/J + K$ $\Big\}$ J = 3, K = 9, L = 10
(e) $I = J + L/K - L$

7 Write the formulas, given the following FORTRAN statements:

(a) Y = SQRT (X ** 2+ 2 . 0) / (1 . 0−X ** N)

(b) X = THETA + SIN (THETA)

(c) Y = 1 . 0 /X

(d) E = ((A ** 2+B ** 2) ** (1 . 0 / 2 . 0)) /A

(e) X = A ** B * C+D * E / F * G ** 2

8 Write the FORTRAN statement to solve the formula for each of the following:

(a) $j = \sqrt{v}$

(b) $a = |x + y|$ where $|\ |$ means the absolute value

(c) $x = a(-b)/c(-d)$

(d) $s = \dfrac{p}{q} + \dfrac{3r}{s}$

9 Eliminate mixed-mode arithmetic in the following by the use of intrinsic functions:

(a) I X = A + J X

(b) N = XK + J X

(c) X = I X ** K

(d) X = X ** I

(e) X = R ** X+N I X

10 Write a program segment to find the value of COST when COST is a step function of volume (a) first without a block IF and then (b) with a block IF.

If VOL is between 0 and 100	COST = 2 0 0+ 0 . 3 × VOL
If VOL is over 100 but not 1000	COST = 3 0 0+ 0 . 3 × VOL
If VOL is over 1000 but not over 5000	COST = 3 5 0+ 0 . 2 5 × VOL

11 Identify and correct the logical errors in the following:

(a)　　　　IF (A .GT . B) SMALL=A
　　　　　SMALL = B

(b)　　　　IF (HOURS . LT . 0 . 0 .OR . HOURS . GT . 6 5 . 0)GOTO 1 5 0
　　　　　PAY=HOURS * 2 . 5
　　　1 5 0 PRINT * , HOURS , 'ZERO OR NEG INPUT'
　　　　　STOP
　　　　　PRINT * , 'HOURS' , HOURS , 'PAY' , PAY

12 Write data validation statements for the quadratic formula—read the necessary variables from cards and validate the data as suitable for processing, i.e., validate that $b^2 - 4ac$ is not negative (which would result in an error in attempting to take the square root). Print the input variables (with labels). Print error messages if data is invalid. The formula is:

$$\frac{-b \pm \sqrt{b^2 - 4ac}}{2a}$$

13 Write a program segment to validate an input data item PRICE. If it is zero, negative, or greater than 30.0, it is to be rejected. Print an error message which gives the value and specifies for which of the reasons it was rejected.

CHAPTER

2B

EXAMPLE PROGRAMS AND PROGRAMMING EXERCISES WHICH USE INTRINSIC FUNCTIONS, IF SELECTION, AND DATA VALIDATION

The two example programs are for the same applications as the two example programs in Chapter 1B, but additional requirements have been added which utilize the features presented in this chapter. The two examples again provide variety in the type of applications being illustrated: a general example of payroll computation and a statistical example of calculating the ordinates of the normal curve. The example programs illustrate a disciplined style using principles of structured programming. The documentation contains both a pseudocode description and flowcharting to provide experience in the two techniques. Following the examples are programming exercises.

General Notes on Chapter 2 Examples

The two examples utilize intrinsic functions, IF selection, and data validation. Statement numbers are also used as labels on some statements. Additional style considerations are the use of more than one numbered, logical block of processing statements, the use of pointer comments with backward GOTOs, and a convention for GOTOs in pseudocode. The examples use simple IF loops to read and process several sets of input data.

Numbered Processing Blocks

As the number of processing statements becomes larger and the number of processing functions increases, it is good programming style to divide a program into more than one group of statements. These groupings (logical blocks) are identified with a heading. It is also useful to assign a number to each of the blocks. The number also identifies the number series allowed for statements in the block. We have chosen to number the initialization block as 0000. The first block after that is numbered 0100, and any statements in the block are between 101 and 199; the next block is 0200 and the statements, if numbered, use labels ranging between 201 and 299. The block number can be placed anywhere in the block heading; we have placed it in the ten columns (63–72) at the right side of the block heading line as BLOCK nnnn.

It is frequently useful to have a separate block for error messages. A convention we have chosen is to assign 900 (or 9000 for larger programs) as the error block number. This means that any reference to a 900 or 9000 number is to an error message.

The advantage of the block number and block number series is in clearly identifying the statement to which a GOTO (or other transfer statement) transfers control. A statement GOTO 310 anywhere in the program is immediately understood as transferring control into block 300.

Pointer Comments for Backward GOTOs

The most understandable design for a computer program is usually a program that has no backward transfers of control, i.e., no GOTOs transferring to earlier program statements. It is virtually impossible to achieve such a program design for all FORTRAN programs. Many FORTRAN programs will need to transfer backward (essentially a GO BACK statement). It is necessary, for example, when the program is to be repeated with new input data. This case is illustrated in both example programs.

In order to make a backward GOTO very clear, we include a comment line just before the GOTO describing what the GOTO is to accomplish (with a blank comment line on either side of the GOTO comment). The words GO BACK may be used in the comment to clearly mark a backward GOTO.

In the flowcharts, some of the backward GOTOs use a connector to avoid too many lines on the chart. The small circle has an identifying letter in it. The GOTO point has an arrow plus the circle ⟶(A) and the point A to which control is going has the same letter plus an arrow to the entry point

(A)⟶

Terminating the Program

The two example programs read more than one set of data. They read and process input data until termination is indicated (usually by reaching the end of the data to be processed). There are several ways to program tests for end-of-data termination. Two simple ways are illustrated in the two example programs:

1 Test for the maximum number of input data items that should be read (general example 2).

2 Test for a data value that terminates the program (statistical example 2).

In the first example (general example 2), the maximum number of input items (MAXCDS) is initialized at 5 (in line 3). A card counter (NCNTR) is set to 1 in line 7. Each time a card is read, the counter is incremented by 1 (line 9). The counter is tested and if less than or equal to the maximum, the program goes back to read new input data (line 21). In flowchart form, the logic of using a counter is given below:

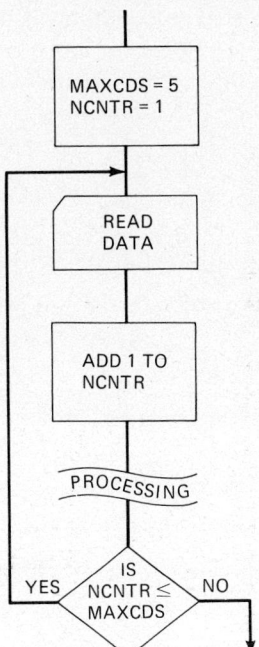

The second example program (statistical example 2) tests for an input data item that is negative (line 5). The input data must contain a data item with a negative value following the last data item to be processed.

In general, a program will be abnormally terminated by the operating system when the program attempts to read data and no more data is available. However, this default option is not good programming practice. It is better to provide for explicit termination with end of program messages as in the example programs. Another method will be explained in Chapter 3.

A GOTO Pseudocode Convention

The pseudocode description needs to provide for transfer of control (same principle as GOTO). The convention used in this text is to use a descriptive name in front of a block of pseudocode description. Any transfer of control in the program is planned with the pseudocode by writing transfer-type pseudocode with the name being the transfer point. The name is underlined. For example, a block of code might be named "Summary", a pseudocode "GOTO Summary" is sufficient description for planning and documenting a program.

The pseudocode convention in the text for an IF test uses the IF block concept. The IF and ELSE are used to identify the possible branches. If a branch has no processing, it is written as "Else continue".

General Program Example 2—Payroll Computation

Problem Description for General Example 2

Paycheck amounts are computed for a specified number of employees. For data validation, input data is printed (echoed). Input data is also validated as being within suitable limits. After calculations, net pay and gross pay are printed, net pay for each employee is checked for a positive pay amount, and negative net pay is noted by an error message. After all employees are processed, the total gross pay and total taxes for all the employees are printed along with the largest single gross pay amount. Values for the following variables are input for each employee:

Identification number

Hours worked

Wage rate

Miscellaneous deductions

The pension rate is 5 percent of gross pay, and taxes are 15 percent of gross pay. The number of employees is specified as 5.

Program Documentation for General Example 2

The documentation consists of a pseudocode description (Figure 2-4), a program listing with sample output (Figure 2-5), and a program flowchart (Figure

	Program Line Numbers
Initialize pension rate at 5%, tax rate at 15%, totaling variables for gross pay and taxes at zero, largest value so far at zero, maximum number of cards at 5, and card counter at 1.	*1–7*
READ data for an employee	*8*
Increment card counter by 1	*9*
PRINT input data for visual validation	*10–11*
Validate input data for out-of-range conditions:	*12*
Hours worked negative or greater than 60	*13*
Wage rate negative or greater than 10.00	*14*
Miscellaneous deductions negative or greater than 15.00	*31–32*
IF input data invalid, print message and go back to READ another card	
Else continue with processing of input data	*15–17*
Compute gross pay, taxes, and net pay	
Select largest gross pay so far	*18*
PRINT net pay and gross pay values for this employee	*19*
Check for negative net pay	*20*
If negative net pay, print warning message and continue with processing	*29–30*
Else continue with processing	
Add gross pay and taxes to accumulating totals	*21–22*
Test card counter against value for maximum number of cards to determine if more cards should be read	*23*
If yes, go back to READ another data card	*23*
Else continue to ending of program	
PRINT summary totals for gross pay and taxes plus largest gross pay	*24–27*
STOP	*28*

FIGURE 2-4 Pseudocode description of program for general example 2—payroll processing.

2-6). Each symbol on the flowchart has at the upper right of the symbol the corresponding line numbers of the listing. This is primarily to aid you in reading the flowchart and comparing it to the program, but in some cases it may be a useful addition to the flowchart documentation.

Planning and Designing the Program for General Example 2 with Pseudocode

The logic for planning a program described in Chapter 2A will be applied to general example 2 using pseudocode as the planning method. The same process can also be used with the program flowchart method.

1   Plan the general logic of processing for one case with normally expected input. Plan to the level of detail needed for the specific problem. For example 2, the appropriate level of detail might be as follows:
READ data for an employee
Compute gross pay, taxes, and net pay
Select largest gross pay so far

```
********* PROGRAM IDENTIFICATION *********
*                                                                       *
*      THIS PROGRAM COMPUTES PAYCHECK AMOUNTS FOR EMPLOYEES             *
*      AND COMPANY TOTALS. IT ALSO FINDS THE LARGEST GROSS             *
*      PAY AMOUNT USING AN INTRINSIC FORTRAN FUNCTION.                 *
*      WRITTEN 04/12/77 BY T. HOFFMANN                                 *
*                                                                       *
*************************************************************************
*                                                                       *
********* VARIABLE IDENTIFICATION *********
*                                                                       *
*      ID      = EMPLOYEE IDENTIFICATION NUMBER                        *
*      HRSWRK  = HOURS WORKED BY EACH EMPLOYEE                         *
*      GRSPAY  = GROSS PAY: $                                          *
*      WGRATE  = WAGE RATE: $/HOUR                                     *
*      PAYCHK  = NET PAYCHECK AMOUNT: $                                *
*      TAXES   = TAXES DUE: $                                          *
*      DEDUC   = MISCELLANEOUS DEDUCTIONS                              *
*      TOTPAY  = TOTAL GROSS PAY FOR COMPANY : $                       *
*      TOTTAX  = TOTAL TAXES FROM ALL EMPLOYEES :$                     *
*      NCNTR   = COUNTER TO LIMIT CARDS READ                           *
*      PLARGE  = LARGEST GROSS PAY FOR ANY EMPLOYEE                    *
*                                                                       *
*****            CONSTANT IDENTIFICATION                           *****
*                                                                       *
*      PNRATE  = PENSION CONTRIBUTION RATE = 0.05                      *
*      TAXRT   = TAX RATE = 0.15                                       *
*      MAXCDS  = CARDS TO BE READ = 5                                  *
*                                                                       *
*************************************************************************
*                                                                       *
********* INITIALIZATION BLOCK                        BLOCK 0000
*                                                                       *
1.          PNRATE = 0.05
2.          TAXRT = 0.15
3.          MAXCDS = 5
4.          PLARGE = 0.0
5.          TOTPAY = 0.0
6.          TOTTAX = 0.0
7.          NCNTR = 1
*                                                                       *
*************************************************************************
*                                                                       *
********* READ-COMPUTE-PRINT DETAIL                   BLOCK 0100
*                                                                       *
8.    101 READ *,ID,HRSWRK,WGRATE,DEDUC
9.          NCNTR = NCNTR+1
10.         PRINT *,' '
11.         PRINT *,' ECHO',ID,HRSWRK,WGRATE,DEDUC
12.         IF((HRSWRK .LT. 0.0) .OR. (HRSWRK .GT. 60.0)) GOTO 905
13.         IF((WGRATE .LT. 0.0) .OR. (WGRATE .GT. 10.0) ) GOTO 905
14.         IF((DEDUC .LT. 0.0) .OR. (DEDUC .GT. 35.0) ) GOTO 905
15.         GRSPAY = HRSWRK*WGRATE
16.         TAXES = GRSPAY*TAXRT
17.         PAYCHK = GRSPAY - TAXES - DEDUC - PNRATE*GRSPAY
*                                                                       *
*           SELECT LARGEST GROSS PAY SO FAR                            *
*                                                                       *
18.         PLARGE = AMAX1(PLARGE,GRSPAY)
*                                                                       *
*           CHECK FOR VALID PAYCHECK AMOUNT                            *
*                                                                       *
19.         PRINT *,' NET PAY = ',PAYCHK,' GROSS PAY = ',GRSPAY
20.         IF(PAYCHK .LE. 0.0) GOTO 901
21.   103 TOTPAY = TOTPAY + GRSPAY
22.         TOTTAX = TOTTAX + TAXES
*                                                                       *
*           IF CARDS READ IS LESS THAN MAXIMUM, GO BACK TO READ ANOTHER*
*                                                                       *
23.         IF(NCNTR.LE.MAXCDS) GOTO 101
*                                                                       *
*************************************************************************
*                                                                       *
********* PRINT SUMMARY AND TERMINATE                 BLOCK 0200
*                                                                       *
24.         PRINT *, ' '
25.         PRINT *, ' TOTAL        TOTAL        LARGEST'
26.         PRINT *, ' PAY          TAX          GROSS PAY '
27.         PRINT *,TOTPAY,TOTTAX,PLARGE
28.         STOP
*                                                                       *
*************************************************************************
```

FIGURE 2-5 Listing of FORTRAN program, sample input, and output for general example 2—payroll processing.

```
       *                                                          *
       *********          ERROR MESSAGE BLOCK              BLOCK 0900
       *                                                          *
29.    901 PRINT *,' NET PAY IS NOT POSITIVE. DO NOT ISSUE CHECK.'
       *                                                          *
       *          GO BACK TO NORMAL PROCESSING                    *
       *                                                          *
30.        GOTO 103

31.    905 PRINT *,' ERROR IN INPUT DATA.'
       *
       *          DO NOT COMPUTE PAY.  GO BACK FOR MORE DATA.
       *
32.        GOTO 101
33.        END
```

ID   HRSWRK
      WGRATE
      DEDUC   SAMPLE INPUT

```
35746,55.5,7.24,30.68
69587,10,2.67,27.50
35649,22,2.75,35.98
15768,37,6.28,24.68
27543,40,3.57,27.95
```

OUTPUT

```
    ECHO            27543  40.0000      3.57000        27.9500
    NET PAY =             86.2900   GROSS PAY =            142.800

    ECHO            15768  37.0000      6.28000        24.6800
    NET PAY =            161.208   GROSS PAY =            232.360

    ECHO            35649  22.0000      2.75000        35.9800
    ERROR IN INPUT DATA.

    ECHO            69587  10.0000      2.67000        27.5000
    NET PAY =            -6.14000   GROSS PAY =             26.7000
    NET PAY IS NOT POSITIVE. DO NOT ISSUE CHECK.

    ECHO            35746  55.5000      7.24000        30.6800
    NET PAY =            290.776   GROSS PAY =            401.820

    TOTAL          TOTAL      LARGEST
     PAY            TAX      GROSS PAY
    803.680       120.552     401.820
```

FIGURE 2-5 *(continued)*

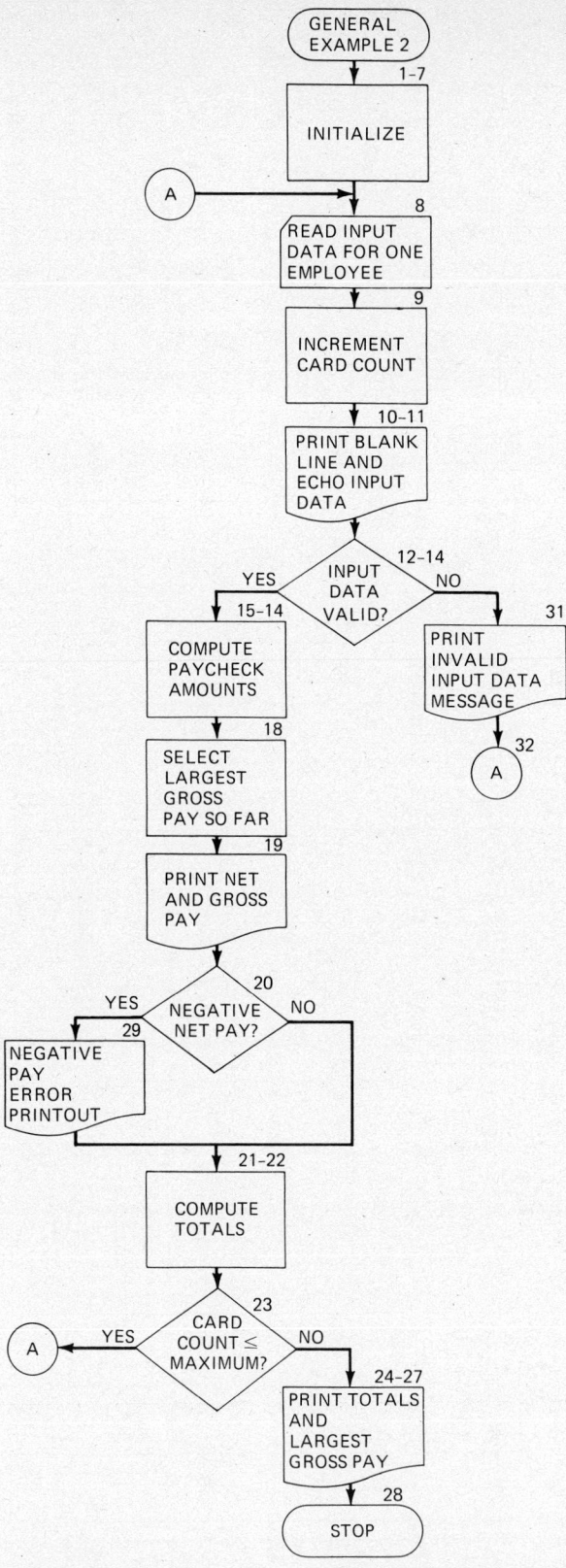

FIGURE 2-6 Program flowchart for general example 2—payroll processing. (Numbers beside symbols refer to line numbers on program listing.)

94

PRINT net pay and gross pay values for this employee
Add gross pay and taxes to accumulating totals
PRINT summary totals for gross pay and taxes plus largest gross pay
STOP

2 Add logic to handle multiple cases. Include logic required for first-time-through and last-time-through processing

---

Statements from Step 1

Statements added to handle multiple cases	Explanation
Initialize pension rate at 5% and tax rate at 15%	As a matter of style, these constants were named instead of the constant values being used in the formula statement. Therefore, they must be set to the desired values.
Initialize totaling variables for gross pay and taxes at zero	Totaling variables must be at zero for first-time-through logic.
Initialize largest value so far at zero	Largest value so far must be less than or equal to gross pay for first-time-through logic. Gross pay will be greater than or equal to zero, so initialize largest value so far at zero.
Initialize maximum number of input cards at 5 and a card counter at 1	Maximum number of inputs is given a variable name and set at 5. Alternatively, the constant 5 could have been coded directly in the IF test. Card counter to keep track of number of repetitions of input reading must be set at 1 for the first-time-through logic of this program.
<u>*READ*</u> *data for an employee*	As a pseudocode convention for this text, underlining one or more words at the beginning of a line means the line of code will be referenced by a transfer of control in another pseudocode statement.
Increment card counter by 1	For first-time-through processing, the card counter was set at 1. After each reading of a card, the card counter is incremented by 1.
Compute gross pay, taxes, and net pay	
Select largest gross pay so far	Current gross pay is compared with largest gross pay so far and the largest of the two is made the new largest gross pay so far. Note the need to initialize for first-time-through with this logic.
PRINT net pay and gross pay values for this employee	
Add gross pay and taxes to accumulating totals	Since current value for gross pay and taxes are being added to accumulated amounts, the totaling variables were set to zero for first-time-through logic.

Statements from Step 1

Statements added to handle multiple cases	Explanation
Test card counter against value for maximum number of cards to determine if more cards should be read *If yes, go back and* **READ** *another card* *Else continue to ending of program* PRINT *summary totals for gross pay and taxes plus largest gross pay* *STOP*	The test is to determine whether the reading of input cards should continue. If the card counter is less than or equal to the maximum, another card should be read and processed. Underlined READ refers back to pseudocode statement to READ data for an employee.

---

3 Add logic for input validation and handling of input errors. The logic for this is placed after the two statements to read data and increment card counter. The input validation consists of two major steps:

PRINT input data for visual validation
Validate input data for out-of-range conditions
  If input data invalid, print error message and **READ** *a new card*
  Else continue with processing of input data

If a programmer desires to specify more detail for the second validation step, the second pseudocode statement can be expanded to:

Validate input data for out-of-range conditions:
  Hours worked negative or greater than 60
  Wage rate negative or greater than 10.00
  Miscellaneous deductions negative or greater than 35.00

4 Add logic for handling exceptions and unusual cases. Review cases in which data may be zero or negative. In this example, a net pay of negative is an unusual case and needs to be provided for. After printing the net pay and gross pay a test for negative net pay is inserted.

Check for negative net pay
  If negative net pay, print warning message and continue with processing
  Else continue with processing

Note that the program logic allows the negative net pay to be printed but a warning message is also printed.

The complete pseudocode for the planning of general example 2 is shown in Figure 2-4. Review the complete pseudocode for the program and then read carefully through the FORTRAN program in Figure 2-6 noting the relationship of the pseudocode statements to the FORTRAN program. To aid in this comparison the pseudocode statements are followed by the corresponding program line reference numbers from the program listing.

Notes for General Example 2

This payroll program is more complex than the one in Chapter 1B and requires additional features. The usual identification blocks are given. Since the program is more complex, the computation has been divided into several blocks. The first block contains all the initialization instructions; given a block number of 0000, it is executed only at the beginning of the program. The grouping of initialization in a separate block assists in the review of this important step. There are additional blocks for read, compute, and print (block 0100), print summary and terminate block 0200), and error messages (block 0900). Note we have written the block numbers at the right of the block name comment line.

Referring to the program listing in Figure 2-6, the output requirements of the program are met as follows:

1 The output for each employee consists of three or four lines
   (a) A blank line to separate each employee output (line 10)
   (b) An echo of input data labeled 'ECHO' (line 11)
   (c) Net pay and gross pay (line 19) or an error message if input is invalid (line 31)
   (d) If net pay is negative, a message to not issue a paycheck (line 29)

2 After all five cards have been read and processed, a summary is printed (lines 24 through 27). The summary line headings consist of two or three words over each value. To line up the headings with the list-directed output for the computer being used, the heading line was written as two outputs (lines 25 and 26)

The AMAX1 intrinsic function is used to select the maximum employee gross pay. The generic MAX name could have been used (if available). Note the program style in the use of the IF statements in lines 12, 13, 14, 20, and 23. The IFs are constructed so that the block of code which is normally expected to execute is placed following the IF and the error condition is a GOTO out of the normal flow.

Statistical Program Example 2—Tables of Ordinates of the Normal Curve

Problem Description for Statistical Example 2

Calculate tables of the ordinates for the normal curve. Input for each table consists of a starting abscissa, an incrementing value, and the number of ordinates to compute. Output from this is a table of X (abscissa) and Y (ordinate) values. The program is to produce a table for each input until a negative input is read for the number of ordinates. The negative value terminates the program. The intrinsic function for exponentiation of e is to be used (EXP). The number of ordinates (table size) should not exceed 50.

Equation: $y = \frac{1}{\sqrt{2\pi}} e^{-(x^2/2)}$

where e is the base for natural logarithms and π has an approximate value of 3.1416.

Program Documentation for Statistical Example 2

The documentation consists of a pseudocode description of the program (Figure 2-7), a program flowchart (Figure 2-8), and a program listing (Figure 2-9).

Initialize constant for $1/\sqrt{2\pi}$ and set problem number counter to 1

PRINT heading

<u>*READ*</u> *starting abscissa value for table (X1), abscissa increment (XINCR) and number of ordinates (NVALUS) to be computed*

Test for end of job (i.e., negative value for number of ordinates)

> *IF (number of ordinates is negative) print end of program message and STOP*
>
> *Else continue*

Validate input values for number of ordinates to be computed:

> *IF (number of ordinates is greater than 50) print error message and go back to <u>READ</u> new data*
>
> *Else continue*

Set abscissa value (XVALU) to starting value (XI)

Set counter (NCNTR) for values in this problem to 1

<u>*Compute ordinate*</u> *(YVALU) as function of abscissa value XVALU*

PRINT abscissa value (XVALU) and ordinate value (YVALU)

Increment abscissa value (XVALU) by abscissa increment (XINCR)

Increment values counter by 1

Check to see whether more ordinates should be computed—values counter is less than or equal to number of ordinates to be computed

> *If yes, go back to <u>Compute ordinate</u>*
>
> *Else PRINT end of problem message, increment problem number counter, and go back to <u>READ</u>*

FIGURE 2-7   Pseudocode description for statistical example 2—tables of ordinates of normal curve.

As in the general example, the line numbers of program statements are placed at the upper right of flowchart symbols as a cross-referencing aid.

Notes on Statistical Example 2

In this program, the value of $1/\sqrt{2\pi}$ is computed, using the square root function (line 1) and a constant value of 6.2832 for 2π (see the constant identification following the list of variables). The structure of the READ-COMPUTE-PRINT block is essentially the same as in statistical problem 1 except that a counter has been inserted to limit the table length to a particular number of values. In addition, the intrinsic exponential function is used (line 9) in place of the constant value for e.

The initialization block contains the printing of the heading which applies to the output (a global heading rather than a heading which applies to a single output or single set of outputs). The first-time-through situation is found in the use of a problem number. Each output table contains as the last line 'END OF PROBLEM problem number'. The problem number is initialized at 1 (line 2) and incremented after the printing of the END OF PROBLEM message but before the next card is read (line 10) for a new problem.

Backward GOTOs are used in the program but are clearly marked by comments before the GOTO statement (lines 13, 17 and 22). Note the use of explicit messages for the end of each table and for the end of the program. The end of program message makes it clear that the program execution is complete. The input data could be echoed, but it is not necessary in this program since the

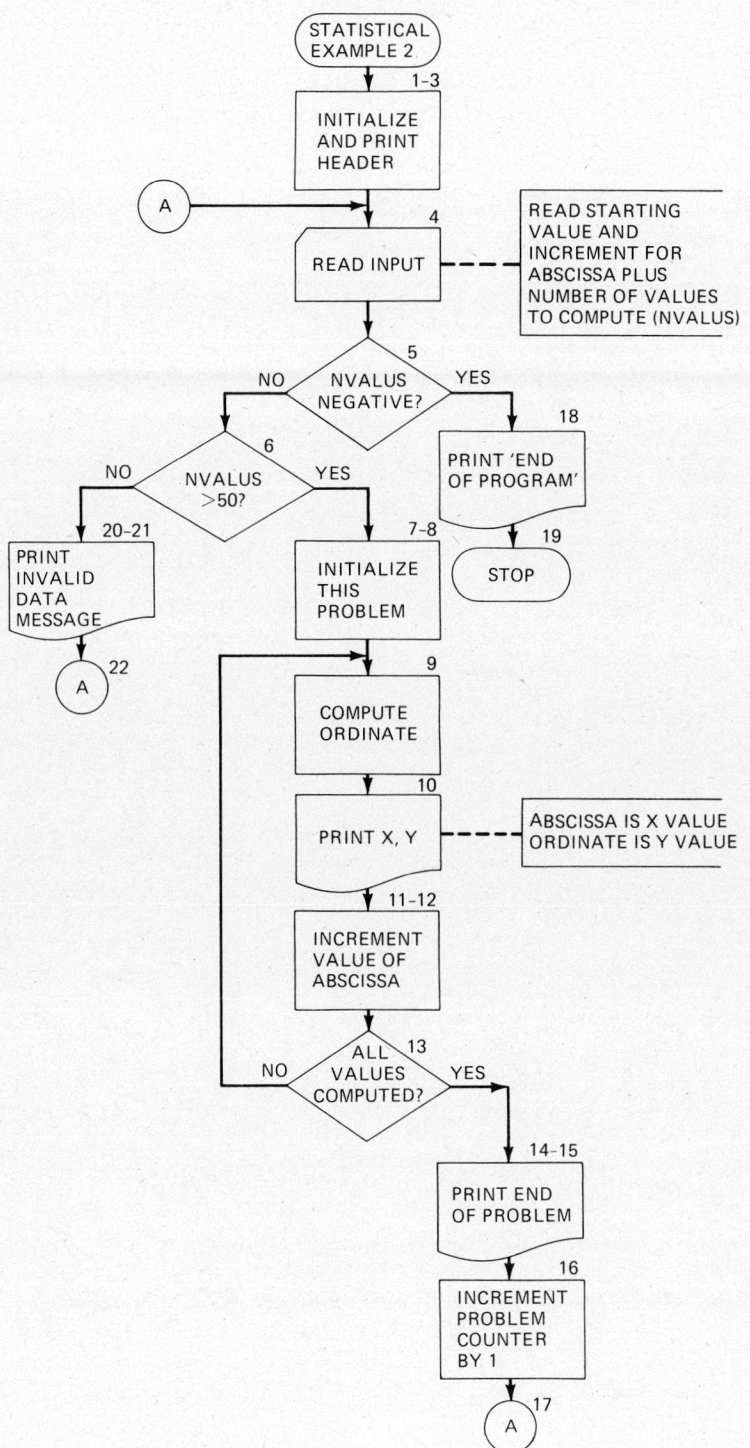

FIGURE 2-8 Program flowchart for statistical example 2—tables of ordinates of normal curve. (Numbers beside symbols refer to line numbers on program listing.

PROGRAM

```
      **********              PROGRAM IDENTIFICATION              **********
      *                                                                   *
      *        CALCULATE TABLES OF ORDINATES OF THE NORMAL CURVE          *
      *        WRITTEN BY T. HOFFMANN 05/03/77.                           *
      *                                                                   *
      *********************************************************************
      *                                                                   *
      **********              VARIABLE IDENTIFICATION              **********
      *                                                                   *
      *        XFIRST    = STARTING VALUE FOR X                           *
      *        XINCR     = INCREMENT OF X                                 *
      *        NVALUS    = NUMBER OF VALUES TO COMPUTE                    *
      *        NCNTR     = COUNTER TO LIMIT AGAINST NVALUS                *
      *        NPROB     = PROBLEM NUMBER                                 *
      *        XVALU     = VALUE OF X TO USE TO COMPUTE YVALU             *
      *        YVALU     = ORDINATE OF XVALU                              *
      *                                                                   *
      *****                   CONSTANT IDENTIFICATION              *****
      *                                                                   *
      *        6.2832    = 2*PI                                           *
      *                                                                   *
      *********************************************************************
      *                                                                   *
      **********             INITIALIZATION BLOCK          BLOCK 0000
      *                                                                   *
 1.          PIROOT = 1.0/SQRT(6.2832)
 2.          NPROB = 1
 3.          PRINT *,' X VALUE       Y VALUE'
      *                                                                   *
      *********************************************************************
      *                                                                   *
      **********           READ - COMPUTE - PRINT BLOCK     BLOCK 0100
      *                                                                   *
 4.      101 READ *,XFIRST,XINCR,NVALUS
      *                                                                   *
      *        NVALUS BEING NEGATIVE SIGNALS END OF DATA                  *
      *                                                                   *
 5.          IF(NVALUS.LE.0) GOTO 201
 6.          IF(NVALUS.GT.50) GOTO 901
 7.          XVALU=XFIRST
 8.          NCNTR=1
 9.      120 YVALU = PIROOT * EXP(-XVALU*XVALU/2.0)
10.          PRINT *,XVALU,YVALU
11.          XVALU = XVALU+XINCR
12.          NCNTR = NCNTR+1
      *                                                                   *
      *        IF NVALUS NOT YET COMPUTED, GO BACK FOR NEXT PAIR.         *
      *                                                                   *
13.          IF(NCNTR.LE.NVALUS) GOTO 120
14.      130 PRINT *,' END OF PROBLEM',NPROB
15.          PRINT *,' '
16.          NPROB = NPROB+1
      *                                                                   *
      *           GO BACK AND READ NEXT DATA SET                          *
      *                                                                   *
17.          GOTO 101
      *                                                                   *
      *********************************************************************
      *                                                                   *
      **********              TERMINATION BLOCK             BLOCK 0200
      *                                                                   *
18.      201 PRINT *,' END OF PROGRAM.'
19.          STOP
      *                                                                   *
      *********************************************************************
      *                                                                   *
      **********             ERROR MESSAGE BLOCK            BLOCK 0900
      *                                                                   *
20.      901 PRINT *,' '
21.          PRINT *,' NVALUS TOO LARGE',NVALUS
      *                                                                   *
      *           END CURRENT PROBLEM AND GO BACK TO READ NEXT DATA SET   *
      *                                                                   *
22.          GOTO 130
23.          END
```

FIGURE 2-9 Listing of FORTRAN program, sample input, and output for statistical example 2—tables of ordinates of normal curve.

```
XFIRST
 XINCR
  NVALUS                    SAMPLE INPUT
-1,-1,-1
1.3,0.3,6
-2.5,0.4,75
-1.4,0.2,7
```

OUTPUT

```
X  VALUE        Y  VALUE
-1.40000         .149727
-1.20000         .194186
-1.00000         .241970
 -.800000        .289691
 -.600000        .333224
 -.400000        .368270
 -.200000        .391042
END  OF  PROBLEM                  1


NVALUS  TOO  LARGE               75
END  OF  PROBLEM                  2

 1.30000         .171368
 1.60000         .110921
 1.90000         .656157E-01
 2.20000         .354746E-01
 2.50000         .175283E-01
 2.80000         .791544E-02
END  OF  PROBLEM                  3

END  OF  PROGRAM.
```

FIGURE 2-9 (continued)

starting value, increment, and number of entries are apparent from the table
output.

Programming Exercises

Description of Assignment

Select one or more problem(s) (or take the problem(s) assigned to you by the
instructor). Use the five statements from Chapter 1 plus the statements ex-

plained in Chapter 2A. The program should be written in good style using the following features (except where inappropriate):

1 Logical IF statement. Use the block IF where appropriate (if available).

2 Use at least one intrinsic function.

3 Echo input data for visual validation if it is not printed out as part of normal output.

4 Use programmed validation of input data when specified in the problem.

5 Use an IF loop to read and process more than one set of input data.

6 Check carefully first-time- and last-time-through logic.

The documentation should consist of the following:

1 Pseudocode description of program

2 Program flowchart

3 Program listing

4 Results of program testing using both valid and invalid input

Chapter 3 will use these same problems but with additional requirements for formatting of output and handling of end and error conditions.

Mathematics and Statistics

1 For the angles given below, compare the value given by the intrinsic sine function with the value obtained using the five terms of the following series expansion for the sine. (*HINT:* x must be in radians—1 degree equals $\pi/180$ radians.) Limit computations to positive angles less than $\pi/2$ radians.

$$\sin(x) = x - \frac{x^3}{3!} + \frac{x^5}{5!} - \frac{x^7}{7!} + \frac{x^9}{9!} - \cdots$$

Angle in degrees
15
95
60
45

2 For each of the following sets of data, compute the standard deviation and mean absolute deviation (average of the absolute deviations from the mean). The means are 2, 8.8, 40.0, and 10.7 for set A, B, C, and D. *HINT:* Read the mean and number of data points in a set and then read each data point in the set from a separate card.

A	B	C	D
−6	1.6	37.25	12.3
−12	6.3	39.4	8.0
8	12.4	45.61	17.4
14	9.3	38.0	6.5
13	8.0	35.78	9.3
7	7.7	42.65	
9	11.6	41.03	
−8	13.5	39.12	
10		43.66	
−15		37.5	

The formula for standard deviation is

$$\sqrt{\frac{\sum_{i=1}^{n} (X_i - \bar{X})^2}{n - 1}}$$

where X_i are the data items and $\bar{X}$ is the mean.

3 The number of combinations (c) of n things taken m at a time is:

$$c = \frac{n!}{n!(n - m)!}$$

For large values of m or n (say k) the factorial can be approximated by Stirling's formula:

$$k! = e^{-k}k^k\sqrt{2\pi k} \qquad e = 2.7183 \quad \text{and} \quad \pi = 3.1416$$

NOTE: This is valid only for positive, nonzero values of k. Compute c for the following using Stirling's approximation formula. Use the FORTRAN function for e.

n	m
6	4
0	5
40	30
50	70

Business and Economics

4 The formula for computing compound interest is:

$$p = a \left(1 + \frac{i}{q}\right)^{nq}$$

where a = initial amount

      i = annual interest rate

      n = number of years

      q = number of times compounded each year

      p = value at end of n years

When q approaches infinity (continuous compounding) the equation becomes:

$$p = ae^{in} \qquad e = 2.7183$$

For each of the following initial amounts and an interest rate of 7 percent, compare the values after 1 and 10 years for compounding quarterly and continuously. Use the FORTRAN exponential function for e.

$$a = 1000, 565, 2045$$

5 The economic order quantity (EOQ) is given by the following:

$$EOQ = \sqrt{\frac{2as}{ic}}$$

where a = annual usage

      s = cost of placing an order

      c = unit cost

      i = annual carrying rate

For each of the following sets of data, compute the EOQ. Note that negative quantities or division by zero inside the square root are errors.

Set	a	s	c	i
1	10000	11.75	.75	.20
2	1000	3.50	1.25	.25
3	8750	15.00	2.00	0
4	7400	37.40	-1.30	.25
5	6000	20.00	1.00	.20

6 Sales commissions (c) are computed as a multiple (f) of sales (s) in excess of quotas (q). If goals are not met, no bonus is paid.

$$c = f(s - q)$$

For each of the following persons, compute the bonus and determine which one is the largest. Print a special message if quotas are not met.

Sales person	Name	Goal	Actual	Bonus factor
1764	C. JONES	$400	$380	.2
2031	A. WHITE	300	340	.1
1885	X. SMITH	375	395	.17
0773	J. ADAMS	380	420	.15
2114	K. JAMES	325	367	.19

Science and Engineering

7 The area of a triangle can be computed by the sine law when two sides of the triangle (a, b) and the angle (θ) between them is known.

$$\text{Area} = ab \, \sin \theta$$

Given the following four triangular pieces of property, find their areas and determine which is largest. Omit computation if angle is outside the range of 0 to 180 degrees.

Plot number	a	b	θ
1	137.4	80.9	.78 radians
2	145.3	91.6	1.35
3	130.4	100.0	4.00
4	128.3	125.4	1.95

8 A projectile fired at an angle (θ) has a horizontal range (R) given by the following:

$$R = \frac{2v^2 \sin \theta \cos \theta}{g}$$

where v = initial velocity
$\quad\quad g$ = 32.2 ft/sec^2

Compute R for each of the following (limit angles to 0 to $\pi/2$ radians and v to positive values):

v	θ
200	20
200	70
200	45
175	160
1750	60

9 The period (p) of a pendulum is given by the following formula:

$$p = 2\pi \sqrt{\frac{L}{g}} \left(1 + \frac{1}{4} \sin^2 \frac{\alpha}{2} \right)$$

where g = 980 cm/sec^2
$\quad\quad L$ = pendulum length
$\quad\quad \alpha$ = angle of displacement

Compute the periods of the following pendulums:

Pendulum number	L (cm)	α (degrees)
1	120	15
2	90	20
3	60	5
4	74.6	10
5	83.4	12

Humanities and Social Sciences

10 From the empirical study of learning, the following relationship was observed:

$$t_x = px^{-l}$$

where x = number of repetitions
t_x = cumulative average task time for the xth repetition
p = time to perform task the first time
l = learning factor
From this:

$$l = - \frac{\log t_x}{\log px}$$

Compute l for each of the following situations (print warning if l is negative):

t_x	p	x
2.7	3.4	100
0.34	1.8	50
0.15	1.4	20
0.74	1.0	500
1.06	.8	400

11 Population growth is often either geometric (e.g., doubles every ten years) or exponential (increasing at an increasing rate). For geometric growth, the equation for population size (p) in year n is:

$$p = a(1 + r)^n$$

where a is the initial population and r is the annual growth rate. For exponential growth a possible equation is:

$$p = ae^{(1+r)^n}$$

Given a = 10,000, for the following situations compute the population in year 10 and the relative increase for both formulas.

Situation number	r
1	.1
2	.2
3	.5
4	.67
5	.7

12 Air pressure is a function of altitude (h). For each of the following locations, compute the air pressure (p) given that the relationship is

$$p = 14.7e^{-0.000038h}$$

Location	Elevation (h in feet)
1. Denver	5280
2. Dead Sea	−1292
3. New York	55
4. New Delhi	760
5. Katmandu	4223

General

13 Given the currency exchange rates, compute the equivalent of each of the following amounts to U.S. dollars (or vice versa). Use a coding scheme such that:

Code	$US	=	Alternate currency
1	1	=	.425 German marks
2	1	=	1.710 English pounds
3	1	=	.213 Hong Kong dollars

and negative codes mean opposite conversion (alternate currency to U.S. dollars). Identify which amount is the largest in U.S. dollars.

	Data
Code	Currency value
1	6.50
3	8.95
2	6.42
−3	12.44
6	8.95
−2	6.43
−1	8.88
4	2.95
1	7.50

Identify erroneous data cards (illegal codes).

14 A customer goes to a food market to buy groceries. Compute item costs, the total grocery bill, and find the most costly purchase for the following purchase list:

Items	Unit cost	Number of units
1. Beef	1.95	1.40
2. Potatoes	.85	6.75
3. Coffee	3.95	1.00
4. Candy	.15	12.00
5. Fruit	.98	7.95

15 Calculate the average temperature for each of the following weeks and determine which is warmest. Omit temperatures greater than 100 or less than 60 degrees Fahrenheit and print a warning message.

Week	Daily temperatures				
1. July 4 –8	85	70	83	77	75
2. July 11 –15	90	78	77	80	77
3. July 18 –22	999	77	85	84	73
4. July 25 –29	77	85	78	0	88

CHAPTER

FORMAT-DIRECTED INPUT AND OUTPUT

The list-directed input and output instructions explained in Chapter 1 are very simple to use but very limiting. FORTRAN provides for more flexible input and output using format-directed input and output. The format-directed method for input and output is frequently the only method available because list-directed input and output is not supported by some older compilers and is not a part of Subset FORTRAN. The commonly used features of format-directed input and output are explained in this chapter; additional features for external files of data on magnetic tape and magnetic disks are explained in Chapter 6.

Format-directed Instructions

In format-directed FORTRAN, obtaining data from an input device or writing data on an output device requires a pair of statements: the input/output statement and the FORMAT statement. The input/output statement specifies what is to be done, what device (unit) is to be used, and what variables are involved. The FORMAT statement specifies the form of the data being read in or written out. The input/output statement and the FORMAT statement are identified as belonging together by assigning a unique statement number to the FORMAT statement and referencing it in the input or output statement. Following the style recommended in this text, the FORMAT statement number will be part of the number series for the block in which it appears. For example, a pair of statements might appear as follows:

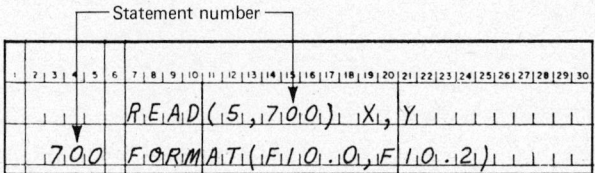

Input/Output Statements for Format-directed Input or Output

The input/output statement with format-directed input/output describes (or implies) four specifications necessary for input or output:

1 The operation (read or write).

2 The device to be used (card reader, printer, disk storage, etc.). FORTRAN assumes these devices have been assigned unit numbers $(1, 2, 3, \ldots, n)$.

3 The FORMAT statement which describes the format of the data to be input or output.

4 The variables to be input or output in the order to be read or written.

There are two basic input/output statements—one for reading (input) and one for writing (output):

READ (*u,fs*) list

WRITE (*u,fs*) list

where *u* refers to the unit number assigned to the input or output device and *fs* refers to the number of the FORMAT statement to be used. The four specifications are provided as follows:

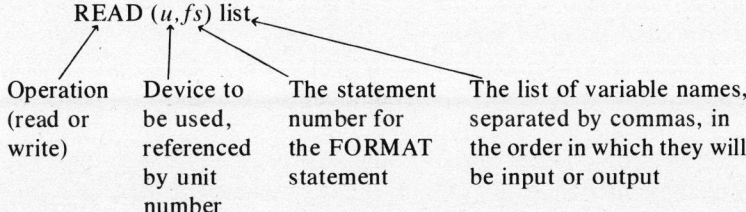

| Operation (read or write) | Device to be used, referenced by unit number | The statement number for the FORMAT statement | The list of variable names, separated by commas, in the order in which they will be input or output |

EXAMPLES

READ (5 , 7 1 0)A , B , X	Read values for A, B, and X (in that order) using unit 5 and FORMAT statement 710.
WRITE (6 , 7 2 0)X , A , B	Write values for X, A, B (in that order) using unit 6 and FORMAT statement 720.

Note that the space following the right parentheses is optional. The text examples of FORMAT statements are numbered in the 700s. This is an arbitrary designation and has no special significance.

The unit specification in the input/output statement can be either an integer constant or an integer variable. Both of the following are correct forms:

READ (5 , 7 0 5)A , B , C
READ (NREAD , 7 0 5)A , B , C

If an integer variable such as NREAD is used, then it must be defined in the program as having a value equal to the desired unit. For example, if the unit number to be used in the above example is 5, then NREAD may be defined by a statement such as:

NREAD = 5

The input or output statement requires a unit number to specify a card reader, printer, etc., but what unit number shall be used? There are no universally agreed-upon unit numbers, nor are any unit numbers specified in the FORTRAN standard. This means that a user of each implementation of FORTRAN must obtain the unit numbers assigned by that implementation. (There is a place to record these unit numbers for your computer on the inside of the back cover.) Although there are no universally agreed-upon standard numbers, the most generally used unit numbers are 5 for card reader and 6 for printer. These unit numbers are used by WATFOR, WATFIV, MNF, and other versions of FORTRAN. Therefore, these commonly used unit numbers will be used in all text illustrations.

One of the desirable features of FORTRAN is its portability such that a program written and run on one computer can be run without significant change on another computer. The use of different unit numbers can inhibit portability, but there are fairly easy ways to handle the differences. One is to write all READ and WRITE systems with variable names for the unit designation (such as NREAD) and merely to change the statement that assigns a value to NREAD. The other method is to assign the desired value to an input or output device by the use of a job control card. In other words, each installation will have assigned default values such as 5 or 6 for the card reader, printer, etc., but other values may be used by a simple job control instruction. These instructions to assign unit numbers are specific to each FORTRAN implementation, so they must be obtained from the computer center being used.

An alternate form of the input and output statement which does not use the unit designation is included in both the full 1966 and the 1977 FORTRAN standard and is provided in most implementations. In the name-description form, READ means read from the standard device (generally card reader), and PRINT means to output using the standard device (generally printer). Note that a comma must follow the FORMAT number in the name-designation form.

Unit-designation form	Name-designation form
READ (5 , 7 0 5)A , B	READ 7 0 5 , A , B
WRITE (6 , 7 1 0)A , B	PRINT 7 1 0 , A , B

The advantage of the name-designation form is that the card reader and printer (or other standard devices such as a terminal) can be specified when the programmer does not know the unit number. However, the name-designation form is not always available in restricted versions such as Subset FORTRAN. Since the unit-designation form is the more general form and always available, it is the preferred form and will be used in all examples in this text.

The unit-designation form can be used for list-directed input or output by writing an asterisk in place of a format statement number. For example, the following are equivalent:

```
READ ( 5 , * )   A , B , C
READ  * ,   A , B , C
```

INPUT/OUTPUT INSTRUCTIONS

Symbols used in description

u = unit designation (integer variable or integer constant) for input/output unit. Unit designations for various devices differ among implementations. Common usage is 5 for card reader and 6 for printer.

fs = statement number of FORMAT statement to be used with the input or output instruction. If * is used in place of a statement number, the instruction is list-directed.

list = list of variables which are to be read, printed, punched, etc., in the order in which they are to be used. The variable names are separated by commas. There need be no spaces between items in the list, but spaces may be used for readability.

Form of instructions

READ (u, fs) list

Reads from an input unit the quantities associated with the listed variable names and puts them into storage for use by the program.

WRITE (u, fs) list

Writes variables using an output unit. Form of output varies with output unit and FORMAT statement having label fs.

Alternate forms without unit designation (not always implemented)

READ fs, list

Reads from a standard input (such as punched card) the quantities associated with the listed variable names and puts them into memory.

PRINT fs, list

Prints a line of output using the quantities represented by the list of variable names in the form specified by FORMAT statement fs.

EXAMPLES

READ (5 , 7 0 5)A , B , C READ 7 0 5 , A , B , C	Read data from the card reader to variable names A, B, and C. Read according to the format specified by statement 705
WRITE(6 , 7 1 0)I , BETA PRINT 7 1 0 , I , BETA	Write on printer the quantities from variable names I and BETA. Use format specified by statement 710

In summary, the basic input/output instructions for format-directed input and output require only four elements: the command word (READ, WRITE), the input/output unit designation, the FORMAT statement reference number, and the list of variable names in the order they are to be read, printed, punched, etc.

Self-testing Exercise 3-1

1 Explain the meaning of the following input-output statements, assuming unit number 5 is card reader and unit number 6 is printer.
   (*a*) READ   (5, 700)A, B, C
   (*b*) PRINT   710, X, Y, Z
   (*c*) WRITE   (NREAD, 720)L, N, O
   (*d*) READ   730, Q, Z, T
   (*e*) WRITE   (6, *) X, Y, IX
2 A FORTRAN program has been written using unit numbers 1 for card reader and 3 for printer. The program is now to be run on a computer with default unit numbers 5 for card reader and 6 for printer. How is this change made?

The FORMAT Statement

The purpose of the FORMAT statement is to describe the specific form of the data being read or written. The FORMAT statement uses a standard method of describing data that is the same for all input/output media. The same FORMAT statement can define data to be read from a card reader, to be punched into cards, or to be printed on the printer as long as the form of the data is the same in all cases. One FORMAT statement can be used by more than one input or output statement. The FORMAT statement does not have to appear next to the input/output statement using it. The statement number is sufficient identification, so that the FORMAT statement can be written before or after the input/ output command using it. Some programmers put a FORMAT statement next to the first input/output statement referencing it; others group all FORMAT statements together at the beginning or end of the program. A convention used in this text is to place each FORMAT statement closely following the first input/output statement which references it and using a statement number from the numbers in the block.

In order to describe the form of the data for input/output, three elements must be specified or implied:

1 *Type of editing*   This can specify real, integer, or real with exponent editing for use with real and integer data. (Other less common types will be explained in Chapter 7.)

2 *Field size*   This is the number of columns on punched cards or printer paper, or character positions on other storage media, that are available for reading, storing or printing the quantity.

3 *Location of decimal point*   This is expressed as the number of places from the right. This element is eliminated from the FORMAT specification for integer quantities (because it has no meaning).

The FORMAT statement consists of the statement number (columns 1 through 5), then the word FORMAT (normally beginning in column 7), followed by sets of specifications separated by commas. The group of specifications is enclosed in parentheses. Spaces may be used freely to improve readability. Examples (to be explained later) are:

1	2	3	4	5	6	7 8 9 10 11 12 13 14 15 16 17 18 19 20	21 22 23 24 25 26 27 28 29 30 31 32 33 34 35 36 37 38 39 40
	1	0	9			FORMAT(F10.2,F5.1)	
	2	0	9			FORMAT(F7.0,I12)	
	3	0	9			FORMAT(E15.8,E15.8,F10.2)	

As illustrated by the examples, each specification set consists of three elements: a single-letter edit descriptor, field size, and decimal location. The three elements in the specification F10.2 are useful in seeing how the three elements are contained in the specification.

$$F10.2$$

Edit descriptor defining   Field size   Two positions allowed to right
real data to be edited   of 10 positions   of decimal point

The first part of the specification is the single-letter edit descriptor. The three most commonly used edit descriptors are F, E, and I.

THREE COMMON EDIT DESCRIPTORS

Letter	Type of quantity	Form	Where
F	Real	Fw.d	w = field size
E	Exponent form of real	Ew.d	d = positions to right
I	Integer	Iw	of decimal

The next part of the FORMAT specification is the field size in numbers of spaces or columns. This is the maximum number of character spaces or columns the quantity can occupy. The data quantity need not use all of the field; the unused positions are left blank. The field size for output should allow space for characters such as the sign and, for real output, a decimal point. For example, the field size for the following real and integer outputs are computed as follows (the E edit will be explained later):

Type of variable	Form of data		Minimum field size					Edit specification
			Sign	Integer digits	Decimal point	Digits in fraction	Total	
Real	±ddd.dd	=	1	3	1	2	7	F7.2
Real	±ddd.	=	1	3	1	0	5	F5.0
Integer	±dddd	=	1	4	0	0	5	I5

The third part of the FORMAT statement (not used with the I edit descriptor), is the location of the decimal point in the field. The field specification and decimal point specification are used in input in a slightly different way than in output. The use in output will be discussed first, and then the differences will be noted.

FORMAT Editing for Output

The handling of data on output is quite simple in the normal case. However, there are special rules for a field size that is too large or too small for the data. Also, the first position on the printed line is not available but is used for vertical spacing control. It will be convenient to separately describe integer data, real data with F edit descriptor, and real data with E edit descriptor. The use of the first print position for vertical spacing will be explained later in the chapter.

For integer data, no decimal point is printed and the quantity is right-justified (number starts at right side of field) and unused positions to the left are blank. A minus sign will print for a negative quantity, but a plus sign will not print for a positive quantity. If the field size is too small for the quantity (for example, a field defined as I4 and a quantity to be output of 39764), there is an error condition called *overflow*. In cases of overflow, the output for the field consists of asterisks to indicate the overflow error.

EXAMPLES

Specification	Data	Output (b indicates blank)
I6	−479	bb−479
I10	3	bbbbbbbbb3
I4	36754	****

Note that a field specification that is larger than needed is one method of leaving space between output items. Another method will be explained later. As an example of the uses of I specifications, the following statements will produce data and blanks in columns as illustrated.

```
    WRITE (6, 700) IX, JIX, KIX
700 FORMAT (I10, I5, I6)
```

where the value for IX is −37454, JIX is 495, and KIX is 1159.

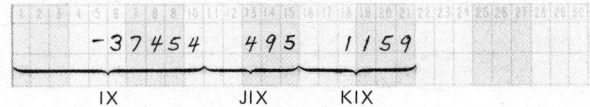

For real output using the F edit descriptor, the computer positions the data in the field by means of the decimal point position. The integer digits are positioned to the left of the decimal point, and the fractional digits are positioned to the right. As an example, in a field of 10 for printing, a specification of F10.3 will position the decimal in the fourth position from the right, i.e., three digits of the fractional part are printed to the right of the decimal point.

$$F10.3 \begin{cases} & \text{Decimal point} \\ \text{6 positions for integer part} & \text{3 positions for fractional part} \\ \overbrace{X \; X \; X \; X \; X \; X} \;\; | \;\; \overbrace{X \; X \; X} \\ 10 \; 9 \; 8 \; 7 \; 6 \; 5 \; 4 \; 3 \; 2 \; 1 \\ \underbrace{\qquad\qquad\qquad\qquad} \\ \text{Field width of 10} \end{cases}$$

The following conditions can occur for the integer portion and fractional portions of the F specification field in output:

1 Digits in result to be output do not fill the field
   (*a*) Integer portion
   (*b*) Fractional portion

2 Digits in result to be output exceed positions in field
   (*a*) Integer portion
   (*b*) Fractional portion

These conditions will be explained and illustrated.

1 Digits do not fill field.
   (*a*) If digits in integer portion do not fill all positions, the unused positions to the left are filled with blanks. For example, 98.5 and F10.1 = bbbbbb98.5. The integer portion must be large enough to include a minus sign when the output quantity is negative. It is good programming practice in writing specifications to allow for a negative sign even when only positive values are expected.
   (*b*) If fractional digits do not fill the fractional portion of the field, the remaining positions to the right are filled with zeros. For example, 347.56 and F10.5 = b347.56000.

2 Digits exceed positions available.
   (*a*) When the number of integer digits exceeds the integer field to the left of the decimal, there will be overflow resulting in output of a field of asterisks. For example, 67943.2 to be printed with a FORMAT statement F8.4 will cause overflow as shown, and the output will be a field of asterisks.

		Field positions
d=4	Fractional digit position (d) =	4
67 943.2000	Decimal point =	1
Field size of 8	Remaining for integer position =	3
Overflow digits	Total =	8

(*b*) If the number of fractional digits exceeds the fractional field size (specified by d portion of specification), the excess digits will be truncated after rounding. No error indication occurs. For example, 7.6543 printed with F8.2 will print 7.65 and 3.9462 with F8.2 will print 3.95.

The E or exponent form of output editing is preferred in all cases where the result is very large or very small or where the result has an unknown range of magnitude. In the E format, the result is expressed as a decimal fraction plus an exponent which indicates the number of places the decimal point of the fraction should be moved to the right (for a positive exponent) or to the left (for a negative exponent). The E specification indicates the number of positions in the E result field and the number of positions (digits) in the fraction.

Ew.d

Exponent form   Field width   Digits in fraction

EXAMPLES

Specification	Quantity	Output
E15.8	375.76001	b0.37576001E+03
E15.8	−.0000037576001	−0.37576001E−05
E13.6	375.76082	b0.375761E+03

The zero to the left of the decimal point in the E form of output is optional, so some implementations of FORTRAN produce it; others do not.

An E specification requires at least seven digit positions more than the size of the fraction to allow for the sign of the fraction, the zero in front, the decimal point, and the E±nn for the exponent. If the field size is more than seven digits greater than fraction size, the result will be right-justified and blank spaces will be inserted at the left. If the number of digits in the specified fraction size is less than the number of digits stored in the computer, the quantity will be truncated after rounding as in the third example above.

The form of the exponent can vary with different implementations of FOR-

TRAN. The following are all standard: E±nn, ±0nn, ±nnn where the n's stand for the digits in the exponent.

The following examples illustrate how data characters and blank spaces will be positioned when integer data items are output with I edit specifications and real data items are output using F and E edit specifications:

```
     WRITE  (6,701) A,B,IX           ⎧A=-493.122
                                     ⎨B= 4.755
701  FORMAT  (F10.3, F8.2,I6)        ⎩IX=5628
```

```
   -493.122      4.76   5628
```
A   B   IX

Note rounding
because d = 2

```
     WRITE  (6,702) X,JIX,Y          ⎧X=1976.43
                                     ⎨JIX=2
702  FORMAT (E16.8,I7,E15.4)         ⎩Y=0.001
```

```
   0.19764300E+04          2      0.1000E-02
```
X   JIX   Y

FORMAT Editing for Input

The FORMAT statement is treated differently with a READ punched-card statement than with a WRITE or PRINT statement in three cases. First, with data in punched cards, no provision need be made for an input sign unless it occupies a column by being punched. If an input value is negative, the sign must be punched as a leading minus sign but if the values to be input are positive, no sign is needed. Within a field, blanks may precede the negative sign, but zeros must not be punched to the left of the sign.

The second difference is in the meaning of the d portion of the specification. In input from punched cards, a decimal point in the data takes precedence over the decimal location specification of the FORMAT statement. If no decimal point is punched, the decimal point location is based on the edit specification in the FORMAT statement. The advantage in punching the actual decimal point (for a real quantity) is that the number may then appear anywhere in the specified field. If the decimal is not punched, the real number must be positioned carefully in the field because the decimal point for an input variable without a decimal punched in it is assumed to be d positions from the right side of the field.

The third difference for input is in the form of input data for E format reading. The E is optional; if E is used, a plus sign is optional. However, clear input forms should be used to avoid mistakes. The following two sets of data are all valid, the items in the set showing different ways to represent the same quantity:

Set 1	Set 2
13795.2E12	.2684E01
13795.2+12	2684.−3
.137952+17	26.84E−1

Note that the exponent changed when the decimal point was moved. A number punched in an E format may also be read by an F specification.

The following examples illustrate the rules for input FORMAT specifications.

1 Several data items are punched on an input card without spaces between. Variable names are assigned as shown. No decimal points are punched, but the locations of the implied decimal points are shown by the carets, e.g., X = 9.8, Y1 = 789.4, YJ = 1.094, YK = 86765.4, and KIX = 88.

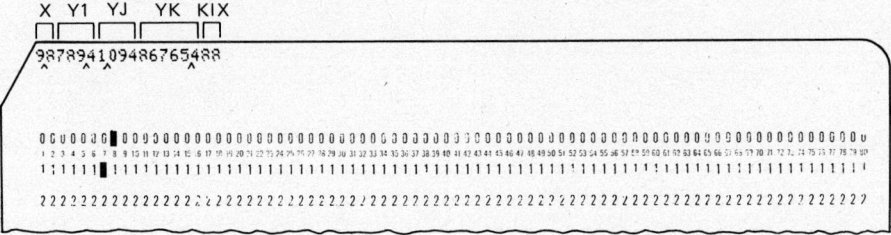

The statement to read these variables is the following (Note that no allowance is made for a sign or a decimal point in the input field size because none appears in the data.):

```
     READ(5,201) X,Y1,YJ,YK,KIX
201  FORMAT(F2.1,  F4.1,  F4.3,  F6.1,  I2)
```

Note that spaces between specifications are optional and for readability only.

2 Applying the rules for reading input, a quantity in a punched card will be read as indicated using the given format:

Quantity in punched card	Format specifications to read data	Read as	Comments
325	I3	000	Because I3 reads only columns 1–3 and data is in columns 8 to 10
325	I10	0000000325	Leading spaces = zeros
325 457	I3, I4	325 and 0457	
325	I10	3250000000	Trailing spaces = zeros
375.56	F5.2, F5.2	000.03 and 75.56	Only first 5 columns read with first format specification
375.56	F10.2	00000375.56	Leading spaces = zeros
375.56	F10.0	0375.5600	Punched decimal overrides format

The basic approach to input and output has now been explained. The rules for the FORMAT statement are summarized in the box.

FORMAT STATEMENT

General form

fs FORMAT (list of specifications separated by commas), where *fs* is a format statement number. Spaces before and after parentheses and between specifications are optional.

Form of specifications

Fw.d	Real variable	w stands for field size
Ew.d	Exponent form	d stands for number of decimal positions to right of
Iw	Integer variable	decimal

Fitting data to field size

1 Data is justified to the right in the field, except in the case of real data being input in which a punched decimal position overrides a FORMAT-specified decimal position.

2 If integer positions of an output are greater than the integer portion field size, an overflow error condition results and a field of asterisks is output.

3 If significant digits in the fractional portion exceed the number of positions in the fraction field to right of decimal point, the quantity to remain is rounded and the excess digits are truncated.

4 Using the E form can ensure maximum accuracy without overflow. The d portion should be the same as the number of significant digits with the field width at least 7 higher.

The next section of this chapter explains how to put headings and other notes on the output from the program. In Chapters 4 and 7, additional input/output methods and specifications are explained.

Self-testing Exercise 3-2

1 Read the following data from a punched card. The card is referenced by the variable names ALPHA, BETA, IOTA, and JIX.

Note that the sizes of the fields, including blank spaces at the left, are:

Variable	Field size	Columns
ALPHA	10	1–10
BETA	9	11–19
IOTA	7	20–26
JIX	7	27–33

2 Print the above variables in reverse order. Leave two spaces between ALPHA and BETA, not counting the sign position. Leave the first position on the line blank (not counting a space for a sign).

3 Print the variables IOTA and BETA. Do not print the fractional portion of BETA. Do not use a field size larger than absolutely necessary, but provide 10 spaces (not counting the space allowed for a sign) before the first quantity and between the actual quantities as printed.

4 What will be the result of the following set of WRITE and FORMAT statements if X = 1.0375 and IYEAR = 95

```
      WRITE (6,701) IYEAR,X
701   FORMAT (I10,F10.2)
```

5 What is the minimum specification for printing the following variables? (Remember to allow for decimal point and one space for sign.) X's stand for nonzero integers.

Form of variable	To be printed as	FORTRAN FORMAT specification
(a) XXXXXXX	XXXX.XX	
(b) XXXX0000	XXXX.0	
(c) −XXXXXXX	−XX.XXXXX	
(d) XXXXXXXX	.XXX	
(e) XXXX	XXXX	
(f) −XXXXXXX0000000	− 0.XXXXXXXXE+ 1 4	

Repetition of FORMAT Specifications

When several variables for input or output have the same specifications, a single specification can be repeated by placing an integer number in front of it. For example, 7F10.3 means that the F10.3 specification is to be used seven times.

By enclosing a set of specifications in parentheses and placing an integer number in front of the set, the set will be repeated the number of times indicated: 3(F10.0, I3) is the same as (F10.0, I3, F10.0, I3, F10.0, I3).

The following examples illustrate the repeat feature. The repeat will stop when the list of variables to be used is exhausted. The program uses only as much of a FORMAT as is needed by the list of variables.

Examples of FORMAT repeat are:

FORMAT	Effect
FORMAT (I 3 , 7 F 1 0 . 0)	I3 and repeat F10.0 up to seven times
FORMAT (5 (I 3 , F 1 0 . 0) , F 1 0 . 0)	Repeat (I3, F10.0) five times then use F10.0
FORMAT (I 3 , 5 (F 1 0 . 0 , I 2))	I3 and repeat (F10.0, I2) up to five times
FORMAT (7 I 2 , 3 (F 1 0 . 0 , I 3))	Repeat I2 up to seven times, and then repeat (F10.0, I3) up to three times

Horizontal Positioning

The use of extra positions in a field specification causes blanks to be inserted in a line, but this is sometimes cumbersome. An alternative is the nX specification which causes n positions to be skipped (and filled with blanks). For example, on output a FORMAT (1X,I3,10X,I3) will put a blank in the first position, print data in the next 3 positions, skip the next 10 (make them blank), and print in the following 3 positions.

A Tc specification is a tabulating specification which positions the input or output device at the cth character position. For example, writing a FORMAT (T50, F10.2) will output starting at position 50 on the line.

The nX and Tc edit specifiers apply to input as well as output. For example, the following read instructions will read the data for Y in columns 51 to 60 and the data for IY in columns 71 to 75.

```
     READ  (5, 100)  Y,  IY
100  FORMAT  (T51,  F10.0,  10X,  I5)
```

HORIZONTAL POSITIONING

nX   Skip n positions to the right.
Tc   Tabulate to position c, i.e., move to position c where next input or output will
     begin. Available only with full FORTRAN.

Self-testing Exercise 3-3

What is the effect of each of the following FORMAT specifications?

1 FORMAT (5(F6.0), 3I4)
2 FORMAT (3I2, 4F10.0, 2E15.8)
3 FORMAT (4(I3, F10.0), I3)
4 FORMAT (I5, 10X, F10.2)
5 FORMAT (19X, F10.2, 20X, I3)
6 FORMAT (T20, F10.2, T50, I3)

Providing Descriptive Labels and Headings on Output

It is frequently desirable to provide descriptive labels and headings on output (primarily printed output). A program to compute the variance and standard deviation of an array of numbers might have an output such as the following:

```
THE VARIANCE IS                        XXXXXX.XX
THE STANDARD DEVIATION IS                XXX.XX
THE NUMBER OF OBSERVATIONS IS               XXX
```

The descriptive character output illustrated above is sometimes termed *Hollerith output*. FORMAT specifications permit any combination of letters, numbers, and special characters on a line of output. There are essentially four methods for providing headings and other character output.

1 Apostrophe edit descriptors in the FORMAT statement

2 H edit descriptor in the FORMAT statement

3 A set of characters in list-directed output enclosed in apostrophes

4 Character data stored internally and referenced by variable names

The first two methods, the apostrophe and H edit descriptors, are essentially identical in purpose and space. The H edit descriptor is the traditional method but tends to be error-prone. The apostrophe method is therefore preferred (but may not be available on older implementations of FORTRAN). The third method was explained in Chapter 1. One approach to method 4 will be explained later in this section.

The Apostrophe Edit Descriptor

The apostrophe method encloses the characters to be output in apostrophes. If the field to be output contains an apostrophe, two consecutive apostrophes are used to specify an apostrophe in the printed output.

EXAMPLES

```
      WRITE(6,700)
700   FORMAT(' NOW IS THE TIME.')

      WRITE(6,710)
710   FORMAT(' I CAN''T DO IT.')
```

The apostrophe specification may be placed among a list of format edit specifications, or it may be the sole output of the WRITE (or PRINT) statement. For example, if the answer is the variable X which has a specification of F10.2, the set of WRITE and FORMAT statements to print

THE ANSWER IS ±XXXXXX.XX

will be:

```
      WRITE(6,700) X
700   FORMAT(' THE ANSWER IS   ',F10.2)

      WRITE(6,700) X
700   FORMAT(' THE ANSWER IS',F12.2)
```

The first apostrophe specification provides for two spaces after IS. The second format shows how the blanks after IS can be provided by making the field size for the output of the variable X two spaces wider. Since the number on output is right-justified, the extra two spaces appear at the left. The Hollerith line starts at the left side with the first position being left blank. A heading such as

ANALYSIS PROGRAM, to be centered on a page with 132 printing spaces, is written with a WRITE or PRINT statement having no variable list, as follows:

```
    WRITE  (6, 700)
700 FORMAT  (58X, 'ANALYSIS  PROGRAM')
```

Note that it was simpler to skip the 58 spaces to the center than to include these in the apostrophe specification. The T specification could also have been used to start the heading in column 59 (same as skipping over 58 spaces).

```
700 FORMAT  (T59,  'ANALYSIS  PROGRAM')
```

The H Edit Descriptor

The use of the H edit descriptor for character output is quite simple. It involves writing out the output exactly as it is to appear (including blanks) and then counting the number of character positions occupied. The number of positions plus an H is written in front of the characters to indicate that the specified number of positions following is not to be translated, but is to be transferred exactly as written to the output line. For example, to print THE ANSWER IS which takes up 14 positions (if the first position is left blank), the H specification is:

```
FORMAT  (14H  THE  ANSWER  IS)
```

Programming errors often occur because the count of the positions is wrong.

The separating comma in the FORMAT statement, necessary after an E, F, and I specification, is optional (but desirable) following the H and apostrophe edit specifications.

CHARACTER OUTPUT FROM FORMAT

Apostrophe edit	Enclose characters to be output in apostrophes. Two consecutive apostrophes are used to specify apostrophe in output.
H edit	Precede the characters to be output by nH where n is the number of characters following H that are to be output.

Comma following apostrophe edit or H edit characters is optional.

Vertical Spacing with Control Characters

On line printers running under FORTRAN, the first column on the line is not printed; that position is used for vertical spacing or carriage control of the printer. The output is written so that column 1 is blank unless vertical spacing control other than single spacing is desired. To implement vertical spacing control, a numeric character is assigned to the first position by an appropriate FORMAT statement. The usual method for including this in the FORMAT is to specify a one-character Hollerith field for output to column 1. The vertical spacing control characters are shown in the box:

VERTICAL SPACING WITH CONTROL CHARACTER

First position on output line is used for vertical spacing control. The character is usually placed in the first position by a character output using either apostrophe or H edit methods.

Character	Vertical spacing before output
Blank	One line (single space)
0 (zero)	Two lines (double space)
1	To first line of next page
+	No advance

NOTE: Some terminals do not use a carriage control character. The character in the first position is displayed.

Either the apostrophe or the H edit descriptor form may be used to specify vertical spacing. The following pairs are identical:

```
700   FORMAT(' ')
700   FORMAT( H )

710   FORMAT('0')
710   FORMAT( H0)
```

The vertical spacing control character can be the only element in the FORMAT or it may be included with other output on the same line. The following are equivalent:

```
700   FORMAT(' ',' THE ANSWERS')
700   FORMAT( H , H THE ANSWERS)
700   FORMAT( 12H THE ANSWERS)
```
Space to top of page and print THE ANSWERS

Since a blank in the first position of any line of output is used for normal single spacing, single-spaced lines should have a format with the first character a space. The following three examples all have the same effect of single spacing.

	2	3	4	5	6	7	8	9	10	11	12	13	14	15	16	17	18	19	20	21	22	23	24	25	26	27	28	29	30	31	32	33	34	35	36	37	38	39	40
		7	0	1		F	O	R	M	A	T	(	'		T	H	I	S		I	S		P	A	G	E		'	,	I	2	)							
		7	0	1		F	O	R	M	A	T	(	1	4	H		T	H	I	S		I	S		P	A	G	E		,	I	2	)						
		7	0	1		F	O	R	M	A	T	(	1	X	,	'	T	H	I	S		I	S		P	A	G	E		'	,	I	2	)					

Self-testing Exercise 3-4

Write a set of WRITE and FORMAT statements to provide the following lines of output. Write each using both the H and apostrophe edit descriptors. A line is assumed to have 132 spaces. Remember that the first space on the line should be blank if there is to be single spacing.

1 ← 25 →THE TOLERANCE IS bbXXX.XX
2 ← 10 →AMOUNT OF SAVINGS IS $ XXX.XX
3 NUMBER IS XXXX
4 THE END. (with vertical spacing of 2 lines before printing.)
5 ← 5 →ITEM← 10 →AMOUNT
6 PAYROLL REPORT centered at top of page.

The A Specification for Input and Output of Characters

There will be situations where characters cannot be placed in a FORMAT statement because the characters to be used are variable. In such cases, it may be desirable to input the characters and store them for later use.

Character data is stored in the computer and therefore can be referenced by a name. The character string GBD can be referred to by NAME just as the data 147.6 can be referred to as VALUE. Each character in the character string occupies one character storage unit. The length of a character data item is the number of character positions (including imbedded blanks) in the string. For example, 'I WILL' occupies six positions.

Variable names identified with a character string do not have any special first letter. Two approaches are used to define variables as referencing character data. The 1977 standard requires explicit identification of each variable name which refers to character data by a special CHARACTER declaration (see Chapter 7). The declaration also specifies the maximum number of characters that can be stored and referenced by a variable name. The accepted method prior to the 1977 standard (and allowed as an extension of 1977 FORTRAN) is to implicitly define variable names as referencing character data by reading character data into them using an A format specification. This implicit method is explained in this chapter because it is used by all pre-1977 FORTRANs, it is implemented by WATFOR, WATFIV, and MNF, and it is likely to continue to be included in most implementations of 1977 FORTRAN. The maximum size in characters of a data item referenced by an implicitly defined character variable depends on the FORTRAN implementation. A common limit is four or six characters.

The A edit descriptor specifies the number of characters to be read from the input and stored in the positions identified with a character variable name. The form is An, where n is the number of characters. The characters to be read can include blanks. For example, if the four-character data strings for NAME1 and NAME2 are being read from a punched card, the READ and FORMAT might be as follows:

```
      READ (5,700) NAME1, NAME2
700 FORMAT (A4,A4)
```

Printing (or other output of character data input by an A edit descriptor) is output with an A edit descriptor. A field larger than the number of characters in the data item results in spaces at the right (the output is left-justified).

THE A EDIT DESCRIPTOR

An   Defines a character variable field containing n characters (including space characters).

When the implicit method of defining character variables is used, there is a maximum size for n which depends on the compiler used. Common limits are four or six characters. See Chapter 7 for the explicit method which removes the length restriction.

Self-testing Exercise 3-5

1 Read a five-character and a six-character field from positions 10 to 14 and 20 to 25 on a punched card and store them in NCHAR and NAME2.
2 Print the data from problem 1 in the form:

```
bTHE DATA 1 IS XXXXX AND DATA 2 IS XXXXXX.
```

Checking for End of Data and Data Error

If the number of data records (such as punched cards) to be input is variable, the program should test for the end of the data. An attempt to read when there are no more input records will cause the operating system to terminate the job abnormally. An explicit method is preferred. The two methods are:

1 Use a special end-of-data data item (explained in Chapter 2).

2 Use an END specification in the READ statement.

The second method of specifying the action to be taken when the end of the data has been reached is the END control item in the input statement. This may not be available in some older FORTRANs. When available, it is very useful. The form of the item is END = s where s is the statement to which control should go when the data has all been read. It is normal practice to have a special end-of-data operating system control card following the last data card. When the computer reads this system control card, the END = s statement is executed. As an example, the READ statement below will be executed until there are no more data cards, at which time control will go to statement 400.

```
READ (5,700,END=400) A,B,C
```

Spaces are optional and used only for readability.

END-OF-DATA SPECIFICATION IN INPUT STATEMENT

END = s   where s is the statement number to which control is to pass when all data has been read.

The specification is placed after the unit number and FORMAT statement number in the input statement.

If a data input, say on a card, is not readable with the specified format, such as, for example, alphabetic characters in an integer field, the operating system will abort the job with some data error message. To avoid this type of termination and to keep the control in the program, full FORTRAN provides a data-type error specification in the READ statement. The form is ERR = s where s is the number of the statement to which control is to transfer if a data error is encountered. This statement should probably print an error message and take appropriate action such as returning to read the next record. For example, if the card shown below is read by the following statement, there will be a data-type error.

```
      READ  (5, 701,  END = 8 0 1,  ERR = 9 0 1)  NIX,  X
7 0 1  FORMAT ( I 5,  F 5 . 0 )
```

The decimal point in an I edit field is a data error.
Reading this card will cause transfer to statement 901.

DATA-TYPE ERROR SPECIFICATION IN INPUT STATEMENT

ERR = s   where s is the statement number to which control is to pass when a data-type error is encountered.

The specification is placed after the unit number and FORMAT statement number (and before or after the END specification if used) in the input statement. Available only in full FORTRAN.

Self-testing Exercise 3-6

1 Write READ and IF statements to read all data cards, each card having variables ID, HOURS, and RATE in columns 1 to 5, 6 to 7, and 8 to 11. There is a trailer card after the last data card with 99999 in the ID field. At end, go to 500.
2 Write a READ statement to perform the same result as problem 1 but using the END feature and omitting the trailer card with 99999 for ID.
3 Write a READ statement to perform the same results as in problem 2 but also with a data error specification transferring to 910 if a data error is encountered.

Handling Physical Records with Slash Editing

One FORMAT statement has thus far been assumed for each line of output, each card read, etc. FORTRAN allows considerably more versatility in input and output. Lines, cards, etc., may be skipped, and a single FORMAT statement may be used for more than one line of output.

The concepts of a physical record and a logical record are useful in understanding how to use FORMAT specifications effectively. A *physical record* is a separable element of a storage or recording medium from which data can be read or on which data can be written. Examples are a punched card and a line on the printer paper. A *logical record* consists of items of data which logically belong together. They may occupy less than one physical record, exactly one physical record, or more than one physical record. For example, a logical record may require two punched cards.

The slash (/) is used in a FORMAT statement to terminate the current physical record. The closing right parenthesis of the FORMAT statement also terminates the current physical record. Using more than one slash causes multiple records to be skipped. The slash can be written anywhere in the FORMAT statement. Examples are:

```
FORMAT ( / / ,  3 F 1 0 . 0 )
FORMAT ( I 2 ,   / ,  F 1 0 . 0 )
FORMAT ( I 2 ,  F 1 0 . 0 ,   / )
```

Since the right, closing parenthesis also terminates a physical record (and therefore can be thought of as a slash), rules can be formulated for the effect of slashes.

USE OF SLASHES IN FORMAT

1 The use of *n* slashes at the beginning or end of a FORMAT cause *n* physical records to be skipped.

2 A slash in the middle of a FORMAT will cause the current record to be terminated, and a new physical record will be brought into use (starting at the beginning of the new record).

3 More than one slash in the middle of a FORMAT will terminate the current record and cause *n* − 1 of the following records to be skipped.

4 Commas before and after the slashes in the FORMAT specifications are optional.

EXAMPLES OF THE USE OF SLASHES

FORMAT (with READ)	Effect
FORMAT (F10.0/I3)	Reads two cards; the first card has a variable specification of F10.0, the second uses I3
FORMAT (3F10.0/)	Reads a card with three F10.0 values, then skips a card
FORMAT (///F6.3)	Skips three cards and uses F6.3 for variable on fourth

FORMAT (with WRITE or PRINT)	Effect
FORMAT (1X, F10.0/)	Prints a line with F10.0 and then skips one line
FORMAT (1X, 3F10.0, /, 1X, I3) Commas optional	Prints three F10.0 values on a line, skips to next line, and prints an I3 value
FORMAT (1X, F10.0, ///)	Prints F10.0, then skips three lines

Note the placement of a blank space as first character of line for vertical spacing control by use of 'b' or 1X specification

Reuse of FORMAT Specifications

At this point, it is appropriate to consider what happens if the number of variables in the input/output list is different from the number of specifications in the FORMAT statement. The rightmost parenthesis in the FORMAT statement acts to terminate the current physical record. When the end of the format specifications are reached without exhausting the list of variables, the current record is terminated, a new record is brought into use, and the format specifications are repeated. However, the program goes back only to the most recent unmodified left parenthesis in the format specifications (a specification in parentheses without a repeat number in front of it) and begins at that point for the repeating of the specifications. For example:

```
      READ  (5, 700) J, A, B, C,
                        ┌──────────────────── Most recent left parenthesis
 700  FORMAT ( I 6 ,  ( F 1 0 . 0 ) )
```

This will read J and A from the first card, but the list is not exhausted, so the specifications must be repeated with a new punched card. Because of the repeat at unmodified parenthesis rule, only F10.0 is repeated in the above example, not the entire specification. The list is still not exhausted, and F10.0 is again repeated with a new card. In other words, the example reads from three cards: J and A on card 1, B on card 2, and C on card 3. The following examples for FORMAT (and a WRITE statement) illustrate the repeat at unmodified parenthesis rule.

(I 3 / (F 10 . 0))	Prints I3 values on one line, goes to next line, and prints an F10.0 value. If more variables, it continues printing one F10.0 to a line until the output list is exhausted.
(I 2 / (3F 10 . 0))	Prints I2 value on one line, then prints three values with F10.0s per line until the output list is exhausted. I 2 F 10 . 0 F 10 . 0 F 10 . 0 F 10 . 0 F 10 . 0 F 10 . 0 F 10 . 0 F 10 . 0 F 10 . 0

The effects of too few or too many specifications can be summarized as:

Condition	Effect	Example
More specifications than variables in the list	Extra specifications are ignored	READ (5 , 7 0 0)A , B , C 7 0 0 FORMAT (5F 10 . 0) Uses only the first three specifications
More variables than specifications	When specifications are exhausted (i.e., the right parenthesis of the FORMAT is reached, which terminates the current record) a new record is brought into use, and the FORMAT specifications are repeated at the most recent unmodified left parenthesis	WRITE (6 , 7 0 0)A , B , C 7 0 0 FORMAT (1X , 2F 10 . 0) Writes output on two lines with A and B on first line and C on second line

What happens if the FORMAT specifications call for a total of field widths (a logical record) greater than one physical record? The first physical record is used in toto, and another record is brought into use for the remainder. For example, if a 160-character line is specified as being written on a 132-character printer paper, the line will have the first 132 characters on the first line and the remaining characters at the beginning of the next line.

Self-testing Exercise 3-7

Explain the effect of each of the following FORMAT specifications.

1 (I 5 /F 10 . 0)
2 (F 10 . 0 / / /F 10 . 0 /)
3 (/ / /F 10 . 0)
4 (F 10 . 0 ,   / / / / /)

Rounding with FORMAT Specifications

Before concluding the discussion of FORMAT editing, the impact of FORMAT rounding needs to be mentioned. It is especially important to be aware of rounding errors in business or accounting reports where totals often need to be the exact sum of individual items. For example, the gross pay amount for each individual listed in a payroll report should be rounded to the nearest penny and the total gross pay for the report should be equal to the sum of the individual pay amounts, yet this may not happen in some situations.

The FORMAT specifications result in rounding in cases where the underlying data contains more digits than are printed out. For example, if pay rate is 5.764 per hour and hours worked are 37, the gross pay is 213.268. If this amount is printed out as dollars and cents for a report, a format of F8.2 will result in an output of 213.27 because the result is rounded and the excess digit is then truncated and not printed. But if the original unrounded data items are used to prepare the sum, there could be small differences. This can be seen from three items.

Gross pay		Printed as F8.2
	213.268	213.27
	312.177	312.18
	249.266	249.27
Total	774.711	(774.72)
	Unrounded sum	Sum of rounded outputs
	(774.71)	
	Rounded sum	

In the majority of programming situations, the rounding of output under format control does not create any special problem. However, when situations arise such as the above example, it is important to understand the reason for it. It is, of course, possible to round and truncate the stored data so that it matches the output. For example, assuming a stored value for GRSPAY of 213ᴧ268 the following statements will round the stored value to the nearest penny:

	GRSPAY
G R S P A Y = G R S P A Y + . 0 0 5	213ᴧ273
G R S P A Y = I F I X (G R S P A Y * 1 0 0 . 0)	21327ᴧ
G R S P A Y = G R S P A Y / 1 0 0 . 0	213ᴧ27

The stored amount for summing is now identical to the amount to print out as dollars and cents. Even though these three statements could be combined, it is rather cumbersome and a different approach to handling the problem is shown in Chapter 5B in connection with the payroll program.

Expressions in Output List

A feature of the 1977 full ANS FORTRAN not found in some older FORTRANs (but available in WATFOR/WATFIV and MNF) is the use of expressions in the output list. The expression, a constant or an arithmetic expression, is evaluated and the resulting value is output as specified by the format. For example, to print the value of a variable called A, its square, and its square root, only an output statement need be used: WRITE(6,700)A, A**2, SQRT(A).

Additional Testing, Debugging, and Quality-control Suggestions

Testing and debugging a program to remove all errors is a significant part of the total programming time, taking perhaps one-fourth to one-third of the time required to produce a complete, tested, documented program. In addition to the test data explained in Chapter 2, the test should include data which violates the input format specifications (if ERR is used).

In general, a program should be written to reject erroneous inputs but to continue processing the rest of the input data. If rejected in validation, the contents of an input should usually be printed; when rejected because of data-type error, the erroneous record contents cannot be printed but are identified by an input record number. Error messages may be printed in place of a regular line of output or may be printed in an error message area (say to the right).

```
NORMAL OUTPUT 999.99

***ERROR MESSAGE***

NORMAL OUTPUT 999.99
```

```
NORMAL OUTPUT:
                          ERROR MESSAGE
NORMAL OUTPUT:

NORMAL OUTPUT:
```

Where the number of input items can be reasonably large (say over 10), it is good programming practice to count the records that are read and to print a message at the end of the ouput identifying the number of records that were processed, perhaps dividing the count into accepted and rejected records.

In debugging, it is often useful to insert temporary debugging statements in the program. These are generally print statements that print out intermediate results prior to and after important program processing or prior to IF statements. It is convenient to use list-directed PRINT statements for this purpose. If there are a number of these PRINT statements, each statement should include a Hollerith output of the number assigned to the debugging statement. For example, debugging statement number 8 outputting results of J and X might be: PRINT *, '8', J, X. When the program is debugged, these PRINT statements are removed. To make removal easy, it is helpful to put an identifying statement number on each temporary statement that clearly marks it as one of the statements to be removed. For example, the statement PRINT *, '8', J, X might be labeled with a 9998:

```
9998 PRINT *, '8', J, X
```

Programming Style Suggestions

Style suggestions related to format-directed input and output are summarized on the next page.

1   Place the FORMAT statement as nearly adjacent to the input/output statement as possible.

2   Use the apostrophe edit descriptor instead of the H descriptor.

3   Print headings as early as possible in the program (say in the initialization block). This output assists in identifying progress of the program during debugging.

4   Remember to leave column 1 blank. Either begin a line with an explicit one blank character specification or skip the first position by an X edit. Do not rely upon an extra width I, F, or E edit descriptor.

5   Use END specification and ERR specification (if available) in formatted READ statements.

6   Use formatted output for more readable results.

7   Use list-directed output for temporary PRINT statements inserted to print out results during debugging.

8   For input, selection of format-directed or list-directed mode is dependent on the data. For example, list-directed data is much simpler to input from a terminal.

9   Where number of input records can be fairly large, keep a record count. Print the record count at the end of the program. The record count can also specify accepted and rejected records.

10 Print error messages which identify the record in error, the reason it is in error, and whether or not it is rejected. Consider a printout of the contents of the rejected input record.

Summary

The chapter has described the FORTRAN instructions to control input and output using the FORMAT statement. When a FORMAT statement is employed in a program, the READ or WRITE statement specifies the FORMAT statement to be used by a FORTRAN statement reference. The FORTRAN statement specifies the form of the data by a set of edit descriptors which include the type of data (integer, real, or exponent form of real data), the number of record positions allowed for the data items, and the decimal point position for real data. Horizontal movement (skipping over record positions) is specified by an X edit descriptor or by a T tabulating edit descriptor.

Providing descriptive labels and headings on output is done mainly with an apostrophe or H edit descriptor which defines the characters to be output. Vertical spacing before printing is specified by a character in column one of a line. Input and output of characters that are assigned to a variable name are specified by A edit descriptor.

It is convenient to be able to operate on data where the number of input records is unspecified. The chapter describes the use of the END specification in the READ statement. Another specifier, ERR, is used for transfer of control when input data does not match format-type specifications. As part of the

FORMAT statement specifications, a slash (stroke) is used to terminate the use of the current physical record and to skip physical records. In addition to variables, the output statement list may contain expressions.

Answers to Self-testing Exercises

Exercise 3-1

1 (*a*) Read from a punched card using card reader (unit 5) values for the variable names A, B, and C. The format of the data is defined by FORMAT statement 700.

(*b*) Print output on the printer consisting of values stored in variable name locations X, Y, and Z. Use format described by FORMAT statement 710.

(*c*) Write values for variables L, N, and O according to FORMAT statement 720 using unit number NREAD. If the printer has a unit number of 6, a value of 6 for NREAD will result in the instruction using the printer.

(*d*) Read, using the card reader (since no unit designation), values to be assigned to variable names Q, Z, and T. The format of the data on the punched card is given by FORMAT statement 730.

(*e*) Write in list-directed form on unit 6 (the printer) the values for variables X, Y, and IX.

2 The input/output statements may be rewritten but this is not necessary. A better approach is to use a job control instruction to assign unit 1 as the card reader and unit 3 as the printer.

Exercise 3-2

```
1       READ  ( 5 , 7 1 0 )  ALPHA ,   BETA ,   IOTA ,   JIX
 7 1 0  FORMAT  ( F 1 0 . 2 , F 9 . 2 , I 7 , I 7 )
2       WRITE  ( 6 , 7 2 0 )  JIX ,   IOTA ,   BETA ,   ALPHA
 7 2 0  FORMAT  ( 1 X , I 7 , I 7 , F 9 . 2 , F 1 2 . 2 )
3       WRITE  ( 6 , 7 3 0 )  IOTA ,   BETA
 7 3 0  FORMAT  ( I 1 7 , F 1 7 . 0 )
```

The result will be (IOTA = 6 for data, 1 for sign, and 10 leading blanks for field size of 17; BETA = 5 for data, 1 for decimal, 1 for sign, and 10 leading blanks for field size of 17)

bbbbbbbbbbb824341bbbbbbbbbbb53429.

4 The result will be:

bbbbbbbb95bbbbbb1.04

5 (*a*) F8.2   (*c*) F10.6   (*e*) I5
   (*b*) F7.1   (*d*) F5.3   (*f*) E15.8

Exercise 3-3

1 Repeat F6.0 five times (parentheses are redundant) and then repeat I4 three times.
2 Uses 3 of I2, 4 of F10.0, and 2 of E15.8.
3 The set I3, F10.0 is used 4 times followed by I3.

4 Use first five positions for integer output, skip next ten positions and then use next ten positions as F10.2.

5 Skip 19 positions. Start at position 20 with F10.2, skip 20 positions to position 50, and then use three positions with I3.

6 Same effect as 5. Start at position 20 with 10.2 then do I3 starting at position 50.

Exercise 3-4

```
1        WRITE  (6, 721)  TOLER
   721   FORMAT  (25X, 16HTHE  TOLERANCE  IS,  F8.2)
   721   FORMAT  (25X  'THE  TOLERANCE  IS',  F8.2)
2        WRITE  (6, 722)  SAVIN
   722   FORMAT  (10X,  'AMOUNT  OF  SAVINGS  IS  $', F7.2)
   722   FORMAT  (10X, 22HAMOUNT  OF  SAVINGS  IS  $,  F7.2)
3        WRITE  (6, 723)  NMBER
   723   FORMAT  (' NUMBER  IS', I5)
   723   FORMAT  (10H NUMBER  IS,  I5)
4        WRITE  (6, 724)
   724   FORMAT  ('0', 'THE  END.')  or  ('0THE  END.')
   724   FORMAT  (1H0,  8HTHE  END.)
5        WRITE  (6, 725)
   725   FORMAT  (5X, 'ITEM', 10X 'AMOUNT')
   725   FORMAT  (5X, 4HITEM,  10X,  6HAMOUNT)
6        WRITE  (6, 726)
   726   FORMAT  ('1',  58X,  'PAYROLL  REPORT')
   726   FORMAT  (1H1,  58X,  14HPAYROLL  REPORT)
```

Exercise 3-5

```
1        READ  (5, 700)  NCHAR,  NAME2
   700   FORMAT  (9X,  A5,  5X,  A6)
```

Note: The implicit method for associating variable names with character data is assumed. If the storage limit for each variable name were four characters, two variable names would be needed.

```
2        WRITE  (6, 701)  NCHAR,  NAME2
   701   FORMAT  (' THE  DATA  1  IS ',  A6,
         'AND  DATA  2  IS ',  A6, '.')
```

Note: Space between NCHAR data and word AND was obtained by making the field size A6 instead of A5 for the five characters of NCHAR; it could also have been coded A5, 'bAND. . . .

Exercise 3-6

```
1        READ  (5, 700)  ID,  HOURS,  RATE
   700   FORMAT  (I5, F2.0, F4.3)
         IF  (ID.EQ.99999)  GO  TO  500
2        READ  (5, 700, END=500)  ID,  HOURS,  RATE
   700   FORMAT  (I5, F2.0, F4.3)
         READ  (5, 700, END=500,  ERR=910)  ID,  HOURS,  RATE
3  700   FORMAT  (I5, F2.0, F4.3)
```

Exercise 3-7

1 I5 is used for value on first card or line, F10.0 for value on second. If list of variables is not exhausted, the next card or line will use I5, etc.

2 First card or line has one value F10.0, the next two cards or lines are skipped, and then F10.0 is used for the next unit record. If list is not exhausted, the next card or line is skipped and the FORMAT is repeated.

3 Skips three cards or lines and then uses F10.0. If repeated, it will skip three cards or lines again.

4 Uses F10.0 and then skips five lines or cards.

Questions and Problems

1 Explain three methods of identifying which input or output unit is to be used with a READ or WRITE statement.

2 Differentiate between physical and logical records.

3 Explain two methods for testing for the end of data.

4 Complete the following table using minimum FORMAT specification:

Data as found on card	Format to read	Desired printing	Format for printing
(a) XXX.XXX		XXX . XXX	
(b) XXX		XXX . 0	
(c) .XXXXE+17		0 . XXXXE+ 1 7	
(d) −.XXXXE+5		−XXXX 0 .	
(e)	F5.2		F5.1

5 What is the effect of the following FORMAT specification sets?
 (a) (` 0 `) or (1H 0)
 (b) (3 F 1 0 . 0 , 3 /)
 (c) (1 F 1 0 . 0)
 (d) (I 6 , 2 (I 7))
 (e) (3 F 1 0 . 0 , 4 (I 3))
 (f) (3 F 1 0 . 0 , 5 E 1 5 . 8)
 (g) (I 6 , F 1 0 . 0)
 (h) (I 6 / F 1 0 . 0)
 (i) (5 (F 1 0 . 0 , I 7))
 (j) (F 1 0 . 4 , F 1 0 . 3 , / / / I 6)
 (k) (I 1 0 , 1 0X , F 1 3 . 2)
 (l) (5 0X , I 3)
 (m) (T 5 0 , I 3)

6 Print a heading XYZ COMPANY centered at the top of a page. Double-space and center 12/31/78 below the heading. Do it two ways—with an apostrophe and with an H edit descriptor.

7 Write sets of WRITE and FORMAT statements to make the following outputs. Leave first position on line blank in all cases.
 (a) ←52 spaces→ ANALYSIS PROGRAM
 (b) CHI SQUARE TEST IS XX.XX

(c) PART NO. ⟵ 20 spaces ⟶ QUANTITY ⟵ 10 spaces ⟶ AMOUNT

(d) PROGRAM DATA IS INCORRECT.

8 Write statements to read a 10-character heading from columns 36 to 45 on a punched card and to print it using the printer at columns 76 to 85.

9 Explain what happens if there are too many format specifications.

10 Explain what happens if there are more variables in the list than there are edit specifications in the FORMAT statement.

CHAPTER

EXAMPLE PROGRAMS AND PROGRAMMING EXERCISES WHICH USE FORMAT-DIRECTED INPUT AND OUTPUT

The example programs and exercises in this chapter use the features presented in Chapters 1 and 2 plus the format-directed input and output explained in Chapter 3A. The two examples—payroll reports and tables of ordinates of the normal curve—show the use of formatting in two different environments. Both examples are instructive, but the payroll report is particularly useful in showing the use of formatting features.

General Notes on Chapter 3 Examples

Examine the sample outputs for the two programs (Figures 3-7 and 3-12). The outputs were formatted to use only 72 spaces instead of the full width of the printer paper. The limit on output size made the output suitable for exhibits in the text without significant reduction in size. Also, many of the programs were written from terminals which had carriages of 72 to 80 spaces.

Use of Input and Output Layouts

The use of input and output layouts is illustrated for the payroll report program but not for the table of ordinates program. In many FORTRAN programs, the input and output is simple enough that layout forms are not needed. As output becomes more complex, layouts are useful, especially output layouts.

The layouts (such as Figure 3-1 and 3-2) allow the placement of data on input and output media to be identified. On output, it helps line up headings and data amounts. A useful convention followed by many programmers is to mark the maximum field to be occupied by each data item by 9s or X's. The 9s are used to indicate numeric digits. Decimal points are written at the position occupied on output. The X's indicate alphanumeric character output such as labels and headings.

Four very important points to remember in regard to input data as illustrated in the example programs are:

1 Data items in FORMAT-directed input are not delineated by commas or blanks (as they were for the list-directed inputs of Chapters 1 and 2).

2 Data items are assigned by the FORMAT statement to a specific set of positions on each punched card used for input. The data items must be placed in the assigned set of positions.

3 For real data, if the decimal point is punched, a data item may be placed anywhere in the set of positions assigned to it on the card. If the decimal point is not punched, the data item must be positioned within the assigned set of positions according to the assumed decimal location specified by the FORMAT statement. Unused positions may be left blank.

4 For integer data, the data item must be right-justified in the field (no blank spaces at the right).

Error-control Features

Both programs use the END and ERR specifications in the input statement. These specifications simplify programming (but may not be available on older compilers). With the END feature, an attempt to read input after the last data card transfers control to the statement number given by the END specification. This is a very clear and effective method for handling an unspecified number of inputs. The ERR feature is used because it allows the program to retain control when input that is incompatible with the format specifications is read. An error in keypunching will often cause such an error.

Both programs print a summary statement stating how many input cards were read. The payroll report program divides this figure into those accepted and those rejected.

Note the use of error messages which print out the card contents or identify the card number of input data cards that are in error. The error message for an input data item that does not meet the validation limit tests is instructive (see lines 16 to 18 in the payroll report program). Although the input data items are tested individually, only a single error output is used. The exact nature of the error is not specified. This is a simple approach and is satisfactory for most fairly simple input validation. However, in more complex validation, it may be useful to have a separate error message for each error detected. The error message shows the output without any special formatting. The printing of the card contents (perhaps with spaces between data items) usually allows the error to be noted; an alternative is to label the parts of the input data being printed out.

General Program Example 3—Payroll Reports

Problem Description for General Example 3

Compute employee pay information for an unspecified number of employees (but less than 15) and print formatted output for each individual and a summary. Input consists of an employee's ID number, the employee name (up to 12 characters long), hours worked, wage rate, and miscellaneous deductions. Hours worked in excess of 40.0 are paid at one and one-half times the regular rate. In addition to miscellaneous deductions, there are deductions for pension (5 percent of gross pay) and taxes (15 percent of gross pay). The total for all employees—hours worked, gross pay, taxes, retirement contributions, deductions, and net pay—are printed on a separate page following the last employee printout. Input data is validated and error messages are printed when errors are detected.

Program Documentation for General Example 3

The documentation consists of an input layout (Figure 3-1), an output layout (Figure 3-2), a pseudocode description of the program (Figure 3-3), a program flowchart (Figure 3-4), a listing of the program (Figure 3-5), a list of input data used in testing the program (Figure 3-6), and a sample output (Figure 3-7) which includes program handling of error inputs.

The input layout (Figure 3-1) is designed for planning and documenting the placement of the input data on a punched card (or a terminal screen). Its use is optional because most FORTRAN programs have simple input. Note the use of

Input Card — General Example 3 — Payroll

FIGURE 3-1 Input card layout for general example 3—payroll reports.

the 9s and X's (as with output layout) to define the contents of the fields and the caret ($\wedge$) to indicate the decimal location (if not punched).

In the input layout, note that the employee name, consisting of 12 characters, is given three separate data names, each referencing four characters. In the implicit method, the storage for a variable is limited, the limit varying with the compiler. This program shows one method of overcoming the storage limit—by dividing the alphabetic item and assigning a data name to each of the smaller items. In this case, the input statement to read all 12 characters from the input card (including any blanks where the employee name is short) requires all three data names to be listed in the instruction, e.g., READ (5, . . .) . . . , NAME1, NAME2, NAME3, ... To write the complete name also requires all three data labels be specified, e.g., WRITE (6, . . .) . . . NAME1, NAME2, NAME3, ...

The output layout (Figure 3-2) has already been mentioned. It is especially helpful in this case in laying out the headings and lining up the data under the

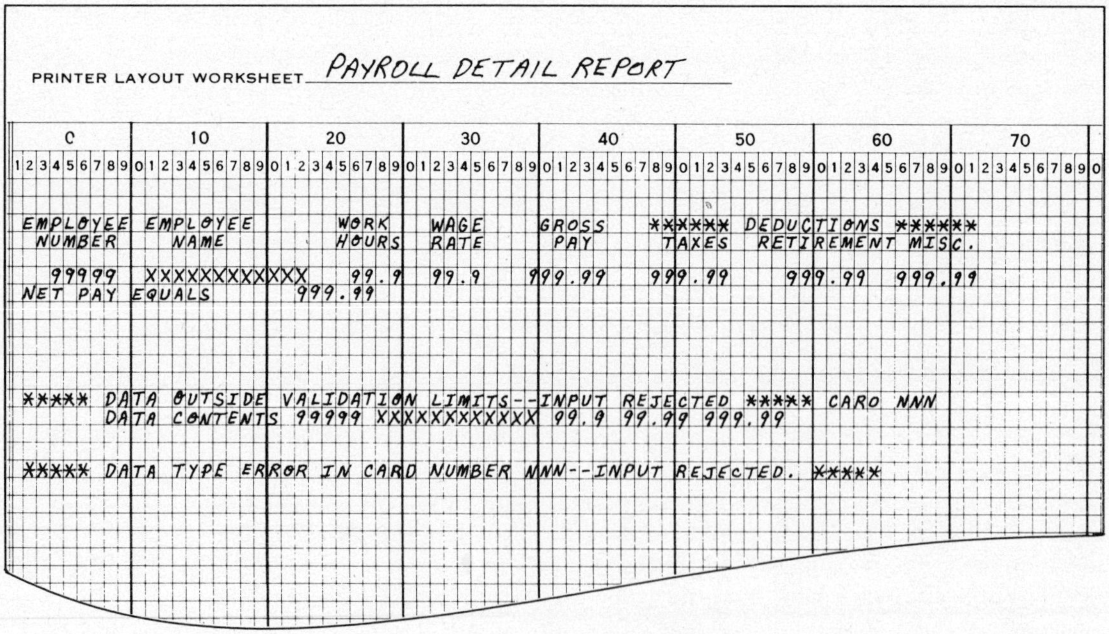

FIGURE 3-2 Layout for detail report for general example 3—payroll reports.

```
PRINT heading for employee data
Initialize counters and constants
READ an employee card
        IF (END) go to Summary
        IF (ERR) PRINT message, increment total card counter, and go back to READ
Increment total card counter
Validate input data
        IF invalid, print data validation message and go back to READ employee card
        Else continue
Increment counter for valid records
Compute overtime hours
IF overtime hours
    Calculate gross pay with overtime at 1.5 regular rate
ELSE
    Calculate gross pay at regular rate
Compute taxes and retirement contribution
Compute total deductions
Compute net pay
Update cumulative totals
PRINT detail for an employee
Test for negative net pay
        IF not valid, print warning message
        Else continue
Go back to READ employee card
Summary
PRINT heading for tables
PRINT cumulative totals
Compute number of invalid records
PRINT number of valid and invalid records
STOP
```

FIGURE 3-3   Pseudocode description of general example 3—payroll reports.

headings. The two types of error messages are also shown on the layout. Layout forms usually have 132 to 140 positions horizontally; the layout form in Figure 3-2 has been trimmed to 80 positions because, as explained, the outputs in the text are all designed to fit on 72 positions.

The list of input data used to test the program is important documentation of the testing performed. At each change or correction in the program, the test data list provides a useful review of the prior testing which can be expanded, if desired, and repeated with the changed program.

Notes on General Example 3

The usual identification blocks are present. The computational section has been divided into six logical blocks with block numbers. In the initialization section, printing the detail report heading is done first. As mentioned in Chapter 3A, this also has advantages for debugging, since it is useful to have some output from a program as early as possible to provide an indication that the program has compiled and begun execution.

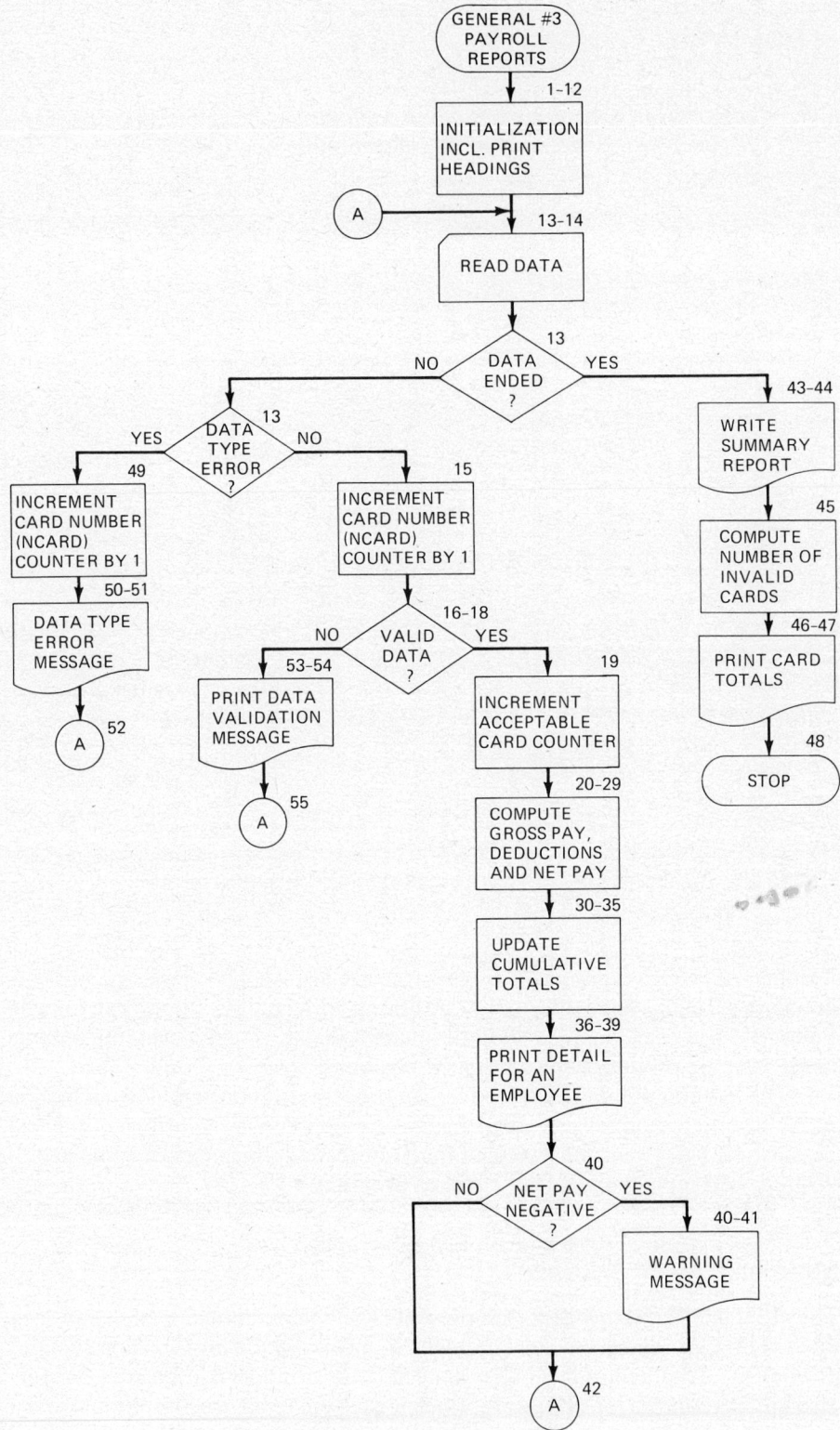

FIGURE 3-4 Program flowchart for general example 3—payroll reports. (Numbers beside symbols refer to line numbers on program listing.)

```
**********          PROGRAM IDENTIFICATION           **********
*                                                             *
*        COMPUTE PAYCHECKS FOR EMPLOYEES AND PRINT FORMATTED   *
*        REPORTS FOR BOTH INDIVIDUALS AND THE COMPANY          *
*        WRITTEN BY T. HOFFMANN      4/22/77                   *
*                                                             *
***************************************************************
*                                                             *
**********          VARIABLE IDENTIFICATION          **********
*                                                             *
*        ID      = EMPLOYEE IDENTIFICATION NUMBER             *
*        HRSWRK  = TOTAL HOURS WORKED                         *
*        GRSPAY  = GROSS PAY: $                               *
*        WGRATE  = WAGE RATE: $/HOUR                          *
*        PAYCHK  = NET PAYCHECK AMOUNT: $                     *
*        TAXES   = TAXES DUE: $                               *
*        DEDUC   = MISCELANEOUS DEDUCTIONS                     *
*        NAME1   = FIRST PORTION OF EMPLOYEE NAME             *
*        NAME2   = SECOND PART OF EMPLOYEE NAME               *
*        NAME3   = LAST PART OF EMPLOYEE NAME                 *
*        OTIME   = HOURS OF OVERTIME WORKED (EXCESS OVER 40.0)*
*        TDEDUC  = TOTAL OF ALL DEDUCTIONS BY EMPLOYEE        *
*        RETIRE  = RETIREMENT CONTRIBUTION BY EMPLOYEE        *
*        TOTHRS  = TOTAL HOURS WORKED BY ALL EMPLOYEES        *
*        TOTRET  = TOTAL RETIREMENT CONTRIBUTION BY ALL EMPLOYEES *
*        TOTPAY  = TOTAL GROSS PAY FOR COMPANY : $            *
*        TOTTAX  = TOTAL TAXES FROM ALL EMPLOYEES :$          *
*        TOTCKS  = TOTAL OF ALL PAYCHECKS                     *
*        TOTDUC  = TOTAL OF ALL DEDUCTIONS                    *
*        NCARD   = NUMBER OF CARDS (RECORDS) READ             *
*        NACEPT  = NUMBER OF ERROR FREE CARDS                 *
*        NOTACP  = NUMBER OF NOT ACCEPTABLE RECORDS           *
*                                                             *
*****               CONSTANT IDENTIFICATION              *****
*                                                             *
*        PNRATE  = PENSION CONTRIBUTION RATE = 0.05           *
*        TAXRT   = TAX RATE = 0.15                            *
*                                                             *
***************************************************************
*                                                             *
**********          INITIALIZATION BLOCK        BLOCK 0000    *
*                                                             *
*        PRINT HEADER/TITLE LINE                              *
*                                                             *
1.            WRITE(6,3)
2.          3 FORMAT(1H1,2('EMPLOYEE '),5X,'WORK   WAGE',4X,'GROSS',3X,6('*'),
             1   ' DEDUCTIONS ',6('*')/2X,'NUMBER',4X,'NAME',8X,'HOURS',
             2   ' RATE',5X,'PAY',4X,'TAXES  RETIREMENT  MISC.')
3.            PNRATE = 0.05
4.            TAXRT = 0.15
5.            NACEPT = 0
6.            TOTPAY = 0.0
7.            TOTTAX = 0.0
8.            NCARD = 0
9.            TOTHRS = 0.0
10.           TOTRET = 0.0
11.           TOTCKS = 0.0
12.           TOTDUC = 0.0
*                                                             *
***************************************************************
*                                                             *
**********      READ AND VALIDATE EMPLOYEE DATA  BLOCK 0100   *
*                                                             *
13.       101 READ(5,102,END=401,ERR=901) ID,NAME1,NAME2,NAME3,HRSWRK,WGRATE,
             1   DEDUC
14.       102 FORMAT(I5,3A4,F4.1,F4.2,F5.2)
15.           NCARD = NCARD + 1
*                                                             *
*        VALIDATE INPUT DATA                                  *
*                                                             *
16.           IF(HRSWRK .LE. 0.0 .OR. HRSWRK .GT. 60.0) GOTO 910
17.           IF(WGRATE .LE. 0.0 .OR. WGRATE .GT. 10.0) GOTO 910
18.           IF(DEDUC .LE. 0.0 .OR. DEDUC .GT. 35.0) GOTO 910
*                                                             *
***************************************************************
*                                                             *
**********         COMPUTE GROSS AND NET PAY     BLOCK 0200   *
*                                                             *
19.           NACEPT = NACEPT + 1
*                                                             *
*        COMPUTE OVERTIME, IF ANY                             *
*                                                             *
```

FIGURE 3-5 Listing of FORTRAN program for general example 3—payroll reports.

```
20.         OTIME = HRSWRK - 40.0
21.         IF(OTIME.GT.0.0) THEN
22.                 GRSPAY = WGRATE*(40.0 + 1.5*OTIME)
23.             ELSE
24.                 GRSPAY = HRSWRK*WGRATE
25.         ENDIF
      *                                                                    *
      *         COMPUTE EACH TYPE OF DEDUCTION AND NET PAY                  *
      *                                                                    *
26.         TAXES = TAXRT*GRSPAY
27.         RETIRE = PNRATE*GRSPAY
28.         TDEDUC = DEDUC + TAXES + RETIRE
29.         PAYCHK = GRSPAY - TDEDUC
30.         TOTPAY = TOTPAY + GRSPAY
31.         TOTTAX = TOTTAX + TAXES
32.         TOTHRS = TOTHRS + HRSWRK
33.         TOTRET = TOTRET + RETIRE
34.         TOTDUC = TOTDUC + TDEDUC
35.         TOTCKS = TOTCKS + PAYCHK
      *                                                                    *
      **********************************************************************
      *                                                                    *
      **********          PRINT DETAIL                        BLOCK 0300
      *                                                                    *
36.         WRITE(6,301) ID,NAME1,NAME2,NAME3,HRSWRK,WGRATE,GRSPAY,TAXES,
           1 RETIRE,DEDUC
37.     301 FORMAT(1H0,2X,I5,2X,3A4,F7.1,F6.2,1X,2F8.2,1X,2(3X,F6.2))
38.         WRITE(6,304) PAYCHK
39.     304 FORMAT(' NET PAY EQUALS',6X,F6.2)
      *                                                                    *
      *         CHECK FOR VALID PAYCHECK AMOUNT                            *
      *                                                                    *
40.         IF(PAYCHK.LE.0.0) WRITE(6,303)
41.     303 FORMAT(1H+,28X,'NET PAY IS NOT POSITIVE.',
           1                 ' DO NOT ISSUE CHECK')
      *                                                                    *
      *         GO BACK AND READ ANOTHER EMPLOYEE DATA CARD                *
      *                                                                    *
42.         GOTO 101
      *                                                                    *
      **********************************************************************
      *                                                                    *
      **********          PRINT SUMMARY AND TERMINATE         BLOCK 0400
      *                                                                    *
43.     401 WRITE(6,402) TOTHRS,TOTPAY,TOTTAX,TOTRET,TOTDUC,TOTCKS
44.     402 FORMAT(1H1,5H*****,18X,'SUMMARY TOTALS'17X,5(1H*)/
           1 ' HOURS',4X,'GROSS    TAXES    RETIREMENT    DEDUCTIONS',
           2 2X,'PAYCHECKS'/' WORKED',4X,'PAY',11X,'CONTRIBUTION'/
           3 1H0,F6.2,2F8.2,5X,F5.2,2X,2(6X,F6.2))
45.         NOTACP = NCARD - NACEPT
46.         WRITE(6,403) NACEPT,NOTACP
47.     403 FORMAT(//10X,'RECORDS ACCEPTED',I3,5X,'RECORDS REJECTED',I3)
      *                                                                    *
      *         NORMAL TERMINATION                                         *
      *                                                                    *
48.         STOP
      *                                                                    *
      **********************************************************************
      *                                                                    *
      **********          ERROR MESSAGE BLOCK                 BLOCK 0900
      *                                                                    *
49.     901 NCARD = NCARD + 1
50.         WRITE(6,902) NCARD
51.     902 FORMAT(//' ***** DATA TYPE ERROR IN CARD NUMBER',I3,
           1 '--INPUT REJECTED. *****')
      *                                                                    *
      *         GO BACK AND READ ANOTHER EMPLOYEE DATA CARD                *
      *                                                                    *
52.         GOTO 101
      *                                                                    *
53.     910 WRITE(6,911) NCARD,ID,NAME1,NAME2,NAME3,HRSWRK,WGRATE,DEDUC
54.     911 FORMAT(1H0,'***** DATA OUTSIDE VALIDATION LIMITS--INPUT ',
           1 'REJECTED ***** CARD',I3/7X,'DATA CONTENTS ',
           2 I5,1X,3A4,1X,F4.1,F5.2,F6.2)
      *                                                                    *
      *         GO BACK AND READ ANOTHER EMPLOYEE DATA CARD                *
      *                                                                    *
55.         GOTO 101
      *                                                                    *
56.         END
```

FIGURE 3-5 *(continued)*

INPUT TEST DATA

ID	NAME	HOURS	WAGE RATE	MISC. DEDUC- TIONS	PURPOSE OR EXPECTED OUTPUT
23456	T. HOFFMANN	40.0	3.57	27.95	NET PAY SHOULD BE 86.29
15786	RALPH JONES	37.0	6.28	24.68	GROSS PAY SHOULD BE 232.36
15968	W. RONG	14.4	2)KM	45.68	ERROR-NONNUMERIC DATA IN NUMERIC FIELD
36985	J. JOHNSON	22.00	275	03598	FORMAT SETS DECIMAL POINT. ERROR-DEDUCTIONS EXCEED LIMITS
JKLUIONA					ERROR-NONNUMERIC DATA IN NUMERIC FIELD
69852	T. NAMAN	10.0	2.67	27.50	NET PAY NEGATIVE
35748	L. SMITH	55.5	7.24	30.68	GROSS PAY = 457.93
					4 RECORDS-ACCEPTED
					3 RECORDS-REJECTED

FIGURE 3-6 Input test data with purposes noted for general example 3.

DETAIL OUTPUT

```
    EMPLOYEE EMPLOYEE       WORK    WAGE    GROSS    ****** DEDUCTIONS ******
    NUMBER    NAME          HOURS   RATE    PAY      TAXES  RETIREMENT  MISC.

    23456  T. HOFFMANN      40.0    3.57    142.80   21.42     7.14     27.95
  NET PAY EQUALS       86.29

    15786  RALPH JONES      37.0    6.28    232.36   34.85    11.62     24.68
  NET PAY EQUALS      161.21


  ***** DATA TYPE ERROR IN CARD NUMBER  3--INPUT REJECTED. *****

  ***** DATA OUTSIDE VALIDATION LIMITS--INPUT REJECTED ***** CARD  4
        DATA CONTENTS 36985 J. JOHNSON   22.0 2.75 35.98


  ***** DATA TYPE ERROR IN CARD NUMBER  5--INPUT REJECTED. *****

    69852  T. NAMAN         10.0    2.67     26.70    4.00     1.34     27.50
  NET PAY EQUALS        -6.14  NET PAY IS NOT POSITIVE. DO NOT ISSUE CHECK

    35748  L. SMITH         55.5    7.24    457.93   68.69    22.90     30.68
  NET PAY EQUALS      335.66
```

SUMMARY OUTPUT

```
    *****                SUMMARY TOTALS               *****
    HOURS    GROSS    TAXES   RETIREMENT   DEDUCTIONS  PAYCHECKS
    WORKED   PAY              CONTRIBUTION

    142.50   859.79   128.97     42.99       282.77     577.02


         RECORDS ACCEPTED   4     RECORDS REJECTED   3
```

FIGURE 3-7 Sample output for general example 3—detail and summary payroll report.

The variable, NCARD, has been created to keep count of the cards read. This assists in locating erroneous data cards and in ensuring that all cards which were intended to be processed have been processed by comparing the final count to the intended value. The initial value and the locations of the increment instructions for the counter must be carefully considered. Note that this is done right after reading the card (line 12) but if there is a data error, the ERR specification causes a transfer and this line is never reached. Therefore, the counter is alternatively incremented with statement 901 at line 49 just before the data error printout. Separate counters are also kept for rejected and accepted records.

The block IF is used in the program (lines 21 to 25). As an alternative, the logic can be coded with a simple logical IF statement as follows:

```
      IF (OTIME.GT.0.0) GOTO 204
      GRSPAY=WGRATE * HRSWRK
      GOTO 205
204   GRSPAY=WGRATE * (40.0+1.5 * OTIME)
205   TAXES=
```

Updating the totals could be done before or after the printing of the pay information. However, grouping the computations in a block makes the program more readable and easier to debug.

Output formatting can be a very lengthy and tedious job. It is useful to use lines of asterisks, but writing out long lines of them in FORMAT statements can be time consuming and error prone. An alternative is the use of repetition counts. The following are equivalent methods for programming a set of five asterisks:

```
FORMAT  ('  '*****')
FORMAT  ('  ',5('*'))
FORMAT  (1H ,  5H*****)
FORMAT  (1H ,5(1H*))
```

Vertical spacing is controlled in several ways in the program. In the FORMAT statement 3 at line number 2 the page is set to the top (1H1); in the FORMAT statement 303 at line 41, no spacing takes place before the print (1H+), so that the message is printed on the same line as the amount; in FORMAT statement 301 at line 37, double spacing takes place before printing (1H0); and in FORMAT statement 403 at line 47, double spacing is accomplished by issuing two line feeds before printing (///). Horizontal spacing is accomplished by having blanks in Hollerith fields (FORMAT statement 902 at line 51), using the nX field (FORMAT statement 304 at line 39), and by specifying a larger than necessary I or F field (FORMAT statement 301 at line 37).

Multiple print lines are contained in FORMAT statement 402 at line 44 by separating them with one or more slashes. Note also that column 1 is left blank in all cases where an H control character is not printed (e.g., the 5X on the second line of FORMAT statement number 3 at line number 2 and the blank in the Hollerith field of statement number 902 at line 51).

The problem of rounding with the format on output is illustrated in this program. The payroll detail is printed out as dollars and cents using a format with two places to the right of the decimal point. The printed totals are the same as the sum of the individual outputs rounded at printing except for total taxes. The sum of the individual taxes as printed is 128.96, whereas the total is shown as 128.97. The result comes about as follows:

Unrounded taxes (Gross pay × .15)	Rounded output
21.42|00	21.42
34.85|40	34.85
4.00|50	4.00
68.68|95	68.69
Totals 128.96|85	128.96
Output 128.97	

The rounding difference is not corrected in this simple program. An approach to correcting this type of rounding error situation is described in Chapter 5.

Statistical Program Example 3—Tables of Ordinates of the Normal Curve

Problem Description for Statistical Example 3

Produce formatted tables of the ordinates of the normal curve based upon an initial value, an incremental value, and the number of entries desired. Validate input data for number of entries not zero, negative, or greater than 50. Use END and ERR specifications. Keep a record count and print this count at the end of the program.

Program Documentation for Statistical Example 3

The documentation consists of a pseudocode description of the program (Figure 3-8), a program flowchart (Figure 3-9), a program listing (Figure 3-10), and a list of input data used in testing the program (Figure 3-11). Sample output is given in Figure 3-12. For the simple formatted output of this program it was not considered useful to use a printer layout form.

Notes on Statistical Example 3

The constant PIROOT used in the formula was computed using the SQRT function. The value of 2π used in computing PIROOT (i.e., 6.2832), is not used elsewhere in the program, so no variable name was assigned to it (see line 3). The overall report heading (global header) was printed as early as possible in the program execution (line 1). It is logical to do so and, as mentioned previously, it aids in debugging because the printout of the heading lets the author

---

WRITE global heading
Initialize problem counter and constants
<u>*READ*</u> *starting X value, X increment, number of values to compute (NVALUS)*
      IF no more data then <u>*Terminate*</u>
      IF data-type error, increment record count, print error message, and GO back
         to <u>*READ*</u>
Increment record count by 1
IF input data for number of values to compute not valid
      Print error message and GO back to <u>*READ*</u>
ELSE
      Continue
WRITE problem title
Initialize step counter to one
<u>*IF step counter*</u> *greater than NVALUS*
      GO back to <u>*READ*</u>
ELSE
      Compute ordinate Y
      WRITE X, Y
      Increment X by X increment and step counter by one
      GO back to <u>*IF step counter*</u>
<u>*Terminate*</u> *with WRITE end of program and number of cards read*
STOP

FIGURE 3-8 Pseudocode description of statistical example 3—tables of ordinates of normal curve.

know the program has been compiled and begun execution. Reading of cards is terminated by the END specification in the READ statement rather than by a specially punched card. Note how a single FORMAT statement with slash editing prints both heading lines for each problem.

Counters can be initialized to either 1 or 0 and checked at either the beginning or end of an execution loop. In this program, the choice is to set the record count to 0 and increment after reading. When a data error causes a transfer of control (ERR = 901), the record count following the READ is not executed, so another increment statement is needed at line 22. NCNTR (the counter for numbers of table entries) is set to 1 at the beginning of the instructions to do the table. As long as NCNTR is less than or equal to NVALUS (the number of entries to be printed), the computation and printing is performed, the counter is incremented by 1 and control is returned to the beginning of the loop.

As an alternative to the block IF (lines 11 through 20), the section could be coded with a single logical IF as follows (note reversal of test to use GT instead of LE):

```
104  IF (NCNTR.GT.NVALUS) GOTO 101
     YVALU=PIROOT * EXP (-XVALU * XVALU/2.0)
     WRITE (6,105) XVALU, YVALU
105  FORMAT (6X, F6.2, 5X, F6.4)
     XVALU=XVALU+XINCR
     NCNTR=NCNTR+1
     GOTO 101
```

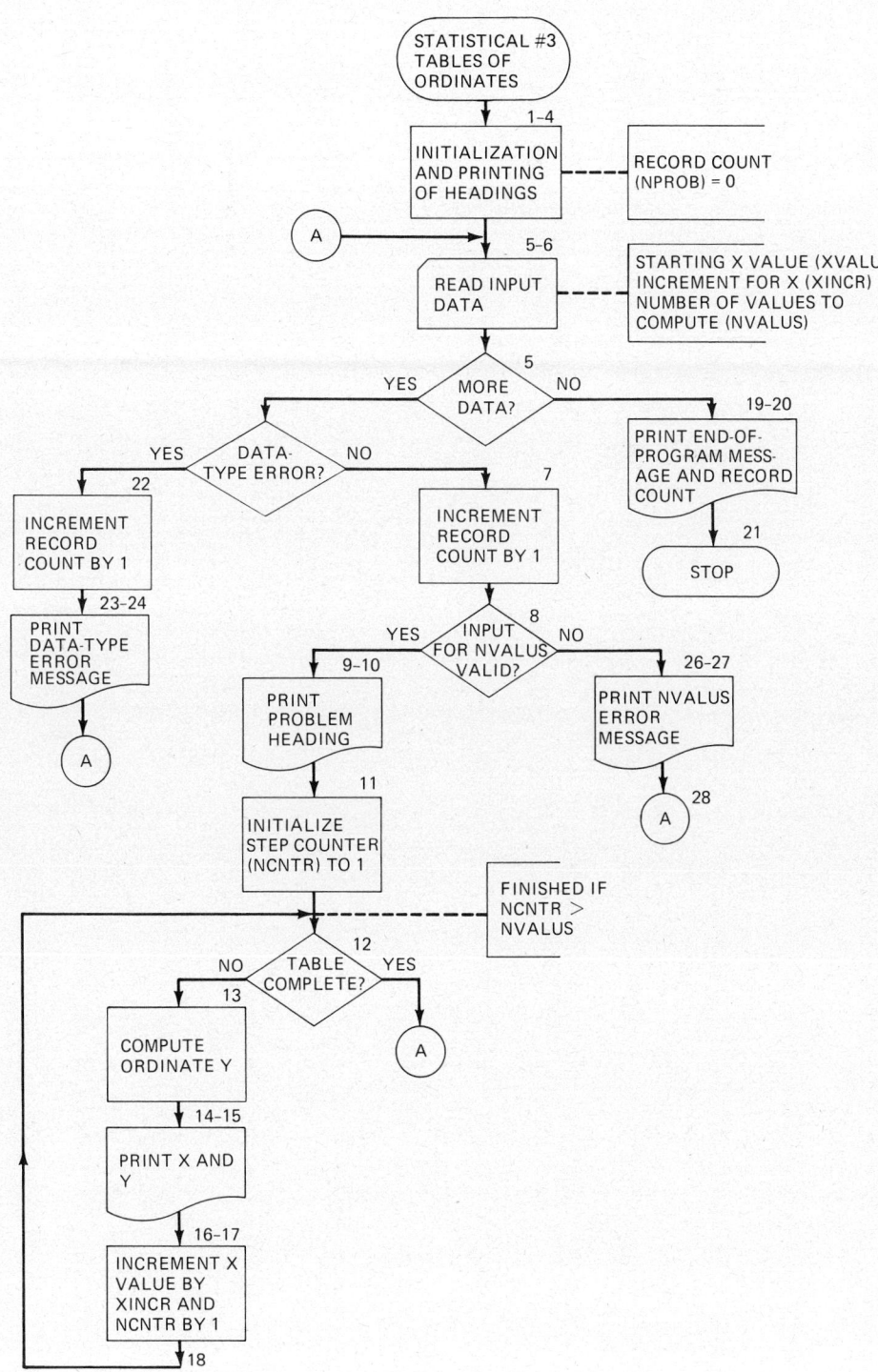

FIGURE 3-9 Program flowchart for statistical example 3—tables of ordinates of normal curve. (Numbers beside symbols refer to line numbers on program listing.)

```
********** PROGRAM IDENTIFICATION **********
*                                                                    *
*          CALCULATE TABLES OF ORDINATES OF THE NORMAL CURVE         *
*          WRITTEN BY T. HOFFMANN 05/03/77                           *
*                                                                    *
**********************************************************************
*                                                                    *
********** VARIABLE IDENTIFICATION **********
*                                                                    *
*          NVALUS = NUMBER OF VALUES TO COMPUTE                       *
*          NCNTR  = COUNTER TO LIMIT AGAINST NVALUS                   *
*          NPROB  = PROBLEM NUMBER COUNTER                            *
*          XVALU  = VALUE OF X TO USE IN COMPUTATION OF YVALU         *
*          YVALU  = VALUE OF THE ORDINATE CORRESPONDING TO XVALU      *
*          XINCR  = INCREMENT OF X                                    *
*                                                                    *
*****          CONSTANT IDENTIFICATION                          *****
*                                                                    *
*          PIROOT = RECIPROCAL OF THE SQUARE ROOT OF TWO PI           *
*                                                                    *
**********************************************************************
*                                                                    *
********** INITIALIZATION BLOCK            BLOCK 0000
*                                                                    *
1.          WRITE(6,1)
2.        1 FORMAT(1H1,7X,'TABLES OF ORDINATES OF THE NORMAL CURVE')
3.          PIROOT = 1.0/SQRT(6.2832)
4.          NPROB = 0
*                                                                    *
**********************************************************************
*                                                                    *
********** READ - COMPUTE - PRINT BLOCK    BLOCK 0100
*                                                                    *
5.      101 READ(5,102,END=200,ERR=901) XVALU,XINCR,NVALUS
6.      102 FORMAT(2F4.1,I2)
*                                                                    *
*          STEP PROBLEM COUNTER                                      *
*                                                                    *
7.          NPROB = NPROB + 1
8.          IF(NVALUS .LE. 0 .OR. NVALUS .GT. 50) GOTO 910
9.          WRITE(6,103) NPROB
10.     103 FORMAT(1H0,5X,'PROBLEM NUMBER',I3/5X,7HX VALUE,4X,7HY VALUE)
11.         NCNTR = 1
*                                                                    *
*          IF NVALUS NOT COMPUTED, CALCULATE NEXT ORDINATE.          *
*          IF THEY HAVE BEEN, THEN READ A NEW PROBLEM CARD.          *
*                                                                    *
12.     104 IF(NCNTR.GT.NVALUS) GOTO 101
13.         YVALU = PIROOT*EXP(-XVALU*XVALU/2.0)
14.         WRITE(6,105) XVALU,YVALU
15.     105 FORMAT(6X,F6.2,5X,F6.4)
16.         XVALU =  XVALU + XINCR
17.         NCNTR = NCNTR + 1
18.         GOTO 104
*                                                                    *
**********************************************************************
*                                                                    *
********** NORMAL TERMINATION BLOCK        BLOCK 0200
*                                                                    *
19.     200 WRITE(6,201) NPROB
20.     201 FORMAT(///' END OF PROGRAM'/3X,I3,' CARDS READ')
21.         STOP
*                                                                    *
**********************************************************************
*                                                                    *
********** ERROR MESSAGE BLOCK             BLOCK 0900
*                                                                    *
22.     901 NPROB = NPROB + 1
23.         WRITE(6,902) NPROB
24.     902 FORMAT(1H0,'***** DATA ERROR IN CARD NUMBER ',I3,6H *****)
*                                                                    *
*          GO BACK AND READ NEXT PROBLEM                             *
*                                                                    *
25.         GOTO 101
*                                                                    *
26.     910 WRITE(6,911) NPROB,XVALU,XINCR,NVALUS
27.     911 FORMAT(1H0,'***** DATA LIMIT ERROR FOR NUMBER OF VALUES *****'/
        1    7X,'CARD NUMBER ',I2,3X,'CONTENTS ',F4.1,2X,F4.1,2X,I2)
*                                                                    *
*          GO BACK AND READ NEXT PROBLEM                             *
*                                                                    *
28.         GOTO 101
*                                                                    *
29.         END
```

FIGURE 3-10 Listing of FORTRAN program for statistical example 3—tables of ordinates of normal curve.

154

```
                        INPUT TEST DATA

    X    STEP  S
  VALUE  SIZE  T  PURPOSE OR EXPECTED OUTPUT
               E
               P
               S
1 -1.4 00020 8 FIRST OUTPUT VALUE = .1497, LAST IS A ZERO AND = .3989
2 03.0 0001. 3 ERROR-DECIMAL POINT IN INTEGER FIELD
3 00000 0.1 75 ERROR-TOO MANY STEPS
4 -2.7 00.7 12 FIRST OUTPUT VALUE = .0104
5              4 DATA CARDS
6
7
```

FIGURE 3-11 Input test data with purpose noted for statistical example 3.

```
          TABLES OF ORDINATES OF THE NORMAL CURVE

       PROBLEM NUMBER  1
       X VALUE    Y VALUE
        -1.40      .1497
        -1.20      .1942
        -1.00      .2420
         -.80      .2897
         -.60      .3332
         -.40      .3683
         -.20      .3910
          .00      .3989

 ***** DATA ERROR IN CARD NUMBER   2 *****

 ***** DATA LIMIT ERROR FOR NUMBER OF VALUES *****
       CARD NUMBER  3   CONTENTS    0   .1  75

       PROBLEM NUMBER  4
       X VALUE    Y VALUE
        -2.70      .0104
        -2.00      .0540
        -1.30      .1714
         -.60      .3332
          .10      .3970
          .80      .2897
         1.50      .1295
         2.20      .0355
         2.90      .0060
         3.60      .0006
         4.30      .0000
         5.00      .0000

 END OF PROGRAM
    4 CARDS READ
```

FIGURE 3-12 Sample output for statistical example 3—tables of ordinates of normal curve.

Programming Exercises

In this chapter, no new problems are given; rather the assignment is to use the problems in Chapter 2B expanded to include features explained in Chapter 3A. Augment the data of Chapter 2B, if necessary, to include at least one validation violation and one data-type error (if you use ERR).

Description of Assignment

Select one or more problems from Chapter 2B (or take the problem(s) assigned to you by the instructor). Write the program including the following features.

1 A heading for the output
2 Labels and/or headings on lines of output
3 Use END, if available, to control program transfer at end of data.
4 Data validation with error message. Include some form of printout of input data. (ALTERNATIVE: Rather than rejecting some data, you may wish to accept the data and give a warning message.)
5 Error message for data-type error. Include record number. If ERR is not available on your compiler, omit this step as well as the test data item with a data-type error.
6 Keep a record count. Print the count at the end of the program. If appropriate, print a separate count for accepted and rejected items.

CHAPTER

THE REPETITION PROGRAM STRUCTURE, SUBSCRIPTED VARIABLES, AND DO LOOPS

A very important program design and coding element is the repetition structure used to program the repeated execution of a block of instructions. The repetition structure is implemented in FORTRAN by the DO loop. Many repetition problems are simplified by the use of subscripted variables, so the FORTRAN notation for subscripted variables will be explained before describing the DO loop.

Subscripted Variables

Subscripts are frequently used in mathematical formulations and therefore it is important to understand this method of identifying data items. The mathematical concept of subscripts can be directly applied to FORTRAN.

Arrays and Matrices

A list of quantities which can be classed together can be thought of as a one-dimensional array. A quantity in the list is identified by a name given to the entire list, plus a number which refers to the position in the list occupied by the quantity. Mathematical notation uses a lowered number, hence the term subscript. For example, sales by customers would form a single-dimension array as shown in Figure 4-1. If S is used to denote sales, the sales to customer 3 can be identified as an array element S_3, to customer 4 as S_4, etc.

A two-dimensional array, or rectangular array (often called a *matrix*), provides a twofold classification. For example, a classification of persons by height and weight would result in a rectangular array. A single name can be used to refer to the matrix, and when any particular element or classification in the array is referred to, the name is used with a subscript. By convention, the row is always written first and the column second.

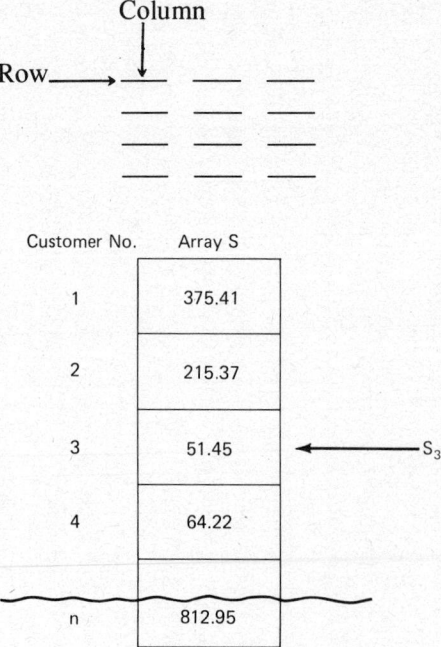

FIGURE 4-1 Single-dimension array.

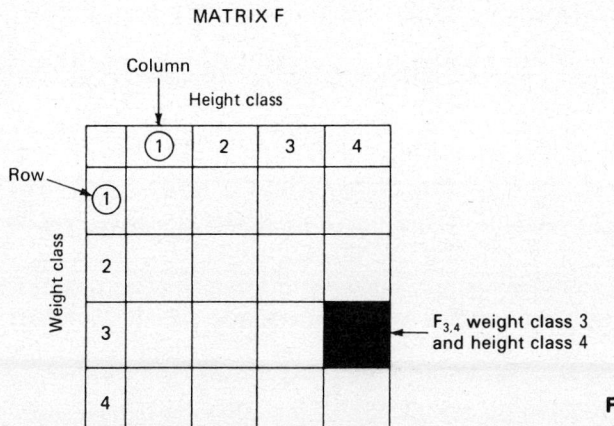

FIGURE 4-2 Two-dimensional array.

For example, if F is used to refer to the twofold classification of females, $F_{3,4}$ refers to the number of those who are in weight class 3 and height class 4, as illustrated in Figure 4-2.

A threefold classification uses three subscripts. The first subscript refers to the row, the second to the column, and the third to the level. For example, a classification by weight, height, and age will result in the three-dimensional array shown in Figure 4-3. If the entire classification by weight, height, and age is termed C, persons falling into weight class 2, height class 4, and age class 1 are identified as $C_{2,4,1}$. The classifications are listed as subscripts in order by row, column, and level.

In short, subscripts are used to identify one out of a related set of items. All items in an array have the same name because they are all in the same category. All items in an array are of the same data type (integer or real); the first letter convention identifies the type of the array. The subscript identifies a specific element within the array. The name of an array must *not* be the same as the name of a simple variable.

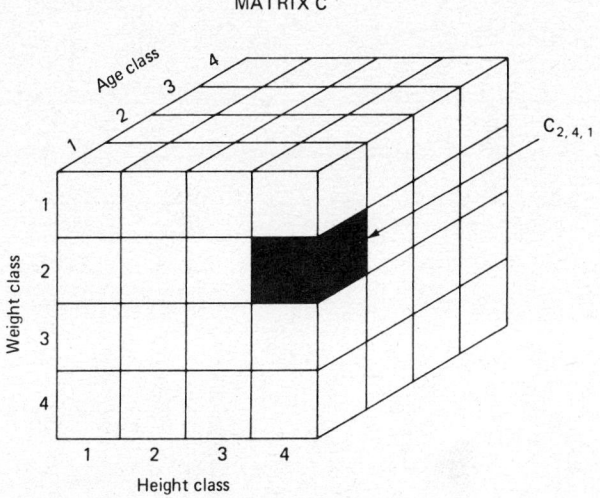

FIGURE 4-3 Three-dimensional array.

Form of FORTRAN Subscripts

Standard mathematical notation for subscripts uses numbers or letters written below the level of the symbol to which they apply, but since neither the keypunch nor the printer in a computer system is usually equipped to handle lowered characters, subscripts are represented in FORTRAN as a set of numbers enclosed in parentheses which follow immediately after the name. The subscripts are separated by commas. The previous array examples would appear in FORTRAN as S(3), F(3,4), and C(2,4,1).

Subscripts must have an integer value, since positions in an array can only be whole numbers. Therefore, subscripts can be only integer variables, integer constants, or integer expressions. The number of subscripts is limited to three in Subset FORTRAN and to seven in full FORTRAN.

In some older FORTRANs (but not the 1977 standard) the integer arithmetic expressions are limited to multiplication, subtraction, and addition, in the following forms, where k is an integer constant and i is an integer variable:

Addition or subtraction	$i \pm k$
Multiplication	$k * i$
Combinations	$k * i \pm k$

THE GENERAL FORM OF SUBSCRIPTS

$A(iek_1)$
$A(iek_1, iek_2)$
$A(iek_1, iek_2, iek_3)$

A = any array name. First letter of array name identifies array variables as integer or real in same way as variable names.

iek = integer variables, integer expressions, or integer constants as subscripts. Full FORTRAN also allows array element references as subscripts.

Subscripts are separated by commas. The number of subscripts is limited to three in Subset FORTRAN and to seven in full FORTRAN. Spaces are optional for readability.

EXAMPLES OF ALLOWABLE SUBSCRIPTS

Subscripted variable	Comments
ALPHA (9)	References 9*th* element in array ALPHA
BETA (1,7)	References the element in row 1 and column 7 of array BETA
IOTA (I,J,K)	References element in I*th* row, J*th* column and K*th* level of array IOTA. In order to locate the element, the program must have values for I, J, and K
GAMMA (M,3)	References M*th* row and 3*rd* column of array GAMMA
Y(7*KIX,8)	Value of KIX is multiplied by 7 to arrive at row; column is 8*th*
Z(NIX + 3, JIX)	Add 3 to value of NIX to compute row number; number of column is the value of JIX

EXAMPLES OF SUBSCRIPTS NOT ALLOWED

Variable	Why not allowed
ALPHA (X)	Cannot be real subscript. Code as ALPHA (INT(X))
X(NIX, YIX)	Cannot be real subscript. Code as X(NIX, INT(YIX))

EXAMPLES OF SUBSCRIPTS NOT ALLOWED BY SUBSET OR BY OLDER FORTRANs

Variable	Why not allowed
SALES (1+I,J)	Wrong form for older FORTRANs; should be I + 1
JIX (KIX*7)	Wrong form for older FORTRANs; should be (7*KIX)
CLASS (I,J,K,L)	Too many subscripts for limited Subset version of FORTRAN

The Use of Subscripts

Each time the compiler program translating the FORTRAN source statement to machine language encounters a variable name, it assigns a memory location to it. A subscripted variable name presents a problem because the number of memory locations to be assigned to it is not always apparent from the program. In fact, the number may vary, depending on the problem being run. To allow the compiler to assign the correct number of memory locations for a subscripted variable, the programmer must specify the maximum size of the subscripts, i.e., the maximum size of the array. The statement for doing this is the DIMENSION statement, which may appear any place in the program before the first use of the subscripted variable. However, it is usually good practice to put all DIMENSION statements at the beginning of the program in a STORAGE ALLOCATION block. The basic form of DIMENSION is given here; the standard full FORTRAN also allows dimensions to be integer constant expressions and to be expressed as lower and upper bounds (see Chapter 7).

BASIC FORM FOR DIMENSION FOR SUBSCRIPTED VARIABLES

DIMENSION A(k), A(k_2,k_2), A(k_1,k_2,k_3), A($k_1,k_2, \ldots , k_n$)

If more than one array is dimensioned, the variables are separated by commas.

A = any array name
k = an integer constant
$k_1,k_2,k_3, \ldots$ = the maximum number of rows, columns, levels, etc.

1977 Standard FORTRAN allows up to 7 dimensions; 1977 Subset FORTRAN allows up to 3 dimensions.

Examples of DIMENSION statement are:

```
DIMENSION A(100)
DIMENSION A(100),B(50),C(10,10)
DIMENSION NIX(10,10,5),KIX(50,10)
```

Care should be taken not to dimension larger than will be necessary for the maximum set of data. A DIMENSION X(100, 100, 100) calls for $100 \times 100 \times 100$ memory locations. Although valid in form, this requirement for 1 million memory locations exceeds the internal capacity allowed for most problems.

When an array name is used in an executable statement, it must always be used with a subscript to identify which location is desired. The only exception to this rule is a specialized input/output situation in which a variable name without a subscript references the entire array (to be explained later in the chapter). Two short sample problems will illustrate two types of uses for the subscripted variable.

Subscript Example 1

The first problem is a program to tally the number of students whose grade-point averages fall into each of five categories. The subscripted variable will be called TALLY. TALLY has five categories:

Category	Grade point
TALLY(1)	0.0 to 0.99
TALLY(2)	1.0 to 1.99
TALLY(3)	2.0 to 2.99
TALLY(4)	3.0 to 3.99
TALLY(5)	4.0

The program reads a card with the grade-point average for a student given on it. This variable, called GPA, is in the form X.XX. The END condition causes the tallies to be printed. After reading the input, the next step is to determine which category the student's grades are in and to add 1 to the tally for that category (Figure 4-4). Note that the data itself is used to provide the subscript category by which it is classified. The statement I = INT(GPA + 1.0) thus provides the proper integer for the tally statement. (The INT or IFIX function is redundant but clarifies the logic.)

Subscript Example 2

The second problem is to sum 100 quantities stored in an array called X. They have been read and placed in the array by instructions not shown. A simple IF loop is used to repeat the processing using a new value at each repetition, as shown in Figure 4-5. The test for termination of the loop is an IF statement which is placed at the beginning of the loop. If subscripts were not available, the program to add 100 numbers would require statements listing all 100 vari-

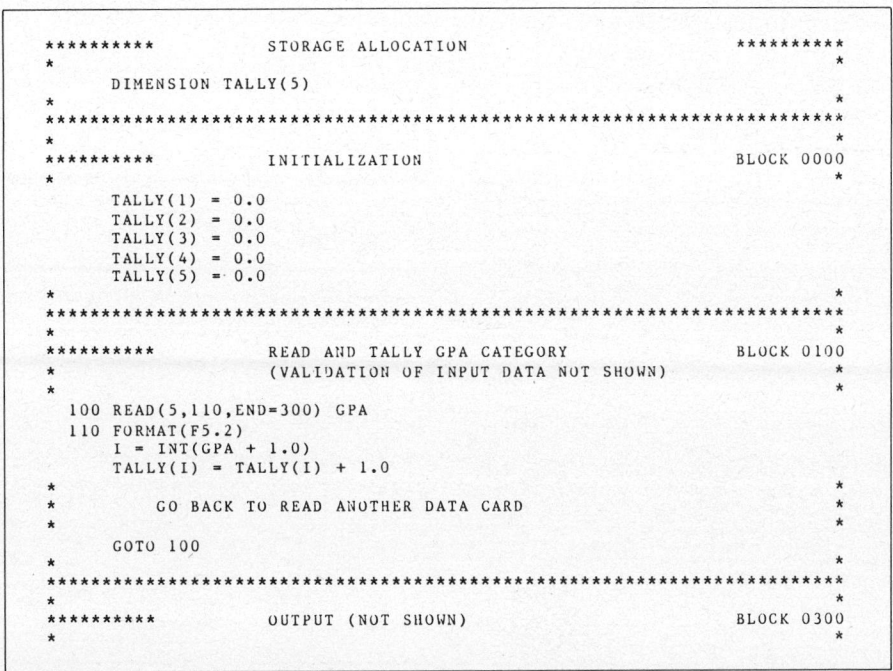

```
**********              STORAGE ALLOCATION              **********
*                                                              *
      DIMENSION TALLY(5)
*                                                              *
*****************************************************************
*                                                              *
**********              INITIALIZATION              BLOCK 0000
*                                                              *
      TALLY(1) = 0.0
      TALLY(2) = 0.0
      TALLY(3) = 0.0
      TALLY(4) = 0.0
      TALLY(5) = 0.0
*                                                              *
*****************************************************************
*                                                              *
**********         READ AND TALLY GPA CATEGORY         BLOCK 0100
*              (VALIDATION OF INPUT DATA NOT SHOWN)            *
*                                                              *
  100 READ(5,110,END=300) GPA
  110 FORMAT(F5.2)
      I = INT(GPA + 1.0)
      TALLY(I) = TALLY(I) + 1.0
*                                                              *
*         GO BACK TO READ ANOTHER DATA CARD                   *
*                                                              *
      GOTO 100
*                                                              *
*****************************************************************
*                                                              *
**********              OUTPUT (NOT SHOWN)              BLOCK 0300
*                                                              *
```

FIGURE 4-4 Program segment for tally grade-point problem.

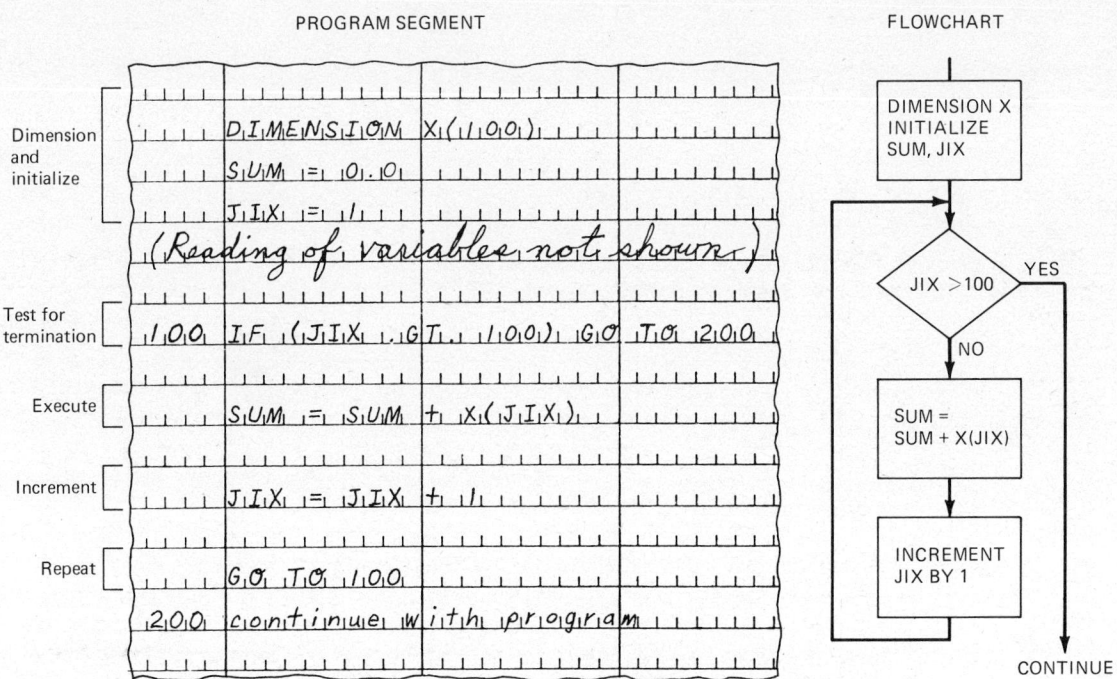

FIGURE 4-5 Program segment to sum quantities stored as subscripted variables.

able names. In order to understand the logic of Figure 4-5, trace the value of JIX and SUM when data values for X(1), X(2), and X(3) are 9.0, 11.0, and 20.0.

Self-testing Exercise 4-1

1 State whether the following statements or expressions are valid, and if invalid for some FORTRANs, state why.

Statement or expression	Valid or invalid for full 1977 FORTRAN	Versions of FORTRAN for which invalid and why
(a) DIMENSION C(100), NIX(100)		
(b) A(14,NIX,X)		
(c) A(JIX*KIX)		
(d) ALPHA(10, 10, 5)		
(e) DIMENSION ALPHA (100), BETA(100, 10)		
(f) GAMMA(A+5.0)		
(g) DELTAS(5*I)		
(h) Y(5, 10, 4, 3)		

2 Write the DIMENSION statements for the following arrays:
   (a) An array of 100 sample observations
   (b) A two-dimensional array to classify persons by sex and by one of ten occupations
   (c) An array to classify business firms by one of eight size groups, one of 15 types of business groups, and one of five location classes
   (d) Four arrays A, B, C, and D, each having 15 entries
3 Give the subscripted variable names by which the following matrix array elements are identified.

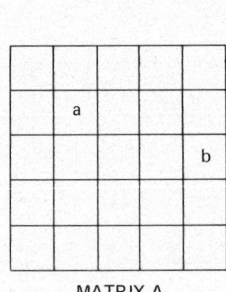

MATRIX A

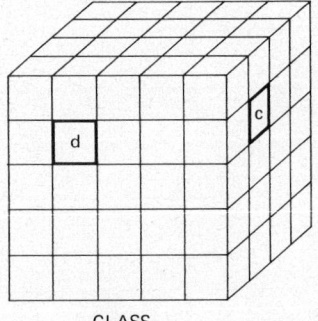

CLASS

4 Give the DIMENSION statements for the arrays in question 3.
5 Using logic similar to that in Figure 4-5, write program segments to initialize a loop counter, dimension three arrays (A, B, and C) for five values, and then read pairs of numbers from five input cards (F10.2,F10.2) into two arrays A and B. Multiply the arrays A and B to create an array C. The DO statement to be presented next is a simpler way to code these operations, but the exercise is a useful learning experience.

The DO Statement

The DO statement or DO loop is one of the most powerful features of FOR-TRAN. It greatly simplifies the writing of program repetition (also called program loops).

Concept of Repetition or Looping

Looping is repetition based on program modification. A set of one or more instructions is executed a number of times, each time altering one or more variables in the set, so that each execution is different from the preceding one. The effect of looping is to reduce substantially the number of instructions required for a program.

The repetition structure (looping) is implemented in FORTRAN by the DO statement, but loops can be written in FORTRAN without the DO statement by coding all the loop control statements. Since an IF statement is used, this might be termed an IF loop. The example in Figure 4-5 was an IF loop. Although the DO loop is preferred for repetition, it may be useful to study the characteristics of an IF loop in order to understand the assumptions and actions imbedded in the more simple approach of a DO loop.

An IF loop requires the following steps for a repetition structure which follows the DO WHILE logic explained in Chapter 1 (Figure 4-6). The repeti-

1977 STANDARD FORTRAN DO WHILE

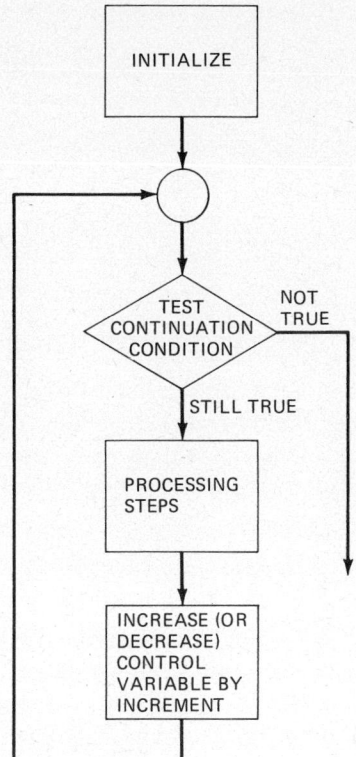

FIGURE 4-6 Flowchart of DO WHILE repetition structure.

tion is said to continue WHILE the condition governing the loop is true; when it is not true, the repetition ceases.

1 Initialize to the first value the loop control variable being modified.

2 Test to see if the loop control variable is within the limit for continuation. If within the limit, continue with the loop; if the limit is exceeded, branch out of the loop.

3 Execute the set of statements in the loop.

4 Modify the loop control variable.

5 Go back to beginning of loop (step 2).

A program segment to sum the quantities identified by odd-numbered subscripts (1, 3, 5, . . .) in an array of 210 numbers will illustrate the IF loop procedure. The array is called DELTA and is assumed to have already been placed in memory.

Program	Comment
Previous statements	
SUM = 0	Initialize accumulator variable ⎫
K = 1	Initialize control variable ⎬ Initialize
100 IF (K .GT. 210)GOTO 200	Test control variable against limit; if continuation limit is exceeded, exit from loop ⎫ Test for continuation. Continue or branch out
SUM = SUM + DELTA (K)	Statement to be executed ⎬ Execute
K = K + 2	Increment control variable ⎬ Modify and return to beginning of loop
GOTO 100	
200 Next statement after loop	

Note that the program can be altered to start with the tenth variable merely by changing the initial value of the control variable; the program can be altered to sum every third value by changing the value of the increment to 3, and changing the limit constant to another value would alter the times the loop would be executed.

Form of the DO Statement

The DO statement is a repetition command which simplifies the writing of loops. It automatically initializes the loop variable, tests to see if the variable is within the limit for continuation, passes control to the statements to be executed (or branches out of the loop), modifies the loop variable, and branches back to the start of the loop.

The DO loop begins with a DO statement which defines the last statement included in the loop, the variable which controls the loop, the limit of continuation value for the loop variable, and the increment. The last statement in a loop can be any executable statement except a transfer of control (DO, GOTO, etc.). The use of a logical IF statement as the last statement in the loop is prohibited in older FORTRANs and restricted in 1977 FORTRAN. To avoid ending with a transfer of control, a CONTINUE statement is written as the last loop statement in these cases. As a matter of style, we have chosen to write a CONTINUE statement as the last statement in every DO loop because it adds clarity to the program structure. Also, for a clear style, the statements between the DO and the CONTINUE statements may be indented (say four spaces) to visually show the range of the loop. For example:

```
DO     150  I = 1, 10, 2
            C ( I ) = A ( I ) * B ( I )
            WRITE ( 6, 700 )  A ( I ),  B ( I ),  C ( I )
150  CONTINUE
```

The example DO statement says that the statements between the DO statement and the statement with a label of 150 should be executed repeatedly based on a loop variable called I. The loop is repeated as long as I is less than or equal to 10. The general form of the DO is summarized in the box.

THE DO STATEMENT

The DO Statement in Subset and Older FORTRANs

DO s $i = ik_1, ik_2, ik_3$ s = the statement label (number) of the last statement
If $ik_3 = 1$, then   in the loop (the terminal statement).
DO s $i = ik_1, ik_2$ i = an integer variable as the index or control variable
                                                             ik = integer variable or integer constant
                                                             ik_1 = the initial parameter, i.e., the initial value of the
                                                                        loop variable.
                                                             ik_2 = the terminal parameter, i.e., the maximum value
                                                                        the loop variable can be and have the loop process-
                                                                        ing continue.
                                                             ik_3 = the incrementation parameter, i.e., the increment
                                                                        value by which the loop variable is to be modified.
                                                                        If ik_3 is not stated, it is assumed to be 1.

In Subset, but not in older FORTRAN, parameters may be negative. In the older 1966 FORTRAN, a comma between s and i is an error; in the newer standard, a comma between s and i is optional; for example, DO s, i = ... For compatibility, do not use the comma.

The DO Statement in 1977 Full FORTRAN

DO s $v = vek_1, vek_2, vek_3$ v = the index or control variable which may be
                                                                either a real or integer variable.
                                                      vek = parameters which may be integer or real vari-
                                                                ables or constants or real or integer expres-
                                                                sions. Parameters may be negative.

In flowcharting a DO loop, the programmer can write the flow diagram in terms of the DO loop statement itself. The terminal statement number, control variable, initial value, terminal value, and incrementation value are specified within a special processing symbol. A dotted line may be used to visually define the range of the DO loop as shown in Figure 4-7.

The range of a DO loop is the set of statements starting with the statement following the DO statement and ending with the termination statement. A DO loop can contain DO loops within its range. This is termed nesting. When nesting one DO loop inside another, the inner DO loop must be entirely contained within the range of the outer DO loop. The loops may, however, have the same termination statement, but, as a matter of clear style, we use a separate CONTINUE for each loop. There is no specified limit to the number of DO loops which may be nested. The inner loop is repeated the specified number of times each time the loop in which it is contained is incremented. For clarity of program design, the inner DO is indented to show the relationship and range of the inner DO loop to the outer DO loop. As an example, assume a program segment to sum the elements in an N by 5 matrix.

```
     SUM = 0 . 0
     DO  110  I = 1 , N
         DO  100  J = 1 , 5
             SUM = SUM + A ( I , J )     Range of inner DO     Range of
100          CONTINUE                                          outer DO
110  CONTINUE
```

For each time the outer loop is executed, the inner loop is executed 5 times. Therefore, the outer loop will be executed N times and the inner loop 5*N times.

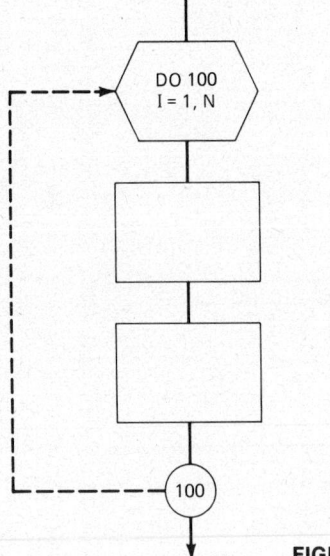

FIGURE 4-7 Flowcharting a DO loop.

Use of the DO Statement

Five examples will illustrate and explain the way the DO statement is used in programming the repetition structure. The examples will also illustrate the rules for DO loops and the style suggestions for clarity in programming.

DO Example 1

Write a DO loop to execute the same processing as the IF loop example, i.e., to sum the variables with odd-numbered subscripts between 1 and 210 (Figure 4-8).

DO Example 2

Multiply two arrays A and B, with N entries in each, to form a new array C (Figure 4-9).

DO Example 3

Read K punched cards with a variable X in each card in columns 1 to 10 in the form 99.99. Find the arithmetic mean (average) of the numbers (Figure 4-10).

DO Example 4

Add two 4×6 matrices called A and B to form matrix C; that is $C(1,1) = A(1,1) + B(1,1)$, etc. (Figure 4-11). The order in which the program

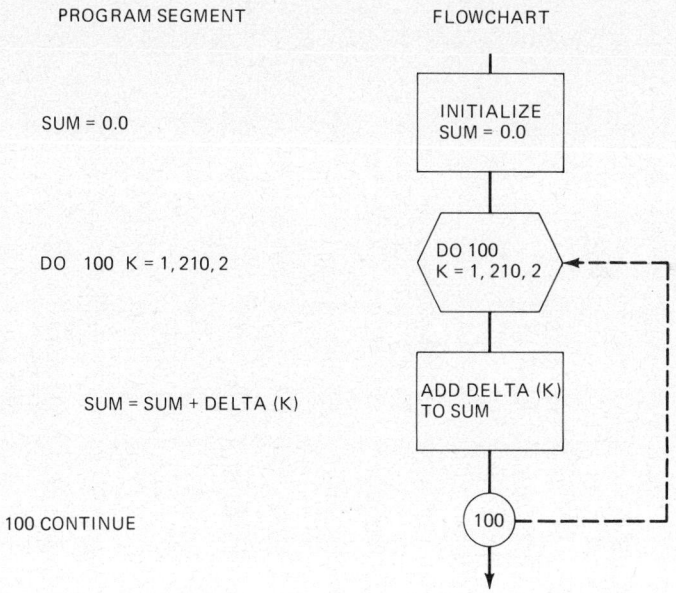

PROGRAM SEGMENT   FLOWCHART

SUM = 0.0   INITIALIZE
                                   SUM = 0.0

DO 100 K = 1, 210, 2   DO 100
                                   K = 1, 210, 2

SUM = SUM + DELTA (K)   ADD DELTA (K)
                                   TO SUM

100 CONTINUE   100

Note that SUM has to be set to zero before the loop is entered if it is to be used as the accumulator variable.

FIGURE 4-8 DO example 1.

PROGRAM SEGMENT   FLOWCHART

DO   100 JIX = 1, N

C(JIX) = A(JIX) * B(JIX)

100 CONTINUE

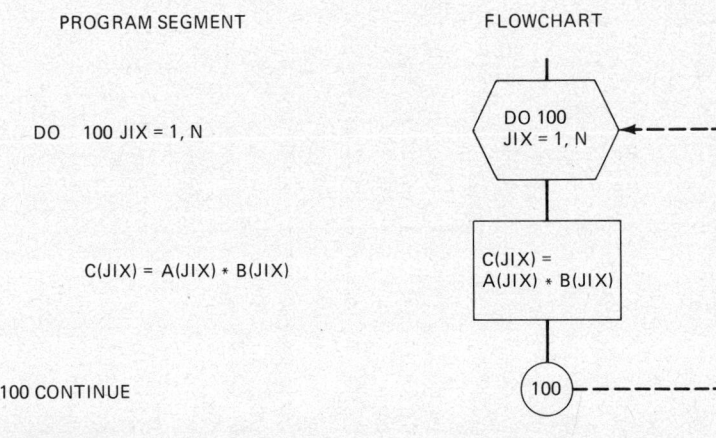

FIGURE 4-9   DO example 2.

PROGRAM SEGMENT   FLOWCHART

SUMX = 0.0

DO   100 I = 1, K

105   READ (5, 105) X
          FORMAT (F10.2)

          SUMX = SUMX + X

100 CONTINUE

110 AMEAN = SUMX/FLOAT (K)

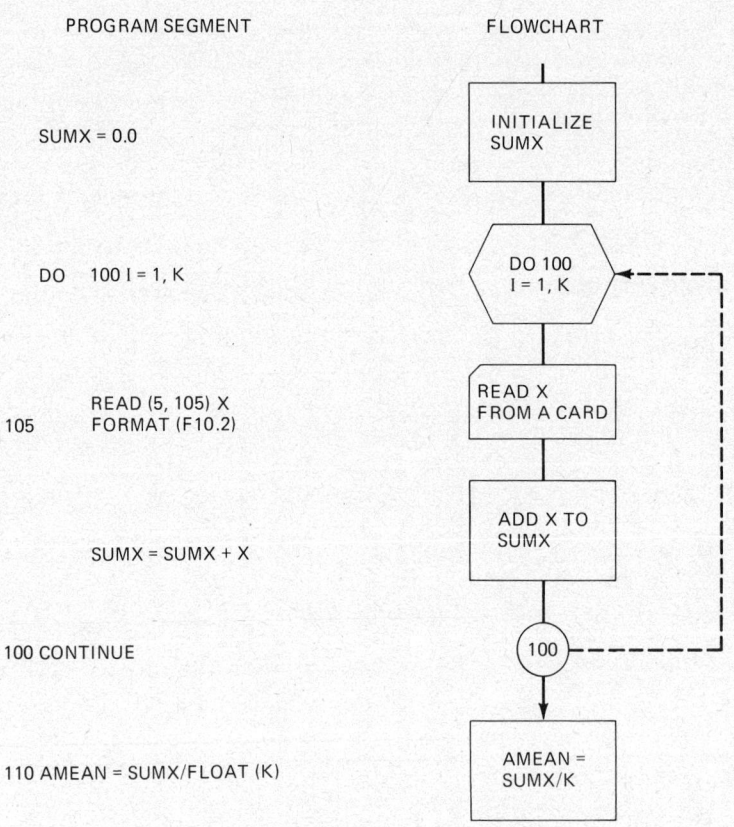

Note that the loop index I was not used in any loop statement but simply as a loop counter

FIGURE 4-10   DO example 3.

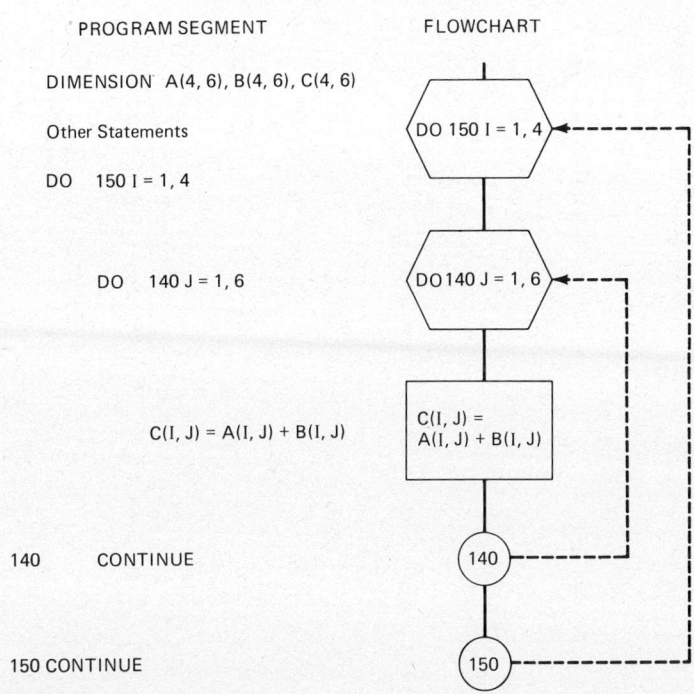

PROGRAM SEGMENT

DIMENSION A(4, 6), B(4, 6), C(4, 6)

Other Statements

DO   150 I = 1, 4

DO   140 J = 1, 6

C(I, J) = A(I, J) + B(I, J)

140   CONTINUE

150 CONTINUE

FLOWCHART

DO 150 I = 1, 4

DO 140 J = 1, 6

C(I, J) =
A(I, J) + B(I, J)

140

150

FIGURE 4-11   DO example 4.

will perform the computation is defined by the DOs. The J values go through a cycle from 1 to 6 each time I changes by 1. Thus the order of computations in Example 4 will be:

C (1 , 1) = A (1 , 1) + B (1 , 1)   ⎡ I is set to 1
C (1 , 2) = A (1 , 2) + B (1 , 2)   ⎢ J loops from 1 to 6
C (1 , 3) = A (1 , 3) + B (1 , 3)   ⎣
  .   .
  .   .

C (2 , 1) = A (2 , 1) + B (2 , 1)   ⎡ I is set to 2
C (2 , 2) = A (2 , 2) + B (2 , 2)   ⎣ J loops from 1 to 6 again
  .   .
  .   .

C (4 , 5) = A (4 , 5) + B (4 , 5)   ⎡ I is set to 4
C (4 , 6) = A (4 , 6) + B (4 , 6)   ⎣ J loops from 1 to 6 for the fourth time

DO Example 5

A company manufactures three types of wooden widgets—economy, standard, and super. Varying amounts of wood, hardware, and labor go into each widget. These specifications are given by matrix SPEC. The cost of each element is given by an array COST. The amount of production is given by an array VOL. A FORTRAN program is to find unit cost (UCOST) for each type of

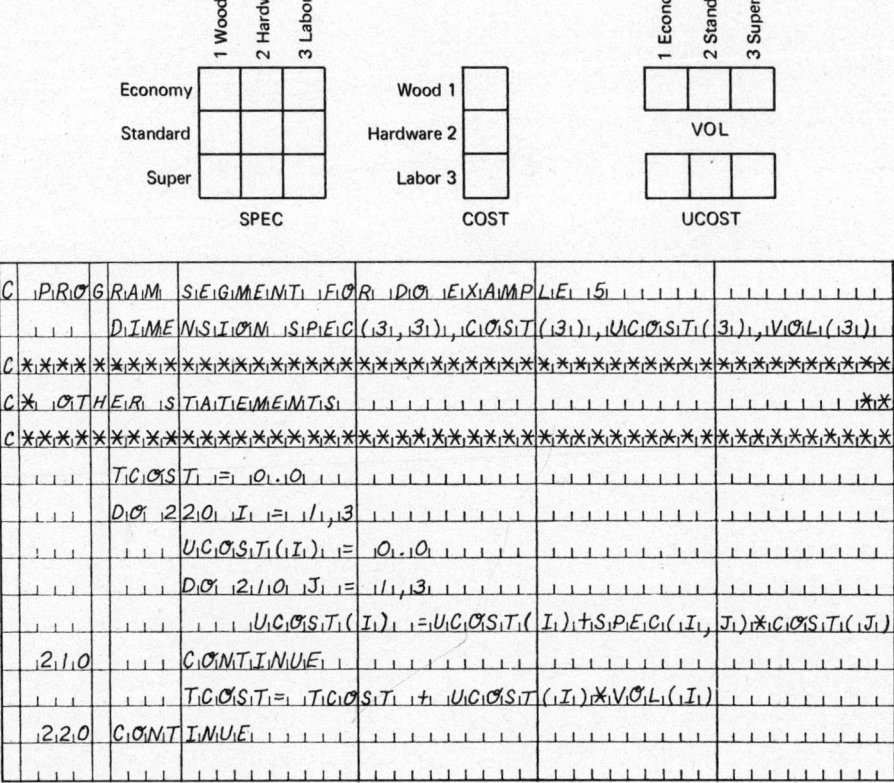

FIGURE 4-12 DO example 5.

widget and to find total cost for the production (TCOST). The program segment is shown in Figure 4-12.

Although stated in terms of matrix multiplication, this problem illustrates the concept of setting up arrays to make FORTRAN coding simple. The program has the same coding if there are 100 products and 50 cost elements. Essentially, any list or array of quantities which can fit in a single classification should probably be subscripted and handled as an array.

Rules for Using the DO Statement

A DO loop is initialized by the execution of the DO statement, and the loop makes a normal exit after it has been executed the requisite number of times. The end-of-range statement (the CONTINUE statement if the pattern described here is followed) must be executed in order for the incrementation and return action of the loop mechanism to be activated. The DO loop in 1977 FORTRAN is based on a DO WHILE logic, so the test for termination is performed prior to any execution. Some older compilers test for termination at the end of the loop.

RULES FOR DO LOOPS

1 A DO statement's parameters must not be altered by statements within the range of the DO. This encompasses the values for the index variable, the initial value, terminal value, and increment.

2 The index variable can be used in statements inside the range of the DO loops or it may be used only as a repetition counter. If an exit other than a normal exit is made from the loop (such as a GOTO out of the loop), the current value of the index variable is available for use outside the loop. After a normal exit (the loop has been completed), it is not available.

3 DO loops must be entered only through the DO statement because that execution establishes the loop controls. Never transfer from a statement outside the range of a DO to the inside of the range of a DO. An inner nested DO can transfer into the range of an outer DO because the inner DO is already in the range of the outer DO.

4 The iteration count for number of times the loop will execute is established as the integer value from ((terminal value − initial value + increment)/increment). If negative, the count is set to zero. A count of zero means the loop will not be executed at all. (Older FORTRANs may execute the loop once.) Note that the iteration count formula allows an initial value larger than a terminal value if there is a negative increment value. (Older FORTRANs do not allow a negative increment.)

5 Older, pre-1977 FORTRANs require that an executable statement should be used as the first statement following the DO statement. This excludes DIMENSION, FORMAT, etc., from following immediately after the DO statement.

Rule 4 regarding the iteration count means that a DO statement DO 100 I = 5,3,1 will not be executed at all (processing will continue with the statement following the CONTINUE for the loop) because the iteration count is $(3 - 5 + 1)/1 = -1$. As mentioned, in some older FORTRANs, the loop might execute once. This may affect portability of programs, and so the prudent programmer will code in a way such that the program will operate properly no matter which logic the compiler follows.

In writing loops, there are efficiency considerations. A computation can often be performed outside the loop once and the result furnished to the loop, thereby reducing processing time. However, such efficient coding should be carefully used because it tends to make the program logic less clear.

Efficiency Example

A program is to produce a table of interest rates for $1 using the formula $A = 1.0(1 + i)^n$ where i is the interest rate (called XI) and n is the number of periods. Since $1 + i$ is the same for each computation, it can be computed once outside the loop for efficiency. But unless the tables are very large, the efficiency is not significant enough to justify loss of clarity.

Clear coding of loop	More efficient coding of loop

DO   150 I = 1, N
      A = (1 . 0 + X 1) * * I
      (other statements)
150 CONTINUE
	FACTR = 1 . 0 + X 1
	DO 150 I = 1, N
	      A = FACTR * * I
	      (other statements)
	150 CONTINUE

Self-testing Exercise 4-2

1 Complete the table:

DO statement	Valid or invalid for 1977 full FORTRAN	If invalid for Subset or for older FORTRANs, explain why
(a) DO N I X I = 1 , 7		
(b) DO 1 2 0 , I = 1 , N I X		
(c) DO 2 3 0 M I X = 1 , J , K		
(d) DO 3 5 0 J A N E = J O E , + 7		
(e) DO 4 5 0 K = 1 0 , 8		
(f) DO 5 6 0 L U C K = 7 , 7		
(g) DO 6 7 0 I L L = 7 , 1 5 , 3		
(h) DO 7 8 0 I = 1 , N − 1		
(i) DO 8 9 0 X = 1 , 1 0 , 2		

2 At the completion of the following program loops, what will be the value of K, L, and M?

```
      M  =  0
      DO    1 5 0  I  =  1 , 1 0
            K  =  I
            DO    1 4 0  J  =  1 , 5
                  L  =  J
                  M  =  M + 1
1 4 0         CONTINUE
1 5 0  CONTINUE
```

3 How many times will the loops defined by the following DO statements be executed? Note where the answer for common pre-1977 FORTRAN versions may differ from the answer with the 1977 standard. Which statements are allowed by the 1977 standard FORTRAN but not allowed by 1977 Subset FORTRAN standard? Show computation for iteration count using the formula.

(a) DO   3   I = 5 , 5
(b) DO   3   I = 5 , 1
(c) DO   3   I = 1 , 5
(d) DO   3   I = 1 , 5 , 3
(e) DO   3   A = 0 . 1 , 0 . 5 , 0 . 2
(f) DO   3   A = 0 . 0 3 , 0 . 3 0 , 0 . 0 5
(g) DO   3   I = 5 , 1 , − 2

4 In what order will the following program segment print out the subscripted variables from a three-dimensional array?

```
DO      120  I = 1 , 2
        DO      110  J = 1 , 2
                DO      100  K = 1 , 2
                        WRITE  ( 3 , 9 0 0 )  ARRAY  ( I , J , K )
100             CONTINUE
110         CONTINUE
120 CONTINUE
```

5 What will the following program segment do?

```
DO      150  I = 1 , 3 0
        SUM = 0 . 0
        SUM = SUM + A ( I  ) * B ( I  )
150 CONTINUE
```

6 Which of the DO loop nests in Figure 4-13 are valid?

7 Write a program segment to sum the products from multiplying the elements in array LIX by the corresponding elements in array MIX. There are N entries in each.

8 Write a program segment to find the largest number of an N-entry array called X. Assume at least one positive number. Put the largest one in BIG.

9 Write a program segment to print out every other entry in a K-entry array called DAD, starting with the second entry.

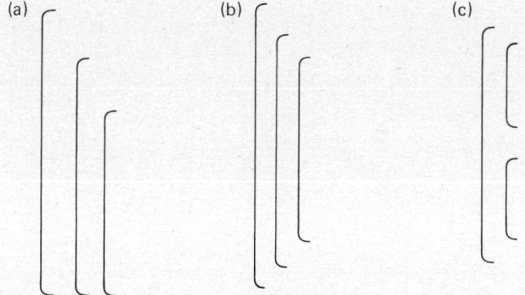

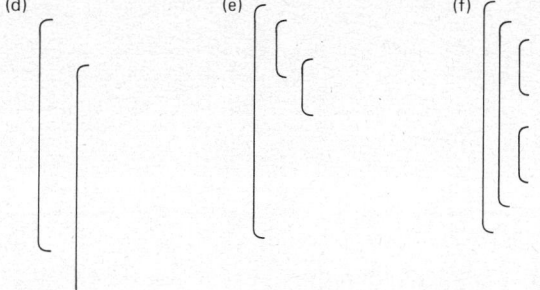

FIGURE 4-13 Loop nesting for question 6 in Self-testing Exercise 4.2.

10   Write a program segment to shift the values in an array A so that A(1) = A(2), A(2) = A(3), etc. A(N) should contain original value of A(1). Be careful with A(1).

11   Write a program segment to shift the values in a 25-entry array called ALPHA so that A(2) = A(1), A(3) = A(2), etc., and A(1) = A(25). Be sure to check your logic carefully.

Implied DO Loops in Input/Output

In reading or writing subscripted variables, each subscripted variable may be listed, but this is very cumbersome. Another method is to include the READ or WRITE statement inside a DO loop, but this method is limited by the fact that each loop initiates a repeat of the input/output command. A very useful FORTRAN feature which may simplify input and output of subscripted variables is a form of the input/output statement called an *implied* DO *loop*.

The form of the implied DO loop input or output statement is similar to that of the DO loop. In fact, as many as three implied loops may be nested. The form is shown by the following examples:

```
READ  ( 5 , 7 0 0 )  ( A ( I ) ,  I = 1 , N )
READ  ( 5 , 7 0 0 )  ( ( A ( I , J ) ,  J = 1 , M ) ,  I = 1 , N )
```

Note that each of the loop parameter specifications is enclosed in parentheses. Note also the placement of the commas, particularly after the parentheses.

In addition to the fact that it is a shorter form, the advantage of the implied DO loop over the regular DO loop is that the resulting variables are treated as a single list so that input or output from physical records is entirely under FORMAT control. For example, READ (5,700)(A(I),I = 1,100) will read the variable from 2 to 100 cards, depending on the format specifications. Keep in mind that the closing parenthesis of the FORMAT statement terminates the current physical record. If more variables are still available in the list to be read or written and the format specifications have been exhausted, the format specifications are used again with a new record.

FORMAT	READ instruction READ(5,700)(A(I),I = 1,100)
7 0 0 FORMAT (F 1 0 . 0)	One value per card (100 cards)
7 0 0 FORMAT (8 F 1 0 . 0)	Eight values per card (13 cards but only 4 values from the 13*th*)
7 0 0 FORMAT (2 F 1 0 . 0 / F 1 0 . 0)	Two values from first card, one variable value from second card, two variable values from third card, etc., because slash terminates use of a record (skips to next record).

The above example applies equally well to output. A program statement of the form WRITE(6,700)(A(I),I = 1,100) will write 100 values as specified by the FORMAT statement, e.g., one value per line, eight values per line, etc.

The implied DO loop can therefore be considered as a DO loop which creates a list of input or output variables to be input or output under FORMAT control. Nested loops can be used in implied input or output DO loops. The outer loop is written last, and the innermost DO (the one which changes most rapidly) is placed next to the variable. The loops should be listed so that they match the arrangement of the data.

Implied DO loop	Order in which variables are read or written
READ (5 , 7 0 0) (A (I) , I = 1 , N)	A (1) , A (2) , A (3) , . . . , A (N)
READ (5 , 7 0 0) ((A (I , J) , I = 1 , M) , J = 1 , N)	A (1 , 1) , A (2 , 1) , A (3 , 1) , . . . , A (M , N)
READ (5 , 7 0 0) ((A (I , J) , J = 1 , N) , I = 1 , M)	A (1 , 1) , A (1 , 2) , A (1 , 3) , . . . , A (M , N)
READ (5 , 7 0 0) (((A (I , J , K) , I = 1 , M) , J = 1 , N) , K = 1 , L)	A (1 , 1 , 1) , A (2 , 1 , 1) , A (3 , 1 , 1) , . . . , A (M , N , L)

A special form of the implied DO can be used when an entire array is to be read, printed, punched, etc. The array name is written without subscripts or implied DO loops. The DIMENSION statement will already have specified both the fact that it is an array name and the size of the entire array to be read or written. This input or output form can be used only when the entire array is desired in natural order, i.e., in the column order (row varies most rapidly). For example, array Y dimensioned as (2,2) will be processed by an implied DO in the order (1,1), (2,1), (1,2), (2,2)). This form, in essence, creates a list for the entire array in natural order and, therefore, it is input or output under format control. Reliance upon default procedures such as the array name without subscripts are quite error prone and should be used with caution. The explicit specifications in the implied DO loop are preferred style.

There is no special method for flowcharting of implied DO loops. Since the effect is entirely contained within the READ or WRITE statement, it is probably satisfactory to merely indicate that data is to be read or written by the normal input or output symbol. If additional detail is desired in the flowchart, the implied loop can be noted in the symbol or an annotation symbol can be used to provide more detail.

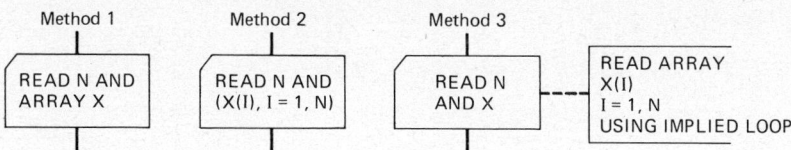

Self-testing Exercise 4-3

Explain the effect of each of the following sets of statements. It may be helpful to review the section on "Reuse of FORMAT Specifications" in Chapter 3.

```
1       DIMENSION A ( 1 0 , 1 0 )
        READ  ( 5 , 7 0 0 ) A
  700 FORMAT  ( F 1 0 . 0 )
```

```
2         DIMENSION  B(5,5)
          READ  (5,710)  ((B(I,J),  J=1,5),I=1,5)
    710  FORMAT  (8F10.0)

3         DIMENSION  C(6,6)
          READ  (5,720)  (C(1,J),J=1,6)
    720  FORMAT  (6F10.0)

4         DO   130  K=1,3
            DO   120  J=1,N
              DO   110  I=1,N
                READ  (5,105)  X(I,J,K)
    105         FORMAT  (F10.0)
    110       CONTINUE
    120     CONTINUE
    130  CONTINUE

5         WRITE  (6,730)((KIX(I,J),  J=1,4),I=1,4)
    730  FORMAT  (4I10,/)
```

Initializing Data Values with the Data Statement

In many programs, there are variables which should be set to an initial value. This may be accomplished by input of data as the first step in the program, by assignment statements, or by a DATA statement. The DATA statement provides initial values for variables, entire arrays, and array elements.

THE DATA STATEMENT

DATA nlist/clist/nlist/clist/   or   DATA nlist/clist/, nlist/clist/

nlist is a list of variable names, array names, or array element names.

clist is a list of the values to be assigned. A value can be repeated by using an integer plus asterisk in front of the value, the integer specifying the number of repetitions of the value. The nlist (in 1977 full FORTRAN but not in 1977 Subset FORTRAN) can be an implied DO statement.

The DATA statement is placed in the program after any specifications (such as DIMENSION statements) but before any executable statements.

EXAMPLES

DATA A, B, I / 5.0, 3.5, 4 /	assigns 5.0 to A, 3.5 to B, and 4 to I.
DATA A, B, C(3) / 3*10.0 /	assigns 10.0 to A, 10.0 to B, and 10.0 to C(3).
DATA ALPHA / 50*0.0 /	places zeros in all 50 elements of array ALPHA.
DATA (BETA(I), I=11, 20) / 10*5.0 /	initializes with the value 5.0 the elements from 11 to 20 in an array BETA. (Note implied DO loop.)
DATA ((IGAMMA(I, J), I=6, 10), J=1, 15) / 75*0 /	initializes to zero the last five rows of elements in a 10 × 15 array.

The DATA statement must be placed after specification statements such as DIMENSION. In the structure used in this text, the DATA statements will be included in a storage assignment block after the DIMENSION statements. It is a useful statement, especially when an entire array or a number of variables used as accumulators are set to zero. For example, setting TALLY1, TALLY2, and a 100-element array GAMMA to 0 can be performed using assignment statements and a DO loop, but it is more efficient and very clear to use a DATA statement.

Without DATA statement	With DATA statement
TALLY 1 = 0 . 0 TALLY 2 = 0 . 0 DO 150 I = 1 , 100 GAMMA (I) = 0 . 0 150 CONTINUE	DATA TALLY 1 , TALLY 2 / 2 * 0 . 0 /GAMMA / 100 * 0 . 0 /

Note that the DATA statement could also have been written as:

DATA TALLY 1 , TALLY 2 , GAMMA / 102 * 0 . 0 /

Self-testing Exercise 4-4

1 Use the DATA statement to initialize A to 40.1, B to 3.7, and C and D to 1.0, and all elements in a 100-element array BETA to 0.
2 Use an implied loop in a DATA statement to initialize to 2.0 every other element between 15 and 49 in an array called ARRAY.

Style Guidelines for Subscripted Variables and DO Loops

As in previous chapters, the style guidelines reflect good practice, but there are alternative styles that may also result in clear, disciplined program coding.

1 Do not over-dimension, especially in multidimensional arrays.

2 Test for use of subscripts that exceed the maximum value dimensioned for the array. Out-of-range subscripts can often yield difficult-to-debug results.

3 In the variable identification block, use a separate array name section to clearly identify array names (see examples in Chapter 4B).

4 Use a separate storage assignment block to clearly specify the DIMENSIONs for all arrays.

5 End each DO loop with a CONTINUE statement. It is not required except when the last statement in the range of the DO loop would be a transfer of control. However, as a matter of style, the CONTINUE clearly marks the range of a DO loop.

6 As a matter of style, statements may be indented between the DO statement and the CONTINUE statement to visually define the range of the DO loop.

7 For nested DO loops, each inner loop may be indented. Each nested loop may end with a separate CONTINUE. Example:

```
DO    130  I  =  1 ,  N
      DO    120  J  =  1 ,  M
            DO    110  K  =  1 ,  5
                  SUM  =  SUM  +  A ( I , J , K )
110               CONTINUE
120         CONTINUE
130   CONTINUE
```

8 Since the single letters I through J are so often used as loop parameters, it is well, as a matter of style, not to use these single letters as simple variable or array names, reserving them for DO loop parameters. In following this suggestion, it is not necessary to define these index variables in the "variable identification block."

Summary

The repetition structure is very important in programming. In FORTRAN, it is implemented by the DO loop. Subscripted variables are frequently used in connection with loops because it simplifies the programming of processing on data items that can be grouped together and assigned a common name. Subscripts indicate data item position in the array. The DIMENSION statement defines the maximum number of entries in an array.

The DO loop begins with the DO statement that specifies the range of the loop, the control variable, the initial value, the terminal value, and the increment. Good practice suggests that a DO loop should always end with a CONTINUE statement and indentation should be used to visually define the statements inside the loop.

An implied DO loop may be contained within a READ or WRITE statement. This is very useful because it allows input and output to be completely under FORMAT control.

Data values, especially arrays, can be initialized to starting values by assignment statements, but a very useful alternative is the DATA statement.

Answers to Self-testing Exercises

Exercise 4-1

1

Valid or invalid	If invalid for some versions of FORTRAN, why
(a) Valid	
(b) Invalid	Real subscript (X) not allowed
(c) Valid	Not allowable subscript form in older FORTRANs
(d) Valid	
(e) Valid	
(f) Invalid	Real subscript expression (A + 5.0) not allowed
(g) Valid	Not allowable form in older FORTRANs; should be I*5
(h) Valid	Subscripts limited to three in subset FORTRAN and many older FORTRANs

2 (*a*) DIMENSION ARRAY (100)
   (*b*) DIMENSION PERSNS (2, 10)
   (*c*) DIMENSION BUSNES (8, 15, 5)
   (*d*) DIMENSION A (15), B (15), C (15), D (15)
3 (*a*) A (2, 2)
   (*b*) A (3, 5)
   (*c*) CLASS (2, 5, 2)
   (*d*) CLASS (2, 2, 1)
4 DIMENSION A (5, 5), CLASS (5, 5, 4)
5 Figure 4-14

Exercise 4-2

1

Full 1977 FORTRAN	If invalid for Subset or older FORTRANs, why
(*a*) Invalid	Because a variable may not be used as a statement number.
(*b*) Valid	Comma after statement number optional in 1977 Standard (or not allowed by older versions).
(*c*) Valid	
(*d*) Valid	Parameters may not be signed for older FORTRANs.
(*e*) Valid	But note that the terminal value is less than initial value. The new standard says execute zero times. Some versions will execute the loop once.
(*f*) Valid	The loop will be executed once; count = $(7 - 7 + 1)/1 = 1$.
(*g*) Valid	Note that the loop stops when the terminal value is exceeded. Therefore, this will be executed three times. Using the iteration count formula, the count = $(15 - 7 + 3)/3 = 11/3 = 3$.
(*h*) Valid	Arithmetic expression not allowed except in 1977 full FORTRAN.
(*i*) Valid	Control variable must be integer in 1977 Subset FORTRAN and in older FORTRANs

2 K = 10, L = 5, M = 50
3 (*a*) 1 $(5 - 5 + 1)/1 = 1$
   (*b*) 0* $(1 - 5 + 1)/1 = -3 = 0$
   (*c*) 5 $(5 - 1 + 1)/1 = 5$
   (*d*) 2 $(5 - 1 + 3)/3 = 2$
   (*e*) 3† $(.5 - .1 + .2)/.2 = 3$
   (*f*) 6† $(.30 - .03 + .05)/.05 = 6$
   (*g*) 3‡ $[1 - 5 + (-2)]/-2 = 3$
4 ARRAY (1, 1, 1), (1, 1, 2), (1, 2, 1), (1, 2, 2),
   (2, 1, 1), (2, 1, 2), (2, 2, 1), (2, 2, 2)
5 The program will end with SUM = A(30)*B(30). The initializing of the accumulating variable name must be done outside the loop in which it is used.
6 Valid: *a*, *b*, *c*, and *f*.
   Invalid: *d* and *e*. Inner DO must be entirely within range of outer.

* Pre-1977 versions often performed one time.

† Not allowed by 1977 Subset FORTRAN and older FORTRANs.

‡ Not allowed by older FORTRANs.

```
*********          STORAGE ALLOCATION                    *********
*                                                               *
      DIMENSION A(5),B(5),C(5)
*                                                               *
*****************************************************************
*                                                               *
*********          INITIALIZATION                    BLOCK 0000
*                                                               *
    I = 1
    J = 1


*                                                               *
*****************************************************************
*                                                               *
*********          READ DATA INTO ARRAYS             BLOCK 0100
*                                                               *
  100 IF(I.GT.5) GOTO 200
      READ(5,150) A(I),B(I)
  150 FORMAT(F10.2,F10.2)
      I = I + 1
*                                                               *
*         GO BACK TO READ ANOTHER DATA CARD                     *
*                                                               *
      GOTO 100                                                  *
*                                                               *
*****************************************************************
*                                                               *
*********          MULTIPLY A TIMES B TO GIVE C      BLOCK 0200
*                                                               *
  200 IF(J.GT.5) GOTO 300
      C(J) = A(J)*B(J)
      J = J + 1
*                                                               *
*         GO BACK TO START OF BLOCK                             *
*                                                               *
      GOTO 200
*                                                               *
*****************************************************************
```

FIGURE 4-14 Program segment which uses loops to read and multiply array values.

```
7        ISUM=0.0
         DO    150 I=1,N
              ISUM=ISUM+LIX(I)*MIX(I)
    150 CONTINUE
8        BIG  =0.0
         DO    100 I=1,N
              IF  (X(I).GT.BIG) BIG=X(I)
   or    BIG  =X(1)
         DO    100 I=2,N
         etc.
    100 CONTINUE
9        DO    160 I=2,K,2
              WRITE  (5,700) DAD(I)
    160 CONTINUE
10       TEMP=A(1)
         DO    100 I=2,N
              A(I-1)=A(I)
    100 CONTINUE
         A(N)=TEMP
11       TEMP=A(25)                Possible alternative in 1977 full
         DO    100 I=1,24          FORTRAN
              K=25-I               TEMP=A(25)
              A(K+1)=A(K)          DO    100 I=24,1,-1
    100 CONTINUE                        A(I+1)=A(I)
         A(1)=TEMP           100 CONTINUE
                                   A(1)=TEMP
```

Exercise 4-3

1 One hundred values for A will be read from cards. One value will be read from each card, arranged in natural order by columns, i.e., the row subscript will vary most rapidly.

   A(1,1), A(2,1), A(3,1), . . .

2 Twenty-five values for B will be read, eight to a card, in row order—

   B(1,1), B(1,2), . . .

3 Six values will be read from a card. These will form the first row of a 6 × 6 matrix.
4 This will read an N × N × 3 array, punched one to a card and arranged in natural order. The row varies most rapidly, column next, and level last.
5 The 16-value array KIX will be printed out with four column values per line, double-spaced between lines (because the closing parenthesis does single spacing and the slash skips a line).

Exercise 4-4

1 D A T A A , B , C , D / 4 0 . 1 , 3 . 7 , 2 * 1 . 0 / , B E T A / 1 0 0 * 0 . 0 /
2 D A T A (A R R A Y (I) , I = 1 5 , 4 9 , 2) / 1 8 * 2 . 0 /

Questions and Problems

1 Define or explain:
   (a) The purpose of the DIMENSION statement
   (b) Array
   (c) Matrix
   (d) Subscript
2 Write the DIMENSION statements for the following:
   (a) An array X with 59 entries
   (b) An array YES with 39 rows and 10 columns
   (c) An array to accept a threefold classification—by state, by one of twenty sizes of cities, and by one of two classes relating to growth in the past ten years.
3 A company wishes to classify SALES by salesmen (ten of them), by size of company (four size categories), and by product sold (eight of these). Set up the classification for SALES, and write a program segment to calculate totals by a salesman.
4 Complete the table below.

DO statement	Valid or invalid for 1977 full FORTRAN	If invalid for Subset or older FORTRANs, why
(a) DO 19 N I X = J I X , K I X , L I X		
(b) DO 100 F I X = 1 , T R I X		
(c) DO 50 I = 1 , N , L + 1		
(d) DO 30 I = 1 , N , K		
(e) DO 17 I = 1 , 4 , 2		
(f) DO X J = I , K		

5 What is the purpose of the CONTINUE statement?

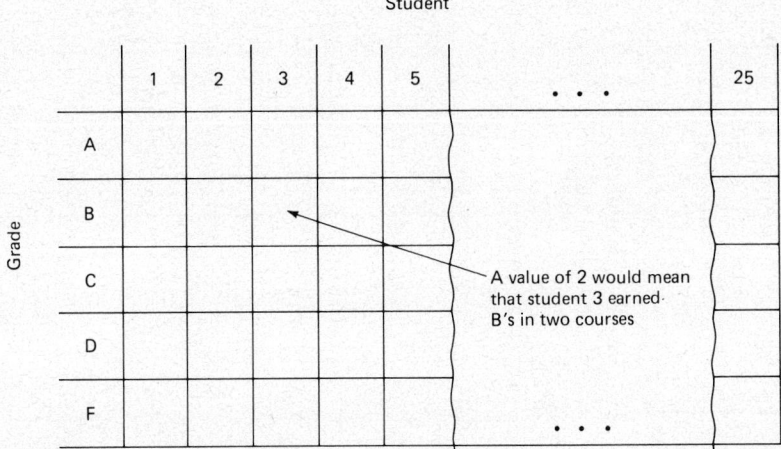

FIGURE 4-15 Course-grade matrix for problem 7.

6 In what order will the first six subscripted variables be processed when N is 2 and M is 3?

```
        DO    1 0 2   I = J , N
            DO    1 0 1   J = 1 , N
                DO    1 0 0   K = 1 , M
                    A  ( K , J , I ) = . . .
1 0 0                   CONTINUE
1 0 1           CONTINUE
1 0 2 CONTINUE
```

7 A matrix contains the number of A's, B's, etc., earned by each student in a class of 25. Each course is three credits. (See Figure 4-15.) Write a program segment to calculate the grade point for each student and the grade-point average for the class.

8 What is the effect of the following statements?

(a)
```
        READ  ( 5 , 7 0 0 )  ( ( ( A ( I , J , K ) , K = 1 , 3 ) ,
        J = 1 , 5 ) , I = 1 , 3 )
  7 0 0 FORMAT  ( F 1 0 . 0 )
```

(b)
```
        DIMENSION  BETA  ( 5 , 5 , 5 )
        READ  ( 5 , 7 0 0 )  BETA
  7 0 0 FORMAT  ( F 1 0 . 0 / )
```

(c)
```
        DIMENSION  IOTA  ( 8 , 8 )
        WRITE  ( 6 , 7 0 0 )  IOTA
  7 0 0 FORMAT  ( I 1 0 )
```

(d)
```
        DO   7 5 0  J = 1 , N
            WRITE  ( 6 , 7 0 0 )  J , A ( J )
  7 0 0       FORMAT  ( I 1 0 , F 1 0 . 2 )
  7 5 0 CONTINUE
```

(e)
```
        READ  ( 5 , 7 0 0 )  B ( 1 , 1 ) , B ( 3 , 2 ) , B ( 4 , 1 )
  7 0 0 FORMAT  ( F 1 0 . 0 )
```

CHAPTER

EXAMPLE PROGRAMS AND PROGRAMMING EXERCISES WHICH USE SUBSCRIPTED VARIABLES AND DO LOOPS

The example programs will illustrate the use of subscripted variables, DO loops, and implied DO loops. The general example of payroll makes use of implied DO loops for input and output; the statistical program output does not require an implied DO, but the computational procedures make effective use of DO loops. Both example programs should be reviewed because they illustrate features in different ways.

General Comments on the Example Programs

Both programs use an array to store data as it is computed. The stored array of data is then used for processing and output. Without the array, it is cumbersome to store tables or matrices of data.

The variable identification block has previously contained only variable names and constant identification. An array names block is added to clearly identify array names. The DIMENSION statements are placed in a *storage allocation block*.

In the flowcharts (which require more than one page), note the use of off-page connector references.

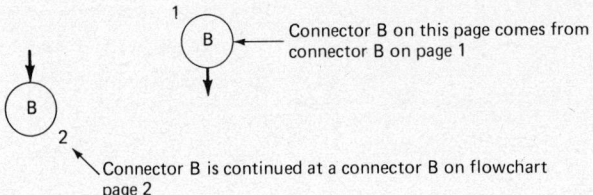

Some programmers use a special off-page connector symbol found on IBM

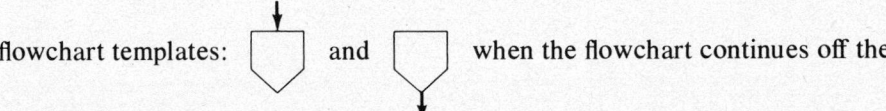

flowchart templates: and   when the flowchart continues off the

page. Either method is satisfactory.

There is no special flowcharting symbol or notation to indicate implied DO loops with input or output. The flowchart need not show all details of the program coding and, in these programs, implied DO loops were not significant for the flow of program logic.

General Program Example 4—Payroll Reports

The program computes gross pay, deductions, and net pay as with the previous programs. However, new techniques are used, such as storing the valid input data in an array. This allows the program to delay the payroll reports until all data has been read. Also, the reports can list the employees in a different order than the order of the input.

Problem Description for General Example 4

The program is to read employee pay data and produce two reports: (1) Error and Control Report (see Figure 4-20, page 195) and (2) Report of Pay Amounts (see Figure 4-21, page 196). There are two sets of input for the program. The first consists of five pairs of department numbers and names, one pair per card. The second set of input data consists of employee data, one card for each employee, giving ID number, name, department number where employed, hours worked, wage rate, and miscellaneous deductions. The program will process 14 or fewer valid employee input cards.

The Error and Control Report produced during input validation consists of three parts (refer to example in Figure 4-20, page 195):

1 An echoing of the table of department numbers and names for visual validation.

2 Error messages identifying errors detected during input validation.
   (a) For invalid data (invalid department number), the error message identifies the cause of the rejection and the card number of the rejected record.
   (b) For data-type errors, the message identifies the card number.
   (c) For array overflow caused by excess employee data cards, an excess data error message is printed and the program is terminated.

3 A record count of total records read and total records rejected.

The Report of Pay Amounts consists of a heading, a line of output for each employee, and a total line (refer to example in Figure 4-21, page 195). The employees are not listed in the order of input; rather, they are listed by department. Because the report does not have space for an error message if net pay is zero, negative, or over $300, there is a column for notes and a code in the column is used to reference an error message at the bottom of the report.

Program Documentation for General Example 4

The documentation of program design is given by a pseudocode description (Figure 4-16) and a program flowchart (Figure 4-17). The program listing is given in Figure 4-18. Test data used for the sample output is listed in Figure 4-19. An example of an Error and Control Report is shown in Figure 4-20 and an example of a Report of Pay Amounts is given in Figure 4-21.

Notes on General Example 4

The outputs from program example 4 are in much better form than previous reports. Error messages are removed from the detail report, headings are more meaningful, and the order of output is under program control. The variable identification block has been enlarged to include a section which names tempo-

---

Dimension arrays for 5 departments and 15 employee records (14 accepted records and 1 potential error case)
WRITE heading at top of page for Error and Control Report
Initialize counters, summing variables and rates
READ set of allowable department numbers and names
WRITE table of department numbers and names for visual validation
WRITE error message heading
READ an employee card and test for end of data and data-type error
    If no more cards, go to Print Detail Report, else continue
    If data-type error, increment record counter, print message, and go back to
      READ, else continue
Increment record counter
Test for invalid department number
    IF invalid department number, print message and go back to READ, else
      continue
Compute payroll data and store in arrays
    Compute overtime
    Compute gross pay, including overtime (if any)
    Compute taxes, pension contribution, all deductions
    Compute net pay
Add employee gross pay, total deductions, and net pay to totals
Increment accepted employee records counter by 1
Test number of accepted records
    If number exceeds limit of array storage, print excess records message and
      stop
    Else go back to READ an employee card
Print Detail Report
WRITE record counts at bottom of Error and Control Report
WRITE heading for Report of Pay Amounts at top of new page
DO for all departments
    Select department numbers in order
    For each employee PRINT detail (Name, ID, Dept. Name, Gross Pay, Deductions, Net Pay)
    IF net pay is outside limits (negative or > 300), PRINT error code on same line
End of DO
WRITE summary totals and error code explanation
STOP

FIGURE 4-16 Pseudocode description of logic of general program example 4—pay reports.

rary variables. These are variable names which are used only in a short block of code and which are not needed either before or after that block is executed. Such variables may arise as temporary counters or, as in this case, to improve readability or efficiency. The reason for listing them is that if the program is later revised and modified, the same name should not be used as a variable name.

A new block has been added to describe storage allocation. DIMENSION and DATA statements (and several other types described in later chapters) appear in this block. Some variables have been initialized by a DATA statement and others by arithmetic assignment statements. Although logically equivalent, they are handled differently by the FORTRAN compiler. The DATA statement method is generally preferred, but there are some restrictions in special cases that will be explained in Chapter 5.

Note in the computation block two counters are incremented (line 22 and line 40). The first (NCARD) keeps track of all cards read while the second (NUM) counts those accepted (error-free). These counters were initialized in line numbers 10 and 11.

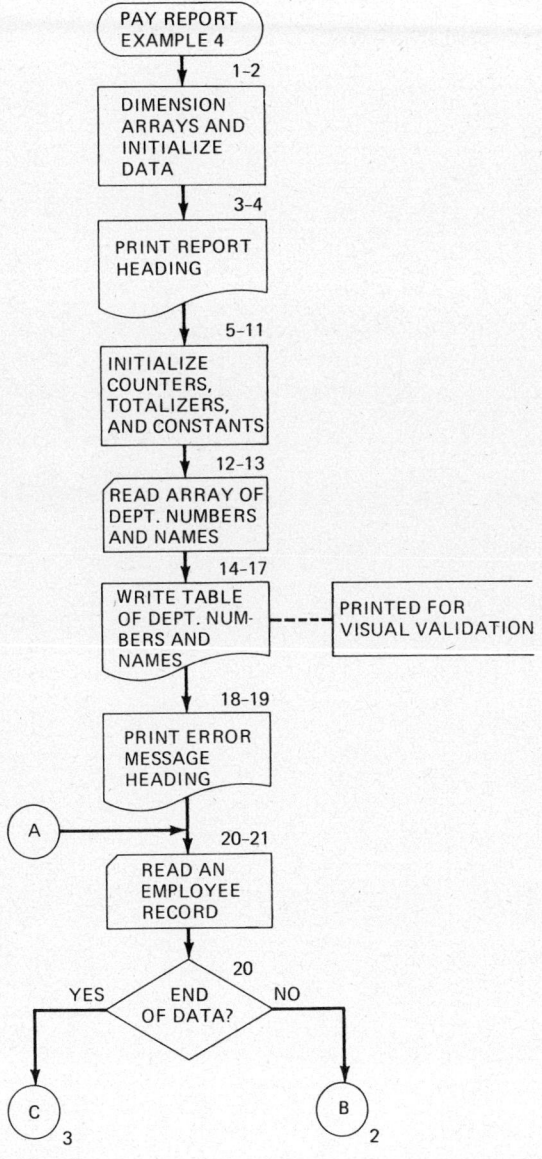

FIGURE 4-17 Program flowchart for general program example 4—pay reports. (Numbers next to symbols are line numbers from program listing.)

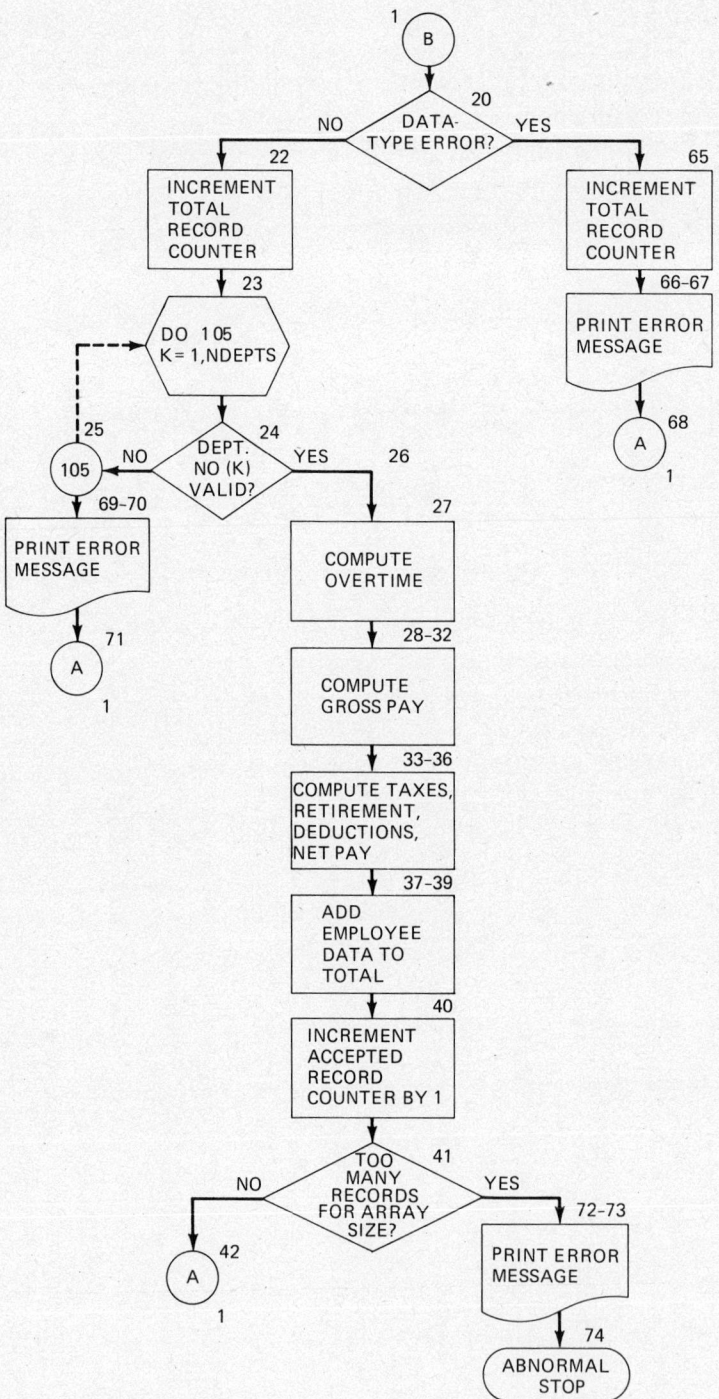

FIGURE 4-17 *(continued)* Program flowchart for general program example 4—pay reports.

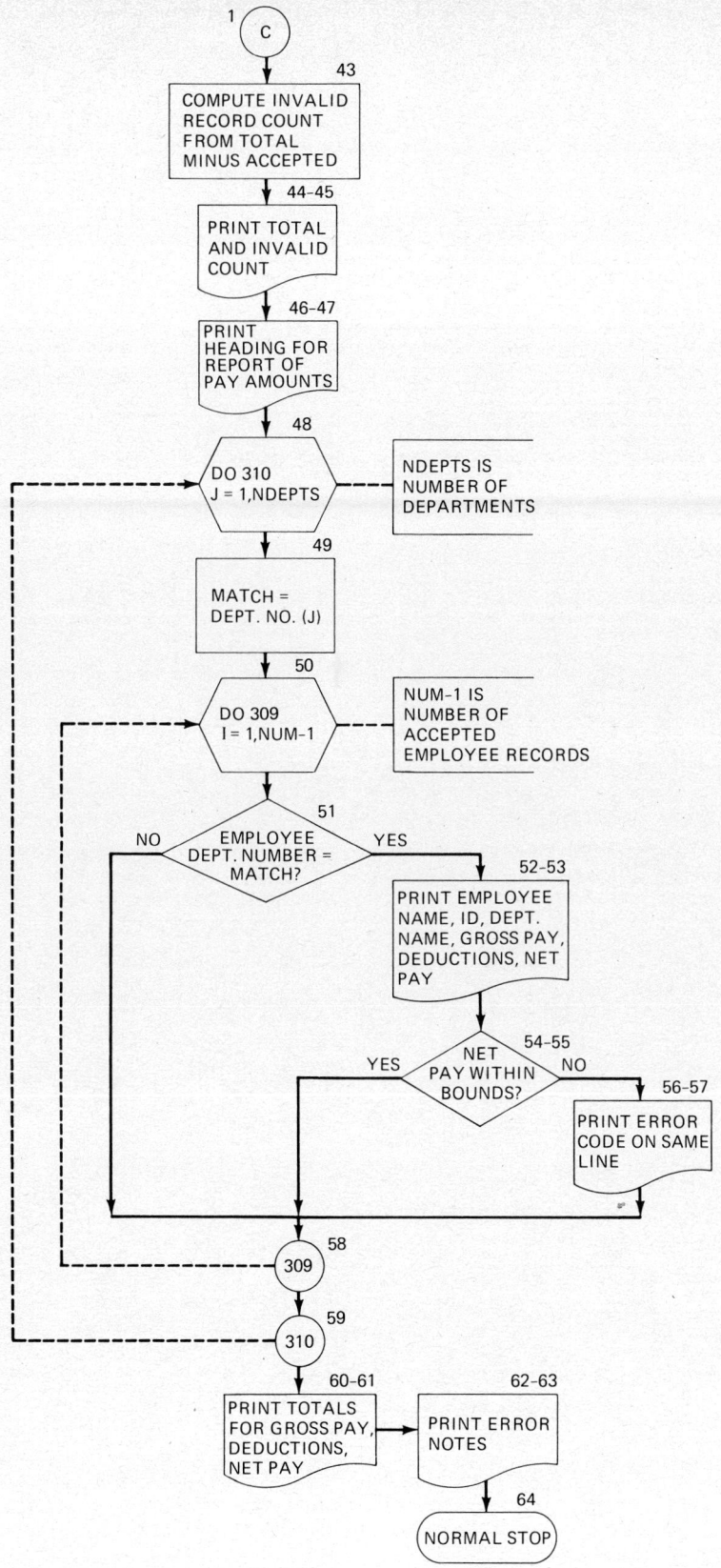

FIGURE 4-17 *(continued)*

```
*********          PROGRAM IDENTIFICATION          *********
*                                                          *
*      THIS PROGRAM COMPUTES EMPLOYEE PAYCHECKS BASED       *
*      UPON HOURS WORKED, WAGE RATE AND VARIOUS DEDUCTIONS.  *
*      IT PRINTS EMPLOYEE DATA GROUPED BY DEPARTMENTS.       *
*      WRITTEN 4/27/77 BY T. HOFFMANN                        *
*                                                          *
************************************************************
*                                                          *
*********          VARIABLE IDENTIFICATION          *********
*                                                          *
*****               ARRAY NAMES                        *****
*                                                          *
*      ID     = EMPLOYEE IDENTIFICATION NUMBER              *
*      GRSPAY = GROSS PAY: $                                *
*      NAME   = EMPLOYEE NAMES                              *
*      NDEP   = DEPT. NUMBER WHERE WORKED                   *
*      NODEPT = LIST OF DEPARTMENT NUMBERS                  *
*      NMDEPT = CORRESPONDING LIST OF DEPARTMENT NAMES       *
*      PAYCHK = NET PAYCHECK AMOUNT: $                      *
*      PAYDAT = PAYROLL INPUT DATA (HRSWRK,WGRATE,DEDUC)     *
*      TDEDUC = TOTAL OF ALL DEDUCTIONS FOR AN EMPLOYEE      *
*                                                          *
*****               SIMPLE VARIABLES                   *****
*                                                          *
*      NCARD  = NUMBER OF CARDS READ                        *
*      NUM    = NUMBER OF VALID EMPLOYEE RECORDS ACCEPTED    *
*      NOTVLD = NUMBER OF NOT VALID EMPLOYEE RECORDS         *
*      OTIME  = HOURS OF OVERTIME (EXCESS OVER 40.0)         *
*      RETIRE = RETIREMENT CONTRIBUTION BY EMPLOYEE          *
*      TAXES  = TAXES DUE: $                                *
*      TOTNET = TOTAL OF NET PAY AMOUNTS                     *
*      TOTPAY = TOTAL GROSS PAY FOR COMPANY: $              *
*      TOTDUC = TOTAL OF ALL EMPLOYEE DEDUCTIONS             *
*                                                          *
*****               CONSTANT IDENTIFICATION            *****
*                                                          *
*      NDEPTS = NUMBER OF DEPARTMENTS (SET AT 5)            *
*      PLIMIT = MAXIMUM PAYCHECK VALUE TO ALLOW = $300.00    *
*      MAXEMP = MAXIMUM NUMBER OF EMPLOYEE RECORDS IN ARRAY = 15 *
*      PNRATE = PENSION CONTRIBUTION RATE = 0.05            *
*      TAXRT  = TAX RATE = 0.15                             *
*                                                          *
*****               TEMPORARY VARIABLE NAMES           *****
*                                                          *
*      MATCH,PAYNET                                         *
*                                                          *
************************************************************
*                                                          *
*********          STORAGE ALLOCATION          *********
*                                                          *
*      MAXIMUM NUMBER OF VALID EMPLOYEE RECORDS IS 14 (MAXEMP-1) *
*      MAXIMUM NUMBER OF DEPARTMENTS IS 5 (NDEPTS)          *
*                                                          *
1.        DIMENSION NODEPT(5),NMDEPT(5),ID(15),NAME(15,3),NDEP(15),
         1     PAYDAT(15,3),GRSPAY(15),TDEDUC(15),PAYCHK(15)
2.        DATA NDEPTS/5/PLIMIT/300.0/MAXEMP/15/
*                                                          *
************************************************************
*                                                          *
*********          INITIALIZATION BLOCK          BLOCK 0000
*                                                          *
*      SET OUTPUT PAGE TO TOP AND PRINT HEADER              *
*                                                          *
3.        WRITE(6,1)
4.      1 FORMAT(1H1/' EMPLOYEE PAYCHECK PROGRAM'//)
*                                                          *
*      SET CONSTANTS AND ZERO ACCUMULATORS                 *
*                                                          *
5.        PNRATE = 0.05
6.        TAXRT = 0.15
7.        TOTPAY = 0.0
8.        TOTNET = 0.0
9.        TOTDUC = 0.0
10.       NCARD = 0
11.       NUM = 1
```

FIGURE 4-18 Listing of FORTRAN program for general program example 4—payroll reports.

```
        *                                                          *
        *          READ AND PRINT DEPARTMENT NUMBERS AND NAMES     *
        *                                                          *
12.          READ(5,7) (NODEPT(K),NMDEPT(K), K=1,NDEPTS)
13.        7 FORMAT(I4,A4)
14.          WRITE(6,9)
15.        9 FORMAT(1H0,'TABLE OF DEPARTMENTS'/' NUMBER    NAME')
16.          WRITE(6,11) (NODEPT(K),NMDEPT(K),K=1,NDEPTS)
17.       11 FORMAT(2X,I4,4X,A4)
        *                                                          *
        *          PRINT ERROR MESSAGE HEADER                      *
        *                                                          *
18.          WRITE(6,13)
19.       13 FORMAT(///6X,'ERROR MESSAGES DURING DATA INPUT'//)
        *                                                          *
        ************************************************************
        *                                                          *
        *********          READ EMPLOYEE DATA            BLOCK 0100
        *                                                          *
20.      101 READ(5,102,END=301,ERR=901) ID(NUM),(NAME(NUM,J),J=1,3),
           1    NDEP(NUM),(PAYDAT(NUM,K),K=1,3)
21.      102 FORMAT(I5,3A4,I4,F4.1,F4.2,F5.2)
22.          NCARD = NCARD + 1
        *                                                          *
        *          CHECK FOR VALID DEPARTMENT NUMBER IN EMPLOYEE CARD *
        *          WHEN FOUND, PROCESS EMPLOYEE DATA                *
        *                                                          *
23.          DO 105 K=1,NDEPTS
24.          IF(NODEPT(K).EQ.NDEP(NUM)) GOTO 201
25.      105 CONTINUE
        *                                                          *
        *          ERROR -- NO MATCH FOUND FOR EMPLOYEE DEPT. NUMBER *
        *                                                          *
26.          GOTO 903
        *                                                          *
        ************************************************************
        *                                                          *
        *********          COMPUTATION BLOCK             BLOCK 0200
        *                                                          *
        *          COMPUTE PAY, INCLUDING OVERTIME, IF ANY.        *
        *                                                          *
27.      201 OTIME = PAYDAT(NUM,1) - 40.0
28.          IF(OTIME.GT.0.0) THEN
29.             GRSPAY(NUM) = (40.0 + 1.5*OTIME)*PAYDAT(NUM,2)
30.          ELSE
31.             GRSPAY(NUM) = PAYDAT(NUM,1)*PAYDAT(NUM,2)
32.          ENDIF
        *                                                          *
        *          COMPUTE EACH TYPE OF DEDUCTION AND NET PAY       *
        *                                                          *
33.          TAXES = GRSPAY(NUM)*TAXRT
34.          RETIRE = GRSPAY(NUM)*PNRATE
35.          TDEDUC(NUM) = PAYDAT(NUM,3) + TAXES + RETIRE
36.          PAYCHK(NUM) = GRSPAY(NUM) - TDEDUC(NUM)
37.          TOTPAY = TOTPAY + GRSPAY(NUM)
38.          TOTDUC = TOTDUC + TDEDUC(NUM)
39.          TOTNET = TOTNET + PAYCHK(NUM)
40.          NUM = NUM + 1
        *                                                          *
        *          TEST TO PREVENT ARRAY OVERFLOW. IF ARRAYS NOT FULL *
        *          RETURN TO READ NEXT EMPLOYEE DATA CARD.          *
        *                                                          *
41.          IF(NUM.GT.MAXEMP) GOTO 906
        *                                                          *
        *          GO BACK TO READ ANOTHER DATA CARD               *
        *                                                          *
42.          GOTO 101
        *                                                          *
        ************************************************************
        *                                                          *
        *********          PRINT DETAIL BY DEPARTMENT GROUPING   BLOCK 0300
        *                                                          *
        *          PRINT SUMMARY OF DATA INPUT MESSAGES            *
        *                                                          *
43.      301 NOTVLD = NCARD - NUM + 1
44.          WRITE(6,302) NCARD,NOTVLD
45.      302 FORMAT(1H0,I4,' CARDS READ'/I5,' CARDS REJECTED')
```

FIGURE 4-18 *(continued)*

```
       *                                                                *
       *             PRINT HEADER/TITLE LINE FOR EMPLOYEE DETAIL         *
       *                                                                *
46.        WRITE(6,303)
47.    303 FORMAT(1H1,4X,8HEMPLOYEE,5X,2HID,3X,4HDEPT,3X,5HGROSS,4X,
       1      5HTOTAL,6X,3HNET,4X,5HNOTES/7X,4HNAME,12X,4HNAME,4X,
       2      3HPAY,3X,10HDEDUCTIONS)
       *                                                                *
       *             FOR EACH DEPARTMENT FIND EACH EMPLOYEE              *
       *                                                                *
48.        DO 310 J=1,NDEPTS
49.        MATCH = NODEPT(J)
50.        DO 309 I=1,NUM-1
51.        IF(NDEP(I).NE.MATCH) GOTO 309
52.        WRITE(6,304)  (NAME(I,N),N=1,3),ID(I),NMDEPT(J),
       1      GRSPAY(I),TDEDUC(I),PAYCHK(I)
53.    304    FORMAT(1H0,2X,3A4,I6,2X,A4,3X,F6.2,3X,F6.2,3X,F6.2)
54.        PAYNET = PAYCHK(I)
       *                                                                *
       *             CHECK FOR VALID PAYCHECK AMOUNT                     *
       *                                                                *
55.        IF(PAYNET.GT.0.0 .AND. PAYNET.LE.PLIMIT) GOTO 309
56.        WRITE(6,306)
57.    306    FORMAT(1H+,57X,'A')
58.    309    CONTINUE
59.    310 CONTINUE
       *                                                                *
       ******************************************************************
       *                                                                *
       *********     PRINT SUMMARY AND TERMINATE         BLOCK 0400
       *                                                                *
60.        WRITE(6,402) TOTPAY,TOTDUC,TOTNET
61.    402 FORMAT(//20X,'TOTALS',3X,F7.2,2F9.2)
62.        WRITE(6,403)
63.    403 FORMAT(///5X,'NOTES'/5X'A - NET PAY IS OUT OF BOUNDS',
       1      '. DO NOT ISSUE CHECK.')
64.        STOP
       *                                                                *
       ******************************************************************
       *                                                                *
       *********          ERROR MESSAGE BLOCK            BLOCK 0900
       *                                                                *
65.    901 NCARD = NCARD + 1
66.        WRITE(6,902) NCARD
67.    902 FORMAT(//6H *****,' ERROR IN DATA CARD NUMBER ',I2,6H *****)
       *                                                                *
       *             GO BACK TO READ NEXT EMPLOYEE DATA CARD             *
       *                                                                *
68.        GOTO 101
       *****                                                        *****
69.    903 WRITE(6,904) NCARD
70.    904 FORMAT(//' ***** ERROR - DEPT. NO. NOT VALID. CARD NO.  ',I4,
       1      2X,5H*****)
       *                                                                *
       *             GO BACK TO READ NEXT EMPLOYEE DATA CARD             *
       *                                                                *
71.        GOTO 101
       *****                                                        *****
72.    906 WRITE(6,907)
73.    907 FORMAT(///' ***** ERROR. ATTEMPTED TO READ ',
       1      'MORE THAN 14 VALID DATA CARDS'/7X,'PROGRAM ABORTED. ')
74.        STOP
75.        END
```

FIGURE 4-18 *(continued)*

INPUT TEST DATA

DEPT NO.	DEPT NAME	PURPOSE
1234	FIN	COLLECTIVELY THESE FORM A DATA SET OF DEPARTMENT
4275	ENGR	NUMBERS AND NAMES. NO ERROR MESSAGES ARE
7269	MKTG	GENERATED.
7531	PROD	
8551	ACCT	

ID	NAME	DEPT NO.	PAYROLL DATA	PURPOSE OR EXPECTED OUTPUT
23456	J. HOFFMANN	7531	40.03.5727.95	NET PAY = 86.29
15786	RALPH JONES	8551	37.06.2824.68	GROSS PAY = 232.36
36985	J. JOHNSON	7269	22.00275035986	GROSS PAY = 12.42
23456	T. HOFFMANN	1596	40.03.5727.95	ERROR-NOT VALID. CARD NO. 4
69852	T. NAMAN	4275	10.02.6727.50	NET PAY NEGATIVE
35748	L. SMITH	4275	55.57.2430.68	NET PAY TOO LARGE-OVER 300.0
1596	GEN			ERROR-NONNUMERIC DATA IN NUMERIC FIELD. CARD NO. 7
42753	R. M. NELSON	1234	40.07.4557.64	NET PAY 180.76
74365	A. PETERSON	7531	54.04.8254.63	GROSS PAY = 294.02
62475	Q. SIBLEY	4275	37.58.2465.34	THIS PERSON IN ENGR DEPT SET
				10 DATA CARDS
				2 REJECTED ON INPUT
				2 ERROR NOTES

FIGURE 4-19 Annotated input test data for general problem 4.

```
EMPLOYEE PAYCHECK PROGRAM


TABLE OF DEPARTMENTS
NUMBER    NAME
 1234     FIN
 4275     ENGR
 7269     MKTG
 7531     PROD
 8551     ACCT




    ERROR MESSAGES DURING DATA INPUT




***** ERROR - DEPT. NO. NOT VALID. CARD NO.     4   *****


***** ERROR IN DATA CARD NUMBER  7 *****

  10 CARDS READ
   2 CARDS REJECTED
```

FIGURE 4-20 Example of Error and Control Report from pay reports program.

```
     EMPLOYEE      ID    DEPT     GROSS      TOTAL        NET    NOTES
       NAME               NAME     PAY    DEDUCTIONS

R. M. NELSON  42753   FIN      298.00     117.24     180.76

T. NAMAN      69852   ENGR      26.70      32.84      -6.14    A

L. SMITH      35748   ENGR     457.93     122.27     335.66    A

Q. SIBLEY     62475   ENGR     309.00     127.14     181.86

J. JOHNSON    36985   MKTG      60.50      48.08      12.42

J. HOFFMANN   23456   PROD     142.80      56.51      86.29

A. PETERSON   74365   PROD     294.02     113.43     180.59

RALPH JONES   15786   ACCT     232.36      71.15     161.21


              TOTALS          1821.31     688.66    1132.65


NOTES
A - NET PAY IS OUT OF BOUNDS. DO NOT ISSUE CHECK.
```

FIGURE 4-21   Example of Report of Pay Amounts from pay reports program.

Arrays are used to store data previously referenced by individual variable names. The arrays are both one- and two-dimensional. Conceptually, there are arrays for the department table, arrays for input data, and arrays for results.

1   The department table arrays consist of two one-dimensional arrays with five entries in each for number and name of each department.

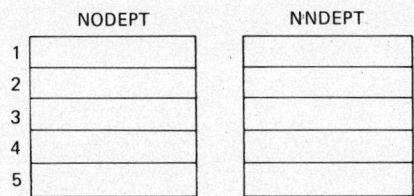

2   Arrays for input data. The use of input data arrays allows all input data to be stored so that the error report can be prepared separately and the output can be in a different order than the input. All arrays have 15 rows to accommodate 14 valid employee records plus a potential error case.

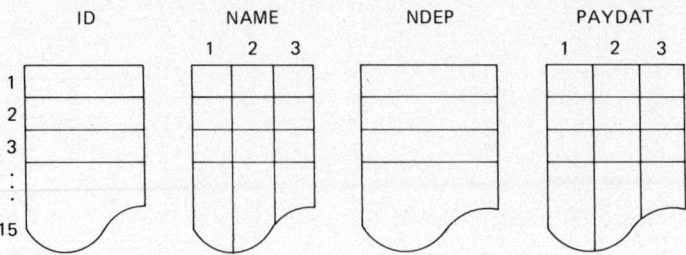

There is an array for identification numbers, a table for the three parts of each name, a number-of-department list, and a table for three different types of payroll data (previously called HRSWRK, WGRATE, and DEDUC). A reference to hours worked for the I*th* valid record is now PAYDAT(I,1).

3 Arrays of results. There are single-dimension, 15-element arrays for gross pay, total deductions, and net pay (called PAYCHK).

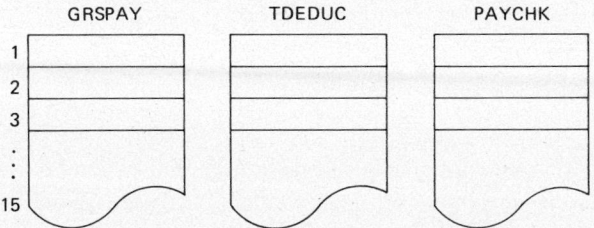

On input, data is assigned to rows in the different arrays by using the value of the valid input counter (NUM). Invalid data is not stored in the arrays. If the current value of NUM is 3, then a statement which reads ID(NUM), NDEP(NUM), etc. will place the ID in element 3 of the ID array, and NDEP in the third element of the array for number of department where employee works. If the data on input turns out to be invalid, the counter NUM does not change and the next input card is stored in the same locations, replacing the invalid input.

If a program attempts to store more data in arrays than has been allocated in the DIMENSION statement, there will be an error which may cause incorrect results or abnormal termination. Therefore, a program should be designed to prevent attempting to store too many data items in arrays. There are various methods for doing this. Note two cases in the sample program.

1 A specified number of data items to be stored. Since the program specifications define five departments, the department table arrays are dimensioned at five cells. The READ statement (line 12) reads and stores only five items by using NDEPTS as the termination value of the implied DO loop. NDEPTS is initialized at 5 (line 2).

2 An unspecified number of data items to be stored. Since the program description calls for an unspecified number of input data cards but not to exceed 14 accepted records, a count is established for accepted records which are stored in the various arrays. This count is tested against a limiting value. If more records are available to be read after the limit has been reached, an error message is printed and the program is aborted. Because the records are read directly into storage arrays rather than into temporary input locations, one extra storage position must be allocated in each array for a possible excess record in process. This is why the program has a limit of 14 accepted records and the arrays are dimensioned at 15.

The program makes use of implied DO loops for input and output. Review these:

		Lines
1	READ table of department names	12
2	PRINT table of department names	16
3	READ employee data	21
4	PRINT employee data (note that WRITE statement is in range of inner, nested DO loop)	52

In the print detail block, note should be made of the use of the local variable MATCH. The value of MATCH (line 49) is a function of the "outside" loop index (J); it does not change with the "inner" loop (I). To reduce execution time (to eliminate the necessity to reevaluate NODEPT(J) for each change in I) a local temporary variable has been used. Similarly, PAYNET (line 54) has been set so that PAYCHK(I) need be referenced only once, not twice, in line 56. In this simple program, these temporary variables are not needed to reduce execution time, but they are used to illustrate the technique of programming for efficiency.

The program uses input and output validation techniques similar to those used in prior programs; an additional technique is the printout of the table of department names. It is good style to print out tables such as these for visual validation. The validation of net pay (line 56) illustrates how to combat those classic $1,000,005.37 "computer errors" described in newspaper articles. It is always good style to test, if possible, critical output data to see if it is in a range of "reasonable" values.

In 1977 full FORTRAN (but not Subset FORTRAN), a constant or an expression may be used in the output list. Note how convenient it was to use this feature in line 83. The alternative would have been to establish a new temporary variable (TEMP = MAXEMP − 1) and print TEMP.

Statistical Program Example 4—Tables of Cumulative Normal Probability

This example illustrates the use of a DO loop in a computational procedure. In this case, the computation is numerical integration. As a review of this procedure, recall that integration means computing the area under a curve within an interval of the function. One approach to this is to divide the interval into small segments and compute the areas of each of these. For example:

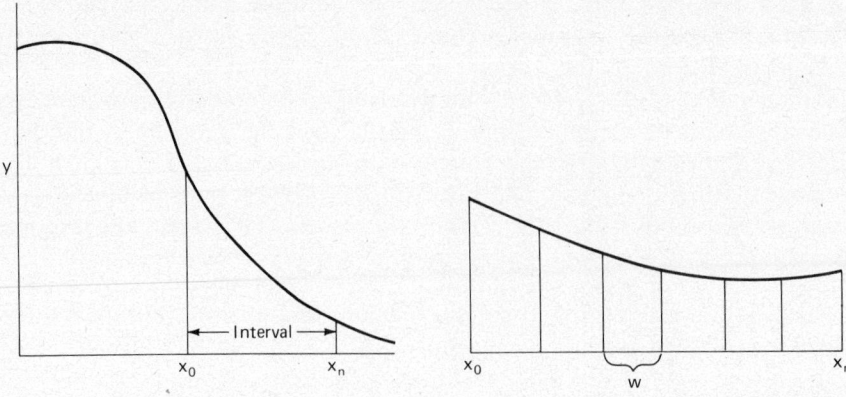

The heights of each segment are given by the ordinates of the curve; the base of each is width w on the x-axis; the curve at the top of each is approximated by a simple curve or straight line. If a straight line is used, then each segment is a trapezoid and the equation for the area is

$$a_n = \frac{y_{n-1} + y_n}{2} w$$

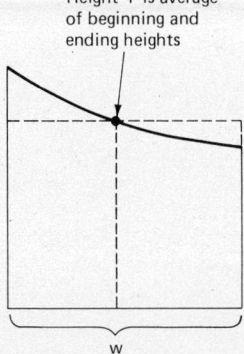

Height Y is average of beginning and ending heights

w

While this is a good approximation, it can be improved. If a second-degree polynomial (or parabola) is used, this gives rise to Simpson's rule, which is a very good approximation.

$$\text{Area} = \frac{w}{3} (y_0 + 4y_1 + 2y_2 + 4y_3 + \cdots + 4y_{n-1} + y_n)$$

(n must be an even number). The 4s and 2s and division by 3 arise from the area equation and the fact that interior ordinates are used many times in computing segment areas.

Problem Description for Statistical Example 4

The program is to calculate and print a normal probability table of Z values and corresponding probability of Z or less for positive values of Z. The positive Z values represent multiples of the standard deviation greater than the mean. The probability of Z or less represents the cumulative probability of an item being included in the range which contains all items up to Z standard deviations greater than the mean.

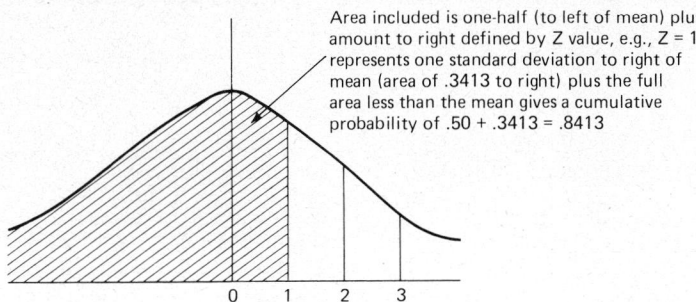

Area included is one-half (to left of mean) plus amount to right defined by Z value, e.g., Z = 1 represents one standard deviation to right of mean (area of .3413 to right) plus the full area less than the mean gives a cumulative probability of .50 + .3413 = .8413

0   1   2   3

The program produces a new table with appropriate headings for each valid input. The input defines the beginning of the table, the end of the table, and the interval between table entries for Z. The input is checked for invalid values—negative values or beginning value greater than ending value. An invalid value results in an error message with card number.

Equation: Probability $= \int_{-\infty}^{Z^*} f(Z) = .5 + \int_0^{Z^*} \frac{1}{2\pi} e^{-(X^2/2)}$

The area under $y = f(Z)$ in the interval 0 to Z^* is to be computed using Simpson's rule. The distance on the x axis between zero and the Z entry for which a probability is being computed is divided into 20 segments. The area is then computed using Simpson's rule with 20 values of y corresponding to the 20 values of x.

Program Documentation for Statistical Example 4

The documentation consists of a pseudocode program description (Figure 4-22), a program flowchart (Figure 4-23), a program listing (Figure 4-24), and an example input (Figure 4-25) and output (Figure 4-26).

Initialize problem counter (one problem per card)
READ start value, end value, and step size
  If out of data, go forward to Terminate
  If data-type error, increment problem counter, write error message and go back
    to READ
Increment problem counter
Validate data
  If invalid data, write error message, and go back to READ
WRITE table heading
Set ZSTAR (Z value being computed) to start value for first entry
Set X to zero
Compute size of 20 X increments from zero to ZSTAR
Initialize sums to zero
Compute 20 ordinates and save in array
Sum first and last ordinate
Sum even-numbered ordinates
Sum odd-numbered ordinates
Compute TOTSUM of first sum plus 2 times second sum plus 4 times third sum
*Probability equals 0.5 + (increment * TOTSUM)/3*
WRITE ZSTAR and probability
Increment ZSTAR by step size to set ZSTAR to next value of Z entry in table
Compare ZSTAR with end value for Z
  IF end value for Z not exceeded, go back to Set X
  ELSE go back to READ another data card
Terminate with message and card count

FIGURE 4-22 Pseudocode description of program for statistical example 4—normal probability tables.

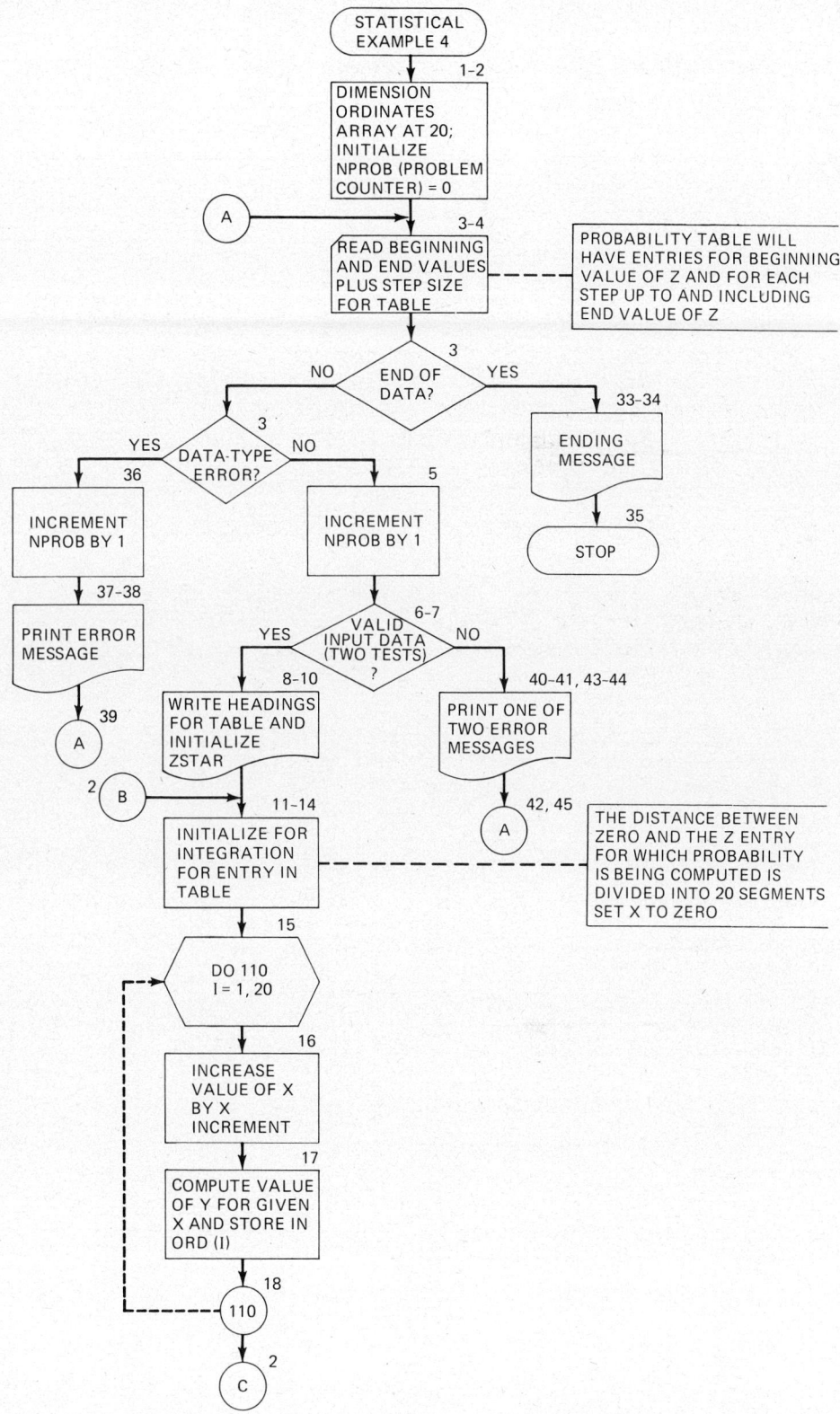

FIGURE 4-23 Program flowchart for statistical program example 4—normal probability tables. (Numbers next to symbols are line numbers from program listing.)

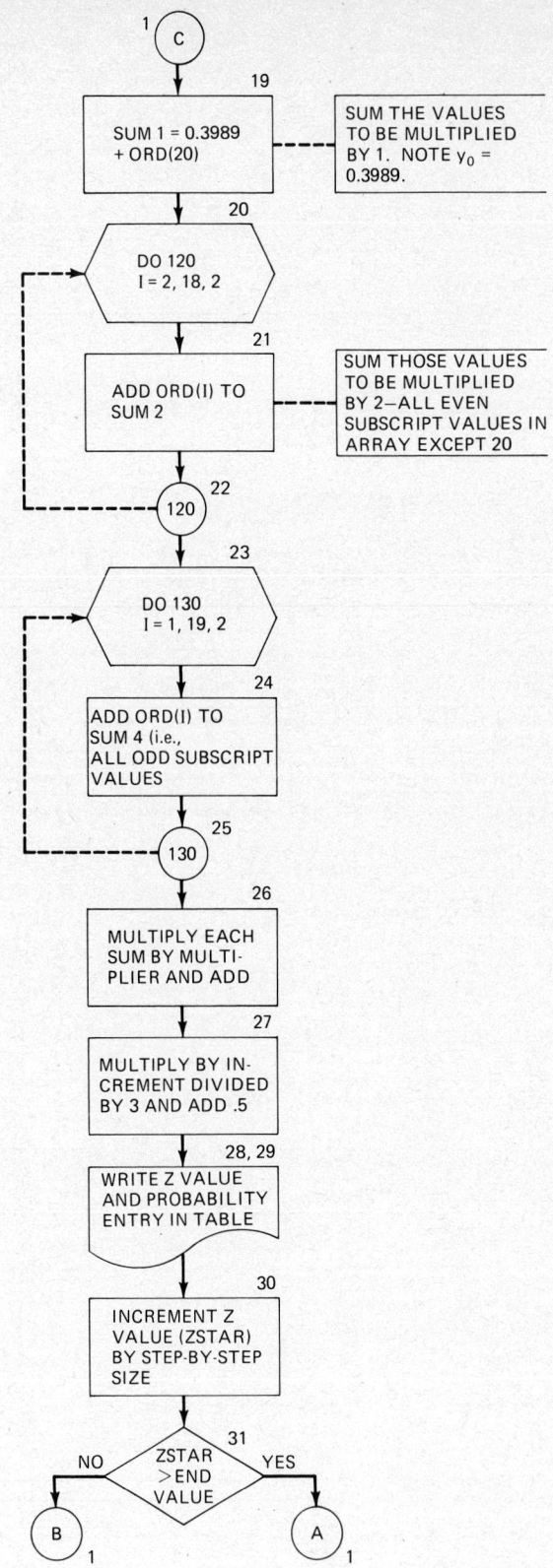

FIGURE 4-23 *(continued)*

```
********** PROGRAM IDENTIFICATION **********
*                                                                    *
*           PROBABILITIES OF VALUES LESS THAN Z (Z GT 0) FOR         *
*           NORMAL PROBABILITY TABLES, BETWEEN LIMITS, ARE           *
*           GENERATED USING SIMPSON'S RULE FOR NUMERICAL INTEGRATION.*
*           WRITTEN 04/30/77 BY T. HOFFMANN                          *
*                                                                    *
**********************************************************************
*                                                                    *
********** VARIABLE IDENTIFICATION **********
*                                                                    *
*****                    ARRAY NAMES                            *****
*                                                                    *
*           ORD     = ORDINATES OF THE NORMAL CURVE                  *
*                                                                    *
*****                 SIMPLE VARIABLES                          *****
*                                                                    *
*           NPROB   = PROBLEM COUNTER                                *
*           VALU1   = STARTING VALUE FOR TABLE                       *
*           VALU2   = ENDING VALUE FOR TABLE                         *
*           STPSIZ  = STEP SIZE (I.E. TABLE INCREMENT)               *
*           ZSTAR   = UPPER BOUND OF INTEGRATION INTERVAL            *
*           X       = ABCISSA VALUES IN SIMPSON'S RULE               *
*           XINCR   = INTEGRATION INTERVAL                           *
*           SUM1    = SUM OF FIRST AND LAST ORDINATE                 *
*           SUM2    = SUM OF EVEN ORDINATES                          *
*           SUM4    = SUM OF ODD ORDINATES                           *
*           TOTSUM  = TOTAL OF SUMS                                  *
*           PROB    = NORMAL PROBABILITY VALUE                       *
*                                                                    *
**********************************************************************
*                                                                    *
********** ALGORITHM - SIMPSON'S RULE **********
*                                                                    *
* PROB=.5+(XINCR/3)*(ORD(0)+4*ORD(1)+2*ORD(2)+...+4*ORD(N-1)+ORD(N)) *
*                                                                    *
**********************************************************************
*                                                                    *
********** STORAGE ALLOCATION **********
*                                                                    *
1.        DIMENSION ORD(20)
**********************************************************************
*                                                                    *
********** INITIALIZATION AND INPUT BLOCK          BLOCK 0000
*                                                                    *
2.        NPROB = 0
3.      6 READ(5,2,ERR=901,END=201) VALU1,VALU2,STPSIZ
4.      2 FORMAT(3F4.2)
*                                                                    *
*         INCREMENT PROBLEM COUNTER                                  *
*                                                                    *
5.        NPROB = NPROB + 1
6.        IF(VALU1.LT.0.0) GOTO 920
7.        IF(VALU1.GT.VALU2) GOTO 910
8.        WRITE(6,11)
9.     11 FORMAT(1H1,5X,'NORMAL PROBABILITY TABLE'//6X,
       1     'Z VALUE    PROBABILITY OF'/,18X,'Z OR LESS'/)
10.       ZSTAR = VALU1
*                                                                    *
**********************************************************************
*                                                                    *
********** COMPUTE PROBABILITY VALUES              BLOCK 0100
*                                                                    *
11.   101 X = 0.0
12.       XINCR = ZSTAR/20.0
13.       SUM2 = 0.0
14.       SUM4 = 0.0
*                                                                    *
*         COMPUTE 20 ORDINATES IN TABLE INTERVAL                     *
*                                                                    *
15.       DO 110 I = 1,20
16.         X = X + XINCR
17.         ORD(I) = 0.3989*EXP(-X*X/2.0)
18.   110 CONTINUE
19.       SUM1 = 0.3989 + ORD(20)
20.       DO 120 I= 2,18,2
21.         SUM2 = SUM2 + ORD(I)
22.   120 CONTINUE
```

FIGURE 4-24 Listing of FORTRAN program for statistical program example 4—normal probability tables.

```
23.          DO 130 I = 1,19,2
24.             SUM4 = SUM4 + ORD(I)
25.      130 CONTINUE
26.          TOTSUM = SUM1 + 2.0*SUM2 + 4.0*SUM4
27.          PROB = 0.5 + XINCR*TOTSUM/3.0
28.          WRITE(6,108) ZSTAR,PROB
29.      108 FORMAT(7X,F6.2,7X,F6.4)                                    *
     *                                                                 *
     *              INCREMENT TABLE VALUE AND REAPPLY RULE             *
     *                                                                 *
30.          ZSTAR = ZSTAR + STPSIZ
31.          IF(ZSTAR.LE.VALU2) GOTO 101
     *                                                                 *
     *              GO BACK TO READ NEXT PROBLEM                       *
     *                                                                 *
32.          GOTO 6
     *                                                                 *
     ******************************************************************
     *                                                                 *
     *********          TERMINATION BLOCK                   BLOCK 0200
     *                                                                 *
33.      201 WRITE(6,202) NPROB
34.      202 FORMAT(1H1,'PROBABILITY PROGRAM TERMINATED NORMALLY.'/
         1     5X,I3,' DATA CARDS READ.')
35.          STOP                                                      *
     *                                                                 *
     ******************************************************************
     *                                                                 *
     *********          ERROR MESSAGE BLOCK                 BLOCK 0900
     *                                                                 *
36.      901 NPROB = NPROB + 1
37.          WRITE(6,914) NPROB
38.      914 FORMAT(1H0,'***** ERROR. CANNOT UNDERSTAND DATA CARD NUMBER',I3)
     *                                                                 *
39.          GOTO 998
     *                                                                 *
40.      910 WRITE(6,907) NPROB,VALU1,VALU2
41.      907 FORMAT(1H0,'***** ERROR IN DATA. CARD NUMBER',I3/
         1     ' STARTING VALUE OF TABLE,',F6.2,
         2     ', MUST BE LESS THAN ENDING VALUE,',F6.2)
     *                                                                 *
42.          GOTO 998                                                  *
     *                                                                 *
43.      920 WRITE(6,905) NPROB,VALU1
44.      905 FORMAT(1H0,'***** ERROR IN DATA CARD NUMBER',I3/
         1     ' STARTING VALUE SHOULD BE POSITIVE, NOT,'F6.2)
     *                                                                 *
     *              GO BACK TO READ NEXT PROBLEM                       *
     *                                                                 *
45.      998 GOTO 6                                                    *
     *                                                                 *
46.          END
```

FIGURE 4-24   *(continued)*

FIGURE 4-25   Annotated input test data for statistical problem 4.

```
        NORMAL  PROBABILITY  TABLE

        Z VALUE     PROBABILITY OF
                      Z OR LESS

            0           .5000
          .25           .5987
          .50           .6914
          .75           .7733
         1.00           .8413
         1.25           .8943
         1.50           .9331
         1.75           .9599
         2.00           .9772
         2.25           .9877
         2.50           .9937
         2.75           .9970
         3.00           .9986

  ***** ERROR IN DATA CARD NUMBER  2
  STARTING VALUE SHOULD BE POSITIVE, NOT, -1.00

  ***** ERROR. CANNOT UNDERSTAND DATA CARD NUMBER  3

  ***** ERROR IN DATA. CARD NUMBER  4
  STARTING VALUE OF TABLE,  2.50, MUST BE LESS THAN ENDING VALUE,  1.50
```

```
  NORMAL  PROBABILITY  TABLE

  Z VALUE     PROBABILITY OF
                Z OR LESS

     .25          .5987
```

```
  PROBABILITY PROGRAM TERMINATED NORMALLY.
       5 DATA CARDS READ.
```

FIGURE 4-26 Example output from statistical program 4—normal probability tables.

Notes on Statistical Example 4

In this case, the variable identification block has been augmented by a special section for listing array names. An algorithm block has been added to explain the methodology. Also a storage allocation block has been inserted for DI-MENSION statements.

The initialization and input block sets counters, reads a data card and checks it for several kinds of potential errors. In this problem, most of the code in this block is executed once for each input card and initializes the upper value of the table for each card read.

The computation block implements Simpson's rule by computing twenty equally spaced ordinates and saving them in an array. (The zeroth ordinate is known to be 0.3989 from setting Z to 0 in the normal equation.) Three partial sums are created: one for those ordinates multiplied by 1 (zeroth and last), a second for the even-numbered ordinates (those to be multiplied by 2), and the third for the odd-numbered ones (those to be multiplied by 4). Note the use of the DO loops and the values of the DO parameters in lines 15 and 20. The total sum is computed (line 26) by multiplying the partial sums by their appropriate values and adding. A less efficient way of doing this would have been to put a 2 multiplier and a 4 multiplier in front of ORD in lines 19 and 21 respectively. This would have caused eighteen multiplications. (Why?)

Programming Exercises

Description of Assignment

Select one or more problems (or take the problem(s) assigned to you by the instructor). Use DO loops in the program to process data and to perform input and output of subscripted variables. Use a DATA statement for initialization where appropriate. Follow the style guidelines and prepare the following:

1 Pseudocode description

2 Program flowchart

3 Program listing

4 List of test data and expected results. Test for both valid and invalid data where appropriate.

5 Sample output including results of testing of all error conditions.

Mathematics and Statistics

1 For each of the following sets of n data points (X, Y), compute the correlation coefficients (r).

$$r = \frac{n\Sigma XY - (\Sigma X)(\Sigma Y)}{\sqrt{[n\Sigma X^2 - (\Sigma X)^2][n\Sigma Y^2 - (\Sigma Y)^2]}}$$

Set 1		Set 2	
X	Y	X	Y
34.22	102.43	20	27.1
39.87	100.93	30	28.9
41.85	97.43	40	30.6
43.23	97.81	50	32.3
40.06	98.32	60	33.7
53.29	98.32	70	35.6
53.29	100.07	80	37.2
54.14	97.08		
49.12	91.59		
40.71	94.85		
55.15	94.65		

2 Pascal's triangle is a set of numbers having some very interesting properties. (Actually, Omar Khayyam wrote about them much before Pascal.) Arranged in

the usual manner (as shown below), each number in the interior is the sum of the numbers on either side of it in the row above. Any row (labeling the top as row zero) contains the coefficients of the expansion $(a + b)^n$ or the ordered set of combinations of n things taken m (0, 1, 2, etc. from left to right) at a time. Write a program to compute and print the first 11 rows ($n = 0$ through 10) of Pascal's triangle. Printing need not be in the symmetric triangle form.

n							
0				1			
1			1		1		
2		1		2		1	
3	1		3		3		1
etc.				etc.			

3 Write a program which uses Simpson's rule to evaluate the gamma function (which is the generalization of the factorial) for the following set of values: $n = 0.5, 1.7, 2.0,$ and 1.5. *HINT:* Since $\log \frac{1}{x}$ where $x = 0$ is undefined, use a very small number in place of zero, such as 1.0E-10.

$$\text{gamma} = \int_0^1 \left(\log \frac{1}{x} \right)^{n-1} \qquad \text{for } n > 0$$

Business and Economics

4 Prepare tables of the form given below which shows the size of a loan that is possible from different monthly payments ($100 to $500 in $50 increments) for a given number of months (m) at annual interest rates of 7, 8, 9, 10, 11, and 12 percent. Assume the monthly rate is one-twelfth the yearly rate. Read in m as 240 and 300.

TERM IN MONTHS   NNN   *NESTED DO LOOP*

12898.25

Monthly payments	Annual interest rate				
	.07	.08	.09	. . .	.12
$100	XXXXX.	XXXXX.			
150	XXXXX.				
200					
250					
300					
.					
.					
.					
500					

5 Prepare a table of the form shown below for given interest rates (i) and 1-year increments from 1 through 10 years showing the effect on an initial amount of $100 compounded annually, quarterly, monthly, weekly (assume exactly 52 weeks per year), daily (assume each year has 365 days), and continuously. Use i values of 7, 9, and 12 percent. (See problem 2-4 for formulas.)

NN INTEREST RATE

| Year | Frequency | | | | | |
	1	4	12	52	365	Cont.
1	XXXX.XX	XXXX.XX				
2	XXXX.XX					
.						
.						
.						
10						

6 A business executive has the following portfolio of stocks at the start of a period and makes the given set of transactions during the period. Prepare a report showing her starting position, a summary of her transactions, and her final position. *HINT:* Reference the stocks by number rather than by name.

STARTING PORTFOLIO

Stock number	Stock	Shares	Price/share
1	International Harvester	100	33.50
2	White Consolidated	200	27.50
3	Texaco	100	29.25
4	Northern Natural Gas	300	44.00
5	National Distillers	500	24.25
6	Public Service of Colorado	200	19.75
7	Middle So. Utilities	200	16.25

TRANSACTIONS

Number	Stock	Action	Shares	Price
3	Texaco	Buy	100	28.75
8	Anheuser-Busch	Buy	200	23.00
4	Northern Natural	Sell	200	45.25
7	Middle So. Utilities	Buy	100	17.00
9	IBM	Buy	100	261.50
1	International Harvester	Sell	100	32.00
3	Texaco	Buy	100	29.50
6	Public Service of Colorado	Sell	200	20.25
10	Control Data Corp.	Buy	100	21.25

FINAL PRICES

Stock	Price	Stock	Price
International Harvester	32.50	Public Service of Colorado	20.00
White Consolidated	30.00	Middle So. Utilities	17.00
Texaco	28.50	Control Data	22.00
Anheuser-Busch	22.25	IBM	255.25
Northern Natural Gas	47.50	National Distillers	26.25

TFST MON
FINAL (COMP)

Science and Engineering

7 A frequently encountered computer science problem is to sort an array of numbers into descending order of magnitude. One procedure for doing this is called the bubble-sort technique. The steps in it are as follows:

(*a*) Compare the first and second number. If the second is larger, switch the order of the numbers.

(*b*) Take the next number in the array and compare it to its predecessor. If it is larger, switch positions and compare it to the next predecessor making a switch if it is larger. Repeat until the selected number is not larger than a predecessor or it is in the first position.

(*c*) Take the next number after the previously selected one and repeat step 2 until the last number has been selected and compared.

For example, the original set is 8, 9, 5, 11, 7. The arrows show exchanges; the dotted lines show comparisons without exchanges.

Column	0	1	2	3	4	5	6
Array	8	9	9	9	9	11	11
	9	8	8	8	11	9	9
	5	5	5	11	8	8	8
	11	11	11	5	5	5	7
	7	7	7	7	7	7	5

Each column shows the array contents after the comparison and/or switch. The underlined number is the one which had been selected for comparison with its predecessor.

Write a program to perform a bubble sort on any set of less than 100 numbers. Use it to sort the following sets of data:

	Set number	
One	Two	Three
66,	−6	.156
85	−87	.951
86	−56	.537
45	−34	.015
77	2	.126
74	6	.672
57	43	
49	18	
62	85	

8 Prime numbers are those divisible without a remainder only by themselves (and one). To find all the primes less than 1000, one can start with two and divide all higher numbers by it, eliminating all which have no remainder and then moving to the next larger which has not been eliminated and dividing by it in the same manner. This is a straightforward method based upon the definition. It is very time-consuming, however, because division is lengthy. A quicker way is to use the *Sieve* *of Eratosthenes* procedure. Fill an array with values from 1 to 1000. Starting with the second entry, set to zero all multiples of it in the array (all multiples of 2). Proceed to the next nonzero number and repeat the process, etc. At the conclusion of this all the nonzero entries will be prime numbers. Write a program to implement this procedure and print out a table of primes.

9   Data is often more meaningful if graphed. Write a program to both tabulate and graph the curve of damped vibration,

$$y = e^{-nx} \sin mx$$

for the following values:

n	m	x Range
0.2	1	0 to 3π
0.2	2	$-\pi$ to 2π
0.3	3	0 to 2π

HINT: Create the graph sideways on the paper, i.e., X is plotted on the vertical direction and Y is plotted across (horizontally) the page. Use an array of one-character variables set to blanks and insert an asterisk in the appropriate Y position for each X.

Humanities and Social Sciences

10   Data from a questionnaire has been punched into cards as follows:

Column	Data
1–2	Age: 0 = no response
3	Sex: 1 = female, 2 = male
4	Homeowner: 1 = yes, 2 = no, 0 = no response
5–7	Income (in thousands): 999 = none, 900 = no response
8	Political preference: 1 = Democrat, 2 = Republican, 3 = Other, 0 = no response

Tally responses and nonresponses and prepare the following tables:

TABLE I

Age, years	Income (in 000)				
	Less than 5	5–9	10–15	15–19	Over 19
Less than 20					
20–29					
30–39					
40–49					
50–59					
60–69					
Over 69					

TABLE II

Age	Sex		Homeowner		Politics		
	F	M	Yes	No	Dem.	Rep.	Other
Less than 20							
20–29							
30–39							
40–49							
50–59							
60–69							
Over 69							

TABLE III

Nonresponses
    Age
    Homeowner
    Income
    Political preference

DATA

Age	Sex	Homeowner	Income	Politics
35	1	1	25	1
19	2	0	18	3
17	1	2	999	3
39	2	1	35	2
54	2	1	17	1
73	2	2	900	1
27	2	1	27	2
72	1	2	8	0
0	2	2	40	2
43	1	1	25	1
55	2	1	27	1
39	2	2	43	3
32	1	0	11	3
23	1	2	900	0
66	1	1	7	1

11 One step in preparing a concordance is to search the text for a selected phrase or word. Write a program which will read a paragraph, calculate the frequency of a selected word, and print a summary. Paragraphs are limited to 800 characters, including spaces and punctuation, appearing on 10 cards. The paragraph is indented 5 spaces. *CAUTION:* Only individual words which match the key word are to be counted, not longer words which contain the key letters. *HINT:* Establish an array of 800 elements and read the characters of the paragraph into it using 80A1 per card. Read in the key word as single characters into another array including a beginning and ending blank as part of the key word. Test for the series of letters, e.g., blank, T, H, E, blank, from the key word array. Watch out for situations where the key word is followed by a period.

Key word: THE

Paragraph:

Now is the time for all good men to come to the aid of their party. But let us not lose heart for there are thirty theocratic parties to console us.

Key word: LOVE

Paragraph:

Love is patient and kind; it is not jealous or conceited or proud; love is not ill-mannered or selfish or irritable; love does not keep a record of wrongs.

12 Given the following data on population and immigration for the United States, produce a table showing, for each decade, beginning population, total increase, net immigration, and percent of increase attributable to immigration.

Period	Beginning population (000)	Net immigration (000)
1870–1880	39,818	2,274
1880–1890	50,156	4,490
1890–1900	62,948	2,531
1900–1910	75,995	5,289
1910–1920	91,972	3,201
1920–1930	105,711	3,089
1930–1940	122,775	1,067
1940–1950	131,669	875
1950–1960	151,326	2,660
1960–1970	179,323	3,282

General

13 A matrix contains the number of A's, B's, etc., earned by each student. Each course is four credits. Write a program to calculate the grade point (A = 4, B = 3, etc.) average for each student and the average student grade point.

Student name	Number of courses for each grade				
	A	B	C	D	E
George Thiel	0	8	2	2	1
Craig Ebert	3	4	9	1	0
Dean Greco	1	5	3	0	0
Paul Hogan	5	8	9	0	1
David Sellman	7	1	0	2	0
Bonnie Link	5	3	3	1	0
Susan Frye	9	6	4	4	0
Larry Maxwell	3	8	2	0	0
Kathy Adams	7	1	4	2	1
Jill Swift	3	3	4	2	0
Rebecca Young	7	5	2	0	1
Dan Johnson	1	1	1	0	0
Mark Snyder	1	3	0	2	0
Steve Fisher	2	4	0	2	0
Sally Crown	6	6	7	1	0

14 Given any amount of a restaurant check up to $25 and any amount tendered up to $40, find the quantity and denomination of paper money and coins to return as change. Print the result in order from smallest to largest denomination. Print an error message if the amount tendered is less than the check.

AMOUNTS

Check	Tendered
$ 2.13	$20.00
6.15	5.00
3.37	3.37
21.95	20.00
17.44	30.00

HINT: Results are obtained from largest to smallest, so save the results in an array for printing in small to large order.

15 Reprogram problem 13 of Chapter 3 and print the conversions in groups ordered by their codes as 3, 2, 1, -1, -2, -3.

CHAPTER

FORTRAN
SUBPROGRAMS
AND THE CASE
PROGRAM STRUCTURE

A subprogram is a separate program unit which is used (called) by a main program or by other subprograms. Some subprograms are included in the FORTRAN language as intrinsic functions. But the intrinsic functions cover only a few common mathematical functions; a programmer may find it desirable to write blocks of code which perform complex or specialized functions. Also, it is often useful to partition a program into individual units that can be tested separately. Since subprograms are separate, independent program units, they can be combined with any program. The subprogram capability is thus a very important feature of the FORTRAN language. It is implemented in two different ways: the function subprogram and the subroutine subprogram, both of which are explained in the chapter.

The three basic programming structures (sequence, selection, and repetition) have been presented in prior chapters. The sequence structure of one statement following another was described in Chapter 1. The selection structure for choosing between two program paths as implemented by the FORTRAN IF was explained in Chapter 2. The repetition programming structure using the DO loop was presented in Chapter 4. Although all programming may be performed using only the three basic structures, it is convenient to use a fourth programming pattern, the case structure, which programs a selection among multiple alternatives. The FORTRAN implementation of the case structure using the computed GOTO also is described in the chapter.

Characteristics of Subprograms

As background for understanding the specific types of subprograms, the purpose and use of subprograms are explained and some general characteristics are described.

Purpose and Use of Subprograms

The purpose of subprograms is to simplify programming. Subprograms aid in programming simplifications in two major ways:

1 *Reusable program elements* Processing functions that will be used more than once in the program (or used by more than one program) are written once and then used by programs needing the processing. Examples are subprograms to:
(*a*) Generate random numbers
(*b*) Calculate statistics (such as mean, variance, etc.)
(*c*) Sort data into ascending or descending order

2 *Decomposition of programming tasks* Sections of the program are written as independent subprograms in order to reduce the complexity of the program design, to aid in testing the program, and to allow different programmers to work on different subprograms concurrently. For example, the instructions to print a report (which may be fairly complex) may be organized into a subprogram separate from the instructions to compute the data to be printed in the report.

The first objective of reusable program elements can be achieved because each subprogram is treated as a separate program. This independence is reflected in the following features of a subprogram.

1 It can be compiled separately from the program using it.

2 The variable names in the subprogram refer to different storage locations (in other words, are different variables) than variables with the same names in programs which use the subprogram. If it is desired that they be the same, special instructions are available to make the names refer to the same storage locations.

3 Use of a subprogram is achieved by a simple program statement in the using (calling) program.

4 Transfer of data between a program using a subprogram (a calling program) and the subprogram is specified by special instructions in the calling program and the subprogram.

The second objective of decomposing programming into smaller, simpler tasks is also possible because the subprograms can be written and tested separately. In this approach, a large program is written as a main control program (the main program) which uses (calls) subprograms. In other words, the main control program ties together the major segments of the program which are written and tested as separate programs.

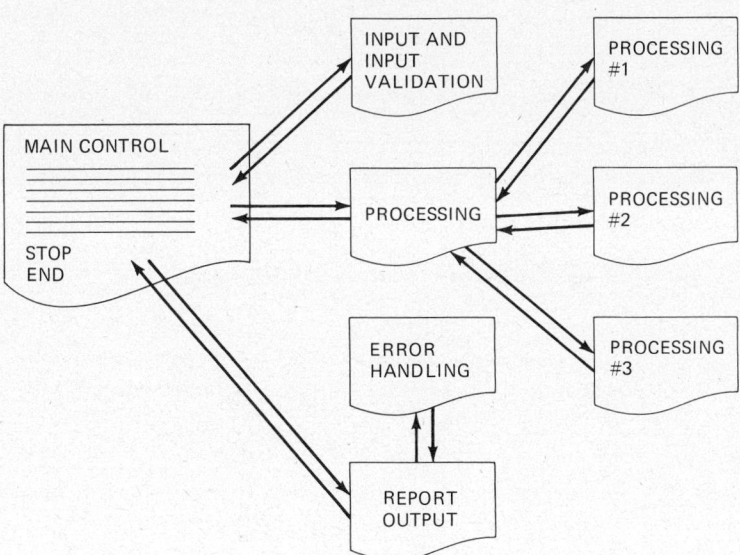

When executing a program which invokes user-written subprograms, the subprograms are included with the main program. The main program and each subprogram has an END as the last statement, so each is compiled separately, but they are enclosed by a set of job control statements which defines them as belonging together in the completed program. For example, in a submission using a card deck:

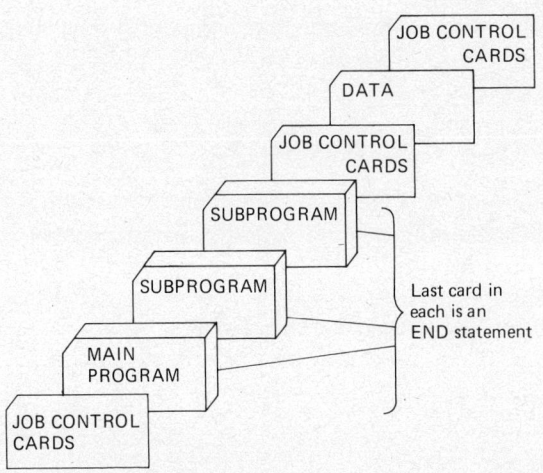

When a large program uses a number of subprograms, it may assist in documentation to list in the comments at the beginning of each subprogram the program units which call upon the subprogram. This is especially helpful if the subprogram is altered, replaced, etc.

Checking on Availability of Prewritten Subprograms

It is very important for the programmer to be aware of the extensive libraries of prewritten subprograms that are easily available for use as part of a program being written. These are in addition to the standard intrinsic FORTRAN functions. A university computer center will usually have several hundred such subprograms either developed by the center or obtained from an outside supplier. For example, a well-known library of subroutines is the IMSL (International Mathematical and Statistical Libraries, Inc.) library of mathematics and statistics subroutines. There are over 400 prewritten subprograms classified as follows:

Analysis of Experimental Design Data

Basic Statistics

Categorized Data Analysis

Differential Equations: Quadrature; Differentiation

Eigensystem Analysis

Forecasting; Econometrics; Time Series

Generation and Testing of Random Numbers; Goodness of Fit

Interpolation; Approximations; Smoothing

Linear Algebraic Equations

Mathematical and Statistical Special Functions

Non-Parametric Statistics

Observation Structure

Regression Analysis

Sampling

Utility Functions

Vector, Matrix Arithmetic

Zeros and Extrema; Linear Programming

It is a wise procedure to always check on the availability of a prewritten routine before taking the time to design, code, and test a new subprogram. Most computer centers maintain a directory of available subprograms plus documentation manuals describing each and the exact procedure for calling them.

Function Subprogram

The function subprogram is the method by which a programmer can write specialized functions. The function is coded as a separate program unit. It is assigned a name by the programmer so that the function can be called using the name as a reference. A function subprogram is called into use by writing the name followed by a list of values (variable names or constants) to be used by the function—the values separated by commas and enclosed in parentheses. The list of values are termed the arguments of the function. For example, a programmer may write a small program routine to find the largest value in a single-dimension array of n elements. The programmer decides to keep the routine as a separate program unit by defining it as a function subprogram and assigning it the name RAYMAX. Another program unit, such as a main program, may use the RAYMAX function by including the function name RAYMAX followed by the arguments enclosed in parentheses in a statement. Assuming the RAYMAX function is to operate on array ALPHA with N entries, the function call would read RAYMAX(ALPHA,N). A function call is not written alone; it is part of a statement. Two separate examples illustrate the way the example RAYMAX function subprogram is invoked by statements in the using (calling) program.

EXAMPLE 1

Arguments of the function

X = RAYMAX (ALPHA, N)+ 6 . 0

This example calculates the maximum value from the N values in array ALPHA, adds 6.0 to it, and stores the result in X.

EXAMPLE 2

I F   (B I G . LE . RAYMAX (Y , 1 0))   GOTO   1 2 0

This statement compares the value of BIG with the largest value in the 10 values in array Y. If BIG is less than or equal to that value, control goes to statement 120.

The statements which invoke the function are in the calling program. The program unit which does the processing is a separate subprogram. The calling program statement identifies the subprogram to be used and defines the data to be used (normally with the argument list). The function subprogram operates upon the data in the argument list and transfers a single value back to the calling program in place of the function call.

The function subprogram is written as a separate subprogram unit beginning with an identifying statement. This first statement consists of the word FUNCTION followed by the programmer-assigned name of the function and an argument list of variables required by the function with the variables separated by commas and the list enclosed in parentheses. The beginning letter of the function name indicates the type of the result to be returned from the function (integer or real). When the function is used, the value of the variables in the argument list in the calling statement of the using program are used in place of each of the corresponding variables in the argument list of the subprogram. For this reason, the variables in the argument list in the function definition are termed dummy variables; they are replaced by the values of the actual variables in the argument list of the calling statement.

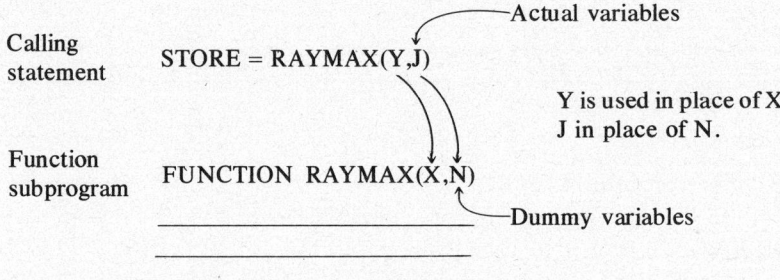

Calling statement   STORE = RAYMAX(Y,J)   —Actual variables

Y is used in place of X
J in place of N.

Function subprogram   FUNCTION RAYMAX(X,N)   —Dummy variables

The actual argument list must correspond in number of values and type (real or integer) with the dummy argument list.

The processing program statements follow the function naming statement. One or more of the assignment statements in the subprogram must define the function name as the result variable, e.g., function name = expression. An example of such a statement for the RAYMAX function is RAYMAX = BIG shown below:

Outline	Example	
FUNCTION f(X₁,X₂,...,Xₙ)	FUNCTION RAYMAX (X,N)	
_____	DIMENSION X(100)	
_____	BIG=-9.99E-10	
_____	DO 100 I=1,N	Function subprogram
_____	BIG=AMAX1(X(I),BIG)	
	100 CONTINUE	
function name = expression	RAYMAX=BIG	
RETURN	RETURN	
END	END	

In the example RAYMAX function subprogram, there is an array named X and the number of entries in the array is N. Any array used in the subprogram must be dimensioned in the subprogram, so array X is dimensioned in the example at a maximum of 100.

The RETURN statement is put at the logical end (or ends if there is more than one logical end) of the function subprogram. It signals that control is to return to the program from which the transfer to the subprogram was made. The END statement is required as the last statement or physical end of the subprogram. The END statement implies the RETURN statement, so the RETURN is optional if it would logically be the last statement before the END (except in older FORTRANs, which require RETURN before END).

EXAMPLE
As a simple case to illustrate both the form of the calling program and the form of the function, a simple program to read two values from a card, sum them, and print the two inputs plus the sum is written with a function subprogram to perform the summing operation.

Calling program	Function subprogram
READ*, A, B	FUNCTION ADDF (X, Y)
SUM = ADDF (A, B)	ADDF = X + Y
PRINT*, A, B, SUM	RETURN
STOP	END
END	

If the calling program reads a value of 4.0 for A and 3.5 for B, these values are provided as argument values to the function ADDF which sums them (uses the value for A in place of X and the value for B in place of Y) and returns the sum of 7.5 to be stored in SUM by the calling program.

EXAMPLE
Several programs may need to calculate the economic order quantity. This is therefore to be written as a function subprogram. The economic order quantity (EOQ) is calculated from the formula:

$$EOQ = \sqrt{\frac{24VS}{AC}}$$

where V = average monthly usage in units
S = setup or order cost
A = carrying cost expressed as a decimal
C = variable cost per unit
The EOQ is the quantity calculated by the formula except that, for this program, it must not be less than 1 month's average usage nor more than 12 months' average usage. If it exceeds the 12 months' supply, the EOQ is set to

12 months' supply; if the EOQ is less than 1 month's supply, EOQ is set equal to 1 month's supply. The function subprogram is shown in Figure 5-1.

    In order to make use of the EOQ formula function program in a statement, it is necessary only to write EOQ (a_1, a_2, a_3, a_4), where the a's stand for actual real arguments (variables or constants) used in place of the dummy real arguments V, S, A, and C of the subprogram. For example:

ORDER = SPECL + EOQ (USAGE, SETUP, CARRY, UNITC)

This statement will obtain the EOQ value using the values for USAGE, SETUP, CARRY, and UNITC as factors in the formula. The single value returned, the EOQ, is used in the replacement statement.

SUMMARY OF SPECIFICATIONS FOR FUNCTION SUBPROGRAM

Notation

    f = function name
    e = expression
    $x_1, x_2, \ldots, x_n$ = dummy arguments of the function
    $a_1, a_2, \ldots, a_n$ = actual calling arguments of the function

Where defined	Externally defined in a separately compiled independent subprogram
How defined	FUNCTION $f(x_1, x_2, \ldots, x_n)$ $f = e$ (at least one statement of this form in program) RETURN (at each logical exit from program) END
How named	Same as variable name—up to six characters, first letter determines type, etc.
How called into use	Appearance of name in an expression $v = f(a_1, a_2, \ldots, a_n)$
Number of outputs	One
Restrictions on form of calling argument	Type, number, and order of calling arguments must agree with the dummy arguments of the definition; argument may be a variable name, subscripted variable, array name, or expression; must have at least one argument

Self-testing Exercise 5-1

1 What do the following programs do?

```
*****  MAIN  PROGRAM  ******          FUNCTION  SUM (X)
       DIMENSION  A (100)             DIMENSION  X (100)
       READ  (5, 700)  A              SUM = 0.0
700    FORMAT  (10F8.0)               DO  100  I = 1, 100
       ANS = SQRT  (SUM (A))             SUM = SUM + X (I)
       WRITE  (6, 700)  ANS      100  CONTINUE
       STOP                           RETURN
       END                            END
```

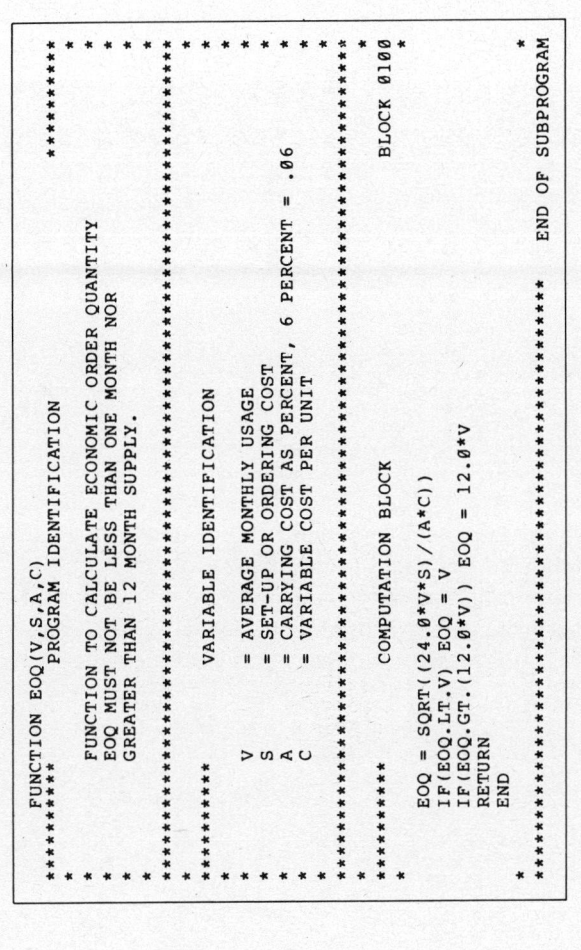

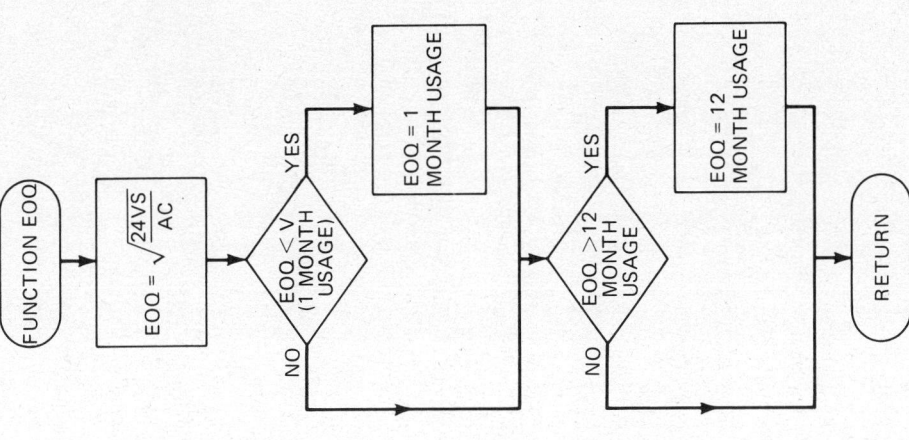

FIGURE 5-1 Function subprogram to calculate economic order quantity.

2 A function is defined as IBOY(X,A,J). What is the type of the result returned by the function? What type are the variables in the calling argument list?

3 Write a function subprogram to find the positive, real root (if it exists) of a quadratic equation. The a term is always positive for this problem. The formula is:

$$\text{ROOT} = \frac{-b + \sqrt{b^2 - 4ac}}{2a}$$

If there are no real, positive roots ($b^2 - 4ac$ is negative), make the answer equal 0.

4 Write a main program statement that uses the function in problem 3.

5 Write a function subprogram to calculate the difference between yearly interest earned using two interest rates for a given amount invested.

6 Write a main program statement to use the function in problem 5. Use variable names XINT1, XINT2, and AMOUNT for main program variables.

Subroutine

A function subprogram always has an argument list and returns a single value to the program statement where it is used. The *subroutine* subprogram removes these restrictions. The subroutine may have arguments, but it does not require them. It does not automatically return a value to the main program.

The subroutine is a separate program which is defined by the word SUBROUTINE followed by a name and dummy arguments (but no dummy arguments are required). The name, up to six characters, has no type (integer or real) significance.

$\text{SUBROUTINE } f(x_1, x_2, \ldots, x_n)$ or $\text{SUBROUTINE } f$

_____
_____
_____
_____
_____
_____

RETURN
END

The arguments of the subroutine definition may include dummy array names as well as single variable names. If a dummy array name is used, the dummy array name must be dimensioned in the subroutine.

The subroutine is used by writing a CALL statement. If an argument list is needed, the actual arguments to be used have the same type and are listed in the same order as the definition or dummy arguments. A subroutine can itself call other subroutines or functions.

CALL $f(a_1, a_2, \ldots, a_n)$ for subroutine defined as having an argument list

or   CALL f for subroutine defined as without argument list

EXAMPLE

To illustrate the form of both the calling program and the subroutine subprogram, the simple example will be used of a program which reads values for A and B, calls a subroutine to sum them, and prints the values for A, B, and the sum.

Calling program	Subroutine
READ * , A , B	SUBROUTINE SUMIT (X , Y , RESULT)
CALL SUMIT (A , B , SUM)	RESULT=X+Y
PRINT * , A , B , SUM	RETURN
STOP	END
END	

When the calling program calls the subroutine, it provides the value of A and B to be used by the subroutine in place of X and Y. It also provides a variable SUM which is equivalent to RESULT (both being third in the list). When the subroutine calculates $X + Y$ and stores it in RESULT, it actually stores the sum in SUM. Compare this form with the previous example using a function.

EXAMPLE

A program requires the ordering of several arrays in descending sequence by magnitude from the largest to the smallest value. The arrays are all one-dimensional, and the number of quantities in an array range from 10 to 100. The subroutine is written so that one of the arguments is the array name and the other is the number of entries. The subroutine program shown in Figure 5-2 is dimensioned to handle the largest array.

Note that the subroutine is general and will work for an array of 100 or less entries. The quantities are arranged by successive comparisons, shifting the larger values to the front until the array is ordered. A program needing to order a J-element array called GRADES merely writes the following statement:

CALL ORDER (J , GRADES)

After the array GRADES is ordered, control is returned to the statement following the CALL. Note that the J in the actual argument is not the same as the J used in the subroutine. These two J's are considered to be entirely different.

In the flowcharting programs with subroutines, the subroutine program or module symbol is used to indicate a subroutine CALL.

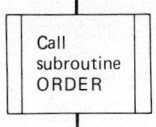

A subroutine does not automatically return a single value to the calling program as does a function. However, the subroutine must be able to com-

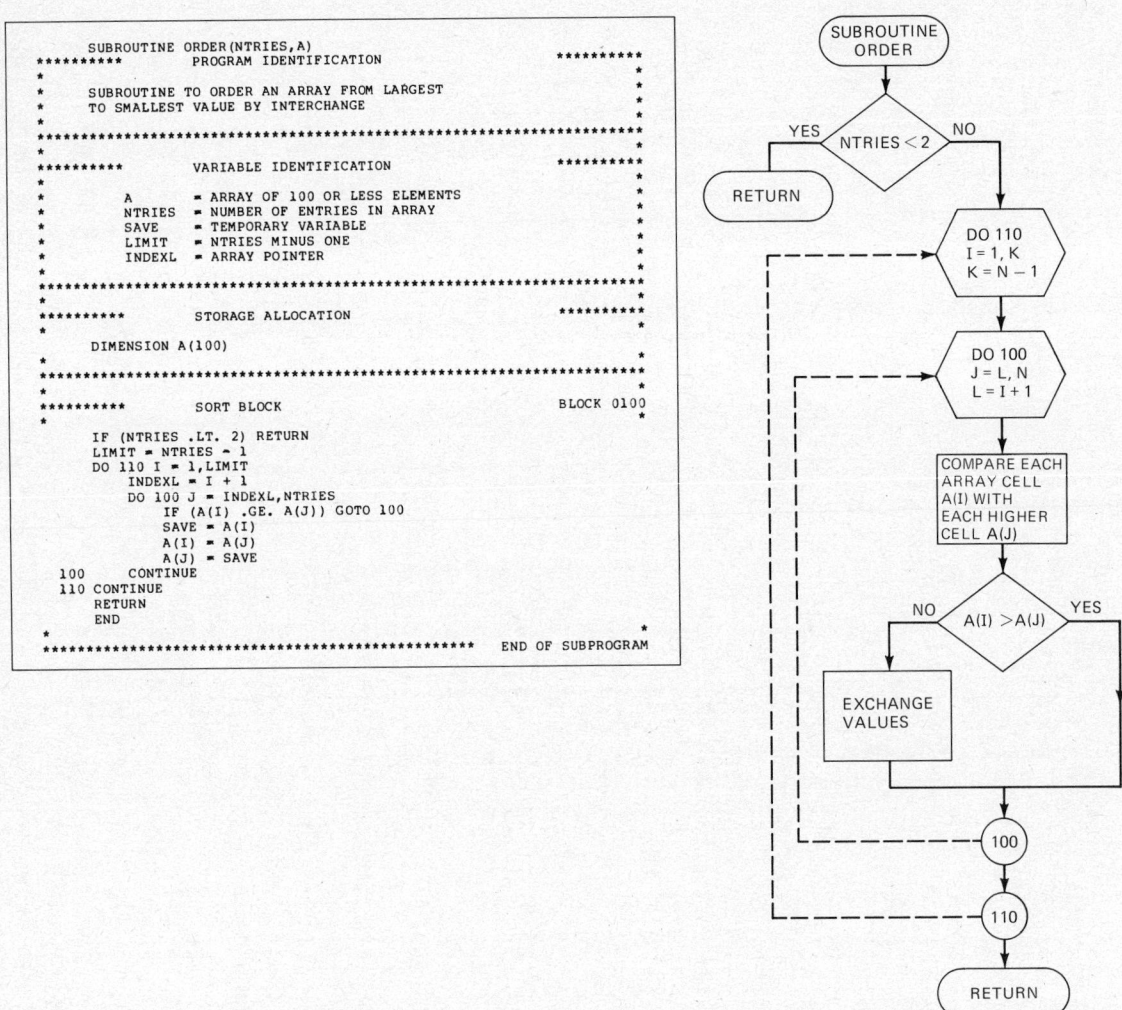

```
      SUBROUTINE ORDER(NTRIES,A)
*********          PROGRAM IDENTIFICATION          *********
*                                                          *
*    SUBROUTINE TO ORDER AN ARRAY FROM LARGEST             *
*    TO SMALLEST VALUE BY INTERCHANGE                      *
*                                                          *
***********************************************************
*                                                          *
*********          VARIABLE IDENTIFICATION         *********
*                                                          *
*      A        = ARRAY OF 100 OR LESS ELEMENTS            *
*      NTRIES   = NUMBER OF ENTRIES IN ARRAY               *
*      SAVE     = TEMPORARY VARIABLE                       *
*      LIMIT    = NTRIES MINUS ONE                         *
*      INDEXL   = ARRAY POINTER                            *
*                                                          *
***********************************************************
*                                                          *
*********          STORAGE ALLOCATION              *********
*                                                          *
      DIMENSION A(100)                                      *
*                                                          *
***********************************************************
*                                                          *
*********          SORT BLOCK             BLOCK 0100       *
*                                                          *
      IF (NTRIES .LT. 2) RETURN
      LIMIT = NTRIES - 1
      DO 110 I = 1,LIMIT
          INDEXL = I + 1
          DO 100 J = INDEXL,NTRIES
              IF (A(I) .GE. A(J)) GOTO 100
              SAVE = A(I)
              A(I) = A(J)
              A(J) = SAVE
100       CONTINUE
110   CONTINUE
      RETURN
      END
*                                              *
*************************************************  END OF SUBPROGRAM
```

FIGURE 5-2 Subroutine program to order an array from largest to smallest value.

municate with the calling program and transmit the results of the subroutine processing. This communication occurs in two ways—via the arguments in the subroutine call or by common storage (to be explained later in the chapter). The use of arguments in the calling list and corresponding dummy arguments in the subroutine declaration to communicate results of computation was illustrated by the first example. In that example, a single result was transferred through the argument list. This method is not limited to one result. For example, assume a subroutine which requires one value (Y) to be sent from the calling program and which provides two values (A1 and A2) returned as results. In the following program segment, the subprogram CALL causes the subroutine to use the storage locations for Y, A1, and A2 as the locations for B, C, and D. When the subroutine executes C = 50, it is actually executing A1 = 50.

Calling program	SUBROUTINE
CALL COMP (Y, A1, A2) A1 and A2 now contain quantities computed by subroutine (identified in subroutine as C and D).	SUBROUTINE COMP (B, C, D) C = D = END

This means that the subroutine is not limited in the number of values which may be communicated back to the calling program by this method. These values may include arrays.

Note that the communication between the subroutine and the main program need not include any computed result. In the sorting example, the subroutine sequenced data that was specified by an argument in the call to the subroutine, but there was no value returned to the calling program.

SUMMARY OF SPECIFICATIONS FOR SUBROUTINE

Notation

f = function name
e = expression
$x_1, x_2, \ldots, x_n$ = dummy arguments in the function
$a_1, a_2, \ldots, a_n$ = actual calling arguments of the function

Where defined	Externally defined in a separately compiled independent program
How defined	SUBROUTINE $f(x_1, x_2, \ldots, x_n)$ or SUBROUTINE f Program steps RETURN (at each logical exit from program) END
How named	Same as variable name (up to six characters, etc.) except the name of subroutine has no type significance
How called into use	CALL statement CALL $f(a_1, a_2, \ldots, a_n)$ or CALL f
Number of results	Any number
Restrictions on form of calling argument	Type, number, and order of actual calling arguments must agree with the dummy arguments of the definition; argument may be a variable name, subscripted variable, array name, or expression; need not have an argument

---

Self-testing Exercise 5-2

1 Why should a subroutine be used instead of a function?
2 Write the function problem 5 from Exercise 5-1 as a subroutine. The problem was to

write a subprogram to calculate the difference between yearly interest earned using two interest rates for a given amount invested.

3 Write a statement to use (call) the subroutine in question 2 if the main program variables are XINT1, XINT2, AMOUNT, and D (for the difference).

4 Write a subroutine that will interchange rows and columns of square matrices. The subroutine should handle matrices from 2×2 to 20×20. Name the routine MOVE (remember that the name of the subroutine does not indicate type).

5 If, with reference to problem 4, the matrix to be rearranged is called ALPHA and is $KIX \times KIX$ in size, what is the statement to perform the move?

The COMMON and EQUIVALENCE Declarations

Use of COMMON Storage

A variable name used in a subprogram is not related to the same variable name used in the main program simply by having the same name. The two variables are assigned to different memory locations, and computations affecting one do not affect the other. The X's in the following example are completely independent (although they can be associated by the subroutine dummy argument list and subroutine call argument list).

Main program	Subprogram
X = A/B	X = Z**2

←————————Not the same————————→

There are many instances in which it is convenient and desirable to have a variable name in both programs refer to the same memory location. This is accomplished by the use of a special storage area designated as COMMON.

The use of common storage allows communication among independent program units. Instead of a list of variable names as arguments in the subroutine definition and subroutine CALL statement to specify data to be used and data names for results, the data required for processing and the results to be stored may be placed in common storage available to both calling program and subprogram.

Blank COMMON

The most frequently used common storage is also termed *blank* COMMON to distinguish it from a special form of common storage called *named* COMMON. A set or block of blank COMMON storage is defined by a blank COMMON declaration:

COMMON nlist

where nlist is a list of variable names or array names common to more than one program unit. An array name in a COMMON declaration defines the entire array as being in common storage.

The blank common storage sequence in all program units starts with the same storage location. The compiler assigns memory locations to the special blank common storage by sequentially assigning the variables listed in the COMMON declaration. The first variable in each list occupies the first position in common, the second (if an array of size 10) occupies the next 10 positions, etc. Because variables are associated by the order of appearance in the COMMON declaration, a COMMON declaration listing all the variable or array names in the same order must be included in each subprogram having any (even one) of these common elements. One cannot list only those variables unique to a particular subprogram. Putting two variables in the same position in the COMMON declaration list of two different program units will result in their using the same memory location. If the variable and array names in all the COMMON declarations are the same (the usual case), the COMMON declarations may be duplicated on the card punch and a copy placed in each subroutine using any of the common variables.

EXAMPLES

Main program COMMON A,B,C Subprogram COMMON A,B,C	A,B,C in main program reference same data as A,B,C in subprogram.
Main program COMMON X,Y,Z Subprogram COMMON A,B,C	X,Y,Z in main program references same data storage locations as A,B,C in subprogram.
Main program COMMON D,G Subprogram 1 COMMON D,G,X Subprogram 2 COMMON D,G,X	If subprograms share X but it is not used by the main program, then main program need not list X (if not required to keep other variables in same sequence), but recommended procedure is to have all COMMON declarations the same list.

An array included in a COMMON declaration must also be dimensioned in each program using the COMMON declaration. The dimensions must be the same for all using programs. Alternatively, the dimensioning may be included in the COMMON declaration for the variable. This is recommended as being less error-prone. For example:

Single declaration (Recommended)	Separate declarations
COMMON X(100),Y(50)	DIMENSION X(100),Y(50) COMMON X,Y

By following the style of including the dimension in the COMMON declaration, dimension statements are used only to dimension noncommon variables. This style aids in keeping common variables and local variables (applying only to a single program unit) clearly identified. Also, an array variable name appearing in a COMMON dimensioned declaration is clearly identified as being an array.

Named COMMON and Block Data Subprogram

Blank COMMON is useful in that it applies to all program units declaring COMMON. Data stored in it is not affected by execution of RETURN or END statements of subprograms using blank COMMON. However, if data is shared only by some but not all of a number of subprograms, blank COMMON requires that the variables be accounted for in the COMMON declaration list of all subprograms with COMMON declarations. Also, variables in blank COMMON may not be initialized using the DATA statement.

An alternative common storage is *named* COMMON. The form of the named COMMON declaration is to have the block name enclosed in slashes preceding the variable name in the COMMON declaration.

COMMON/common block name/nlist

If no name appears between the slashes, the variables that follow are blank COMMON; in other words, // specifies blank COMMON. A named COMMON block has a unique storage sequence which starts at the same location for all COMMON blocks having the same name. Named COMMON blocks having the same name must be the same size.

EXAMPLES

COMMON /A /X , Y , Z /B /M , N , F	Means named common block A contains X,Y,Z and named common block B contains M,N,F
COMMON / /R , S , T (1 0 0)	R, S, and array T are in blank COMMON

Data in named COMMON may be initialized by use of a BLOCK DATA subprogram which contains a DATA statement to provide initial values for variables and array elements. A BLOCK DATA subprogram is defined by the BLOCK DATA statement:

BLOCK DATA [symbolic name for block data subprogram (optional)]

The BLOCK DATA statement is followed by statements which define data (which has been specified in a named COMMON block) such as the DATA statement but DIMENSION, COMMON, and EQUIVALENCE statements may also be used. The last statement is END.

The reason for the BLOCK DATA subprogram is that named COMMON can be used by several program units (but need not be used by the main program), and so no regular program unit can have the data initialization. The BLOCK DATA subprogram defines initialization at the global level of the entire set of programs and subprograms. An example of a BLOCK DATA subprogram is the following:

Example program unit using named COMMON	BLOCK DATA subprogram to initialize named COMMON
SUBROUTINE CALCUL COMMON /BD /ALPHA (5 0), BETA, A _____ _____ RETURN END	BLOCK DATA COMMON /BD /ALPHA (5 0), BETA, A DATA ALPHA / 5 0 * 0 /BETA / 1 . 0 / END

Notice that the 50-element array ALPHA, the variables BETA and A are defined in two or more program units as being in named COMMON (named BD). The BLOCK DATA subprogram initializes ALPHA as zeros and BETA as 1.0. All the variable names in a common block sequence must be named in the named COMMON statement even if they are not initialized in the DATA statement. More than one named COMMON block may be initialized by DATA statements in the same BLOCK DATA subprogram.

COMMON DECLARATIONS AND BLOCK DATA SUBPROGRAM

Blank COMMON Block

COMMON nlist   or   COMMON//nlist

where nlist is a list of variable names, array names, and array declarators. Data may not be initialized with DATA statement.

Named COMMON Block

COMMON/common block name/nlist

Block Data Subprogram

BLOCK DATA [name for block data subprogram] (name optional)
Statements such as DIMENSION, COMMON, EQUIVALENCE, or statements not yet explained (IMPLICIT, SAVE, PARAMETER, TYPE)
DATA statement
END

The block data subprogram is used to provide initial values for variables and arrays in named COMMON. If any variables in a named COMMON are initialized, all variables in the block must be specified in the DATA statement.

The EQUIVALENCE Declaration

The EQUIVALENCE declaration is used in a program to indicate that two variables are to use the same memory location. The reason for using this statement may be that, due to an error, two different names have been written for the same item. Or the reason may be to conserve memory space. Two or more variables used at different points in the program may be assigned to the same memory location if the earlier variable's values do not have to be preserved. Using the same name for all the variables would also cause them to share the memory location, but this may not be consistent with the naming scheme, etc., being used. Other reasons may also arise in individual programs. Two entire arrays, if they are of equal dimension, may be equivalenced. An entry from an array may be equivalenced to a nonsubscripted variable. Two arrays may be overlapped in whole or in part, but two individual array entries may not be equivalenced. The form is:

$$\text{EQUIVALENCE} \quad (v_1, v_2, \ldots, v_n), (A_1, A_2, \ldots, A_n)$$

where all the variable names or arrays listed inside each set of parentheses are to be assigned to the same memory location.

EXAMPLES

EQUIVALENCE (X, Y)	X and Y are to be assigned to the same memory location.
EQUIVALENCE (A(3), X)	X and A(3) are to reference the same location.
EQUIVALENCE (I, J), (R, S)	I and J are the same, and R and S are the same.
Incorrect EQUIVALENCE (A(3), B(9))	This is incorrect because two subscripted variables cannot be equivalenced.

The COMMON and EQUIVALENCE declarations should appear in the program ahead of any statements using the variables which they declare. A recommended order for these declarations (if any of the variables to be equivalenced are in COMMON) is:

1 DIMENSION   } or, as recommended, include dimensioning in
2 COMMON   } COMMON declaration.
3 EQUIVALENCE

The DATA statement follows these specifications.

EXAMPLES

```
DIMENSION A(100),B(50)
                                    or  COMMON A(100),B(50)
COMMON A,B
EQUIVALENCE (VALUE1,A(1)), (VALUE2,B(50))
```

These three statements indicate that the two arrays A and B, are to be located in the COMMON area. The variables A(1) and VALUE1 are different names for the same variable as are VALUE2 and B(50).

Self-testing Exercise 5-3

1 Two subprograms and a main program all refer to the same set of three variables called X, IOTA, and CHI and to a 100-element array called SILLY by the two

subprograms and DILLY by the main program. Write three statements to declare these variables as COMMON (and dimension the arrays) in the three program units.

2   In a subroutine called SORT to sort an array, the array to be sorted is called X and dimensioned as 100. The main program also refers to the array as X and dimensions it as 100. Write statements to associate the two arrays X, (*a*) using the argument lists and (*b*) using COMMON declarations. Also, DIMENSION the arrays.

3   Redo the answers to problem 2 assuming the name of the array is X in the subroutine and A in the main program.

4   Redo the answers to problem 1 putting the variables in named COMMON and initializing all variables to zero.

The Case Program Structure

The case program coding structure is an extension of the selection structure. In the selection structure, there are two program paths, one of which is selected during program execution; in the case structure, there are more than two program paths, one of which is selected (Figure 5-3). The case structure is useful because in many problems there are different processing actions to be performed on different classes or types of data. Each programming path may be termed a case. For example, the selection of a processing path for the different cases may be based on a code or other characteristic of the data. The multiple path selection can be programmed in FORTRAN by a set of IF statements or ELSEIF statements, but is usually more clearly programmed by the computed GOTO statement.

The computed GOTO transfers control to one of several program statements based on the value of an integer variable (or integer expression). The specifications are summarized in the box.

COMPUTED GOTO STATEMENT

GOTO $(s_1, s_2, s_3, \ldots, s_n)[,]i$

i = integer variable (or integer expression in 1977 full FORTRAN)
s_i = statement number

GOTO can also be written as GO TO

If the value of the integer variable (or the integer expression) is 1, control transfers to the first statement listed; if the value is 2, control goes to the second statement, etc. If the integer value is less than 1 or greater than n (number of statements listed), control goes to the statement following the computed GOTO (or may cause a fatal error in some older FORTRANs).

The maximum number of statements is not defined by the standard, but some compilers have limits.

The comma following the right parenthesis, separating it from i, is required by many older compilers; it is optional in 1977 standard.

Integer variable is required by many older compilers and by 1977 Subset FORTRAN; any integer expression is allowed by 1977 full standard.

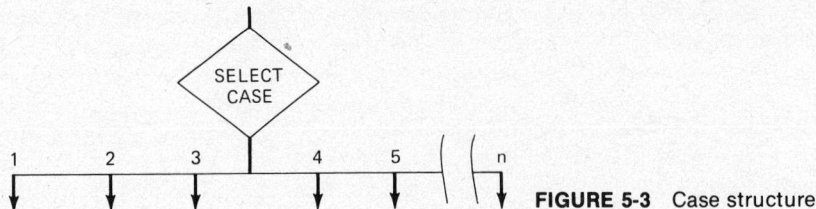

FIGURE 5-3 Case structure.

A statement number can be repeated in the list so that, for example, both a value of 1 and a value of 2 will transfer control to the same statement. An integer value less than one or greater than the number of statements listed will cause the statement following to be executed; this is useful in error control. By always placing an error-control or error-message statement following a computed GOTO, the out-of-range condition is easily detected and reported. But since some older FORTRANs treat the out-of-range condition as a fatal error, it is preferable to explicitly test for out-of-range variable value before executing the computed GOTO. Some simple examples illustrate the form of the statement.

Computed GOTO Example 1

A program will perform one of four types of statistical analysis based on a code of 1 to 4 input by the user. The input value is assigned to ICODE. The statement numbers for the four cases are 201, 301, 401, and 501. The case statement to select the processing path is:

```
GOTO  (201, 301, 401, 501), ICODE
```

Computed GOTO Example 2

A program should transfer control to 410 if JVALUE is 1 or 2, to 450 if JVALUE is 3 or 4, and to 600 if JVALUE is 5. If JVALUE is zero, negative, or more than 5, print an error message.

```
GOTO (410, 410, 450, 450, 600), JVALUE
PRINT*, 'JVALUE OUT OF RANGE', JVALUE
```

Computed GOTO Example 3

A program to analyze the distribution of amount of sales by invoice may set up the following four categories (it is assumed that no sale exceeds $2999):

Less than $500

$500 to $999.99

$1000 to $1999.99

$2000 to $2999.99

If the sales are negative, zero, or over 2999.99, then control should go to an error statement (number 910). The sales are punched on a card in the form XXXX.XX. A partial program and flowchart are shown in Figure 5-4.

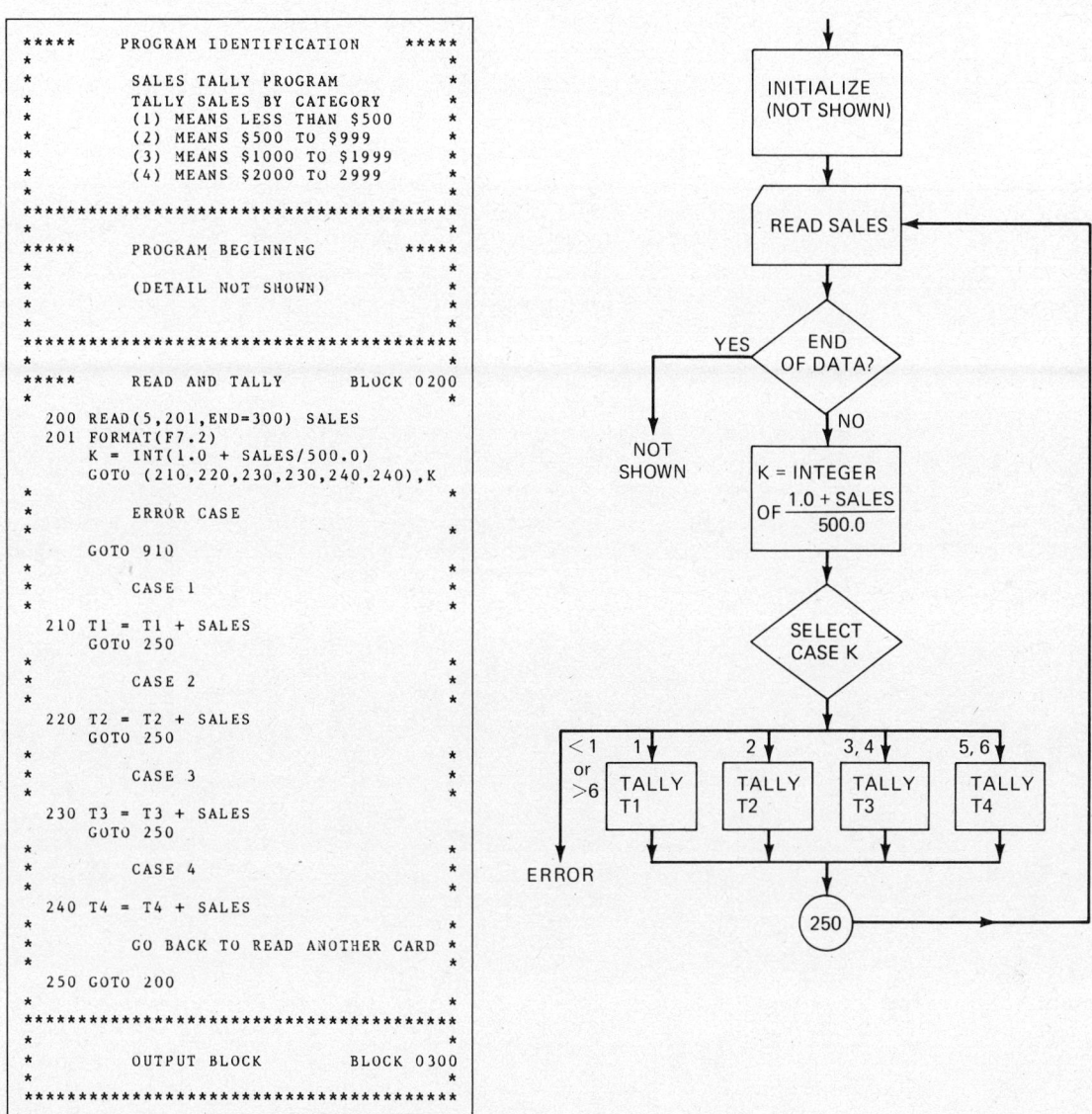

```
*****     PROGRAM IDENTIFICATION     *****
*                                        *
*        SALES TALLY PROGRAM             *
*        TALLY SALES BY CATEGORY         *
*        (1) MEANS LESS THAN $500        *
*        (2) MEANS $500 TO $999          *
*        (3) MEANS $1000 TO $1999        *
*        (4) MEANS $2000 TO 2999         *
*                                        *
******************************************
*                                        *
*****     PROGRAM BEGINNING       *****
*                                        *
*        (DETAIL NOT SHOWN)              *
*                                        *
*                                        *
******************************************
*                                        *
*****     READ AND TALLY      BLOCK 0200 *
*                                        *
  200 READ(5,201,END=300) SALES
  201 FORMAT(F7.2)
      K = INT(1.0 + SALES/500.0)
      GOTO (210,220,230,230,240,240),K
*                                        *
*        ERROR CASE                      *
*                                        *
      GOTO 910
*                                        *
*        CASE 1                          *
*                                        *
  210 T1 = T1 + SALES
      GOTO 250
*                                        *
*        CASE 2                          *
*                                        *
  220 T2 = T2 + SALES
      GOTO 250
*                                        *
*        CASE 3                          *
*                                        *
  230 T3 = T3 + SALES
      GOTO 250
*                                        *
*        CASE 4                          *
*                                        *
  240 T4 = T4 + SALES
*                                        *
*        GO BACK TO READ ANOTHER CARD    *
*                                        *
  250 GOTO 200
*                                        *
******************************************
*                                        *
*        OUTPUT BLOCK        BLOCK 0300   *
*                                        *
******************************************
```

FIGURE 5-4 Partial program and flowchart for sales-tally problem.

The computed GOTO (in the 1977 FORTRAN standard) could have been written as:

GO TO (. . . .), INT (1 . 0+ SALES / 5 0 0 . 0)

It was written in two steps for clarity in the example. In the example, the INT (or IFIX) function which takes the integer portion of the result is redundant because there will be truncation across the equals sign to the integer variable K. However, using an explicit function reduces the chance for error in understanding and maintaining the program. Note how the statement following the computed GOTO specifies transfer to an error-handling block.

To clarify the cases following a computed GOTO, it is useful to precede the beginning of each case (before each statement number specified in the computed GOTO) by a comment line which indicates the case to which the coding to follow applies. This is illustrated in Figure 5-4.

There must be GOTOs following each tally instruction. Note that all of the GOTOs are forward to a single statement at the end of the group which transfers back to begin with a new card. This is usually a clearer programming approach than with frequent backward transfers.

Self-testing Exercise 5-4

1   What happens if X = 4.51 in the execution of

GOTO (1 0 0 , 2 0 0 , 3 1 0 , 4 5 0 , 7 1 0) I N T (X)

2   An input code (called ICODE) is either 2, 3, 4, or 5. Different processing is to be performed in each case (statement 200, 300, 400 and 500). If ICODE is negative, zero, or greater than 5, go to 900. Write a computed GOTO to perform this case selection.

3   The question is the same as question 2 except ICODE is 0, 1, 2, and 3.

4   A programmer following the 1977 FORTRAN standard writes a computed GOTO as follows:

GOTO (1 0 0 ,   2 0 0 ,   4 0 0 ,   6 0 0) ,   I X + 2

The statement is rejected. Rewrite in FORTRAN acceptable to both old and new versions.

5   Code problem 2 using IF statements. This is to illustrate the power and simplicity of the computed GOTO in a case situation.

6   A subroutine is used for all error messages. Before transferring to the error-message subroutine, the calling program defines a code from 1 to 6 for one of six messages plus a value for a variable (call it XERR) that is to be printed with the error message. Write the statements to define the code, to call the subroutine, to define the subroutine, and to select from among the message cases.

Summary

Subprograms are an important programming technique useful for reducing the complexity of large programs, for separate writing and testing of parts of programs, for making use of prewritten routines, etc. The two types of subprograms are function subprograms and subroutines.

The function subprogram returns a single value to the main program. It is used for coding user-defined functions. It is invoked by using the function name, together with arguments, in an expression.

The subroutine is a separate program that is invoked by a CALL statement which lists as the arguments data to be used by the subroutine and data names assigned to receive the results (if not in common storage). A subroutine may return no result, one result, or multiple results.

The COMMON declaration is an alternate method for two programs to communicate. Common storage assignments allow different programs to access the same storage locations and thereby use the same data.

The case structure is an extension of the selection structure in instances where multiple cases can be identified by integers between 1 and n. The case coding structure for selecting among multiple program paths for different cases is implemented in FORTRAN by the computed GOTO.

Answers to Self-testing Exercises

Exercise 5-1

1 The function subprogram SUM sums the elements of a 100-entry array. The main program reads the array, takes the square root of the sum returned by the function, and prints the result.

2 The function IBOY returns an integer result; the variables in the calling argument list are real (X), real (A) and integer (J).

3
```
      FUNCTION ROOT (A, B, C )
      DESCR=B**2  -  4.0*A*C
      IF (DESCR.LE.  0.0)GOTO  100
      ROOT=-B+SQRT (DESCR ) / (2.0*A )
      IF (ROOT.GE.  0.0)RETURN
100   ROOT=0.0
      RETURN  (optional)
      END
```

4 `X=A**2+ROOT (X, Y, Z )`

5
```
FUNCTION DIFF  (RATE1,  RATE2,  AMT )
DIFF=AMT* (RATE2-RATE1 )
RETURN   (optional)
END
```

6 `D=DIFF (XINT1, XINT2, AMOUNT )`

Exercise 5-2

1 The subroutine need not have arguments; the functions must have at least one argument. The subroutine returns any number of results; the function subprogram returns one result. The function is used in an assignment statement; the subroutine is called by a single, separate statement.

2
```
SUBROUTINE DIFF  (RATE1,  RATE2,  AMT,  RESULT )
RESULT=AMT* (RATE2-RATE1 )
RETURN  (optional)
END
```

3 `CALL DIFF  (XINT1, XINT2, AMOUNT, D )`
The result of the call is to make D in the main program equal to the RESULT in the subroutine.

4
```
      SUBROUTINE MOVE  (N, B )
      DIMENSION B (20, 20 )
      DO   110  I=1,N
         L=I+1
         DO  100J=L,N
            TEMP=B (I, J )
            B (I, J )=B (J, I )
            B (J, I )=TEMP
100      CONTINUE
110   CONTINUE
      RETURN (optional)
      END
```

5 `CALL MOVE  (KIX, ALPHA )`

Exercise 5-3

1 Main program	COMMON	X , I O T A , C H I , D I L L Y (1 0 0)
Subprogram 1	COMMON	X , I O T A , C H I , S I L L Y (1 0 0)
Subprogram 2	COMMON	X , I O T A , C H I , S I L L Y (1 0 0)

2 (*a*) Argument list

Subroutine	S U B R O U T I N E S O R T (X)
Main program	C A L L S O R T (X)

(*b*) Common

Subroutine	S U B R O U T I N E S O R T
	D I M E N S I O N X (1 0 0) ⎱ or COMMON X (1 0 0)
	C O M M O N X ⎰
Main program	D I M E N S I O N X (1 0 0) ⎱ or COMMON X (1 0 0)
	C O M M O N X ⎰
	C A L L S O R T

3 (*a*) Subroutine   S U B R O U T I N E   S O R T (X)
   Main program   C A L L   S O R T (A)
   (*b*) Subroutine   S U B R O U T I N E   S O R T

   D I M E N S I O N   X (1 0 0) ⎱ or   COMMON X (1 0 0)
   C O M M O N   X   ⎰

   Main program   D I M E N S I O N   A (1 0 0) ⎱ or   COMMON A (1 0 0)
   C O M M O N   A   ⎰

   C A L L   S O R T

Note that since A and X were both the first item in COMMON, they will occupy the same storage and therefore be equivalent.

4 Main program   COMMON /G 1 /X , I O T A , C H I , D I L L Y (1 0 0)
   Subprogram 1   COMMON /G 1 /X , I O T A , C H I , S I L L Y (1 0 0)
   Subprogram 2   COMMON /G 1 /X , I O T A , C H I , S I L L Y (1 0 0)
   B L O C K   D A T A
   C O M M O N   / G 1 / X , I O T A , C H I , D I L L Y (1 0 0)
   D A T A   X , I O T A , C H I , D I L L Y / 1 0 4 ∗ 0 . 0 /
   E N D

Exercise 5-4

1 It will go to statement 450 because X will be truncated to 4. It could also have been coded in two steps.
   J X = I N T (X)
   G O T O (1 0 0 , 2 0 0 , 3 1 0 , 4 5 0 , 7 1 0) , J X

2 Subtract 1 from ICODE to make it within limits of 1, 2, 3, and 4.
       G O T O (2 0 0 , 3 0 0 , 4 0 0 , 5 0 0) , I CODE – 1
   9 0 0 for out of limits
   or   I CODE = I CODE - 1
       G O T O (2 0 0 , 3 0 0 , 4 0 0 , 5 0 0) , I CODE
   9 0 0 for out of limits

3 Add 1 to ICODE to make it fit form of 1, 2, 3, or 4.

```
        GOTO (200, 300, 400, 500), ICODE+1
 900  for out of limits
or     ICODE=ICODE+1
        GOTO (200, 300, 400, 500), ICODE
 900  for out of limits
```

4
```
I = IX+2
GOTO (100, 200, 400, 600), I
```

5
```
IF (ICODE.LT.2.OR.ICODE.GT.5) GOTO 900
IF (ICODE.EQ.2) GOTO 200
IF (ICODE.EQ.3) GOTO 300
IF (ICODE.EQ.4) GOTO 400
```

6 Main program
```
JCODE=
XERR=
CALL (JCODE, XERR)
```
Subprogram
```
SUBROUTINE (KODE, XMSSG)
GOTO (100, 200, 300, 400, 500, 600), KODE
```

Questions and Problems

1 What is the difference between the function subprogram and subroutine?

2 What is the difference between the COMMON and the EQUIVALENCE statement?

3 What is the effect of each of the following statements or declarations?

(*a*)   `CALL WILMA`

(*b*)   `CALL MOM (DAD, KIDS, SIS)`

(*c*)   `EQUIVALENCE (TEEN, SILLY, CRAZY)`

(*d*)   `FUNCTION NICE (I, J, K)`

(*e*)   `SUBROUTINE COME (X, Y, Z, B)`

(*f*)   `X = TALLY (GAMMA1, GAMMA2)`

4 Make X in a main program equal to $\sqrt[3]{A^2 + B^2}$. Do this step using two different methods: a function subprogram and a subroutine (using two methods for transferring the answer). Write complete subprograms but show only the necessary segment of the main program.

5 Write a main program segment to read n (say, 10) data items in F10.2 fields and print the input. Write a subroutine to order the data items from smallest to largest. Code statements for the main program to call this subroutine and then print out the ordered array. For a small array, interchange sorting is satisfactory. In interchange sorting, the first variable is compared with each of the other variables. If the value being compared is smaller, the two are interchanged. This continues through the array. The result is the smallest value in cell 1. The same procedure is followed for cell 2, etc. See Figure 5-2 for large-to-small sort logic.

CHAPTER

5B

EXAMPLE PROGRAMS
AND PROGRAMMING
EXERCISES
WHICH USE
SUBPROGRAMS
AND THE
CASE STRUCTURE

General Notes on Chapter 5 Examples

The example programs illustrate the use of subroutines and function subprograms, COMMON and EQUIVALENCE statements, and the case structure. The program for general example 5, Payroll Report, makes use of two function subprograms and a subroutine. It includes the case structure plus named and blank COMMON, EQUIVALENCE, DIMENSION, and DATA statements. The program for statistical example 5, Numerical Integration, uses those same features, except for the case structure. We used the optional double slashes without a name for the blank COMMON declaration. This technique more clearly shows the difference between blank and named COMMON declarations. An additional section, *Subroutine and Function Identification,* has been added to the variable identification block.

General Program Example 5—Payroll Reports

The program produces the same sort of reports as its predecessor in Chapter 4 for gross pay, total deductions, and net pay. The report printing logic is the same except that several other error conditions are checked and hence the "Notes" section of the payroll report is altered. Retirement and tax computations are more complex and make use of additional input data. Tax is calculated by a function and retirement calculated by a subroutine. The case structure is used in the pension subroutine. A rounding function is used to adjust all dollar and cents values to the nearest penny.

Problem Description for General Example 5

The program is to read employee pay data and produce two reports: (1) Error and Control Report and (2) Report of Pay Amounts. The Report of Pay Amounts is to contain a line for each employee and a line of totals at the end of the report. The employees are to be grouped by department in the report. In the Report of Pay Amounts, net pay that is negative or over $300.00 is accompanied by a warning note. Also, errors in input code for union/management employees are to be noted.

The first input for the program consists of a set of five department numbers and names, one pair per card. Input validation for this input consists of output which echoes the table for visual verification. Subsequent input data consists of one card for each employee, giving ID number, name, department number where employed, hours worked, wage rate, miscellaneous deductions, number of dependents, and union/management code. During reading of this input data, error messages which reflect the detection of data-type errors or invalid data are printed immediately and the cards are not processed further for the subsequent Report of Pay Amounts. After all records are read and validated for input errors, a total record count and number of rejected cards is printed.

Program Documentation for General Example 5

The documentation of program design is given by a pseudocode description (Figure 5-5) and a program flowchart (Figure 5-6). The program listing is shown in Figure 5-7. Test data is documented in Figure 5-8 and the corresponding Error and Control Report is Figure 5-9 and Report of Pay Amounts is Figure 5-10.

Notes on General Example 5

The variable identification block has been enlarged to include a section to identify any subroutine and function subprograms by name and by a brief description. Note that throughout this entire block, each name must be unique.

MAIN PROGRAM

Establish storage common with other program units
Dimension arrays for 5 departments and 15 employees (14 plus 1 potential error case)
Initialize data for departments, net pay limits, and maximum number of employees
PRINT heading at top of page for Error and Control Report
Zero accumulators and initialize counters and constants
READ and echo department numbers and names for visual validation
PRINT error message heading
<u>READ</u> an employee data card and test for end of data and data-type errors
    If no more cards, go to <u>Print Detail Report</u>, else continue
    If data-type error, increment record counter, print message, and go back to
        READ an employee data card, else continue
Increment record counter
Check for valid department number
    If invalid, print message and go back to <u>READ</u> an employee data card
    Else continue
Compute overtime and gross pay
Compute taxes with tax rate function
Compute retirement contribution with pension subroutine
Compute total deductions
Compute net pay
Add employee gross pay, total deduction, and net pay to totals
Increment accepted employee records counter by 1
Test number of accepted records
    If number exceeds limit of array storage, print excess records message
    Else go back to <u>READ</u> an employee data card
<u>Print Detail Report</u>
Compute invalid record count
Print record counts at bottom of Error and Control Report
PRINT column headings for Report of Pay Amounts at top of new page
DO for all department numbers in order
    Select all employees in that department by matching departmental number
        with department number in employee record
    For each matching employee check for net pay outside limits
        If invalid pay, set error note, else continue
    PRINT detail for matching employee
End of DO
Print summary totals and error code explanations
STOP

FIGURE 5-5 Pseudocode description of general program example 5—payroll reports.

FUNCTION RATE

Establish storage common with other program units
Test dependents code
        IF one dependent use standard rate;
        IF more than one dependent

$$RATE = \left(1 - \frac{N}{N+6} \right) * Standard\ rate$$

        [N = number of dependents]

RETURN

SUBROUTINE PNSION

Establish storage common with other program units
Test for legal employee type code
        If out of bounds, set error note to 2 and set type code to 1 as default option
        Else continue
Select case for employee type
        Case 1 (Union employee)
                Pension contribution = 6 percent of GRSPAY
        Case 2 (Management employee)
                Pension contribution is 5 percent of $200 base pay plus 7.5 percent
                        of pay over base
RETURN

FUNCTION PNYRND

Round a value to nearest penny
RETURN

FIGURE 5-5 *(continued)*

Since COMMON, DIMENSION, and DATA statements all control storage (memory) allocation, they are grouped at the beginning, before any executable code, in a single storage allocation block.

Many of the features of this program are identical to general program example 4. However, the computation block has been altered somewhat to reflect more complex formulas for retirement contributions and taxes. Tax rate has been made a function (called RATE) of the number of dependents. While this relationship could have been inserted directly in the program in place of code line 41, it was felt preferable to code it as a function subprogram so that the specific formula could be isolated from the general program flow. If the formula changes, it is easily identified for changes to be made. Similarly, a subroutine called PNSION has been used to implement the specific procedure for computing pension contributions. The latter makes use of the computed

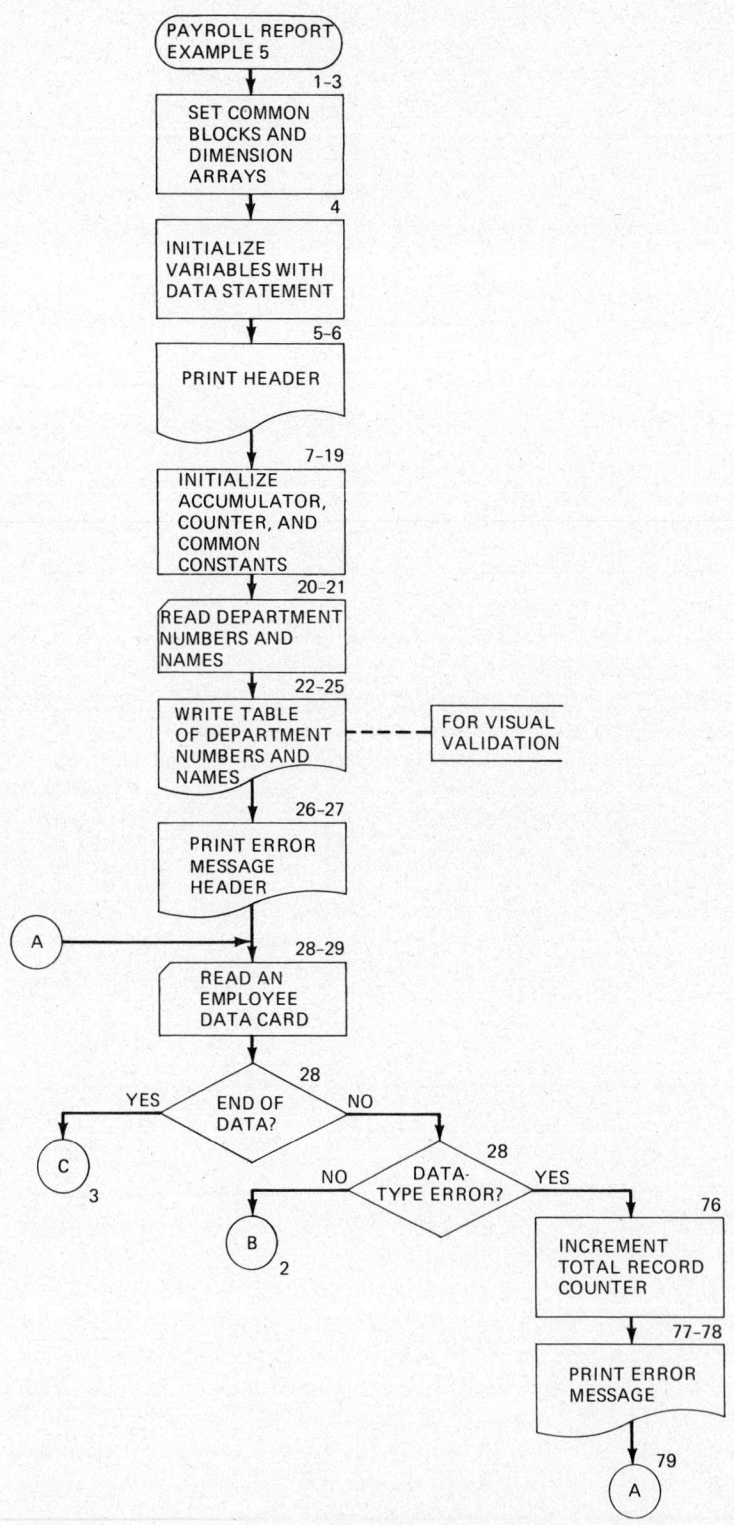

FIGURE 5-6 Program flowchart for general example 5—payroll reports. (Numbers next to symbols are line numbers from program listing.)

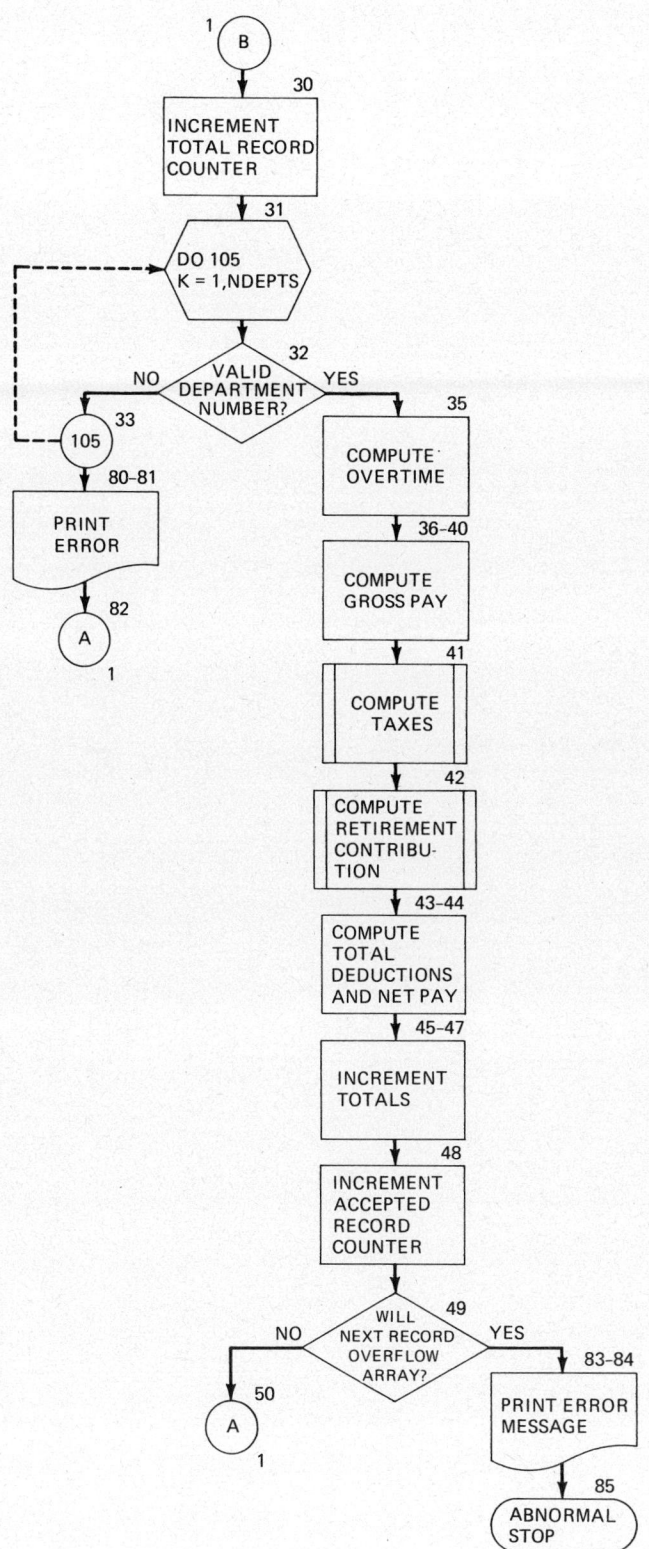

FIGURE 5-6 *(continued)*

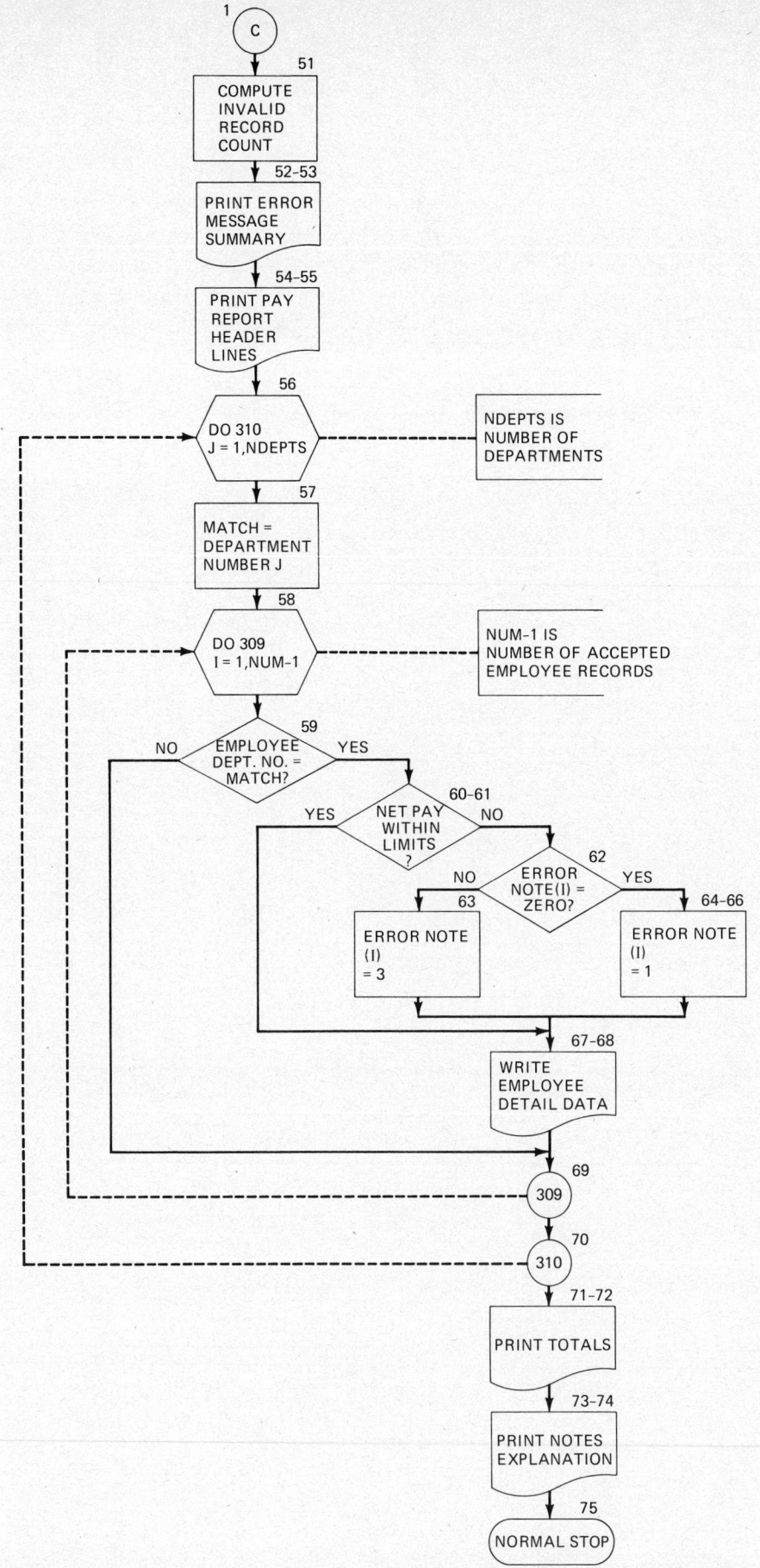

FIGURE 5-6 *(continued)* Program flowchart for general example 5—payroll reports.

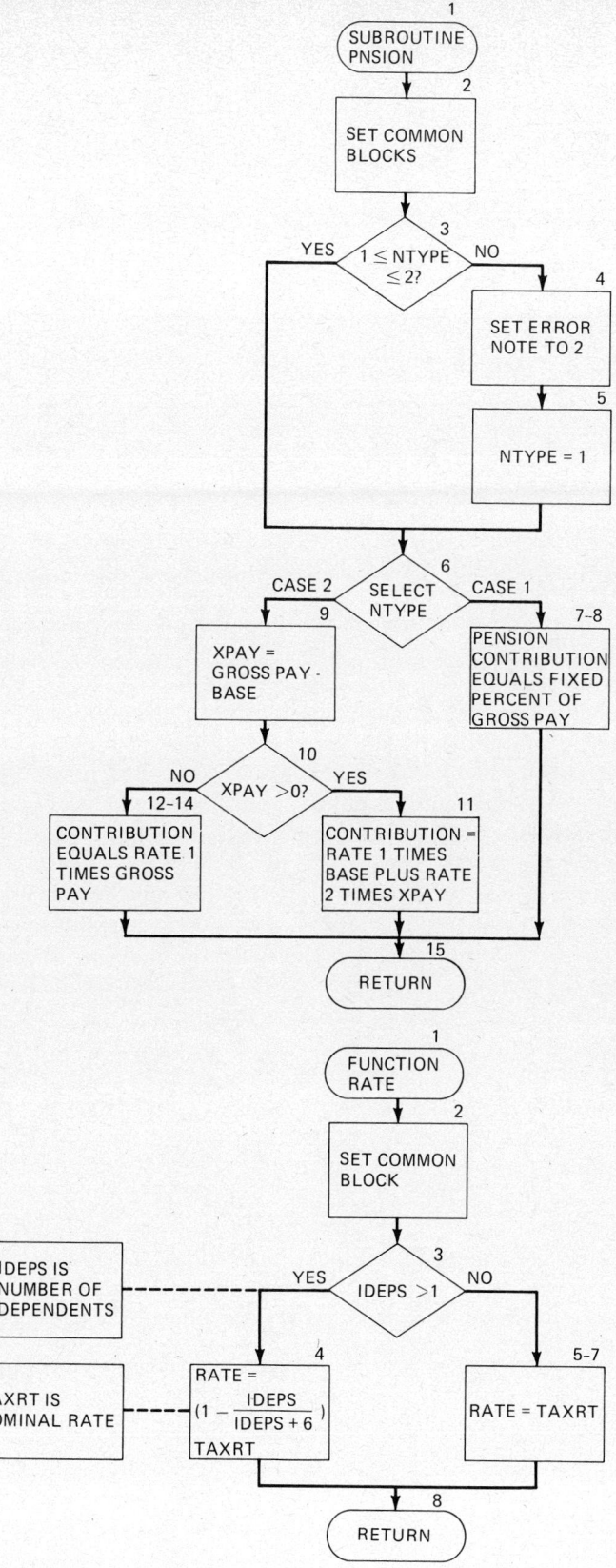

FIGURE 5-6 *(continued)*

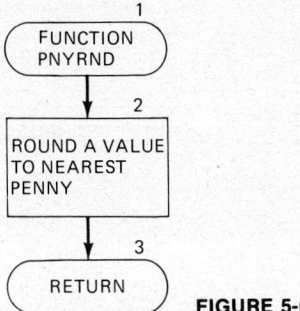

FIGURE 5-6 *(continued)*

GOTO and the case structure. The FORTRAN 1977 standard says that if the selection variable for a computed GOTO is less than one or greater than the number of cases cited, control is to go to the following statement, but many current compilers consider such a condition to be a fatal error causing abnormal program termination. Therefore, a specific test was made in the PNSION subroutine line 3 so that the program will work in either case.

The test for error in union/management code has been placed in the PNSION subroutine. The default option in the case of a code that is neither 1 or 2 is to assume it is 1 (union) and set up an error code for the line being processed. This is an example of the use of default options to allow processing to continue. The most likely value is inserted and a warning message is output to alert the user to check that item.

As a matter of style to clarify program units, the last line of the main program has a note, END OF MAIN PROGRAM, embedded in the last line of asterisks. An END OF SUBPROGRAM message is in the last line of each subprogram. Note that the identification blocks also appear at the beginning of each subprogram and block structuring is used as appropriate.

In Chapters 3A and 3B, the problem was discussed of format rounding in business-type reports which have all figures to the nearest cent and generally foot (add down columns) and crossfoot (add across rows). The result is that the report footing and crossfooting totals may differ slightly from the sum of the columns or rows obtained from unrounded data. One solution is to round all data internally in the same form as it is to be printed out. In the case of the pay report, this is to the nearest penny. It is cumbersome to write the rounding computations as part of every statement where it is applicable. A very easy and straightforward method is to use a rounding function. Such a function, called PNYRND, is part of the pay report program. Note how it consists of only one assignment statement, RETURN, and an END statement. It is used in statements in the main program. One example is line 39:

GRSPAY(NUM) = PNYRND(PAYDAT(NUM,1)*(PAYDAT (NUM, 2))

See also lines 37 and 41.

In summary, review the following features of this pay report program.

1 The use of a function and a subroutine to isolate key computations that may need to change.

```
*********           PROGRAM IDENTIFICATION             *********
*                                                             *
*         THIS PROGRAM COMPUTES EMPLOYEE PAYCHECKS BASED      *
*         UPON HOURS WORKED, WAGE RATE AND VARIOUS DEDUCTIONS.*
*         IT PRINTS EMPLOYEE DATA GROUPED BY DEPARTMENTS.     *
*         VARIABLE TAX AND PENSION RATES ARE COMPUTED         *
*         WRITTEN 7/12/77 BY T. HOFFMANN                      *
*                                                             *
***************************************************************
*                                                             *
*********           VARIABLE IDENTIFICATION            *********
*                                                             *
*****                ARRAY NAMES                       *****
*                                                             *
*         ID     = EMPLOYEE IDENTIFICATION NUMBER             *
*         GRSPAY = GROSS PAY: $                               *
*         NAME   = EMPLOYEE NAMES                             *
*         NDEP   = DEPT. NUMBER WHERE WORKED                  *
*         NODEPT = LIST OF DEPARTMENT NUMBERS                 *
*         NMDEPT = CORRESPONDING LIST OF DEPARTMENT NAMES     *
*         PAYCHK = NET PAYCHECK AMOUNT: $                     *
*         PAYDAT = PAYROLL INPUT DATA (HRSWRK,WGRATE,DEDUC)   *
*         TDEDUC = TOTAL OF ALL DEDUCTIONS FOR AN EMPLOYEE    *
*         NERRS  = LIST OF ERROR CODE NOTES                   *
*         NDEPS  = NUMBER OF CLAIMED DEPENDENTS               *
*         MTYPE  = UNION(=1), MANAGEMENT(=2) TYPE OF EMPLOYEE *
*                                                             *
*****                SIMPLE VARIABLES                  *****
*                                                             *
*         NCARD  = NUMBER OF CARDS READ                       *
*         NUM    = NUMBER OF VALID EMPLOYEE RECORDS           *
*         NOTVLD = NUMBER OF NOT VALID EMPLOYEE RECORDS       *
*         OTIME  = HOURS OF OVERTIME (EXCESS OVER 40.0)       *
*         RETIRE = RETIREMENT CONTRIBUTION BY EMPLOYEE        *
*         TAXES  = TAXES DUE: $                               *
*         TOTNET = TOTAL OF NET PAY AMOUNTS                   *
*         TOTPAY = TOTAL GROSS PAY FOR COMPANY: $             *
*         TOTDUC = TOTAL OF ALL EMPLOYEE DEDUCTIONS           *
*                                                             *
*****                CONSTANT IDENTIFICATION           *****
*                                                             *
*         NDEPTS = NUMBER OF DEPARTMENTS (SET AT 5)           *
*         PLIMIT = MAXIMUM PAYCHECK VALUE TO ALLOW = $300.00  *
*         TAXRT  = BASE TAX RATE = 0.15                       *
*         MAXEMP = MAXIMUM NUMBER OF EMPLOYEE RECORDS IN ARRAYS= 15 *
*         PRATU  = PENSION RATE FOR UNION EMPLOYEES = 0.06     *
*         PRATM1 = BASE PENSION RATE FOR MANAGEMENT = 0.05     *
*         PRATM2 = PENSION RATE FOR $ OVER BASE = 0.075        *
*         BASE   = BASE SALARY FOR MANAGEMENT PENSION = 200.00 *
*                                                             *
*****                TEMPORARY VARIABLE NAMES          *****
*                                                             *
*         MATCH,PAYNET,XPAY,NTYPE                             *
*                                                             *
*****                SUBROUTINE AND FUNCTION IDENTIFICATION  *****
*                                                             *
*         RATE   = CALCULATES PROPER TAX RATE                 *
*         PNSION = COMPUTES PENSION CONTRIBUTION              *
*         PNYRND = ROUNDS COMPUTATIONS TO NEAREST PENNY       *
*                                                             *
***************************************************************
*                                                             *
*********           STORAGE ALLOCATION                 *********
*                                                             *
*         MAXIMUM NUMBER OF VALID EMPLOYEE RECORDS IS 14 (MAXEMP-1) *
*         MAXIMUM NUMBER OF DEPARTMENTS IS 5 (NDEPTS)         *
*                                                             *
1.        COMMON // TAXRT
2.        COMMON /PENCOM/GRSPAY(15),NERRS(15),PRATU,PRATM1,PRATM2,BASE
3.        DIMENSION NODEPT(5),NMDEPT(5),ID(15),NAME(15,3),NDEP(15),
         1    PAYDAT(15,3),TDEDUC(15),PAYCHK(15),NDEPS(15),MTYPE(15)
4.        DATA NDEPTS/5/PLIMIT/300.0/MAXEMP/15/
*                                                             *
***************************************************************
```

FIGURE 5-7 Listing of FORTRAN program for general example 5—payroll reports.

```
       *                                                              *
       **********            INITIALIZATION BLOCK            BLOCK 0000
       *                                                              *
       *        SET OUTPUT PAGE TO TOP AND PRINT HEADER               *
       *                                                              *
 5.           WRITE(6,1)
 6.         1 FORMAT(1H1/' EMPLOYEE PAYCHECK PROGRAM'//)
       *                                                              *
       *        ZERO ACCUMULATORS AND INITIALIZE COUNTERS             *
       *                                                              *
 7.           TOTPAY = 0.0
 8.           TOTNET = 0.0
 9.           TOTDUC = 0.0
10.           NCARD = 0
11.           NUM = 1
12.           TAXRT = 0.15
13.           PRATM2 = 0.075
14.           PRATM1 = 0.05
15.           PRATU = 0.06
16.           DO 6 I = 1,MAXEMP
17.              NERRS(I) = 0
18.         6 CONTINUE
19.           BASE = 200.0
       *                                                              *
       *        READ AND PRINT DEPARTMENT NUMBERS AND NAMES           *
       *
20.           READ(5,7) (NODEPT(K),NMDEPT(K), K=1,NDEPTS)
21.         7 FORMAT(I4,A4)
22.           WRITE(6,9)
23.         9 FORMAT(1H0,'TABLE OF DEPARTMENTS'/' NUMBER    NAME')
24.           WRITE(6,11) (NODEPT(K),NMDEPT(K),K=1,NDEPTS)
25.        11 FORMAT(2X,I4,4X,A4)
       *                                                              *
       *        PRINT ERROR MESSAGE HEADER                            *
       *                                                              *
26.           WRITE(6,13)
27.        13 FORMAT(///6X,'ERROR MESSAGES DURING DATA INPUT'//)
       *                                                              *
       ****************************************************************
       *                                                              *
       **********            READ EMPLOYEE DATA               BLOCK 0100
       *                                                              *
28.       101 READ(5,102,END=301,ERR=901) ID(NUM),(NAME(NUM,J),J=1,3),
           1     NDEP(NUM),(PAYDAT(NUM,K),K=1,3),NDEPS(NUM),MTYPE(NUM)
29.       102 FORMAT(I5,3A4,I4,F4.1,F4.2,F5.2,I2,I1)
30.           NCARD = NCARD + 1
       *                                                              *
       *        CHECK FOR VALID DEPARTMENT NUMBER IN EMPLOYEE CARD     *
       *        WHEN FOUND, PROCESS EMPLOYEE DATA                      *
       *                                                              *
31.           DO 105 K=1,NDEPTS
32.              IF(NODEPT(K).EQ.NDEP(NUM)) GOTO 201
33.       105 CONTINUE
       *                                                              *
       *        ERROR -- NO MATCH FOUND FOR EMPLOYEE DEPT. NUMBER      *
       *                                                              *
34.           GOTO 903
       *                                                              *
       ****************************************************************
       *                                                              *
       **********            COMPUTATION BLOCK                BLOCK 0200
       *                                                              *
       *        COMPUTE PAY, INCLUDING OVERTIME, IF ANY.              *
       *                                                              *
35.       201 OTIME = PAYDAT(NUM,1) - 40.0
36.           IF(OTIME.GT.0.0) THEN
37.              GRSPAY(NUM) = PNYRND((40.0 + 1.5*OTIME)*PAYDAT(NUM,2))
38.           ELSE
39.              GRSPAY(NUM) = PNYRND(PAYDAT(NUM,1)*PAYDAT(NUM,2))
40.           ENDIF
```

FIGURE 5-7 *(continued)* Listing of FORTRAN program for general example 5—payroll reports.

```
      *
      *              COMPUTE TAXES USING RATE FUNCTION                    *
      *                                                                   *
41.        TAXES = PNYRND(GRSPAY(NUM)*RATE(NDEPS(NUM)))
      *                                                                   *
      *              COMPUTE RETIREMENT CONTRIBUTION BASED UPON           *
      *              UNION/MANAGEMENT TYPE                                *
      *                                                                   *
42.        CALL PNSION(MTYPE(NUM),RETIRE,NUM)
43.        TDEDUC(NUM) = PAYDAT(NUM,3) + TAXES + RETIRE
44.        PAYCHK(NUM) = GRSPAY(NUM) - TDEDUC(NUM)
      *                                                                   *
      *              INCREMENT TOTALS AND COUNTER                         *
      *                                                                   *
45.        TOTPAY = TOTPAY + GRSPAY(NUM)
46.        TOTDUC = TOTDUC + TDEDUC(NUM)
47.        TOTNET = TOTNET + PAYCHK(NUM)
48.        NUM = NUM + 1
      *                                                                   *
      *              TEST TO PREVENT ARRAY OVERFLOW. IF ARRAYS NOT FULL   *
      *              RETURN TO READ NEXT EMPLOYEE DATA CARD.              *
      *                                                                   *
49.        IF(NUM.GT.MAXEMP) GOTO 906
      *                                                                   *
      *              GO BACK TO READ ANOTHER DATA CARD                    *
      *                                                                   *
50.        GOTO 101
      *                                                                   *
      *********************************************************************
      *                                                                   *
      *********           PRINT DETAIL BY DEPARTMENT GROUPING    BLOCK 0300
      *                                                                   *
      *              PRINT SUMMARY OF DATA INPUT MESSAGES                 *
      *                                                                   *
51.    301 NOTVLD = NCARD - NUM + 1
52.        WRITE(6,302) NCARD,NOTVLD
53.    302 FORMAT(1H0,I4,' CARDS READ'/I5,' CARDS REJECTED')
      *                                                                   *
      *              PRINT HEADER/TITLE LINE FOR EMPLOYEE DETAIL          *
      *                                                                   *
54.        WRITE(6,303)
55.    303 FORMAT(1H1/5X,8HEMPLOYEE,5X,2HID,3X,4HDEPT,3X,5HGROSS,4X,
      1         5HTOTAL,6X,3HNET,4X,5HNOTES/7X,4HNAME,12X,4HNAME,4X,
      2         3HPAY,3X,10HDEDUCTIONS,3X,'PAY')
      *                                                                   *
      *              FOR EACH DEPARTMENT FIND EACH EMPLOYEE               *
      *                                                                   *
56.        DO 310 J=1,NDEPTS
57.           MATCH = NODEPT(J)
58.           DO 309 I=1,NUM-1
59.              IF(NDEP(I).NE.MATCH) GOTO 309
60.              PAYNET = PAYCHK(I)
      *                                                                   *
      *                 CHECK FOR VALID PAYCHECK AMOUNT                   *
      *                                                                   *
61.              IF(PAYNET.GT.0.0 .AND. PAYNET.LE.PLIMIT) GOTO 307
62.              IF(NERRS(I) .NE. 0) THEN
63.                 NERRS(I) = 3
64.              ELSE
65.                 NERRS(I) = 1
66.              ENDIF
67.    307       WRITE(6,304) (NAME(I,N),N=1,3),ID(I),NMDEPT(J),
      1             GRSPAY(I),TDEDUC(I),PAYCHK(I),NERRS(I)
68.    304       FORMAT(1H0,2X,3A4,I6,2X,A4,3X,F6.2,3X,F6.2,3X,F6.2,I6)
69.    309    CONTINUE
70.    310 CONTINUE
      *                                                                   *
      *********************************************************************
```

FIGURE 5-7 *(continued)*

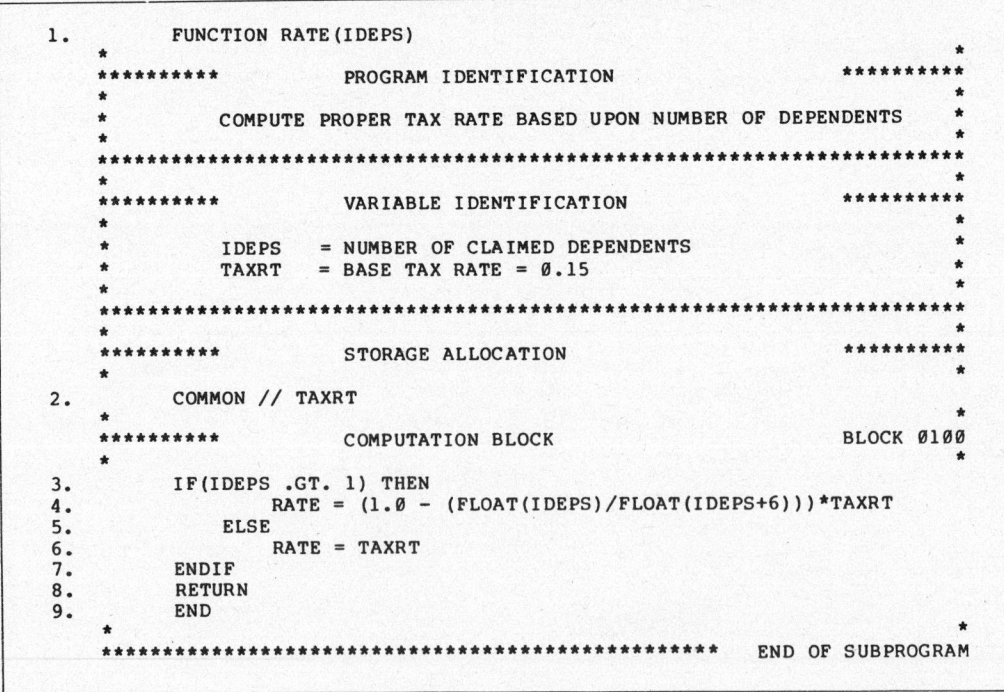

```
         *                                                              *
         **********                PRINT SUMMARY AND TERMINATE              BLOCK 0400
         *                                                              *
71.          WRITE(6,402) TOTPAY,TOTDUC,TOTNET
72.     402 FORMAT(//20X,'TOTALS',3X,F7.2,2F9.2)
73.          WRITE(6,403)
74.     403 FORMAT(///5X,'NOTES'
        1   /5X,'0 - NO ERRORS'
        2   /5X,'1 - NET PAY IS OUT OF BOUNDS. DO NOT ISSUE CHECK.'
        3   /5X,'2 - UNION/MANAGEMENT CODE ERROR. UNION ASSUMED.'
        4   /5X,'3 - BOTH TYPE 1 AND 2 ERRORS.')
75.          STOP
         *                                                              *
         ****************************************************************
         *                                                              *
         **********                ERROR MESSAGE BLOCK                   BLOCK 0900
         *                                                              *
76.     901 NCARD = NCARD + 1
77.          WRITE(6,902) NCARD
78.     902 FORMAT(//6H *****,' ERROR IN DATA CARD NUMBER ',I2,6H *****)
79.          GOTO 908
         *****                                                    *****
80.     903 WRITE(6,904) NCARD
81.     904 FORMAT(//' ***** ERROR - DEPT. NO. NOT VALID. CARD NO.  ',I4,
        1       2X,5H*****)
         *                                                              *
         *          GO BACK TO READ NEXT EMPLOYEE DATA CARD             *
         *                                                              *
82.     908 GOTO 101
         *****                                                    *****
83.     906 WRITE(6,907) MAXEMP-1
84.     907 FORMAT(///' ***** ERROR. ATTEMPTED TO READ ',
        1       'MORE THAN',I3,'VALID DATA CARDS'/7X,'PROGRAM ABORTED. ')
85.          STOP
86.          END
         *                                                              *
         ************************************************** END OF MAIN PROGRAM
```

```
 1.          FUNCTION RATE(IDEPS)
         *                                                              *
         **********              PROGRAM IDENTIFICATION              **********
         *                                                              *
         *     COMPUTE PROPER TAX RATE BASED UPON NUMBER OF DEPENDENTS   *
         *                                                              *
         ****************************************************************
         *                                                              *
         **********              VARIABLE IDENTIFICATION             **********
         *                                                              *
         *     IDEPS   = NUMBER OF CLAIMED DEPENDENTS                    *
         *     TAXRT   = BASE TAX RATE = 0.15                           *
         *                                                              *
         ****************************************************************
         *                                                              *
         **********                STORAGE ALLOCATION                **********
         *                                                              *
 2.          COMMON // TAXRT
         *                                                              *
         **********                COMPUTATION BLOCK                   BLOCK 0100
         *                                                              *
 3.          IF(IDEPS .GT. 1) THEN
 4.              RATE = (1.0 - (FLOAT(IDEPS)/FLOAT(IDEPS+6)))*TAXRT
 5.          ELSE
 6.              RATE = TAXRT
 7.          ENDIF
 8.          RETURN
 9.          END
         *                                                              *
         **************************************************** END OF SUBPROGRAM
```

FIGURE 5-7 *(continued)* Listing of FORTRAN program for general example 5—payroll reports.

```
1.          SUBROUTINE PNSION(NTYPE,CASH,NUM)
    *                                                                    *
    **********           PROGRAM IDENTIFICATION           **********
    *                                                                    *
    *       COMPUTE PENSION CONTRIBUTION BASED UPON TYPE OF EMPLOYEE.    *
    *           UNION = 1     MANAGEMENT = 2      ERROR = OTHER          *
    *                                                                    *
    ******************************************************************
    *                                                                    *
    **********           VARIABLE IDENTIFICATION          **********
    *                                                                    *
    *****               SIMPLE VARIABLE NAMES                  *****
    *                                                                    *
    *       NTYPE    = CODE FOR TYPE OF EMPLOYEE                         *
    *       CASH     = RETIREMENT CONTRIBUTION                          *
    *       NUM      = EMPLOYEE NUMBER                                   *
    *       PRATU    = PENSION RATE FOR UNION EMPLOYEES = 0.06           *
    *       PRATM1   = BASE PENSION RATE FOR MANAGEMENT = 0.05           *
    *       PRATM2   = PENSION RATE FOR $ OVER BASE = 0.075              *
    *       BASE     = BASE SALARY FOR MANAGEMENT PENSION = 200.00       *
    *       XPAY     = PAY OVER BASE                                     *
    *                                                                    *
    *****                   ARRAY NAMES                        *****
    *                                                                    *
    *       GRSPAY   = GROSS PAY: $                                     *
    *       NERRS    = LIST OF ERROR CODE NOTES                          *
    *                                                                    *
    **********           FUNCTION IDENTIFICATION          **********
    *                                                                    *
    *       PNYRND   = ROUNDS COMPUTATIONS TO NEAREST PENNY             *
    *                                                                    *
    ******************************************************************
    *                                                                    *
    **********             STORAGE ALLOCATION             **********
    *                                                                    *
2.          COMMON /PENCOM/GRSPAY(15),NERRS(15),PRATU,PRATM1,PRATM2,BASE
    *                                                                    *
    **********             COMPUTATION BLOCK                  BLOCK 0100
    *                                                                    *
3.          IF(NTYPE.GE.1 .AND. NTYPE.LE.2) GOTO 102
    *                                                                    *
    *       CASE ERROR - SET ERROR INDICATOR AND ASSUME NTYPE IS 1      *
    *                                                                    *
4.          NERRS(NUM) = 2
5.          NTYPE = 1
6.      102 GOTO (103,104),NTYPE
    *                                                                    *
    *       CASE ONE - UNION TYPE EMPLOYEE                              *
    *                                                                    *
7.      103 CASH = PNYRND(PRATU*GRSPAY(NUM))
8.          GOTO 106
    *                                                                    *
    *       CASE TWO - MANAGEMENT TYPE EMPLOYEE                          *
    *                                                                    *
9.      104 XPAY = GRSPAY(NUM) - BASE
10.         IF(XPAY.GT.0.0) THEN
11.             CASH = PNYRND(PRATM1*BASE + PRATM2*XPAY)
12.         ELSE
13.             CASH = PNYRND(PRATM1*GRSPAY(NUM))
14.         ENDIF
15.     106 RETURN
16.         END
    *                                                                    *
    ****************************************************** END OF SUBPROGRAM
    *                                                                    *
```

FIGURE 5-7 *(continued)*

```
1.          FUNCTION PNYRND(VALUE)
   *                                                                          *
   ********** PROGRAM IDENTIFICATION                              **********
   *                                                                          *
   *          VALUES ARE ROUNDED TO THE NEAREST PENNY                         *
   *          CALLED FROM MAIN AND PENSION                                    *
   *                                                                          *
   ************************************************************************
   *                                                                          *
   ********** VARIABLE IDENTIFICATION                             **********
   *                                                                          *
   *          VALUE  = VALUE OF EXPRESSION TO BE ROUNDED                      *
   *                                                                          *
   ************************************************************************
   *
2.          PNYRND = FLOAT((INT(100.0*(VALUE + 0.005))))/100.0
3.          RETURN
4.          END
   *                                                                          *
   ****************************************************** END OF SUBPROGRAM
```

FIGURE 5-7 *(continued)*

FIGURE 5-8 Annotated input test data for general program example 5—payroll reports.

```
EMPLOYEE PAYCHECK PROGRAM


   TABLE OF DEPARTMENTS
   NUMBER    NAME
    1234     FIN
    4275     ENGR
    7269     MKTG
    7531     PROD
    8551     ACCT




      ERROR MESSAGES DURING DATA INPUT




***** ERROR - DEPT. NO. NOT VALID. CARD NO.      4  *****


***** ERROR IN DATA CARD NUMBER  7 *****

   10 CARDS READ
    2 CARDS REJECTED
```

FIGURE 5-9 Example of Error and Control Report from payroll reports program.

254

```
     EMPLOYEE      ID    DEPT    GROSS     TOTAL       NET     NOTES
       NAME              NAME     PAY    DEDUCTIONS    PAY

  R. M. NELSON   42753   FIN     298.00   104.79     193.21      0

  T. NAMAN       69852   ENGR     26.70    30.70      -4.00      1

  L. SMITH       35748   ENGR    457.93    99.37     358.56      3

  Q. SIBLEY      62475   ENGR    309.00   118.28     190.72      0

  J. JOHNSON     36985   MKTG     60.50    48.69      11.81      0

  J. HOFFMANN    23456   PROD    142.80    52.59      90.21      0

  A. PETERSON    74365   PROD    294.02   116.37     177.65      2

  RALPH JONES    15786   ACCT    232.36    59.53     172.83      0


         TOTALS    1821.31   630.32   1190.99



  NOTES
  0 - NO ERRORS
  1 - NET PAY IS OUT OF BOUNDS. DO NOT ISSUE CHECK.
  2 - UNION/MANAGEMENT CODE ERROR. UNION ASSUMED.
  3 - BOTH TYPE 1 AND 2 ERRORS.
```

FIGURE 5-10 Example of Report of Pay Amounts from payroll reports program.

2 The identification list in the main program of all functions and subroutines called by the main program.

3 The use of blank COMMON (line 1) and named COMMON (line 2).

4 The style of dimensioning all common arrays in the COMMON declaration and only local arrays in a DIMENSION statement (lines 2 and 3).

5 Use of a PNYRND rounding function.

6 The use of the case structure in the pension subroutine.

7 The use of a default value and warning message as shown in the pension subroutine.

Statistical Program Example 5—Numerical Integration

Problem Description for Statistical Example 5

The program compares different methods of numerical integration. The basic concept of computing small areas defined by the function is still followed, but the area segments are approximated by three different methods and the results compared. The three methods are a simple rectangle method, a trapezoid method, and Simpson's rule. Each of the three methods is a separate subroutine; the function to be integrated is defined in a function subprogram.

Program Documentation for Statistical Example 5

The documentation consists of a pseudocode program description (Figure 5-11), a program flowchart (Figure 5-12), a program listing (Figure 5-13), sample test data (Figure 5-14), and sample output (Figure 5-15).

Notes on Statistical Example 5

The variable identification block has been augmented with a section listing subroutine and function names. Note that all of the names in this block are unique. The storage allocation block now contains DIMENSION, blank and named COMMON, and DATA statements because they all affect memory (storage) allocation. Following the style suggestions in Chapter 5A, arrays used only in a particular program unit are defined in a DIMENSION statement. Arrays which are common to several program units are dimensioned in a COMMON statement. The named COMMON (line 2) is used to group variables which are logically associated.

The initialization block sets constants, zeros storage, and prints the output header. The block containing the main program's computation is quite short and explicit. The loop in lines 19 to 22 sets up the necessary ordinate values in the array ORD which are then used by the several subroutines. This separation of functions allows easy program modification. The placing of the function in a separate function subprogram makes it quite easy to modify the total program to test the efficiency of the several integration techniques on different functions by simply replacing the function subprogram with a different one. Note that a change in the function does not affect line 18 or line 21 which process the function. Similarly, other integration techniques could easily be used by replacing or substituting a different subroutine. The connection with the main program is through the CALL statement (lines 23 to 25).

MAIN PROGRAM

Dimension and initialize at zero array to hold error card sequence numbers
Establish storage common with other program units
PRINT heading at top of page
Initialize card counter, error card counter, and array to hold ordinates
READ a data card with beginning and ending x values and number of intervals for
    integration
    If no more cards, go to Termination, else continue
    If data-type error, increment card counter and bad record count, set number
        of error card in error array, and go to READ, else continue
Increment card counter
Test for even number of intervals (steps)
    IF number of segments is not even, print error message and go back to READ
    Else continue
Set initial abscissa to initial x value
Compute interval size based on beginning and ending value of x and number of intervals in range
Compute ordinates in range
Call Subroutines RECT, TRAP, and SIMP in order
PRINT results of three methods of integration
Go back to READ a data card
Termination
Print card counts and card numbers with data-type error
STOP

FIGURE 5-11 Pseudocode description of statistical example program 5—numerical integration.

SUBROUTINE RECT

> *Establish storage common with other program units*
> *Set initial sum to value of ordinate zero*
> *Add sum of ordinates for second through next to last one to initial sum*
> *Area = interval size times sum of all ordinates*
> *RETURN*

SUBROUTINE TRAP

> *Establish storage common with other program units*
> *Set initial sum to average of zeroth and last ordinate*
> *Add sum of balance of ordinates to initial sum*
> *Area = interval size times sum of all ordinates*
> *RETURN*

SUBROUTINE SIMP

> *Establish storage common with other program units*
> *Set SUM1 to sum of zeroth and last ordinate*
> *Initialize SUM2 and SUM4 to zero*
> *Compute SUM2 as sum of even ordinates*
> *Compute SUM4 as sum of odd ordinates*
> *Area = (SUM1 + 2*SUM2 + 4*SUM4)*(interval width/3)*
> *RETURN*

FUNCTION ANYF(X)

> *Any function in x may be used here*
> $ANYF = \sin x - \log x + e^x$
> *RETURN*

FIGURE 5-11 *(continued)*

The variable identification and storage allocation blocks are similar in form in both the main and subprograms. As a matter of style, each program unit has a suitable END OF PROGRAM UNIT comment embedded in the last line of the program unit.

In order that error messages for cards with data-type errors will not clutter the principal output table, the card numbers for the unreadable cards are saved in an error array and printed at the end of the program. Line 12 is the READ statement with an ERR = 901 which tests for data-type errors. Lines 36 to 38 store the card numbers in an error array (NERRS), and lines 29 to 34 in the termination block print out the card numbers having type errors.

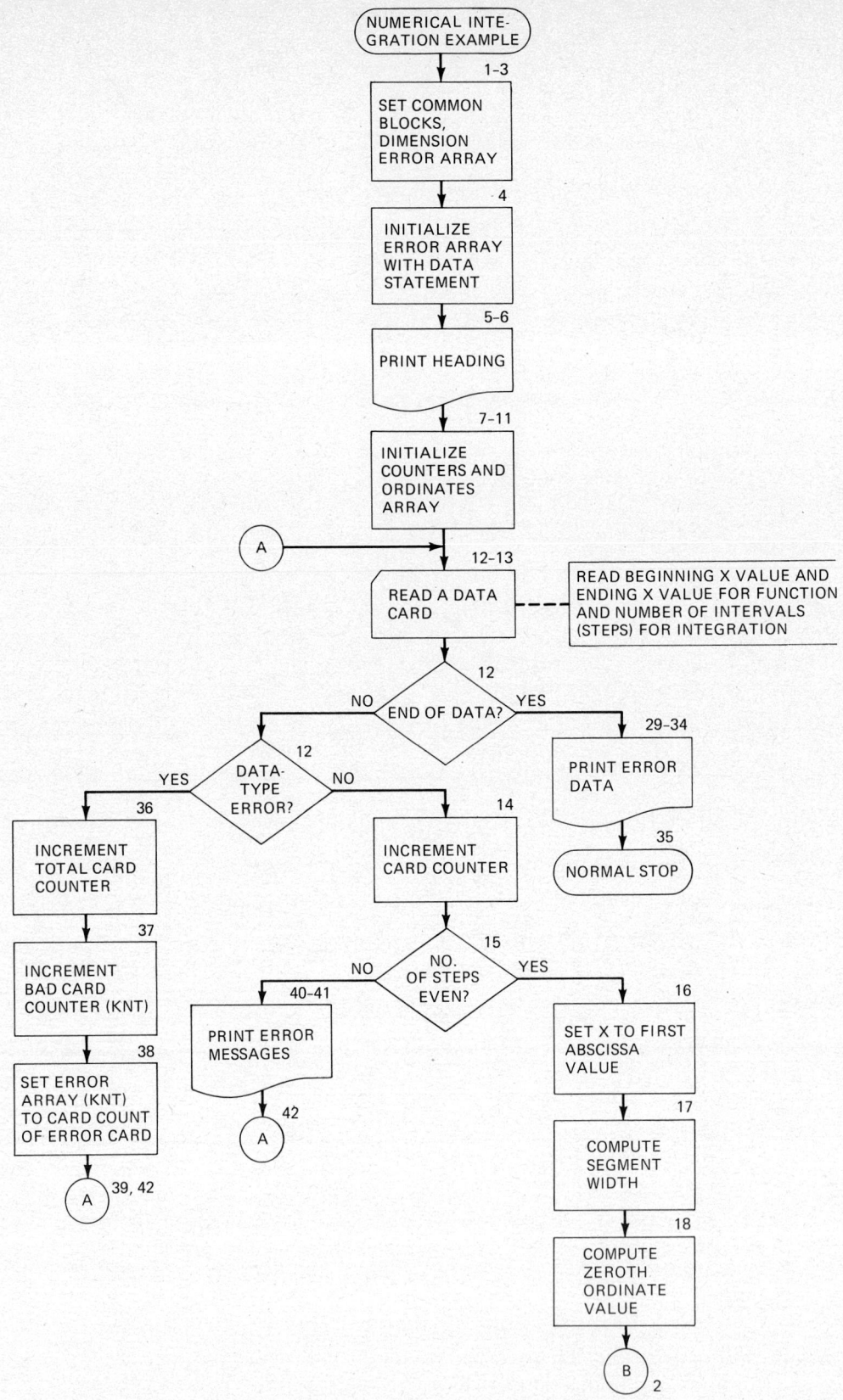

FIGURE 5-12 Program flowchart for statistical example 5—numerical integration. (Numbers next to symbols are line numbers from program listing.)

258

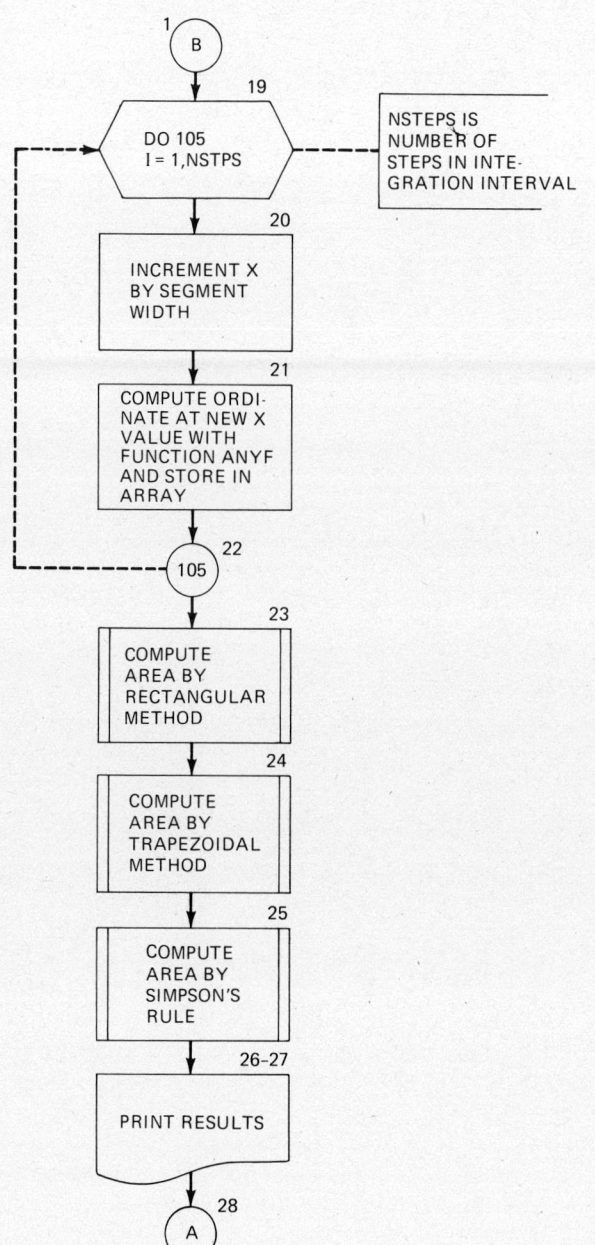

FIGURE 5-12 *(continued)*

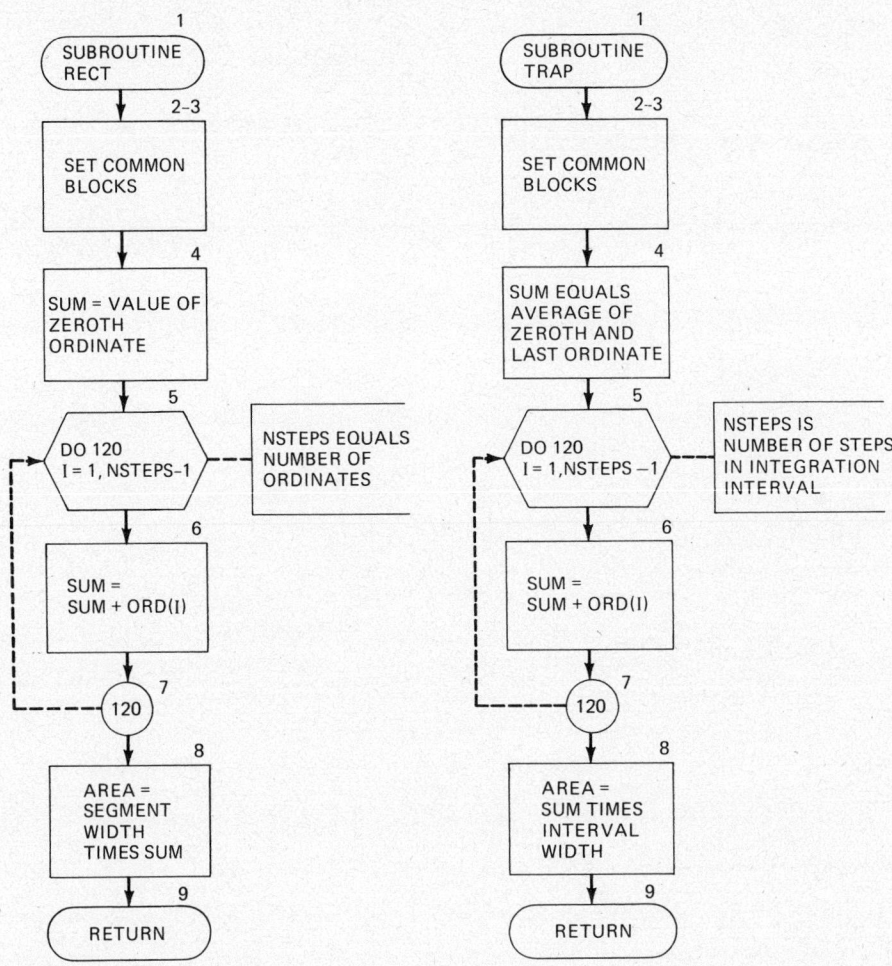

FIGURE 5-12 *(continued)*

In summary, the program has certain style characteristics that should be noted in reviewing it:

1 The list of subroutine and function names in the main program identifies the purpose of each subroutine and function used by the main program.

2 The DIMENSION statement is used only for arrays not in named or blank COMMON. Arrays in COMMON are dimensioned in the COMMON declaration (lines 1 to 3).

3 Data in common storage cannot be initialized by a DATA statement. However, data in named COMMON could have been initialized by a DATA statement in a BLOCK DATA subprogram, but we chose to initialize by assignment statements in the main program (lines 9–10).

4 Input validation is performed to make sure the number of steps is even. Line 15 uses the MOD intrinsic function. MOD(NSTEPS,2) provides the remainder from division by 2. If the remainder is not zero, the number was an odd

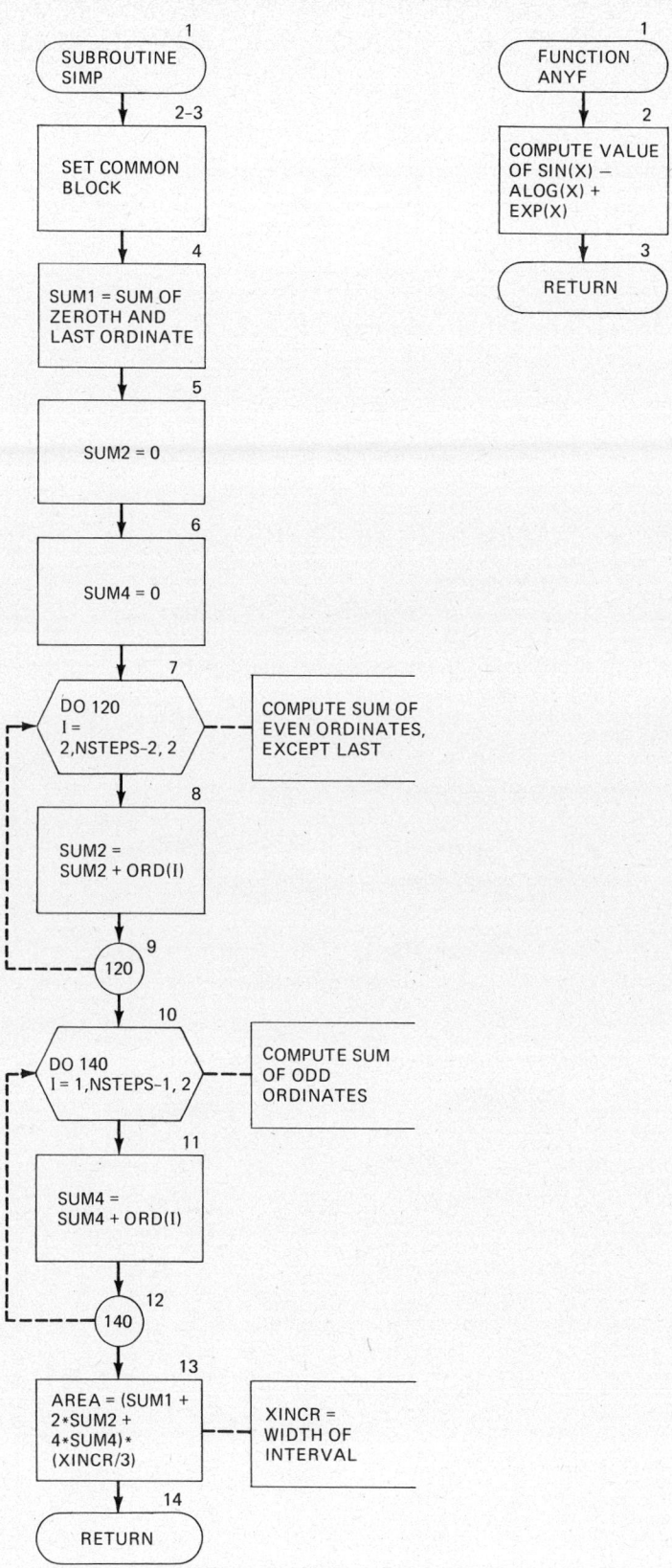

FIGURE 5-12 *(continued)*

```
*********          PROGRAM IDENTIFICATION              *********
*                                                             *
*        PROGRAM TO COMPARE NUMERICAL INTEGRATION TECHNIQUES  *
*        RECTANGULAR, TRAPEZOIDAL, AND SIMPSON'S RULE --      *
*        BY USING ALL THREE FOR THE SAME FUNCTION OVER        *
*        VARIOUS INTERVALS AND WITH DIFFERENT NUMBERS OF      *
*        SEGMENTS. THE NUMBER OF SEGMENTS MUST BE EVEN.       *
*        WRITTEN BY T. HOFFMANN  07/11/77                     *
*                                                             *
****************************************************************
*                                                             *
*********          VARIABLE IDENTIFICATION              *********
*                                                             *
*        NSTEPS    = NUMBER OF SEGMENTS IN INTEGRATION INTERVAL*
*        XINCR     = WIDTH OF SEGMENT                          *
*        ORD0      = VALUE OF ZERO'TH ORDINATE                 *
*        VALU1     = VALUE OF LEFT BOUNDARY OF INTEGRATION INTERVAL*
*        VALU2     = VALUE OF RIGHT BOUNDARY OF INTEGRATION INTERVAL*
*        X         = X VALUES (ABCISSAS) OF INTERVALS          *
*        NCARD     = NUMBER OF CARDS READ                      *
*        RAREA     = AREA USING RECTANGULAR TECHNIQUE          *
*        TAREA     = AREA USING TRAPEZOIDAL RULE               *
*        SAREA     = AREA USING SIMPSON'S RULE                 *
*        KNT       = NUMBER OF DATA ERROR CARDS                *
*                                                             *
*****              ARRAY IDENTIFICATION                 *****
*                                                             *
*        ORD       = ORDINATES OF THE FUNCTION                 *
*        NERRS     = STORES CARD NUMBER OF UNREADABLE CARDS     *
*                                                             *
*****            SUBROUTINE AND FUNCTION NAMES          *****
*                                                             *
*        RECT      = COMPUTES AREA USING RECTANGULAR PROCEDURE *
*        TRAP      = COMPUTES AREA USING TRAPEZOIDAL PROCEDURE *
*        SIMP      = COMPUTES AREA USING SIMPSON'S RULE        *
*        ANYF      = FUNCTION TO BE INTEGRATED                 *
*                                                             *
****************************************************************
*                                                             *
*********          STORAGE ALLOCATION                   *********
*                                                             *
1.        DIMENSION NERRS(10)
2.        COMMON /YBLOCK/ ORD(1000),ORD0
3.        COMMON // NSTEPS,XINCR
4.        DATA NERRS/10*0/
*                                                             *
****************************************************************
*                                                             *
*********          INITIALIZATION BLOCK          BLOCK 0000
*                                                             *
5.        WRITE(6,3)
6.      3 FORMAT(1H1,12X,'COMPARISON OF NUMERICAL INTEGRATION TECHNIQUES'/
         1   1H0,'INTEGRATION OF SIN(X) - ALOG(X) + EXP(X)'//
         2   1X,'FROM   TO  STEPS  STEP ',3X,6(1H*),11X,'METHOD',
         3   10X,6H******/19X,'SIZE',5X,'RECTANGLE',7X,
         4   'TRAPEZOID',7X,'SIMPSON'//)
7.        NCARD = 0
8.        KNT = 0
9.        DO 9 I = 1,1000
10.          ORD(I) = 0.0
11.     9 CONTINUE
*                                                             *
****************************************************************
*                                                             *
*********          INPUT AND COMPUTATION BLOCK   BLOCK 0100
*                                                             *
12.   101 READ(5,103,ERR=901,END=301) VALU1,VALU2,NSTEPS
13.   103 FORMAT(2F4.2,I3)
14.       NCARD = NCARD + 1
15.       IF(MOD(NSTEPS,2).NE.0) GOTO 905
16.       X = VALU1
17.       XINCR = (VALU2 - VALU1)/FLOAT(NSTEPS)
18.       ORD0 = ANYF(X)
19.       DO 105 I = 1,NSTEPS
20.          X = X + XINCR
21.          ORD(I) = ANYF(X)
22.   105 CONTINUE
23.       CALL RECT(RAREA)
24.       CALL TRAP(TAREA)
25.       CALL SIMP(SAREA)
*                                                             *
****************************************************************
```

FIGURE 5-13 Listing of FORTRAN program for statistical example 5—numerical integration.

```
       *                                                                *
       *********            DETAIL PRINT BLOCK                  BLOCK 0200
       *                                                                *
26.          WRITE(6,203) VALU1,VALU2,NSTEPS,XINCR,RAREA,TAREA,SAREA
27.      203 FORMAT(1X,F4.1,F7.2,I5,F5.3,2X,3E15.8)
       *                                                                *
       *            GO BACK TO READ ANOTHER DATA CARD                   *
       *                                                                *
28.          GOTO 101
       *                                                                *
       ******************************************************************
       *                                                                *
       *********            TERMINATION BLOCK                   BLOCK 0300
       *                                                                *
29.      301 WRITE(6,305) KNT
30.      305 FORMAT(1H0,'THERE WERE',I3,' UNREADABLE DATA CARDS.'/
        1       ' THE FOLLOWING WERE NOT PROCESSED:')
31.          DO 303 I = 1,KNT
32.              WRITE(6,302) NERRS(I)
33.      302     FORMAT(5X,'CARD NUMBER ',I2)
34.      303 CONTINUE
35.          STOP
       *                                                                *
       ******************************************************************
       *                                                                *
       *********            ERROR MESSAGE BLOCK                 BLOCK 0900
       *                                                                *
36.      901 NCARD = NCARD + 1
37.          KNT = KNT + 1
38.          NERRS(KNT) = NCARD
39.          GOTO 907
       *                                                                *
40.      905 WRITE(6,906) NSTEPS,NCARD
41.      906 FORMAT(1H0,'ERROR -- NUMBER OF STEPS MUST BE EVEN, NOT',
        1       I3,' AS IN CARD',I3/)
       *                                                                *
       *            GO BACK TO READ ANOTHER DATA CARD                   *
       *                                                                *
42.      907 GOTO 101
       *
43.          END
       *                                                                *
       **********************************************  END OF MAIN PROGRAM
```

```
1.           SUBROUTINE RECT(AREA)
       *                                                                *
       *********            PROGRAM IDENTIFICATION              *********
       *                                                                *
       *        THIS SUBROUTINE INTEGRATES THE AREA UNDER A CURVE       *
       *        USING THE METHOD OF RECTANGLES.  ORDINATES OF THE       *
       *        CURVE MUST HAVE BEEN PREVIOUSLY STORED IN THE           *
       *        ARRAY ORD.                                              *
       *                                                                *
       ******************************************************************
       *                                                                *
       *********            VARIABLE IDENTIFICATION             *********
       *                                                                *
       *        AREA     = AREA UNDER CURVE                             *
       *        SUM      = SUM OF ORDINATES OF CURVE                    *
       *        ORD      = ORDINATES OF CURVE                           *
       *        NSTEPS   = NUMBER OF SEGMENTS IN INTEGRATION INTERVAL   *
       *        XINCR    = WIDTH OF SEGMENT                             *
       *        ORD0     = VALUE OF THE ZERO'TH ORDINATE                *
       *****                ARRAY IDENTIFICATION                *****
       *                                                                *
       *        ORD      = ORDINATES OF THE FUNCTION                    *
       *                                                                *
       ******************************************************************
       *                                                                *
       *********            STORAGE ALLOCATION                  *********
       *                                                                *
2.           COMMON /YBLOCK/ ORD(1000),ORD0
3.           COMMON // NSTEPS,XINCR
       *                                                                *
       ******************************************************************
```

FIGURE 5-13 *(continued)*

```
      *                                                                    *
      **********                    COMPUTATION BLOCK                  BLOCK 0100
      *                                                                    *
  4.         SUM = ORD0
  5.         DO 120 I = 1,NSTEPS-1
  6.            SUM = SUM + ORD(I)
  7.     120 CONTINUE
  8.         AREA = XINCR*SUM
  9.         RETURN
 10.         END
      *                                                                    *
      ***************************************************   END OF SUBPROGRAM
```

```
  1.          SUBROUTINE TRAP(AREA)                                        *
      *                                                                    *
      **********                 PROGRAM IDENTIFICATION          **********
      *                                                                    *
      *        THIS SUBROUTINE INTEGRATES THE AREA UNDER A CURVE           *
      *        USING THE METHOD OF TRAPEZOIDS.  ORDINATES OF THE           *
      *        CURVE MUST HAVE BEEN PREVIOUSLY STORED IN THE               *
      *        ARRAY ORD.                                                  *
      *                                                                    *
      ********************************************************************
      *                                                                    *
      **********                 VARIABLE IDENTIFICATION         **********
      *                                                                    *
      *        AREA      = AREA UNDER CURVE                                *
      *        SUM       = SUM OF ORDINATES OF CURVE                       *
      *        ORD       = ORDINATES OF CURVE                              *
      *        NSTEPS    = NUMBER OF SEGMENTS IN INTEGRATION INTERVAL      *
      *        XINCR     = WIDTH OF SEGMENT                                *
      *        ORD0      = VALUE OF THE ZERO'TH ORDINATE                   *
      *                                                                    *
      *****                    ARRAY IDENTIFICATION                   *****
      *                                                                    *
      *        ORD       = ORDINATES OF THE FUNCTION                       *
      *                                                                    *
      ********************************************************************
      *                                                                    *
      **********                 STORAGE ALLOCATION              **********
      *                                                                    *
  2.         COMMON /YBLOCK/ ORD(1000),ORD0
  3.         COMMON // NSTEPS,XINCR                                        *
      *                                                                    *
      ********************************************************************
      *                                                                    *
      **********                 COMPUTATION BLOCK                  BLOCK 0100
      *                                                                    *
  4.         SUM = (ORD0 + ORD(NSTEPS))/2.0
  5.         DO 120 I = 1,NSTEPS-1
  6.            SUM = SUM + ORD(I)
  7.     120 CONTINUE
  8.         AREA = SUM*XINCR
  9.         RETURN
 10.         END                                                          *
      *                                                                    *
      ***************************************************   END OF SUBPROGRAM
```

```
  1.          SUBROUTINE SIMP(AREA)                                        *
      *                                                                    *
      **********                 PROGRAM IDENTIFICATION          **********
      *                                                                    *
      *        THIS SUBROUTINE INTEGRATES THE AREA UNDER A CURVE           *
      *        USING SIMPSON'S RULE.  ORDINATES OF THE                     *
      *        CURVE MUST HAVE BEEN PREVIOUSLY STORED IN THE               *
      *        ARRAY ORD.                                                  *
      *                                                                    *
      ********************************************************************
      *                                                                    *
      **********                 VARIABLE IDENTIFICATION         **********
      *                                                                    *
      *        AREA      = AREA UNDER CURVE                                *
      *        SUM       = SUM OF ORDINATES OF CURVE                       *
      *        ORD       = ORDINATES OF CURVE                              *
      *        NSTEPS    = NUMBER OF SEGMENTS IN INTEGRATION INTERVAL      *
      *        XINCR     = WIDTH OF SEGMENT                                *
      *        ORD0      = VALUE OF THE ZERO'TH ORDINATE                   *
      *                                                                    *
```

FIGURE 5-13 *(continued)*

```
*****               ARRAY IDENTIFICATION                                 *****
*                                                                            *
*        ORD        = ORDINATES OF THE FUNCTION                              *
*                                                                            *
******************************************************************************
*                                                                            *
**********          STORAGE ALLOCATION                                **********
*                                                                            *
      COMMON /YBLOCK/ ORD(1000),ORD0
      COMMON // NSTEPS,XINCR
*                                                                            *
******************************************************************************
*                                                                            *
**********          COMPUTATION BLOCK                               BLOCK 0100
*                                                                            *
      SUM1 = ORD0 + ORD(NSTEPS)
      SUM2 = 0.0
      SUM4 = 0.0
      DO 120 I = 2,NSTEPS-2,2
          SUM2 = SUM2 + ORD(I)
  120 CONTINUE
      DO 140 I = 1,NSTEPS-1,2
          SUM4 = SUM4 + ORD(I)
  140 CONTINUE
      AREA = (SUM1 + 2.0*SUM2 + 4.0*SUM4)*XINCR/3.0
      RETURN
      END
*                                                                            *
****************************************************         END OF SUBPROGRAM
*                                                                            *
```

```
      FUNCTION ANYF(X)
*                                                                            *
**********          ANYF CAN BE EQUATED TO ANY FUNCTION                **********
*                                                                            *
      ANYF = SIN(X) - ALOG(X) + EXP(X)
      RETURN
      END
*                                                                            *
****************************************************         END OF SUBPROGRAM
```

FIGURE 5-13 *(continued)*

INPUT TEST DATA

START VALUE	END	STEPS	PURPOSE OR EXPECTED OUTPUT
00.2	01.4	020	VALUE OF ABOUT 4.05095
00.2	01.4	998	IMPROVEMENT IN PRECISION
00.2	01.4	006	POORER ESTIMATE
JKL			ERROR-REJECT CARD (NONNUMERIC DATA)
0001	1.00	050	VALUE OF ABOUT 3.11188
0001	1.00	100	IMPROVED ESTIMATE
0001	1.00	010	POORER ESTIMATE
0001	1.00	.01	ERROR-REJECT CARD (DECIMAL POINT IN INTEGER FIELD)
1.40	1.90	031	ERROR-NUMBER OF STEPS NOT EVEN
1.40	1.90	060	VALUE OF ABOUT 2.87549
			10 DATA CARDS
			2 REJECTED FOR DATA-TYPE ERROR
			1 ERROR MESSAGE FOR INVALID DATA

FIGURE 5-14 Annotated input test data for statistical example 5—numerical integration.

```
                COMPARISON OF NUMERICAL INTEGRATION TECHNIQUES

      INTEGRATION OF SIN(X) - ALOG(X) + EXP(X)

      FROM   TO  STEPS  STEP      ******          METHOD         ******
                        SIZE     RECTANGLE       TRAPEZOID       SIMPSON


        .2  1.40    20 .060    .40025963E+01   .40528363E+01   .40509643E+01
        .2  1.40   998 .001    .40499419E+01   .40509487E+01   .40509479E+01
        .2  1.40     6 .200    .39040517E+01   .40715184E+01   .40521335E+01
        .0  1.00    50 .020    .31352949E+01   .31148468E+01   .31122731E+01
        .0  1.00   100 .010    .31228486E+01   .31126245E+01   .31118838E+01
        .0  1.00    10 .099    .32647225E+01   .31624819E+01   .31297218E+01

      ERROR -- NUMBER OF STEPS MUST BE EVEN, NOT 31 AS IN CARD   9

       1.4  1.90    60 .008    .28659777E+01   .28755034E+01   .28754899E+01

      THERE WERE  2 UNREADABLE DATA CARDS.
      THE FOLLOWING WERE NOT PROCESSED:
           CARD NUMBER  4
           CARD NUMBER  8
```

FIGURE 5-15 Example of statistical output from numerical integration program.

number. This could, of course, have been programmed without the MOD function as:

$$NSTEPS = ((NSTEPS / 2) * 2)$$

5 The block structure of the program follows a structured style:

Storage allocation

Initialization

Input and computation

Detail print

Termination

Error message

6 The subroutines have identical COMMON declarations.

7 The function ANYF(X) is separated for ease of change. It is used by only two main program statements and the function could easily have been coded in the main program at lines 18 and 21.

8 A single FORMAT statement is used to print a multiple-line heading. Note the use of slashes and the indentation of the continuation lines (line 6).

Programming Exercises

Description of Assignment

Select one or more problems (or take the problem(s) assigned to you by your instructor). Write each of the computational procedures in the problem as a function and/or subroutine subprogram. Use the case structure where applicable. Follow the style guidelines and prepare the following:

1 Pseudocode description

2 Program flowchart

3 Program listing

4 List of test data and expected results. Test for both valid and invalid data

5 Output including output from error conditions

Mathematics and Statistics

1 For each of the following sets of data, compute the mean and variance of each subset X and Y and the correlation coefficient of the sets. See problem 4-1 for the correlation coefficient formula. The variance for X can be calculated as:

$$\text{Var} = \left(\Sigma X^2 - \frac{(\Sigma X)^2}{n} \right) \Big/ (n - 1)$$

Set 1		Set 2	
X	Y	X	Y
34.22	102.43	20	27.1
39.87	100.93	30	28.9
41.85	97.43	40	30.6
43.23	97.81	50	32.3
40.06	98.32	60	33.7
53.29	98.32	70	35.6
53.29	100.07	80	37.2
54.14	97.08		
49.12	91.59		
40.71	94.85		
55.15	94.65		

2 There are many ways to compute sequences of random numbers; two of these are the inner product or squaring method and the power residue procedure. The inner product method takes a number of digits, say four, squares it, and picks out the central four digits of the product as a random number. The four-digit random number is squared, etc. For example: starting with

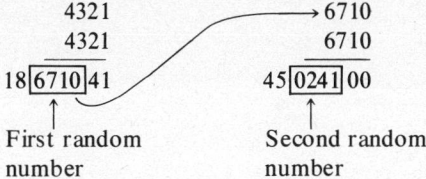

First random number   Second random number

4321 produces the sequence 6710, 0241, etc. The power residue method chooses a starting value, not even nor ending in a 5, and a special constant multiplier (91 is a good choice to obtain a sequence of four-digit random numbers). Form the product of the starting value and the constant and save the low-order four digits as the random number and the base to use for the next multiplication. For example, a starting value of 1907 and a constant of 91 produces the sequence 3537, 1867, etc.

$$
\begin{array}{rcr}
1907 & \longrightarrow & 3537 \\
91 & & 91 \\
\hline
17\;\boxed{3537} & & 32\;\boxed{1867}
\end{array}
$$

Write a program to generate random numbers by each of these procedures and compute the average value of each sequence. Use the following values as test cases:

Length of sequence	Initial value	Constant multiplier (Method two only)
100	4321	91
1000	4321	91
10000	4321	91
500	5023	3219
5000	7023	3219

3 The Newton-Raphson technique can be used effectively to find the real roots of a function by successive approximations. Given a function of x, the following relationship is used:

$$
x_{i+1} = x_i - \frac{f(x_i)}{f'(x_i)}
$$

where x_i = the current estimated value
x_{i+1} = the next estimated value
$f(x_i)$ = the function evaluated at x_i
$f'(x_i)$ = the first derivative of the function evaluated at x_i

An initial estimate, x_0, is required as input to the process and it must terminate when $|x_{i+1} - x_i| <$ some epsilon value. Write a program to compute a root of $f(x) = x^3 - 3x^2 + 5$ to an accuracy of .001 or better. Print out the number of iterations and root. Write the program so that it can be easily modified for other functions and epsilons. Use the following initial estimates: 1.0, −1.0, 0.0, 3.0, −30.0.

Business and Economics

4 Various techniques are used to depreciate capital assets; most common are the straight line, double declining balance, and sum of the years digits. Assuming an initial cost(c), a salvage value (s), and a useful life of N years, the relationships for depreciation (D_n) in year n are as follows:

Straight line:

$$
D_n = \frac{C - S}{N}
$$

Sum of the years digits:

$$D_n = (C - S) \frac{N - n + 1}{\text{sum}}$$

where n is a particular year and

$$\text{sum} = \sum_{i=1}^{N} i = \frac{N(N + 1)}{2}$$

Double declining balance:

$$D_n = \frac{2}{N} \left(C - \sum_{i=1}^{n-1} D_i \right)$$

until $C - \sum_{i=1}^{n} D_i = S$

Write a program to depreciate each of the following assets over their useful lives, showing the annual depreciation by each technique.

Asset number	Initial cost	Salvage value	Useful life
1	$ 10,000.00	$ 3,000.00	6 years
2	37,006.00	4,127.37	8
3	6,000.00	327.00	8
4	75,745.00	8,165.00	7
5	365,000.00	27,500.00	10

5 Modify problem 5 of Chapter 4 by making the interest computations as subprograms.

6 Various intrinsic forecasting techniques can be applied to time series data. Among the simplest of these are exponential smoothing, weighted moving averages, and simple moving averages. These equations are as follows:

Three-period simple moving average:

$$f_{n+1} = \frac{d_n + d_{n-1} + d_{n-2}}{3}$$

where d_i is the ith actual demand and
f_j is the forecast for the jth period

Three-period weighted moving average:

$$f_{n+1} = \frac{3d_n + 2d_{n-1} + d_{n-2}}{6}$$

Exponential smoothing:

$$f_{n+1} = ad_n + (1 - a)f_n$$

where a is a decimal between 0 and 1. (Read in 0.2 for this problem.)

Write a program to compute forecasts by each of these techniques: Start with period 4 and assume f_3 for exponential smoothing equals the mean of the first two values.

Period	Demand series I	Demand series II
1	31.8	100
2	33.7	300
3	32.1	450
4	29.3	570
5	33.9	750
6	37.0	820
8	42.5	915
9	36.7	945
10	31.0	975
11	35.8	1000

Science and Engineering

7 Frequently an experiment results in a set of empirical data which arise because of a functional relationship. Fitting a straight line or curve to the data in order to better understand the relationship is often done. The method of least squares, which minimizes the squares of the differences between actual and fitted function values, is the most common mathematical technique used to do this. The general equation for a straight line is:

$$y = a + bx$$

From a set of x and y paired observations, the desired coefficients can be computed as:

$$b = \frac{n\Sigma xy - (\Sigma x)(\Sigma y)}{n\Sigma x^2 - (\Sigma x)^2}$$

$$a = \bar{y} - b\bar{x}$$

where $\bar{y}$ and $\bar{x}$ are the means of their respective data sets.
Similarly, an equation of the form $y = ax^b$ can be rewritten as:

$$\log y = \log a + b \log x$$

Letting $Y = \log y$
   $X = \log x$
   $A = \log a$
one can see that this is similar to a straight line equation as before:

$$Y = A + bX$$

and thus b and a can be derived with the same equations modified for logarithms. The following data was derived from the pull characteristics of an alternating current magnet. Write a program to compute coefficients for both types of equations.

Pounds pull, Y	Ampere-turns, X
3.0	1.5
4.5	2.0
5.5	3.5
6.0	5.0
7.5	6.0
8.5	7.5
8.0	9.0
9.0	10.5
9.5	12.0
10.0	14.0

8 Referring to problem 8 of Chapter 3, make the degree to radian conversion a function.

9 Referring to problem 9 of Chapter 4, place the graphing routine as a subroutine and the function to be plotted as a function subprogram.

Humanities and Social Sciences

10 Modify problem 10 of Chapter 4 so that alternate printouts are available at the user's choice. That is, the user can request only Table I, only Table II, both Table I and Table II, a Table of Income versus Politics, or a Table of Income versus Sex.

11 The binomial probability distribution is often applicable to sampling situations. For example, among two candidates for office, there does not appear to be a clear winner. A poll is taken of 900 people and 540 prefer candidate A. How likely is this result if indeed the entire population of voters are evenly split? The equation for this is:

$$P\left(\begin{array}{c} n \\ x \end{array}\right) = \frac{n!}{x!(n-x)!} \; p^x(1-p)^{n-x}$$

where $p = 0.5$ for this problem.

Write a program to compute the probabilities for the following situations. If n is less than 10, compute factorials by multiplying, i.e.,

$$n! = 1 \times 2 \times 3 \times \cdots \times n$$

If n is 10 or greater, use Stirling's approximation:

$$n! = e^{-n}n^n\sqrt{2\pi n}$$

for factorials.

Situation number	Sample size	Yes answers
1	9	5
2	90	50
3	90	54
4	10	5
5	100	52

12 The combined effect of wind and temperature on the human body is quite severe, particularly in cold climates. The relative effect of their combination is referred to as the wind-chill factor. Prepare a wind-chill chart for Fahrenheit temperatures from -50 to $+10$ degrees (in 10-degree increments) and windspeeds of 5 to 30 miles per hour. The relevant formulas are:

$V1 = .447$ times windspeed

$V2 = (10.45 + 10\sqrt{V1} - V1) * (33.0 - \text{TEMP}_C)$

Wind-Chill $\text{TEMP}_C = 33.0 - (V2/22.034)$

Note that the temperatures are Celsius and the table is to be in Fahrenheit. (Use a function subprogram for conversion.)

General

13 Refer to problem 13 of Chapter 4 and replace inline code for computing averages with a function subprogram.

14 Write a program to deal three sets of four poker hands of five cards each. Shuffle the deck between each deal. Write the shuffling procedure as a subroutine and use either a random number generator available as a system library subprogram or one of the procedures described in problem 2 of this chapter.

15 Reprogram problem 13 of Chapter 3 to make use of the case structure for currency conversion.

CHAPTER

THE USE OF FILES ON EXTERNAL STORAGE

The FORTRAN problems and programs in the first five chapters assumed that data would be input from punched cards (or at a terminal) and output would be immediately printed or displayed. Data to be saved was placed in arrays in internal storage. These procedures are generally satisfactory for computational problems with relatively little data, but there are situations where large amounts of data need to be input, processed, and saved for later use. The method for storing the data in such cases is a file on external storage. Also called secondary or auxiliary storage, the external storage generally uses magnetic disks or magnetic tape. This chapter will explain how to program the use of files on external storage.

Files in FORTRAN

As background for the input and output instructions, this section will review records and files and explain external storage file-access methods.

Records and Files

A *data item* is a set of numeric (or alphanumeric) characters treated as a unit for processing. In FORTRAN, each data item is uniquely identified by a variable name. Examples are a pay rate, an identification number, a measurement, etc. A collection of related data items constitute a *record*. Examples of a record are data items from a research questionnaire, all of the data items relating to the payroll for one employee, or all of the data describing a chemical process. A collection of records of a given type constitute a *file*. For example, the research questionnaire records make up the research record file, the payroll records make up the payroll file, and the chemical process records are the chemical process data file. This relationship is shown in Figure 6-1.

The records in a file are stored on some medium such as punched cards, magnetic tape, or magnetic disks. Records to be printed are placed on the printer line. Records occupy storage space on the storage medium and each item within the record takes up part of this space. The storage space (described in numbers of character storage positions) for an item is the *field* for the item. +3.758 takes a field of six characters; 3758 requires a field of four characters.

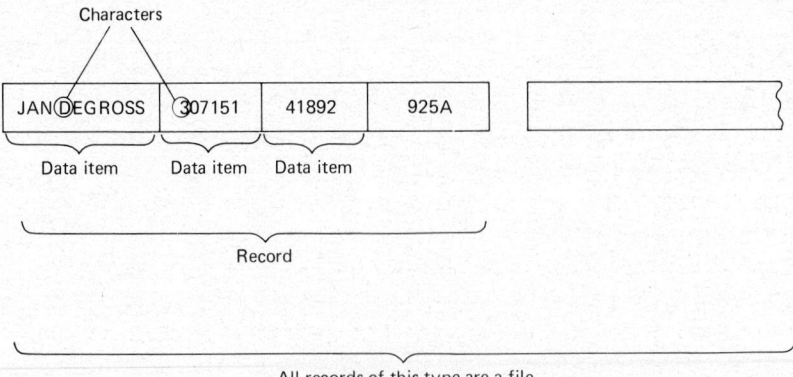

FIGURE 6-1   Relationship of character, item, record, and file.

In FORTRAN, any set of input or output records constitutes a file, but the term is most commonly used to refer to files on external storage. The user of FORTRAN need not understand the technical characteristics of secondary storage because the language handles file storage in a standard manner rather than requiring the programmer to furnish all of the specifications. However, one storage characteristic that the programmer may specify is formatted versus unformatted representation.

Unformatted Input and Output

Two methods for input and output have been used in prior chapters: list-directed input and output and format-directed input and output. Both list-directed and format-directed input and output require considerable computer processing because at input the external representation of data must be converted to the internal representation suitable for processing and for output the internal representation must be formatted. If data is to be written onto a file for subsequent use but there is no human-readable output required, then it is more efficient to write the data record without any conversion to output format. When the records are subsequently read, no conversion to internal representation is required. The writing and reading of data in internal representation without formatting is termed an unformatted read or write. The files are sometimes referred to as binary files. It is specified by a READ or WRITE with a unit number but no FORMAT statement number or asterisk. If unformatted records containing X, Y, I are to be written onto a file on unit 8, the statement is:

WRITE (8) X , Y , I

A subsequent READ statement from this file must use the unformatted form because the records are not formatted:

READ (8) X , Y , I

Because unformatted records are more efficient in terms of processing time, they should be considered for all external FORTRAN files on magnetic tape or magnetic disk.

Storage Media and File-access Methods

The two most common external storage media—magnetic tape and disks—differ in their operation. The magnetic tape is read or written in serial fashion from beginning to end. The first record on the tape is read first, the second record is read second, etc. The second record cannot be accessed without reading the first. It operates very much like a reel of magnetic tape or a tape cassette used for home recording. Records on tape are stored in physical blocks separated by interblock gaps. The gaps allow the tape unit to start and stop between the reading and writing of blocks. The FORTRAN programmer need not be concerned with the physical record on tape because FORTRAN requires only that the programmer define a program record; the compiler arranges physical record storage.

The disk file can access any part of the storage by an access arm (or arms) which moves to the set of storage positions (on a track) where a record is stored. Records on disk storage may be written and read serially, or records may be accessed directly by taking advantage of the direct-access capabilities of the disk. The direct access requires each record to have an identifier that specifies its location in the file. The identifier is not an actual disk address. The connection between the record address identifier and an actual address is performed automatically by the operating system.

In files to be read serially, it is common to have some method for noting the end of a set (file) of records. This is frequently accomplished by a special record containing an end-of-file character (or characters) but other methods may be used such as a record counter maintained by the system.

The file-access methods available in standard FORTRAN are sequential access and direct access. A file must be defined as either one or the other and may be used only in the defined access mode. However, a file on disk storage can be defined as sequential for one use and defined as direct-access for a different use, assuming the records are stored so that both methods are feasible.

1 *Sequential access* Records are read in serial fashion in the same order they were written. The data records in a file must be all formatted or all unformatted. An end file record may be used to mark the end of the file. Sequential-access files can be implemented on either tape or disk storage.

2 *Direct access* This can be implemented only on direct-access storage such as disks. Direct-access input/output statements must be used to write or read, but records may be read or written in any order. Each record must have a unique positive integer identifier called a *record number,* specified when the record is first written. The records can be accessed in order by this record number. The records must have the same length and must be either all formatted or all unformatted. List-directed input or output cannot be used. Endfile records are not used.

Sequential files and direct-access files differ in the procedure for changing or updating a single record in the file. In general, to alter the contents of any record in a sequential file on magnetic tape, the entire file is read and rewritten, making the required change (delete a record, add a record, or change part of the record). In a direct-access file, the contents of a single record may be altered without rewriting the file. A complete discussion of file updating procedure is available in data processing references.[1]

Self-testing Exercise 6-1

1 Classify the following as probably a record or a file.
  (*a*) Height and weight observations for 1000 men from an experiment.
  (*b*) Height and weight for one man.
  (*c*) Income, age, children, and occupation for one family.
  (*d*) Income, age, etc., for all of the families in a study.

---

[1] See discussion in Davis, *Introduction to Computers,* Third Edition, pages 248–283, McGraw-Hill Book Company, New York, 1977; and Davis, Olson, and Litecky, *Elementary Structured COBOL,* pages 159–170, McGraw-Hill Book Company, New York, 1977.

2 True or false.

    (*a*) A formatted file is generally more efficient for processing.

    (*b*) Both tape and disk storage can be used for sequential access.

    (*c*) Tape storage can be used for direct access.

    (*d*) A record number is required for direct access.

    (*e*) Secondary storage and auxiliary storage are the same.

3 Complete the table:

Access method	Order records read	File medium	Use of list-directed I/O	Use of end-of-file record
Sequential	Same order as written	Tape or disk	Allowed	Yes
Direct				

Sequential-access Processing

READ and WRITE Statements for Sequential Access

In simple sequential access, the READ or WRITE statement is the same as those used in previous chapters, but the unit number identifies the auxiliary storage device. The unit number to be used for tapes or disks may be preassigned by the installation or be specifically assigned by the job control cards the programmer places with the program.

Example 1

Read a record from magnetic tape unit 10 based on the FORMAT statement 700.

```
READ (10,700) A,B,X
```

This instruction specifies a formatted, sequential-access processing and assumes the records were written using a formatted WRITE statement.

Example 2

Read the three items in list-directed sequential access (that were written using a list-directed output statement).

```
READ (10,*) A,B,X
```

Note the use of the asterisk in place of the format to specify list-directed input.

    The general form of the READ and WRITE statements is the same as presented in Chapter 3, with square brackets indicating an optional element.

```
READ  (control list) [I/O variables list]
WRITE  (control list) [I/O variables list]
```

The elements in the control list consist of an alphabetic identifier, e.g., UNIT, FMT, etc., followed by an equals sign and a number which identifies a unit, a statement label, or a variable name. Five specifications useful for sequential access are shown in the box. The alphabetic identifier is optional

---

SPECIFIERS FOR SEQUENTIAL-ACCESS CONTROL LIST

[   ] means optional part of specifier

[UNIT =]   unit number of device
 [FMT =]   FORMAT statement number for specific formatting and * for list-directed formatting
     ERR = statement number to which control goes if there is an I/O error
    END = statement number to go to if end-of-file
 IOSTAT = integer variable to hold error code. 0 = no error, negative = end-of-file, and positive = error type code.

---

with the unit number and the format number specifications, but if the alphabetic identifier is not used, the unit number must be first and the FORMAT statement second. The following are identical in their effect:

```
READ   ( 5 , 7 0 0 )  ALPHA
READ   (UN I T = 5 ,   FM T = 7 0 0 )  AL PHA
READ   ( 5 ,   FM T = 7 0 0 )  AL PHA
```

The ERR and END specifications have been explained in Chapter 3; the new specification is IOSTAT. The IOSTAT defines an integer variable to which the program will automatically move an error code in the event of an error. A zero means no error, a positive error code identifies different errors, and a negative integer signifies an end-of-file condition. The positive and negative integers to be used as error codes are defined by the FORTRAN implementor and will usually vary for different compilers.

The IOSTAT specifier is normally used in conjunction with the ERR specifier. An input or output error will send control to the statement number specified by ERR = s. If IOSTAT is also used, the processing statements specified by the transfer on ERR can be executed to analyze the error code of IOSTAT to determine the exact reason for the I/O error. Thus, a combination of ERR and IOSTAT can provide for more information and diagnostic messages than the use of ERR alone.

The END statement has been used in prior chapters to signal the end of input data. This condition has initiated a transfer of control to cause the printing of totals, end-of-program messages, etc. In the case of a sequential file to which records are going to be added, the END statement signals the end of the existing file (an endfile record is detected); new records may then be added.

File-positioning Statements

In a sequential file, reading or writing is performed serially. In order to start over at the beginning of the file, the file is rewound. The term *rewind*, when applied to a file on magnetic tape, is physically implemented, i.e., the tape is rewound. In the case of a disk file, rewind means to position the read/write arms at the first record in the file. To go back only to a previous record, the file must be backspaced. The last logical record of a sequential file may be an end-of-file record. The existence of the end-of-file record is necessary for the use of the END feature with the READ statement. The logical end-of-file record is not always a separate physical end-of-file record since the system may implement end-of-file detection in other ways.

File-positioning statements are used to backspace, write an end-of-file record, or rewind back to the beginning. These statements, given in the box, apply to both tape and disk files.

FILE-POSITIONING STATEMENTS

BACKSPACE unit	or	BACKSPACE (alist)
ENDFILE unit	or	ENDFILE (alist)
REWIND unit	or	REWIND (alist)

where alist contains:

[UNIT =] unit number ([Unit =] is optional)
ERR = statement number

Backspace Example

```
      READ   (7,700)  JIM
700  FORMAT  (I 5)
      BACKSPACE  7
      READ   (7,700)  JON
```

The preceding program segment reads from unit 7 into a variable named JIM. The backspace and subsequent read does a re-read of the same value that was read into JIM, placing it into JON. (It is, of course, not efficient to do it this way, since JON = JIM will accomplish the same effect.)

Endfile Example

```
ENDFILE  8  or  ENDFILE (UNIT = 8)
```

This statement writes an end-of-file record at the end of a sequential file on tape unit 8.

The rewind instruction positions a file at the beginning. There are occasions when the programmer may wish to read the data more than once (perhaps doing searching or using the data differently each time). It is often a good practice to rewind sequential files on auxiliary storage at the beginning of the program to ensure proper positioning. If the file is already rewound, no action is taken. It is generally a desirable procedure to rewind all files prior to terminating the program.

Self-testing Exercise 6-2

1 Write statements to read the variables X, Y, Z from punched cards and write them onto a magnetic tape (use unit 8) in a list-directed, sequential input and output method.

2 Rewrite the list-directed statements from problem 1 to write onto a sequential file on a disk (unit 10), and the UNIT and FMT specifiers.

3 Rewind the file written in problem 1 and read the data.

4 Repeat problems 1 and 2 using format-directed input and output and FORMAT statement 700.

5 Backspace the file(s) in problem 1 and then read the data.

6 Would using rewind in place of backspace in problem 5 have the same effect? Explain.

Direct-access Processing

A direct-access file in FORTRAN consists of a set of storage locations; each location is capable of storing one record and each location has an identifying number. The storage locations are numbered from 1 to N (where N is the maximum number of records in the file). If, for example, the direct-access file is to hold a maximum of 100 records, the record locations are numbered 1 to 100. A numbered location can be empty—with no record currently being stored.

1	Storage for 1 record
2	Storage for 1 record
3	Storage for 1 record
n	Storage for 1 record

Storage and retrieval of records is based on the record location numbers. Using the record number, the records can be read or written in any order. For example, in building a file, the records could be written in the order 3, 7, 2, 1, 5, 9, ... Direct-access files are sometimes called random-access files (in contrast to serial-access sequential files).

The records in a direct-access file must all be the same length. The direct-access records can be formatted or unformatted, but not both in the same file. List-directed input and output is not allowed. An endfile record is not used because it has no purpose.

A direct-access file may be established and defined by job control cards or by OPEN statements (to be explained later in the chapter). The instructions for the direct-access file READ and WRITE are the same as sequential file READ and WRITE except for one new control list specification and dropping the END control specifier, as shown in the box.

SPECIFIERS FOR DIRECT-ACCESS CONTROL LIST

[   ] means optional part of specifier

[UNIT =] unit number of direct-access storage device

[FMT =]   FORMAT statement number for formatted input or output

REC   = variable holding record number of record storage location to be accessed. This is required.

IOSTAT = integer variable to hold error code. 0 = no error, positive = type of error code

ERR   = statement number to go to if I/O error

The ERR and IOSTAT are optional and are used as with sequential files. The REC specifier is required because the program must have a variable name where the record number of the record storage location to be accessed will be stored. For example,

```
    READ ( 5 ,   1 0 )   I R ,   V A L
1 0   FORMAT ( I 3 ,   F 3 . 2 )
    WRITE ( 7 ,   REC = I R )   VAL
```

The preceding reads two values, IR and VAL, from the card reader and then writes VAL in unformatted form onto unit 7 (a disk file) at the record location specified by IR.

Once an individual record storage location in a direct-access file has been occupied by storing a record there, the location may be referenced to read the record or a new record may be stored there, replacing the existing record. Of course, a record may not be read before it has been written. Backspace and rewind are not meaningful in the context of direct-access processing.

Self-testing Exercise 6-3

1 Read 12 records with the variables ID, NAME, and PAY in a format of (I2, A10, F6.2). Write them unformatted onto a direct-access file (unit 10) using a DO loop. Use IOSTAT and ERR, but the statements referenced need not be written.
2 Read record number 5 from the file created in problem 1.
3 Read every other record from the file in question 1 and print them with identifying labels.

OPEN, CLOSE, and INQUIRE Statements

The previous file-handling statements have all assumed devices that were pre-specified as having file space available (probably based on default specifications by the operating system or specified by job control instructions). The OPEN and CLOSE statements are provided by the new standard FORTRAN as facilities for the program to specify files, associate files with devices, disconnect files, etc. The INQUIRE statement allows the program to obtain characteristics and status of a file. The effects of these statements are often dependent on the specific FORTRAN compiler. Hence, they should be used only after reading the appropriate implementor reference manual(s). Because of the implementor dependent status and advanced nature of the instructions, the discussion will survey the capabilities of the OPEN, CLOSE, and INQUIRE statements, but will not describe them in detail.

Opening and Closing a File

The OPEN statement is used to associate (connect) an existing file to an input/output unit or create a new file on a unit. If an option is not specified, the compiler selects the most common or default option. The CLOSE statement terminates the connection.

THE OPEN STATEMENT

OPEN(olist)

The olist is a list of specifiers for the features of the file, the unit number always being required, others being optional except record length which is required for a direct-access file:

[UNIT =]   unit number (UNIT = is optional)
IOSTAT   = integer variable for input/output status
FILE   = name of the file
ERR   = statement label for transfer if error
STATUS   = OLD, NEW, SCRATCH, or UNKNOWN. NEW is default option
ACCESS   = SEQUENTIAL or DIRECT. SEQUENTIAL is default option
FORM   = FORMATTED or UNFORMATTED default option is FORMATTED
              for sequential file and UNFORMATTED for direct-access file
RECL   = record length for a direct-access file (required)
BLANK   = NULL or ZERO to specify handling of blanks. ZERO is default

A new direct-access unformatted file on unit 12 might be opened by the following:

OPEN (1 2 , I O S T A T = I N D I K , E R R = 6 0 0 , F I L E = S A M P L E ,
S T A T U S = N E W , A C C E S S = D I R E C T , R E C L = 2 0 0)

where the specifications indicate that the file is named SAMPLE, it is a new file, it is direct-access, and the length of each record is 200 characters. If an error is encountered in opening the file, control transfers to statement 600 and the variable INDIK receives an error code.

THE CLOSE STATEMENT

CLOSE(clist)

where the clist is a list of specifiers, unit number being the only one required:

[UNIT =]   unit number (UNIT = is optional)
IOSTAT   = input/output status specifier variable
ERR   = statement label
STATUS   = KEEP or DELETE. KEEP is default option

If a file on unit 8 is to be released for other use (it will no longer be available), the CLOSE might read:

C L O S E (8 , S T A T U S = D E L E T E)

Obtaining Data About a File

All the specifiers for an existing file are stored with the file, so information about a file can be obtained by using the INQUIRE statement.

INQUIRE STATEMENT

There are two forms of the INQUIRE statement: file and unit. The form of the file inquiry is:

INQUIRE(FILE = file name and possibly other specifiers)

This returns specifications for the named file.

The form of the unit inquiry is:

INQUIRE(unit number, and possibly other specifiers)

The list of specifiers is used by the programmer to assign a value such as a variable name of the correct type to be used to store each specifier that is included in the list.

Specifier	Value assigned	Values returned or result
IOSTAT	Integer variable	0, negative or positive
ERR	Statement number	Transfer if error
EXIST	Logical variable (See Chapter 7)	True (exists) or false (does not exist)
OPENED	Logical variable	True (opened) or false (not open)
NUMBER	Integer variable	Number of unit connected to file
NAMED	Logical variable	True (named) or false (no name)
NAME	Character variable	Name of file
ACCESS	Character variable	"SEQUENTIAL" or "DIRECT"
DIRECT	Character variable	"YES", "NO," or "UNKNOWN"
FORM	Character variable	"FORMATTED," "UNFORMATTED," or "UNKNOWN"
FORMATTED	Character variable	"YES", "NO," or "UNKNOWN"
UNFORMATTED	Character variable	"YES", "NO," or "UNKNOWN"
RECL	Integer variable	Record length of records in file
NEXTREC	Integer variable	Number of next record in direct-access file
BLANK	Character variable	"NULL" or "ZERO" (zero blank control)

EXAMPLE

INQUIRE   (UNIT = 16,   FORM = FRM,   RECL = LENGTH)

After execution, FRM will contain the characters FORMATTED, UNFOR-MATTED, or UNKNOWN, and LENGTH will contain the length of the records in the file connected to unit 16. The definition of character variables for use with these instructions is explained in Chapter 7A.

Self-testing Exercise 6-4

1 Write the statements to OPEN and to WRITE a record containing PAYNO and PAYRTE onto a new direct-access file called PAY on unit 8. The record number is

IRNO, the error routine label is 900, and the record length is 250. The record is formatted.

2 Inquire what the next record number is after the one just written in question 1.

3 Write the statements to OPEN a formatted sequential file on disk unit 9 and to write a record composed of COURSE and GRADES. Backspace and read the record just written and print it. Close the file. The name of the file is STUDNT.

Summary

FORTRAN programs do not need auxiliary storage if card or terminal input is processed as entered and the results are then displayed or printed. The need for files on external storage arises when input data is to be stored for later use or data is to be used repeatedly by the same program or different programs or the data exceeds the storage space available for arrays. Under these conditions, storing the data as a file on external storage is a desirable approach.

A record in FORTRAN consists of a set of data items that is read or written by a READ or WRITE statement. All records of a given type (same data items) constitute a file. The file may be sequential-access or direct-access. The common storage media of magnetic tape and magnetic disks both support sequential access; direct access requires a direct-access device such as a disk.

In the simplest case of sequential access, reading or writing from the file is the same as for card reader or printer except for a different unit number. It is possible to add additional specifications by the control list. The file may be positioned (rewound or backspaced) by file-positioning statements.

A direct-access file consists conceptually of a numbered set of fixed length storage locations numbered from 1 to N. The file may be predefined by the operating system, defined by job control statements, or by an OPEN statement. Direct-access READ and WRITE statements require a record number specification in the control list. Other specifications may be included.

The 1977 FORTRAN standard provides additional, very flexible facilities for specifying files, connecting files to devices, disconnecting files, inquiring about the status of a file, etc. These will be useful in situations requiring extensive file handling. Their use requires access to the implementor manual for the compiler being employed.

Answers to Self-testing Exercises

Exercise 6-1

1 (*a*) File   (*b*) Record   (*c*) Record   (*d*) File
2 (*a*) False   (*b*) True   (*c*) False   (*d*) True   (*e*) True

3

Access method	Order records read	File medium	Use of list-directed I/O	Use of endfile record
Sequential	Same order as written	Tape or disk	Allowed	Yes
Direct	Random order	Disk	Not allowed	No

Exercise 6-2

1 READ (5 , *)X , Y , Z
   WRITE (8 , *)X , Y , Z
2 READ (5 , *)X , Y , Z
   WRITE (UNIT= 10 , FMT= *)X , Y , Z
3 REWIND 8
   READ (8 , *)A , B , C
4 (1)   READ (5 , 700)X , Y , Z
               WRITE (8 , FMT= 700)X , Y , Z
       700 FORMAT (3F 2 . 0)
   (2)   READ (5 , 700)X , Y , Z
               WRITE (10 , 700)X , Y , Z
       700 FORMAT (3F 2 . 0)
5 BACKSPACE 8
   READ (8 , *)X , Y , Z
6 Yes, it would be the same, but only if there is only one record on the file. If there were
   two records, rewind would always position to read the first, while backspace would
   position to read the second.

Exercise 6-3

1   DO   100 J= 1 ,   12
              READ (5 , 20 , ERR= 30 , IOSTAT=ENCODE) ID , NAME , PAY
       20   FORMAT (I 2 , A 10 ,   F 6 . 2)
              WRITE (10 , REC=ID) NAME , PAY
   100 CONTINUE
2 READ (10 , REC= 5) NAME , PAY
3   DO 10 I= 1 ,   10 , 2
              READ (10 , REC=I) N , P
              PRINT 30 , I , N , P   or
              WRITE (6 , 30)I , N , P
       30   FORMAT (` ID=  ` I 2 , ` NAME=  ` A 10 , ` PAY=  ` F 6 . 2)
   10 CONTINUE

Exercise 6-4

1 OPEN   (8 , ERR= 900 , FILE= PAY , STATUS=NEW ,
   ACCESS=DIRECT , RECL= 250)
   WRITE   (8 , 700 , REC= IRNO , ERR= 900)PAYNO ,   PAYRTE
2 INQUIRE   (UNIT= 8 , NEXTREC= INEXT)
   where record number of next record will be placed in INEXT.
3 OPEN   (9 , ERR= 900 , FILE= STUDNT , FORM=FORMATTED ,
   STATUS=NEW ,   ACCESS=SEQUENTIAL)
   Note that form, status, and access are not required because these specifications are
   default options.
       WRITE   (9 , 700 , ERR= 900) COURSE , GRADES
   700 FORMAT   (2F 10 . 2)
       BACKSPACE 9
       READ   (9 , 700 , ERR= 900) COURSE , GRADES
       WRITE   (6 , 700) COURSE , GRADES
       CLOSE   (9)

Questions and Problems

1 Define the following terms:
  (a) character
  (b) data item
  (c) direct-access storage
  (d) end-of-file record
  (e) field
  (f) file
  (g) record
  (h) sequential-access storage

2 Differentiate between:
  (a) Use of magnetic tape and disks for FORTRAN files
  (b) Formatted and unformatted records and the impact on FORTRAN file use

3 A researcher has 1000 sets of data that will be processed by a number of different programs over a period of 7 months. The data consists of sets of research observations (call them X's) with 9 observations in each set (X_1 through X_9). Each card has an integer number from 1 to 1000 that identifies the set. The data is now in punched cards with each set on a separate card (as I4,9F8.2).
  (a) Write statements to create a sequential file on device 10 (say a magnetic tape).
  (b) Write statements to read half of the data, rewind, and repeat the reading of the first 500 sets of observations.

4 Assume a file as in problem 3.
  (a) Create a direct file. Use the set number as the direct-access file record number.
  (b) Read the sets of data having record numbers equal to the number created by a sampling function. The function is ISAMPL(SEED) where SEED has already been defined.

5 Assume a file as in problem 4, but create an unformatted file and then read the second 10 cards.

6 Assume a file as in problem 3 but list-directed data on cards separated by commas. Read the data, create a file, rewind, and then read the first five records.

CHAPTER

EXAMPLE PROGRAMS AND PROGRAMMING EXERCISES WHICH USE EXTERNAL FILES

The example programs illustrate typical use of external files. The program for general example 6, Payroll Reports, uses an external file to hold reference data which is matched with variable data read in on cards; the program for statistical example 5, Inventory Simulation, uses a temporary file to hold a large data file for use on successive problem runs.

General Notes on Chapter 6 Examples

External data files are used in several ways. In some sense they are just a different form of an array. If the array must be saved between runs of the program, its contents can be written to a file and read in the next time the program is run. Such a run may simply extract data from the file or update it or perform a combination of these procedures. In some cases storing all data to be available for use by the program creates an array that is too large for storage in the main memory and so the data sets which for a small problem would be stored in an array are written as records on an external file.

General Program Example 6—Payroll Reports

The program produces the same reports as its predecessor in Chapter 5. The report printing logic and the computational procedures are identical to those in Chapter 5. The difference is that only the variable data, departments to be included in these reports and the hours worked by each employee, are read from cards. The reference data on each employee is kept on an external file.

In other words, the program illustrates one of the uses for files: retention of reference data. The reference file (also called master file) is a sequential-access file which is sequenced on the employee identification numbers (Figure 6-4). In order to avoid having to search the file from the beginning each time an employee data card is read, the data cards (Figure 6-4) also have been presorted on the ID numbers.

Problem Description for General Example 6

The program is to read employee pay data and produce two reports: (1) Error and Control Report and (2) Report of Pay Amounts. The Report of Pay Amounts is to contain a line for each employee and a total line at the end of the report. The employees are to be grouped by department in the report. In the Report of Pay Amounts, net pay that is negative or over $300.00 is accompanied by a warning note. Also, errors in input code for union/management employees are to be noted.

The first input to the program consists of a set of five department numbers and names, one pair per card. Input validation for this data consists of an output table which echoes the values for visual verification. Subsequent input data consists of one card for each employee, giving ID number, department where worked, and hours worked. These cards are arranged in ascending order on employee ID number. Errors detected on input are noted immediately with a suitable message. Following the reading of each employee card, one or more records are read from the reference file until reference data concerning the particular employee is found or it is established that the matching record is missing or a data error is present. When a matching record is found, it is retained in an array for use in computation and output. The reference file records consist of employee ID number, name, department number, pay rate, miscellaneous deductions, number of dependents, and type of employee (union/management). After all employee input records or cards have been read, a total record count and number of rejected records is printed.

Program Documentation for General Example 6

Since there are very few differences between this program and general example 5, only a portion of the flowchart (Figure 6-5) and two blocks with code segments which are changed will be shown here (Figures 6-2 and 6-3). No pseudocode is given. New test data is documented in Figure 6-4. The Error and Control Report is shown in Figure 6-6, and the Report of Pay Amounts, identical to Figure 5-10, is not shown here.

Notes on General Example 6

The principal difference between this program and general example 5 is in block 100 where the employee data is read. Lines 28 through 30 of general example 5 have been replaced with lines 29 through 36 of general example 6 (Figure 6-2). Three new variable names have been added to name the employee data read from cards. These have been added to the list of variables at the beginning of the program (not shown). The reference master file is on unit 7; it was written by another program not shown.

   Three additional error messages have been added in block 900 (Figure 6-3) to reflect possible file errors. Data-type errors and invalid input data errors print on the Error and Control Report (Figure 6-6); errors which cause the program to

```
****************************************************************
*                                                              *
**********            READ EMPLOYEE DATA              BLOCK 0100
*                                                              *
29.     101 READ(5,103,END=301,ERR=901) IDNUM,NDEPT,HOURS
30.     103 FORMAT(I5,I4,F4.1)
31.         NCARD = NCARD + 1
32.     102 READ(7,104,END=920,ERR=930) ID(NUM),(NAME(NUM,J),J=1,3),
        1       NDEP(NUM),PAYDAT(NUM,2),PAYDAT(NUM,3),NDEPS(NUM),MTYPE(NUM)
33.     104 FORMAT(I5,3A4,I4,F4.2,F5.2,I2,I1)
34.         IF(ID(NUM).LT.IDNUM) GOTO 102
35.         IF(ID(NUM).GT.IDNUM) GOTO 910
36.         PAYDAT(NUM,1) = HOURS
*                                                              *
*           CHECK FOR VALID DEPARTMENT NUMBER IN EMPLOYEE CARD *
*           WHEN FOUND, PROCESS EMPLOYEE DATA                  *
*                                                              *
37.         DO 105 K=1,NDEPTS
38.             IF(NODEPT(K).EQ.NDEP(NUM)) GOTO 201
39.     105 CONTINUE
*                                                              *
*           ERROR -- NO MATCH FOUND FOR EMPLOYEE DEPT. NUMBER  *
*                                                              *
40.         GOTO 903
*                                                              *
****************************************************************
```

FIGURE 6-2 Program block 100 as changed from general example 5 to general example 6 for payroll report program.

```
         ***********************************************************************
         *                                                                     *
         **********               ERROR MESSAGE BLOCK                BLOCK 0900
         *                                                                     *
82.      901 NCARD = NCARD + 1
83.          WRITE(6,902) NCARD
84.      902 FORMAT(//6H *****,' ERROR IN DATA CARD NUMBER ',I2,6H *****)
85.          GOTO 908
         *****                                                            *****
86.      903 WRITE(6,904) NCARD
87.      904 FORMAT(//' ***** ERROR - DEPT. NO. NOT VALID. CARD NO.  ',I4,
             1    2X,5H*****)
         *                                                                     *
         *         GO BACK TO READ NEXT EMPLOYEE DATA CARD                     *
         *                                                                     *
88.      908 GOTO 101
         *****                                                            *****
89.      906 WRITE(6,907) MAXEMP
90.      907 FORMAT(///' ***** ERROR. ATTEMPTED TO READ ',
             1    'MORE THAN',I3,' DATA CARDS'/7X,'PROGRAM ABORTED. *****')
91.          GOTO 939
         *****                                                            *****
92.      910 WRITE(6,911) IDNUM,NDEPT,HOURS
93.      911 FORMAT(//5X,'***** DATA CARD OUT OF ORDER OR NOT ON '/
             1    10X,'PERMANENT FILE.'/10X,2I5,F5.1,' IN DATA CARD.'/
             2    10X,'RUN ABORTED.')
94.          GOTO 939
         *****                                                            *****
95.      920 WRITE(6,921) NCARD
96.      921 FORMAT(//5X,'***** ATTEMPTED TO READ PAST END OF FILE 7.'
             1    /10X,I4,' CARDS READ. RUN ABORTED.')
97.          GOTO 939
         *****                                                            *****
98.      930 WRITE(6,931)
99.      931 FORMAT(//5X,'***** BAD DATA ON PERMANENT FILE. RUN ABORTED.')
         *                                                                     *
         *         ABNORMAL ERROR STOP                                         *
         *                                                                     *
100.     939 STOP
101.         END
         *                                                                     *
         ************************************************* END OF MAIN PROGRAM
```

FIGURE 6-3 Program block 900 as changed from general example 5 to general example 6 for payroll report program.

be terminated are not shown on the error output. Since each employee number is supposed to be on the reference file and both the reference file and data cards have been sorted in ascending order, an error is indicated if a higher ID number is found in the reference file than on the current input card. Also an error occurs if the reference file comes to an end without finding the ID number for the current input record. If the error were an improper sort or a mispunched data card rather than a missing employee record, more elaborate coding could be done to repeat the search of the file. For simplicity's sake, the example program makes an abnormal stop after printing a suitable message and attempts no recovery or diagnostic procedure.

Statistical Program Example 6—Inventory Simulation

This example illustrates the use of a file for temporary storage of data to be read by a separate, subsequent problem from a set of simulation problems executed by the program. The data stored on the file is written in unformatted form because this method requires less computer time to write (and subsequently read) the data.

The program also shows some additional examples of the use of sub-routines and functions as well as the simulation technique of obtaining data for the simulation by sampling from discrete distributions. In other words, there are a limited number of values in each distribution, all of which are specified by the input.

Problem Description for Statistical Example 6

The program is to simulate a situation in which a supply of items is received at the beginning of each period (such as a day) and withdrawals (issues or sales) take place during the period, e.g., fresh dairy products in a grocery store. There is no carryover from one period (day) to the next. The supply received may be either a fixed amount each period or a variable amount selected from a discrete distribution of supply amounts. Demand (withdrawals) arises when customers request the items. Both the number of customers and the size of individual customer orders are described by discrete distributions. Two options exist in running each simulation problem. One is that the detail transactions, day by day, of the simulation are printed (or not printed). The other option is that, as an aid in comparing alternative policies, the supply generated in one simulation problem can be used in a succeeding problem.

A run of the program consists of one or more separate simulation problems each having different characteristics. Inputs to each problem in the run processed consist of a set of problem cards. Each problem set begins with a problem

INPUT DATA FROM CARDS

```
1234FIN     ⎫
4275ENGR    ⎬ Department numbers and names
7269MKTG    ⎪
7531PROD    ⎪
8551ACCT    ⎭
15786855137.0
23456753140.0
23457159640.0  Department number not valid
35748427555.5
36985726922.0
42753123440.0
4592.427537.5
62475427537.5  Invalid. Data-type error
69852427510.0
74365753154.0
```

DATA RECORDS ON EXTERNAL STORAGE FILE

```
15786RALPH JONES  85516.2824.68041
19834JOHN SMITH   24673.5730.93022
23456J. HOFFMANN  75313.5727.95021
23457T. HOFFMANN  15963.5727.95032
35748L. SMITH     42757.2430.68044
36985J. JOHNSON   7269027503598011
40865OSCAR JAMES  75314.5744.74042
42753R. M. NELSON12347.4557.64032
54309B. GRUENZEL  15964.85707.9021
62475Q. SIBLEY    42758.2465.34022
69852T. NAMAN     42752.6727.50091
74365A. PETERSON  75314.8254.63000
```

FIGURE 6-4 Test data from card input and external file for general example 6 program. See also Figure 5-10.

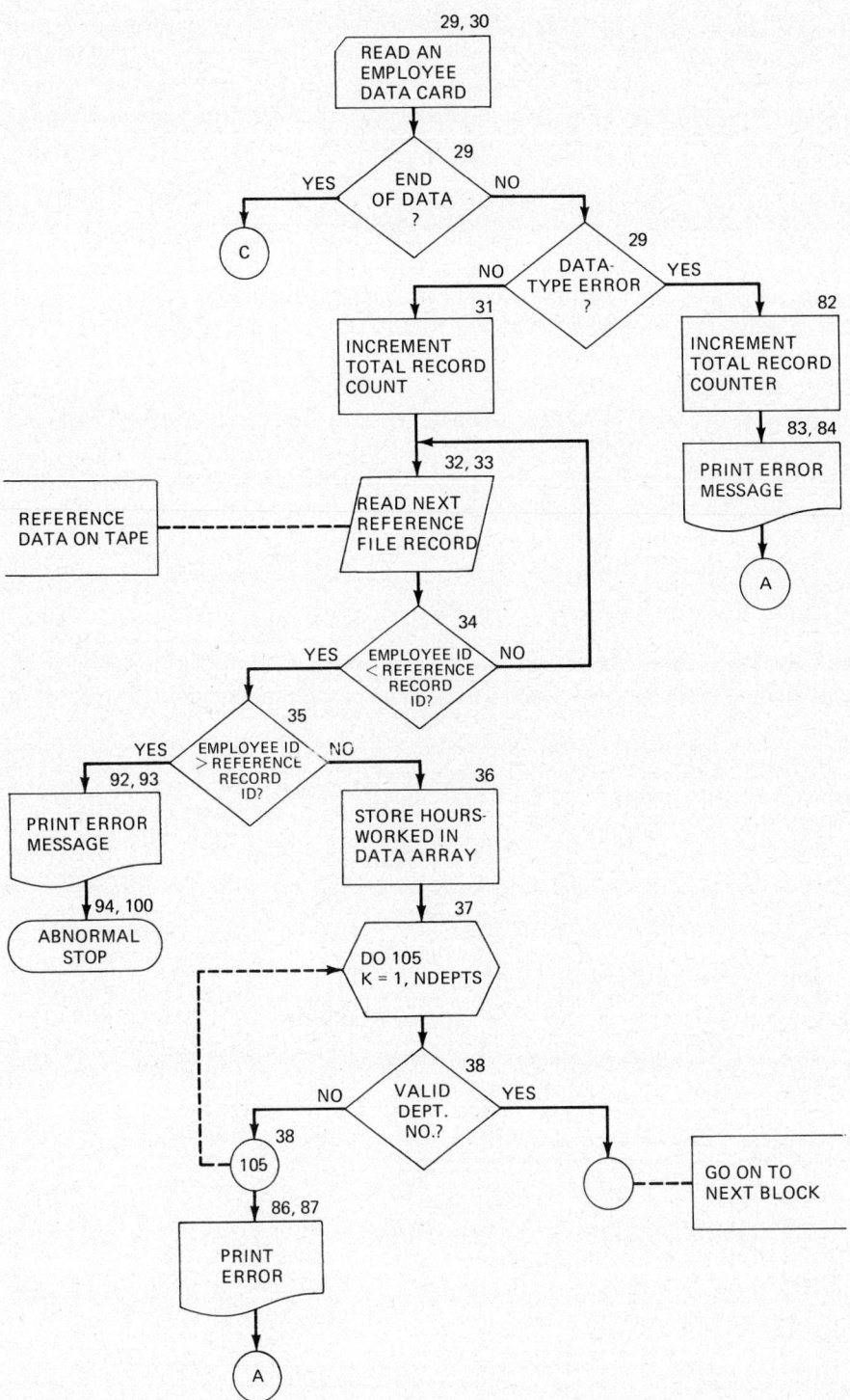

FIGURE 6-5 Flowchart showing file processing in block 100 of general example 6 program and associated error messages in block 900.

```
   EMPLOYEE PAYCHECK PROGRAM


   TABLE OF DEPARTMENTS
   NUMBER   NAME
    1234    FIN
    4275    ENGR
    7269    MKTG
    7531    PROD
    8551    ACCT



       ERROR MESSAGES DURING DATA INPUT



   ***** ERROR - DEPT. NO. NOT VALID. CARD NO.    3  *****


   ***** ERROR IN DATA CARD NUMBER  7 *****

    10 CARDS READ
     2 CARDS REJECTED
```

FIGURE 6-6 Error and Control Report for general example 6 program using external storage.

card with a title in columns 1 to 20. Columns 21 through 24 of this card contain a value defining the number of days to simulate. Column 25 contains a one or zero (for yes or no) to select the detail print option, and column 26 contains a one or zero to select the use of previously generated supply data. Following this title card are cards defining the three discrete distributions for supply, customers, and demand per customer in list-directed format. Each distribution consists of from one to nine pairs of data items, one pair per card, in the form: quantity, frequency. Each set of distribution cards is terminated with a card containing the pair −1,0. If only a −1,0 card is present, the distribution is to be unchanged from the corresponding one given in the data set for the previous problem (valid only after the first problem of the run). The distribution data must follow some simple rules:

1 The frequencies are stated as decimal fractions. The frequencies in a set must sum to 1.00.

2 The quantities must be input in order from smallest to largest.

For example, a supply distribution in which 20 percent of the time the supply is 4 units, 30 percent of the supply is 8 units, and 50 percent of the time the supply is 6 units would be input as follows:

Card No.	Values
1	4,.20
2	6,.50
3	8,.30
4	−1,0

The output for each problem consists of a title and a message showing whether or not the supply reuse option was selected. Summary information is printed showing the length of the simulation and totals for customers, demand, supply, shortages, and excesses. In order to indicate sample validity, the theoretical averages and sample averages for the various distributions are also printed.

MAIN PROGRAM

Establish common arrays for quantities, frequencies, and cumulative density function
Dimension arrays for means of distributions and problem name
READ title and options card
       If no more cards, STOP
       If data error, print message and go back to READ title and options card
Print title and options selected
Print column headings
REWIND supply data tape
Initialize counters and accumulators
Test option to reuse supply data from previous problem
       If reusing supply data, go to READ customers
           else READ supply data distribution (quantities and frequencies)
READ customers per day distribution (quantities and frequencies)
READ demand per customer distribution
When distribution input data has been read, zero rest of array holding quantities and
       frequencies
Compute distribution means for all distributions
Compute cumulative frequency distributions
DO simulation for number of days specified
    If not reusing supply data, get sample supply from distribution
       else read sample supply from tape
    Sample to get number of customers for today
    Set daily demand accumulator to zero
    Set daily count of unsatisfied customers to zero
    DO sampling from demand/customer distribution for each customer
       Accumulate daily demand
       If daily demand exceeds quantity available, increment daily count and
           total count of customers shorted
       End of DO sampling
    Compute today's excess supply
       If excess is negative, then increment stockout accumulator, else continue
    Add to other totals
    Test for output option
       If detail print selected, print detail, else continue
End of DO simulation
Compute and print totals
Compute and print sample and theoretical averages
Go back to READ title and option card for new problem

FIGURE 6-7 Pseudocode description of logic for statistical example 6—inventory simulation.

FUNCTION SAMPLE

Set common block
Get a random number
DO comparison of random number to entries in successive rows of cumulative distribution
    If random number less than array entry for index row, set SAMPLE value to corresponding value in frequency distribution
End of DO comparison
RETURN

FUNCTION RANDOM

Initialize variables
Compute large random digit number
Compute high order digits with MOD function
Compute low order digits by subtraction of high order digits
Scale random digits to between 0–1 (or bias interval)
RETURN

FIGURE 6-7 *(continued)*

Program Documentation for Statistical Example 6

The documentation consists of a pseudocode program description (Figure 6-7), a program flowchart (Figure 6-8), a program listing (Figure 6-9), sample test data (Figure 6-10), and a sample of results from four sets of data (Figure 6-11).

Notes on Statistical Example 6

The general programming style conventions have been followed and the program conforms to all FORTRAN 1977 standards except for the first card. For the particular compiler used in this case, a nonstandard PROGRAM card is needed to relate the logical files in the program with physical file devices. In other systems, this equating of file references with file devices might be accomplished with system job control cards.

The external file usage (number 9 is the number assigned to the file) is coded at lines 11, 49, and 51. In line 11, the file is rewound (from its use in the previous simulation). If the file is already rewound, as it should be for the first simulation, the rewind or return to beginning instruction has no effect. In line 47 the code for the option to reuse supply data is tested; if the code is zero, a new supply data item is generated for use by the function SAMPLE (line 48) and also stored on a file for possible use by the succeeding problem (line 49). If the reuse code is not zero, a supply data item is read from the file on which it was placed by the preceding simulation problem (line 51). Both the write and read file instructions use an unformatted read or write because this is more efficient for internal computer use. The computer does no formatting but merely writes the record on the file in the binary representation used for internal purposes and reads it back in the same form.

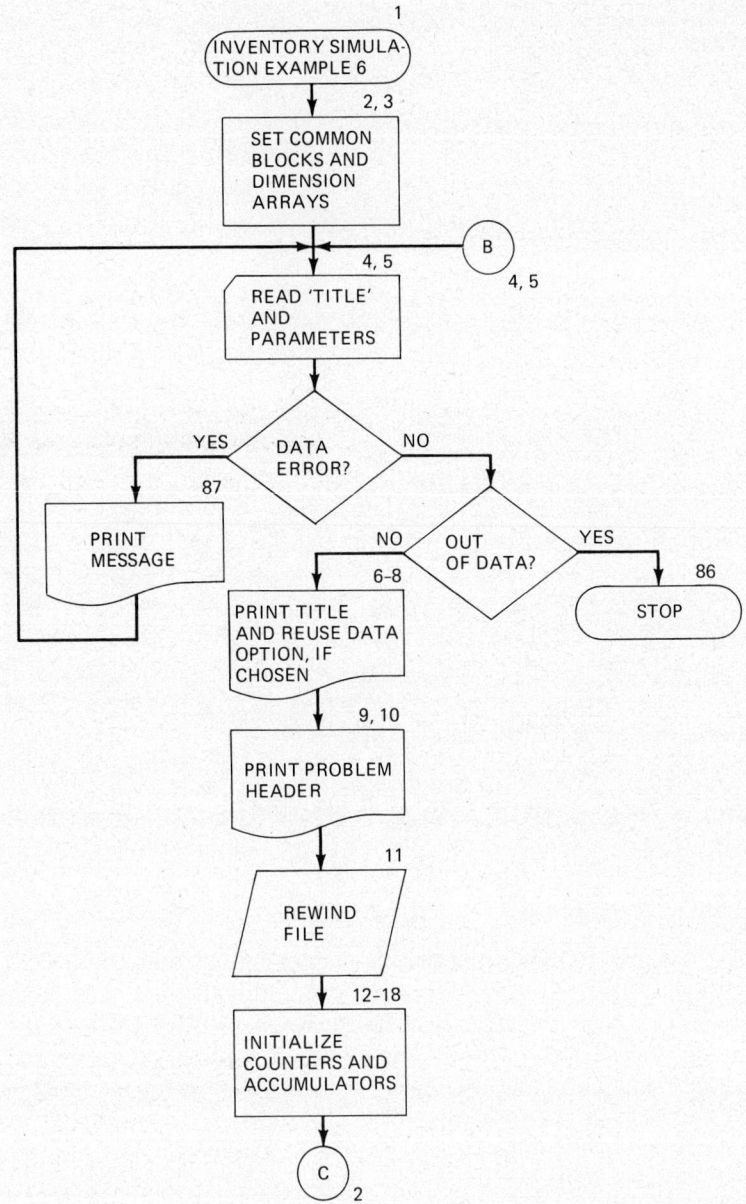

FIGURE 6-8 Program flowchart of statistical example 6 program—inventory simulation.

List-directed input is used for reading the input data and for error messages. Note the use of the unit designation form of list-directed input/output. On line 22, the instruction is written READ(5, *) DX, FX which means to read in list-directed mode from unit 5. If unit 5 is the card reader, the instruction could also be written as READ *, DX, FX. See also lines 87 and 89.

Sampling of each distribution involves the same logic at different points in the program. By placing the logic in a function, the overall program logic is clarified. Communication between the main program and the SAMPLE func-

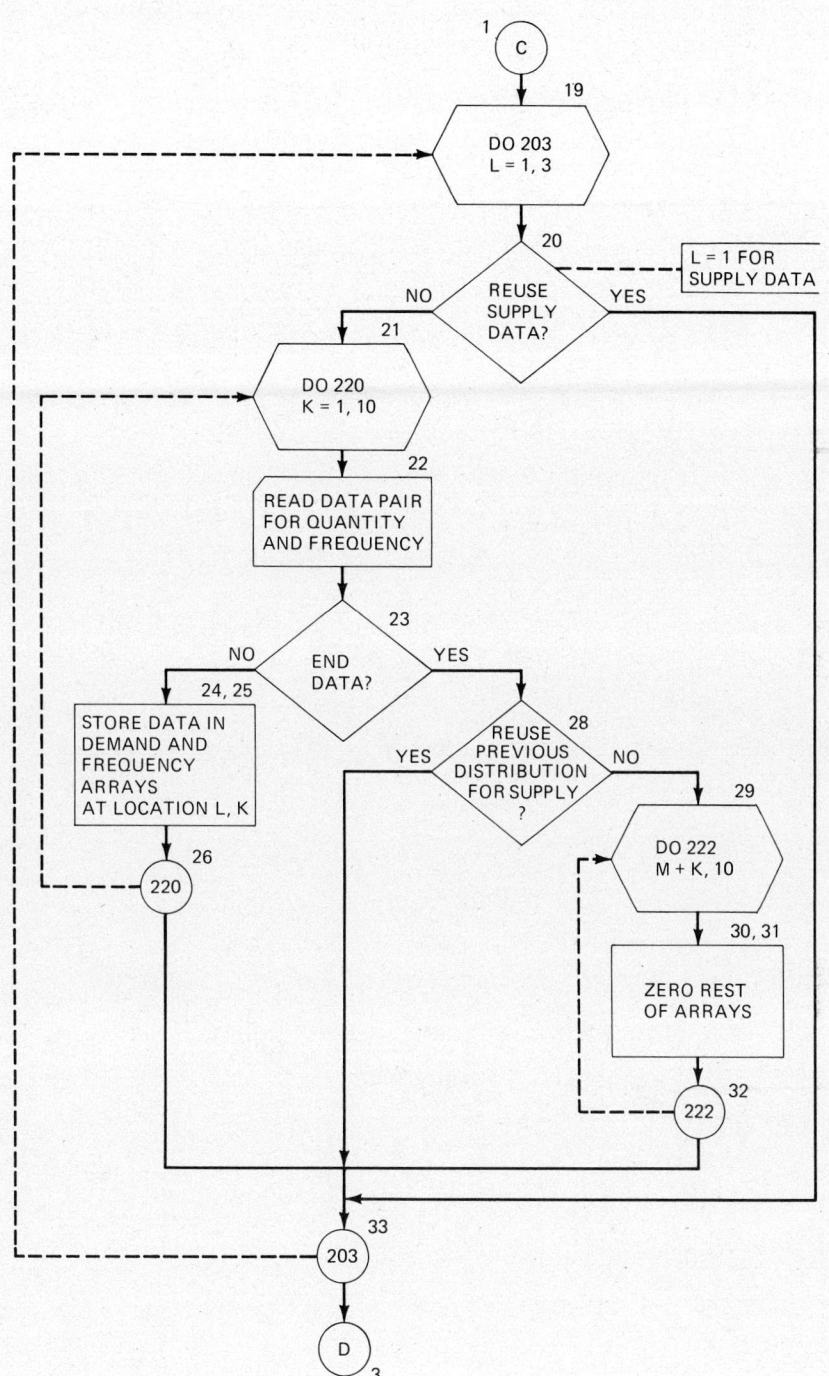

FIGURE 6-8 *(continued)*

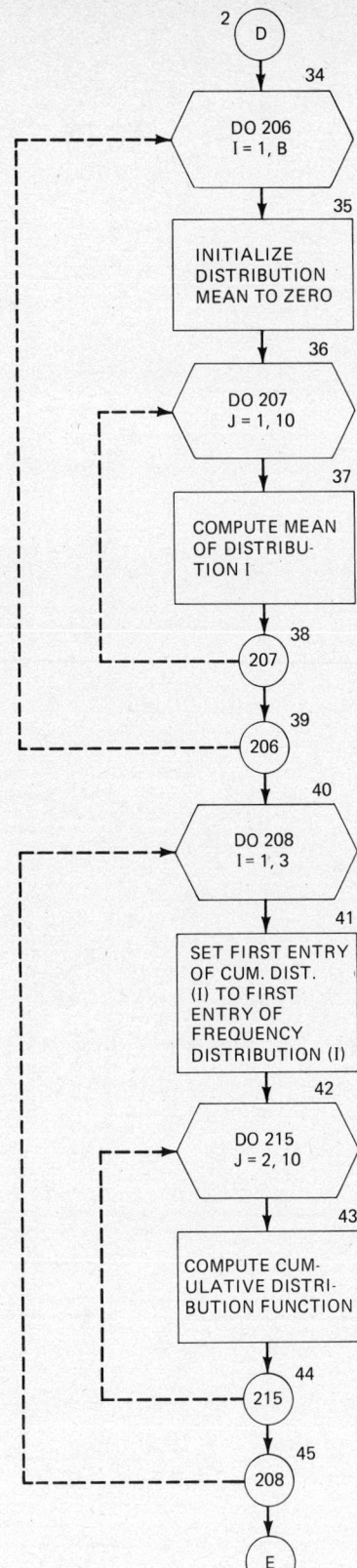

FIGURE 6-8 *(continued)* Program flowchart statistical example 6 program—inventory simulation.

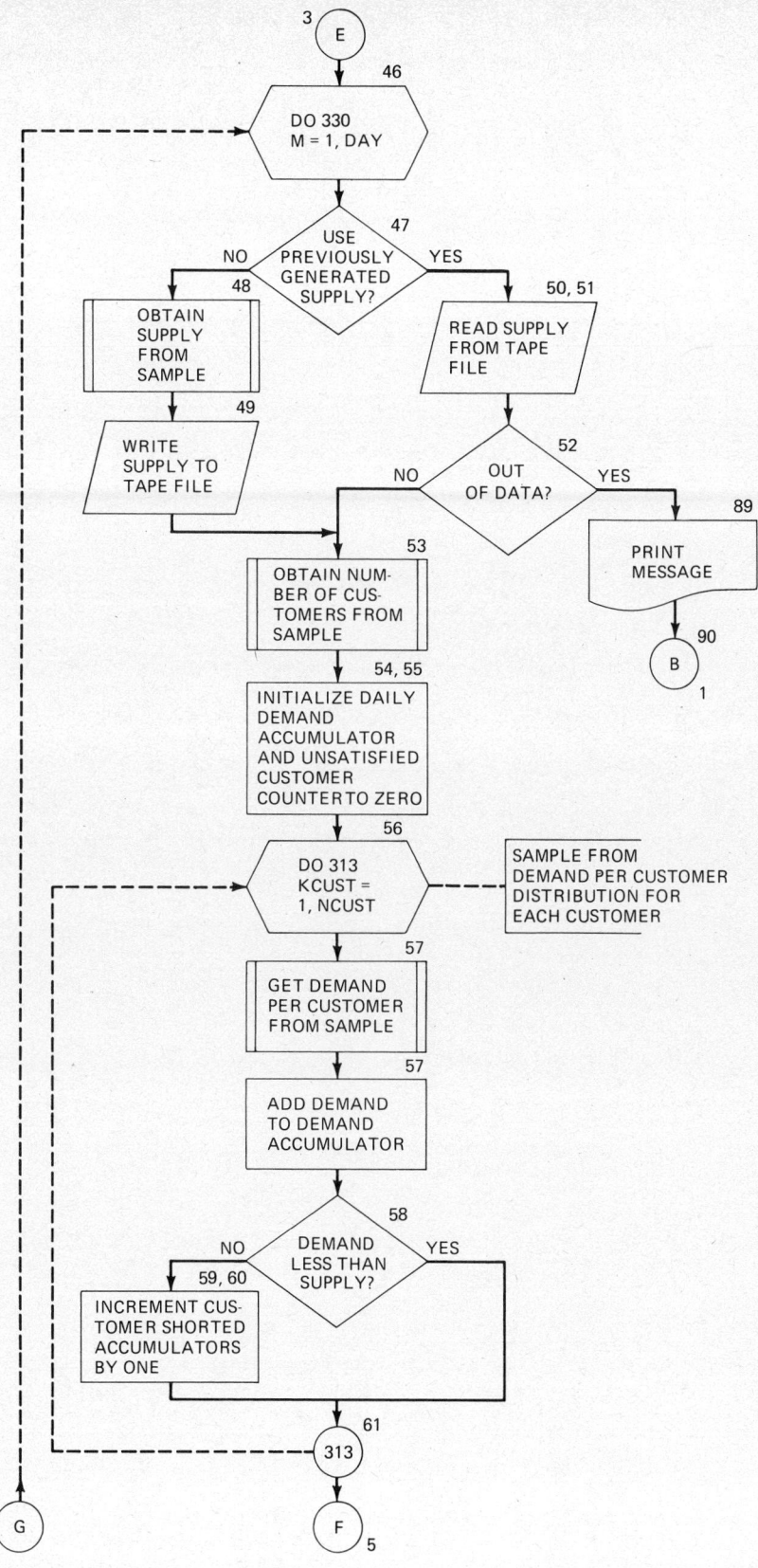

FIGURE 6-8 *(continued)* Program flowchart of statistical example 6 program—inventory simulation.

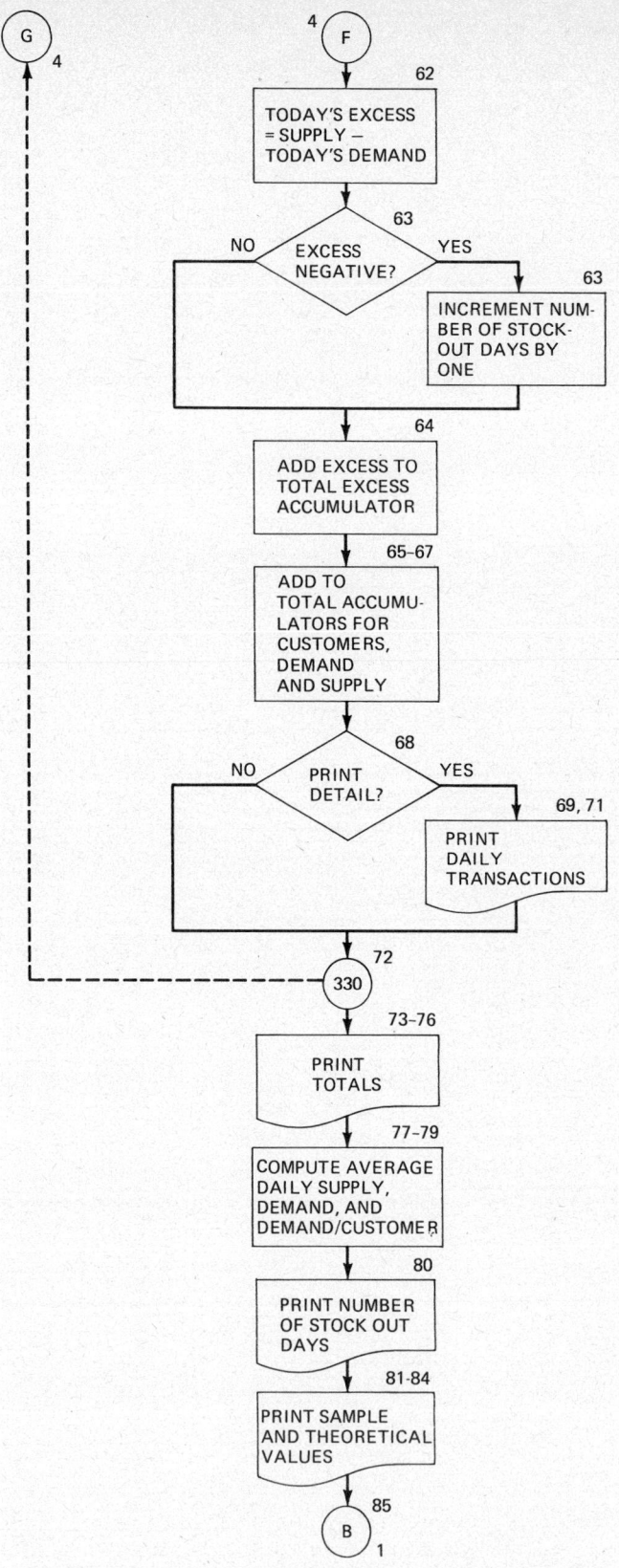

FIGURE 6-8 *(continued)* Program flowchart of statistical example 6 program—inventory simulation.

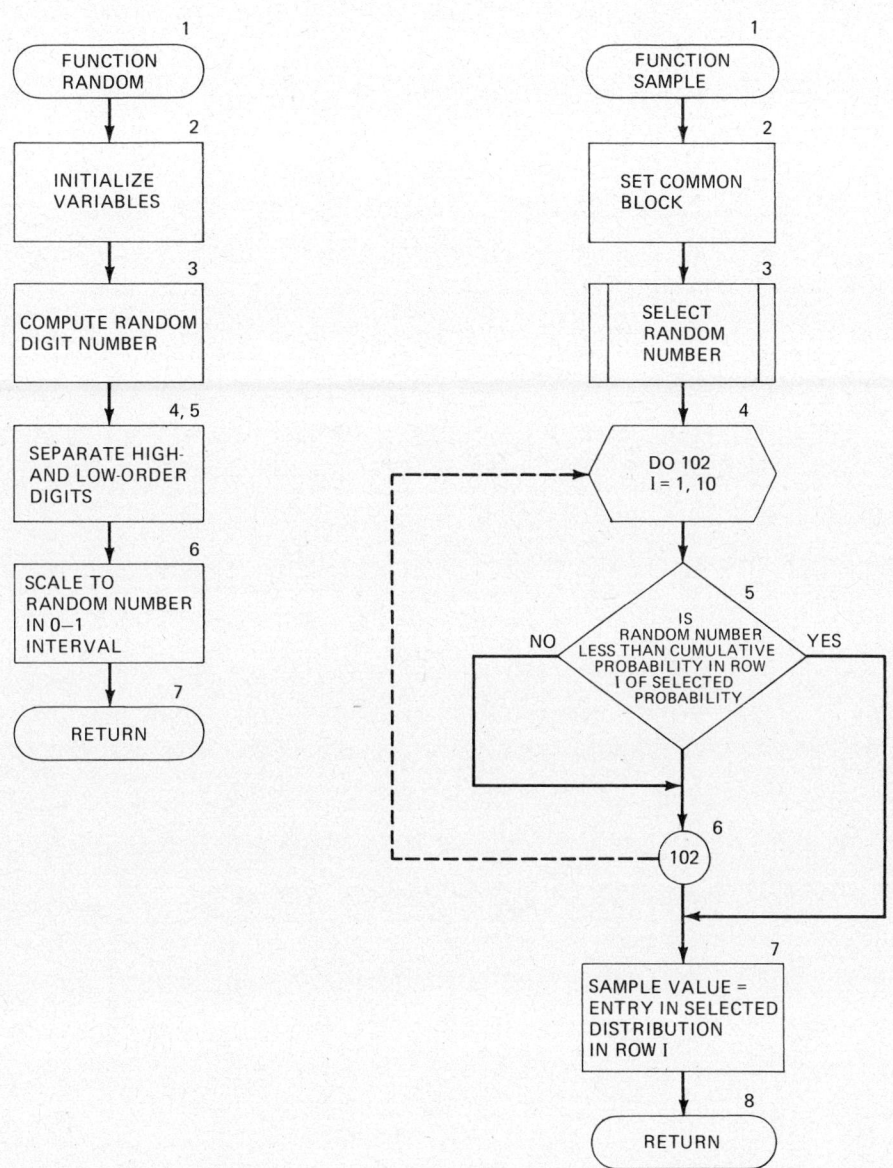

FIGURE 6-8 *(continued)*

tion is facilitated by use of common storage allocation. See line 2 in both routines.

The function RANDOM is an implementation of the power residue method described in problem 5-2. Note particularly the use of the DATA statement and the absence of the COMMON statement which had appeared in the other subprograms. Since this function does not reference any of the variables in common storage, the COMMON statement is not needed.

The program illustrates the use of a switch in programming. A program switch is a method for delaying branching. In other words, at one point in a program, there is a determination of the branch to be taken later. The switch is

```
  1.          PROGRAM SIMPLE (INPUT,OUTPUT,TAPE5=INPUT,TAPE6=OUTPUT,TAPE9)
         **********          PROGRAM IDENTIFICATION                    **********
         *                                                                     *
         *          SIMPLE INVENTORY SIMULATION PROGRAM                        *
         *          WRITTEN BY T. HOFFMANN  7/20/77                            *
         *                                                                     *
         ***********************************************************************
         *                                                                     *
         **********          VARIABLE IDENTIFICATION                 **********
         *                                                                     *
         *          DAY     = NUMBER OF DAYS TO SIMULATE                       *
         *          DEM     = DEMAND BY EACH CUSTOMER                          *
         *          TUSC    = TOTAL UNSATISFIED CUSTOMERS                      *
         *          DUSC    = DAILY COUNT OF UNSATISFIED CUSTOMERS             *
         *          NCUST   = NUMBER OF CUSTOMERS IN A DAY (INTEGER)           *
         *          DCUST   = NUMBER OF CUSTOMERS IN A DAY (REAL)              *
         *          LPR     = DETAIL PRINT SWITCH                             *
         *          NREP    = REPEAT SWITCH FOR REUSE OF SUPPLY DATA           *
         *          NSTOUT  = NUMBER OF STOCKOUT DAYS                          *
         *          SUP     = SAMPLE DAILY SUPPLY                              *
         *          TUXCES  = TOTAL UNITS EXCESS                               *
         *          TOTC    = TOTAL CUSTOMERS                                  *
         *          TOTDEM  = TOTAL DEMAND                                     *
         *          TOTSUP  = TOTAL SUPPLY                                     *
         *          XS      = DAILY EXCESS                                     *
         *          DX      = QUANTITY VALUE                                   *
         *          FX      = FREQUENCY OF 'DX'                                *
         *                                                                     *
         *****               ARRAY IDENTIFICATION                       *****
         *                                                                     *
         *          AMEAN   = MEAN OF EACH DISTRIBUTION                        *
         *          CDF     = CUMMULATIVE DENSITY FUNCTION                     *
         *          NAME    = NAME OF PROBLEM                                  *
         *          XD      = DISTRIBUTIONS OF QUANTITIES                      *
         *          FD      = FREQUENCIES CORRESPONDING TO 'XD'                *
         *                                                                     *
         *****               FUNCTION NAMES                             *****
         *                                                                     *
         *          SAMPLE  = SAMPLES FROM THE DISTRBUTIONS                    *
         *          RANDOM  = RANDOM NUMBER GENERATOR                          *
         *                                                                     *
         ***********************************************************************
         *                                                                     *
         **********          STORAGE ALLOCATION                      **********
         *                                                                     *
  2.          COMMON XD(3,10),FD(3,10),CDF(3,10)
  3.          DIMENSION AMEAN(3),NAME(5)
         *                                                                     *
         ***********************************************************************
         *                                                                     *
         **********          READ DATA CARD AND INITIALIZE          BLOCK 0100
         *                                                                     *
  4.     101 READ(5,102,ERR=901,END=599) (NAME(I),I=1,5),DAY,LPR,NREP
  5.     102 FORMAT(5A4,F4.0,2I1)
  6.          WRITE(6,105) (NAME(I),I=1,5)
  7.     105 FORMAT(1H1,20X,5A4/)
  8.          IF(NREP .NE. 0) WRITE(6,*) ' REUSE SUPPLY DATA'
  9.          WRITE(6,109)
 10.     109 FORMAT(/41X,6(1H*),7HSERVICE,7(1H*)/1X,
        1     5H DAY,4X,9HCUSTOMERS,3X,6HDEMAND,3X,6HSUPPLY,
        1     4X,6HEXCESS,3X,11HUNSATISFIED/42X,5HUNITS,4X,9HCUSTOMERS/)
 11.          REWIND 9
 12.          TOTC = 0.0
 13.          TOTDEM = 0.0
 14.          TOTSUP = 0.0
 15.          TUXCES = 0.0
 16.          DUSC=0.0
 17.          TUSC = 0.0
 18.          NSTOUT=0
         *                                                                     *
         ***********************************************************************
```

FIGURE 6-9 Program listing for statistical example 6—inventory simulation.

```
       *                                                              *
       **********         READ DISTRIBUTIONS AND SET ARRAYS      BLOCK 0200
       *                                                              *
19.        DO 203 L = 1,3
20.           IF(NREP .NE. 0 .AND. L .EQ. 1) GOTO 203
21.           DO 220 K = 1,10
22.              READ(5,*) DX,FX
23.              IF(DX .LT. 0.0) GOTO 221
24.              XD(L,K) = DX
25.              FD(L,K) = FX
26.   220     CONTINUE
27.           GOTO 203
28.   221     IF(K .EQ. 1) GOTO 203
29.           DO 222 M = K,10
30.              XD(L,M) = 0.0
31.              FD(L,M) = 0.0
32.   222     CONTINUE
33.   203 CONTINUE
34.        DO 206 I = 1,3
35.           AMEAN(I) = 0.0
36.           DO 207 J = 1,10
37.              AMEAN(I) = XD(I,J)*FD(I,J) + AMEAN(I)
38.   207     CONTINUE
39.   206 CONTINUE
40.        DO 208 I = 1,3
41.           CDF(I,1)=FD(I,1)
42.           DO 215 J = 2,10
43.              CDF(I,J) = CDF(I,J - 1) + FD(I,J)
44.   215     CONTINUE
45.   208 CONTINUE
       *                                                              *
       ****************************************************************
       *                                                              *
       **********            PERFORM SIMULATION                 BLOCK 0300
       *                                                              *
46.        DO 330 M = 1,INT(DAY)
47.           IF(NREP .EQ. 0) THEN
48.              SUP = SAMPLE(1)
49.              WRITE(9) SUP
50.           ELSE
51.              READ(9,END=910) SUP
52.           ENDIF
53.           NCUST = SAMPLE(2)
54.           DEM=0.0
55.           DUSC = 0.0
56.           DO 313 K=1,NCUST
57.              DEM = DEM + SAMPLE(3)
58.              IF(DEM .LE. SUP) GOTO 313
59.              TUSC=TUSC+1.0
60.              DUSC=DUSC+1.0
61.   313     CONTINUE
62.           XS=SUP-DEM
63.           IF(XS .LT. 0.0) NSTOUT = NSTOUT + 1
64.           TUXCES = TUXCES + XS
65.           TOTC = TOTC + FLOAT(NCUST)
66.           TOTDEM = TOTDEM + DEM
67.           TOTSUP = TOTSUP + SUP
68.           IF(LPR .EQ. 0) GOTO 330
69.           DCUST = FLOAT(NCUST)
70.           WRITE(6,322) M,DCUST,DEM,SUP,XS,DUSC
71.   322     FORMAT(1X,I5,5F10.0)
72.   330 CONTINUE
       *                                                              *
       ****************************************************************
       *                                                              *
       **********         COMPUTE AVERAGES AND PRINT THEM       BLOCK 0400
       *                                                              *
73.        WRITE(6,443)
74.   443 FORMAT(1X,'TOTALS')
75.        WRITE(6,442) DAY,TOTC,TOTDEM,TOTSUP,TUXCES,TUSC
76.   442 FORMAT(1X,F5.0,3F10.0,2F10.0/)
77.        TOTSUP = TOTSUP/DAY
78.        TOTDEM = TOTDEM/TOTC
79.        TOTC = TOTC/DAY
80.        WRITE(6,*) NSTOUT,' STOCKOUT DAYS'
81.        WRITE(6,410)
82.   410 FORMAT(/' AVERAGES',8X,'THEORETICAL',5X,'SAMPLE')
83.        WRITE(6,406) AMEAN(2),TOTC,AMEAN(3),TOTDEM,AMEAN(1),TOTSUP
84.   406 FORMAT(' CUSTOMERS ',5X,2F12.6/' DEM.CUST.',5X,2F12.6/
     1      ' SUPPLY/DAY',5X,2F12.6)
```

FIGURE 6-9 *(continued)*

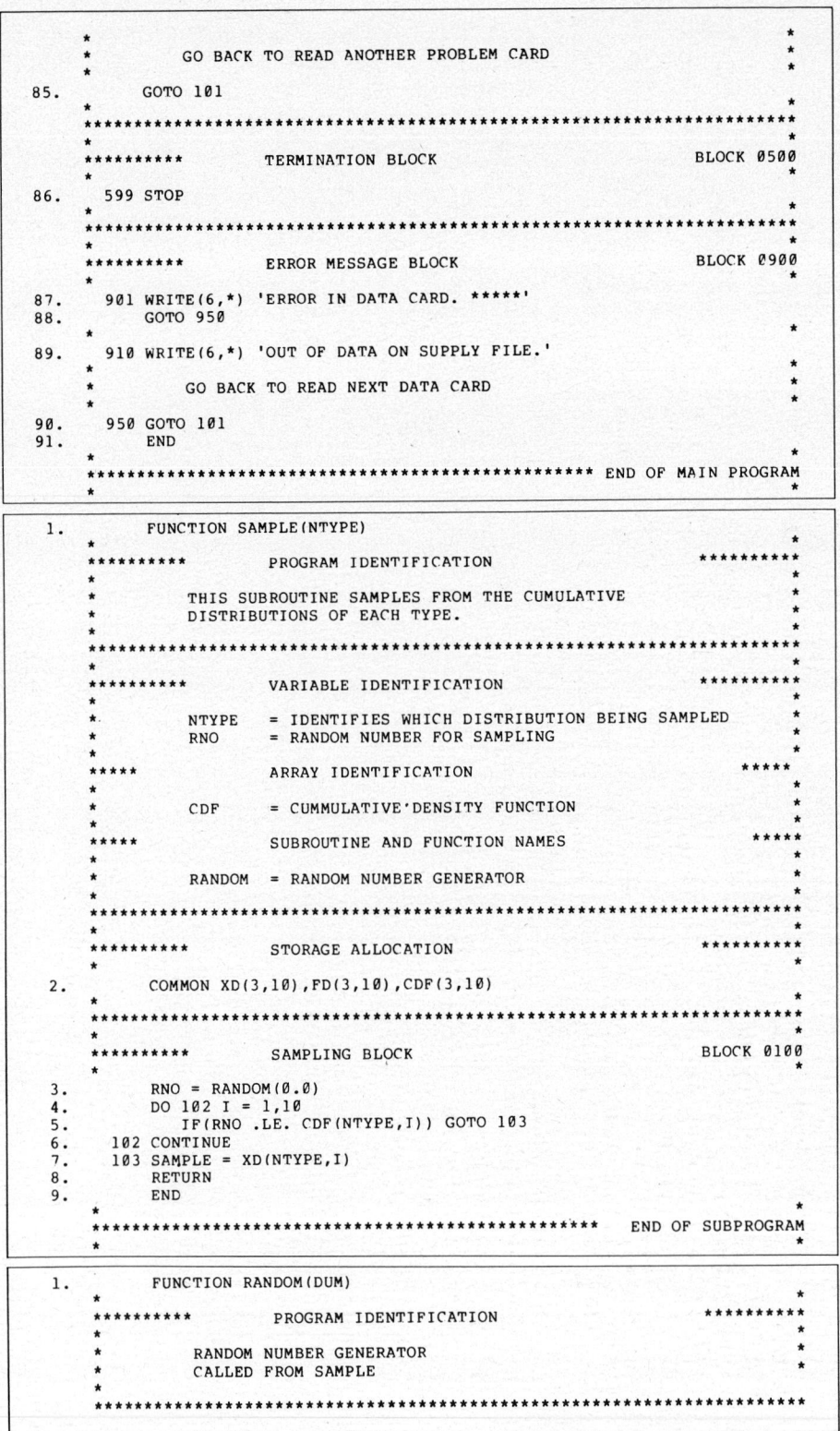

```
        *                                                          *
        *          GO BACK TO READ ANOTHER PROBLEM CARD            *
        *                                                          *
85.         GOTO 101
        *                                                          *
        ************************************************************
        *                                                          *
        **********          TERMINATION BLOCK          BLOCK 0500
        *
86.     599 STOP
        *                                                          *
        ************************************************************
        *                                                          *
        **********          ERROR MESSAGE BLOCK        BLOCK 0900
        *
87.     901 WRITE(6,*) 'ERROR IN DATA CARD. *****'
88.         GOTO 950
        *                                                          *
89.     910 WRITE(6,*) 'OUT OF DATA ON SUPPLY FILE.'
        *                                                          *
        *          GO BACK TO READ NEXT DATA CARD                  *
        *                                                          *
90.     950 GOTO 101
91.         END
        *                                                          *
        ********************************************** END OF MAIN PROGRAM
        *                                                          *
```

```
1.          FUNCTION SAMPLE(NTYPE)
        *                                                          *
        **********          PROGRAM IDENTIFICATION     **********
        *                                                          *
        *          THIS SUBROUTINE SAMPLES FROM THE CUMULATIVE     *
        *          DISTRIBUTIONS OF EACH TYPE.                     *
        *                                                          *
        ************************************************************
        *                                                          *
        **********          VARIABLE IDENTIFICATION    **********
        *                                                          *
        *.         NTYPE    = IDENTIFIES WHICH DISTRIBUTION BEING SAMPLED  *
        *          RNO      = RANDOM NUMBER FOR SAMPLING           *
        *                                                          *
        *****              ARRAY IDENTIFICATION             *****
        *                                                          *
        *          CDF      = CUMMULATIVE DENSITY FUNCTION         *
        *                                                          *
        *****              SUBROUTINE AND FUNCTION NAMES     *****
        *                                                          *
        *          RANDOM   = RANDOM NUMBER GENERATOR              *
        *                                                          *
        ************************************************************
        *                                                          *
        **********          STORAGE ALLOCATION         **********
        *                                                          *
2.          COMMON XD(3,10),FD(3,10),CDF(3,10)
        *                                                          *
        ************************************************************
        *                                                          *
        **********          SAMPLING BLOCK             BLOCK 0100
        *                                                          *
3.          RNO = RANDOM(0.0)
4.          DO 102 I = 1,10
5.             IF(RNO .LE. CDF(NTYPE,I)) GOTO 103
6.      102 CONTINUE
7.      103 SAMPLE = XD(NTYPE,I)
8.          RETURN
9.          END
        *                                                          *
        ********************************************** END OF SUBPROGRAM
        *                                                          *
```

```
1.          FUNCTION RANDOM(DUM)
        *                                                          *
        **********          PROGRAM IDENTIFICATION     **********
        *                                                          *
        *          RANDOM NUMBER GENERATOR                         *
        *          CALLED FROM SAMPLE                              *
        *                                                          *
        ************************************************************
```

FIGURE 6-9 *(continued)*   Program listing for statistical example 6—inventory simulation.

```
       *                                                              *
       **********          VARIABLE IDENTIFICATION          **********
       *                                                              *
       *          B        = CONSTANT MULTIPLIER = 3213.0             *
       *          C        = HIGH ORDER DIGITS OF PRODUCT             *
       *          D        = LOW ORDER DIGITS OF PRODUCT              *
       *          F        = CONSTANT SCALE FACTOR = 1.0E7            *
       *          S        = CONSTANT SCALE FACTOR = 10000.0          *
       *          DUM      = DUMMY ARGUMENT OR BIAS FACTOR            *
       *          R        = RANDOM DIGITS                            *
       *                                                              *
       ****************************************************************
       *                                                              *
       **********          STORAGE ALLOCATION               **********
       *                                                              *
  2.        DATA S/10000./F/1.0E7/B/3213.0/C/1230000./D/4567./
       *                                                              *
       **********          GENERATE RANDOM NUMBER            BLOCK 0100
       *                                                              *
  3.        R = AMOD((AMOD(B*C,F) + AMOD(B*D,F)),F)
  4.        D = AMOD(R,S)
  5.        C = R - D
  6.        RANDOM = R/F + DUM
  7.        RETURN
  8.        END
       *                                                              *
       ****************************************************** END OF SUBPROGRAM
```

FIGURE 6-9   *(continued)*

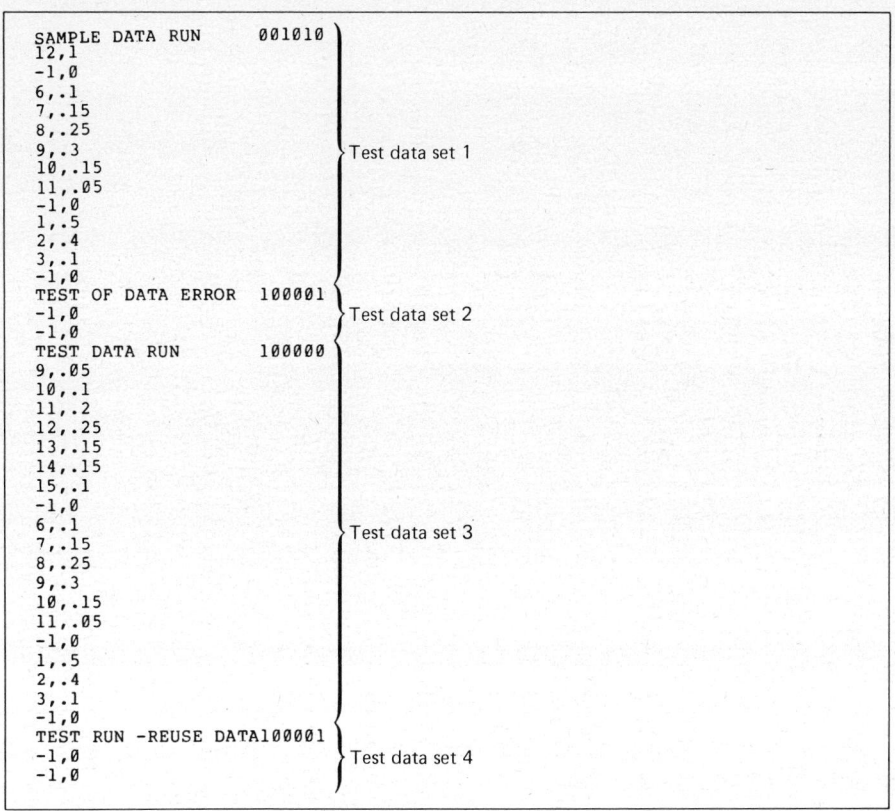

```
SAMPLE DATA RUN       001010
12,1
-1,0
6,.1
7,.15
8,.25
9,.3                              Test data set 1
10,.15
11,.05
-1,0
1,.5
2,.4
3,.1
-1,0
TEST OF DATA ERROR   100001
-1,0                              Test data set 2
-1,0
TEST DATA RUN        100000
9,.05
10,.1
11,.2
12,.25
13,.15
14,.15
15,.1
-1,0
6,.1                              Test data set 3
7,.15
8,.25
9,.3
10,.15
11,.05
-1,0
1,.5
2,.4
3,.1
-1,0
TEST RUN -REUSE DATA100001
-1,0                              Test data set 4
-1,0
```

FIGURE 6-10   Four sets of sample test data for statistical example 6—inventory simulation.

```
                        SAMPLE DATA RUN


                                              ******SERVICE*******
        DAY    CUSTOMERS   DEMAND    SUPPLY    EXCESS    UNSATISFIED
                                              UNITS     CUSTOMERS

         1        6.         10.      12.        2.          0
         2       11.         22.      12.      -10.          5.
         3        6.         11.      12.        1.          0
         4        8.         12.      12.        0           0
         5        9.         14.      12.       -2.          1.
         6        6.         10.      12.        2.          0
         7        9.         16.      12.       -4.          3.
         8        9.         16.      12.       -4.          3.
         9        7.         11.      12.        1.          0
        10        9.         15.      12.       -3.          2.
       TOTALS
        10.      80.        137.     120.      -17.         14.

                      5 STOCKOUT DAYS

       AVERAGES       THEORETICAL       SAMPLE
       CUSTOMERS        8.400000       8.000000
       DEM.CUST.        1.600000       1.712500
       SUPPLY/DAY      12.000000      12.000000
```

```
                      TEST OF DATA ERROR

       REUSE SUPPLY DATA

                                              ******SERVICE*******
        DAY    CUSTOMERS   DEMAND    SUPPLY    EXCESS    UNSATISFIED
                                              UNITS     CUSTOMERS

       OUT OF DATA ON SUPPLY FILE.
```

```
                        TEST DATA RUN


                                              ******SERVICE*******
        DAY    CUSTOMERS   DEMAND    SUPPLY    EXCESS    UNSATISFIED
                                              UNITS     CUSTOMERS

       TOTALS
       1000.    8461.     13551.    12198.    -1353.       1386.

                     595 STOCKOUT DAYS

       AVERAGES       THEORETICAL       SAMPLE
       CUSTOMERS        8.400000       8.461000
       DEM.CUST.        1.600000       1.601584
       SUPPLY/DAY      12.200000      12.198000
```

```
                    TEST RUN -REUSE DATA

       REUSE SUPPLY DATA

                                              ******SERVICE*******
        DAY    CUSTOMERS   DEMAND    SUPPLY    EXCESS    UNSATISFIED
                                              UNITS     CUSTOMERS

       TOTALS
       1000.    8354.     13411.    12198.    -1213.       1285.

                     575 STOCKOUT DAYS

       AVERAGES       THEORETICAL       SAMPLE
       CUSTOMERS        8.400000       8.354000
       DEM.CUST.        1.600000       1.605339
       SUPPLY/DAY      12.200000      12.198000
```

FIGURE 6-11 Test results from four sets of test data for statistical example 6 program—inventory simulation.

used to transmit this information within the program. In the program, the selection of the options uses the switch concept. The value of zero results in one branch; the value of one in another. (However, they are programmed as zero or nonzero.) The two switches are tested in lines 20, 47, and 68 and one of two programming paths selected.

The program does not include all data validation because it was important to keep the program simple and focus on file use and the simulation problem. Examples of additional validation tests that could have been performed are:

1 Frequencies in input set must sum to 1.00.

2 Quantities must be input in order by size. If not in order, the cumulative frequency table will not be correct.

3 Selection of "reuse data" option not allowed for first problem.

In addition to the input data shown in Figure 6-10, it is desirable to test errors which lead to abnormal terminations. Data to make these additional tests and related outputs are not documented here. Proof of the correctness of the sampling procedure and randomness of the random number generator are particularly difficult within a simulation program. Instead, the random number algorithm was separately tested with a program not given here (see problem 6-3). The sampling procedure logic is tested in a somewhat intuitive manner by comparing the theoretical means of the distributions, which can be verified manually, with the sample means. The value shown in the output behaves in a satisfactory manner.

Programming Exercises

Description of Assignment

Select one or more problems [or take the problem(s) assigned to you by your instructor]. Write each of the programs in such a manner as to make use of an external file. Follow the style guidelines and prepare the following:

1 Pseudocode description

2 Program flowchart

3 Program listing

4 List of test data and expected results; provide validity checks

5 Output including error detection

Mathematics and Statistics

1 Sometimes data sets may be quite large and hence they are stored on external files. Modify the program for problem 1 of Chapter 5 to read the data sets from a file, each record of which contains a number pair.

2 When forming the product of two square matrices, it may be desirable to store the product in the location of one of the original matrices. An easy way to accomplish this is to form the product a vector at a time on a file and then read the completed product back into the location of one of the original matrices. (For small matrices an array could be used, but that would not be practical for large matrices because of storage limitations.) Write a program which accomplishes this procedure. Print out the final matrix. As demonstration data use the following two pairs of matrices and form A × B and B × A (if defined).

A						B				
1	2	7	11			1	5	7	11	
	3	9	−3			−2	9	−3	4	
	4	−1	4			6	5	−2	1	
	−6	3	8			0	6	9	2	
2	17	24	1	8	15	2	3	9	−10	−4
	23	5	7	14	16	−5	1	7	8	−11
	4	6	13	20	22	−12	−6	0	6	12
	10	12	19	21	3	11	−8	−7	−1	5
	11	18	25	2	9	4	10	−9	−3	−2

3 Random number generators can be tested in a variety of ways to assure that they are not biased. One way is a χ^2 (chi square) test for uniform distribution of the numbers. In theory, if N random numbers distributed between 0 and 1 are generated and divided into n classes of equal size, there should be N/n values in each class. For example, if 20 classes were established they would be as follows:

Class number	Internal boundaries
1	0.00 through 0.04999 . . .
2	0.05 through 0.09999 . . .
3	0.10 through 0.14999 . . .
.	.
.	.
.	.
20	0.95 through 0.99999 . . .

Assuming 2000 numbers were used, they should be distributed with 100 values in each class. The conformance of actual (A_i for the ith class) to theoretical can be tested by computation of the following:

$$X^2 = \sum_{i=1}^{n} \frac{(A_i - (N/n))^2}{N/n} = \sum_{i=1}^{20} \frac{(A_i - 100)^2}{100} \quad \text{for the example}$$

This value can be compared to the appropriate χ^2 value for $n - 1$ degrees of freedom and a 5 or 10 percent significance level. If X^2 is greater than the appropriate χ^2 value, the random number generator is biased.

Write a program to test the mid-square number generator described in problem 5-2, the one shown as part of statistical example 6, and the random number generator provided as a system or local library function on your computer. Write the program so that the number of values generated is from 100 to 10,000 and the number of cells from 10 to 30. The program should contain the capability of printing the computed X^2 and χ^2 values for 5 and 10 percent significance levels. Prepare a file containing a table of χ^2 values that might be needed and read the appropriate values from it.

Business and Economics

4   Write a program designed to maintain the personnel data file of general example 6. It should be capable of correcting data errors (such as the incorrect union/ management codes), deleting entire records, or adding new records in their appropriate place. A report should accompany each such update run which tells what alterations were made and accounts for the cards read, records changed, and new and old file sizes (in numbers of records).

5   Refer to problem 4-6. Write the program so that the portfolio is maintained as a direct-access file and only the transactions are from cards. Program it in such a way that both a summary report of the transactions and a final position statement are printed.

6   Do problem 5 above using a sequential file.

Science and Engineering

7   A common utility package available at each computer installation is an external file sorting program. The sorting program is frequently used by many other programs and hence is called a system utility. Various techniques exist for doing sorting; one of these is the following. Assume first that two strings of presorted data exist and they are to be merged into one long, sorted string. This can be accomplished by comparing just two records at a time as illustrated in Figure 6-12. If there were two such pairs of strings initially, each pair could be merged into a long string and then those long strings could be merged into a final sorted string. The initial strings can be established by taking a relatively small set of records and sorting them internally by a method such as the bubble sort described in problem 4-7. Write a program which will take a file of unsorted four-digit numbers and sort it as described above. For sample data use either 80 randomly generated numbers or numbers taken from a phone directory. Internally sort groups of 10 numbers to generate the initial strings. Print out the initial unsorted data and the final sorted data.

8   Editing of data files is a common task, and many installations have text editors. As a very rudimentary form of text editing, write a program which will operate upon your program deck from Chapter 5 and separate all comment lines from the rest of the program. Print out three listings: full deck, comments only, and balance of program. Use external files so this can be accomplished in only one run.

9   External files are often established when data sets are expected to become very large. Write a program which can take as input hourly temperatures and add them to a data file on a daily basis. The program should also prepare periodic summary reports on daily maximum, minimum, and average temperatures.

In addition, it should print out the cumulative number of heating or cooling degree-days for the period. These are defined as:

$$\bar{t} = \text{mean temp} = \frac{\text{max temp} - \text{min temp}}{2}$$

degree-day (cooling) $= \bar{t} - 65$

degree-day (heating) $= 65 - \bar{t}$ [Fahrenheit temperatures used here]

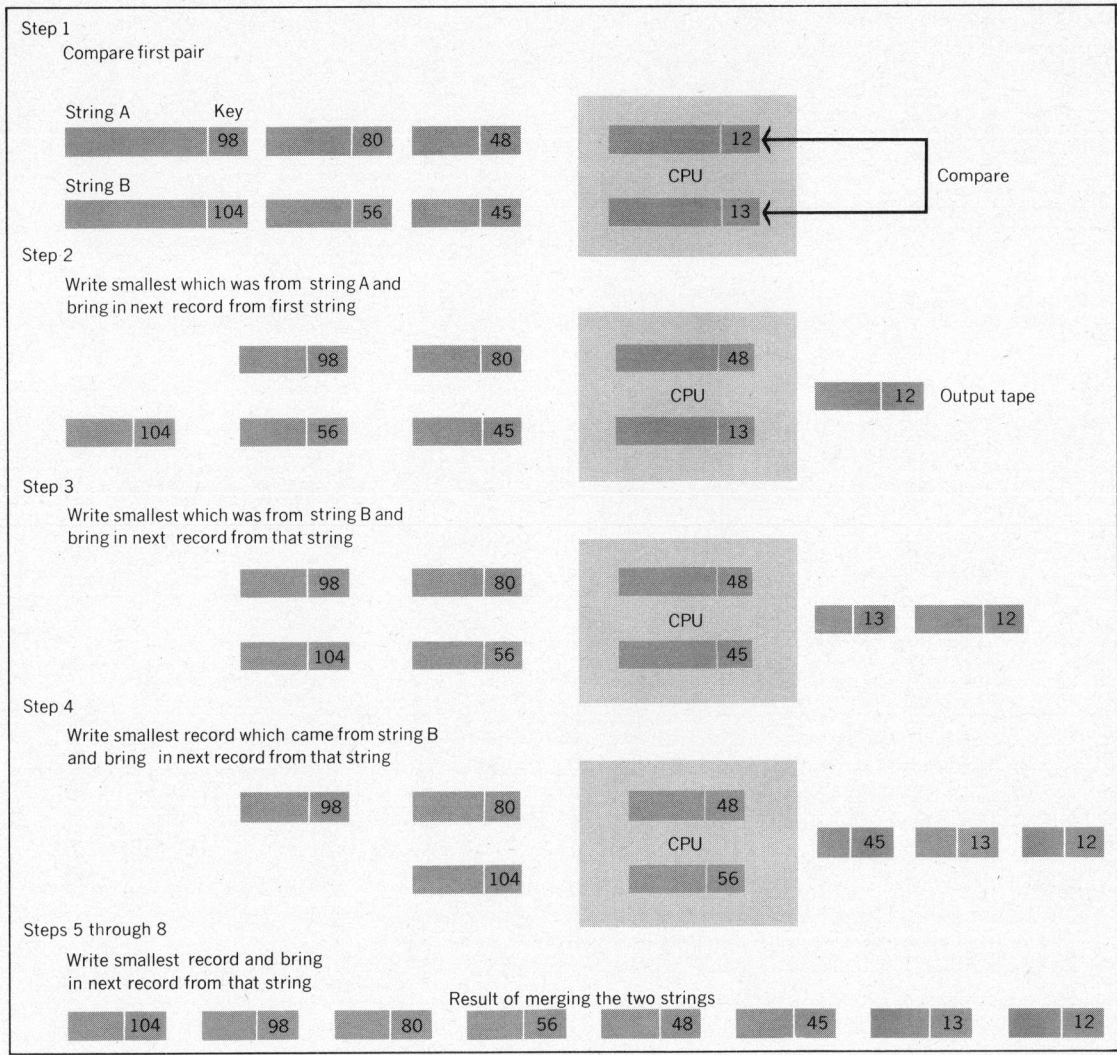

FIGURE 6-12 Logic of merge sorting of presorted strings.

Humanities and Social Science

10 Since the number of respondents to a survey is initially unknown and responses may come in over time, it is often useful to store the data on an external file. Create the file and reprogram problem 10 of Chapter 5 to read response data from such a file.

11 Concordances are usually not done on short texts such as given in problem 11 of Chapter 4. In fact the volume of data may be quite large. Create a text file and reprogram that problem·to read the source text from an external file one line at a time.

12 A study is to be made of the eating habits of a target population. Create two programs: one which will add, correct, and maintain the data file and another which will summarize its contents. The file contains a record for each meal eaten by an individual. The record simply indicates whether or not something from each of the following food groups was eaten at a particular meal.

Dairy products

Cereals

Fruit

Meat

Vegetables

The survey data should indicate the percent of time, for each major meal, that each category was consumed. The summary should be for all subjects or, alternatively, for a selected subject.

General

13 Student grades are a function of homework scores and grades on quizzes and a final exam. Write a program which creates, corrects, and adds to a file of student grades. Consider each of the following columns of data to be update information for the file which must be handled by separate runs of the program.

Name	HW1	Q1	Q2	F
Anderson, Alan	95	67	70	74
Brown, Stewart	95	87	70	80
Carr, David	100	60	80	70
Daly, William	60	65	65	68
Erickson, Jane	45	79	90	87
Gruenzel, Lorna	90	93	87	95
Kohler, Wayne	95	82	80	78
Nelson, Joyce	75	73	75	84
Ray, Ruth	100	85	65	87
Taylor, Alice	50	73	60	75

In addition the following corrections had to be made after the original grade was recorded.

Name	Action
Carr, David	HW1 from 100 to 90
Kohler, Wayne	Q1 from 82 to 87
Ray, Ruth	Q2 from 65 to 73

14 External data files are often maintained because new data is being added over an extended period of time. Write a program which will create and maintain a file of batting statistics for a baseball team. Include times at bat, runs batted in, and hits. Print out updated totals with each change of a record.

15 A personalized dictionary of words or names can be quite useful. In the forthcoming age of personal computers, such files can be quite common. Write a program which will create, correct, and maintain such a file. It should be capable of adding or deleting definitions and, of course, searching for words already in it and printing out the definition. As minimum test data select 15 FORTRAN words or commands from this text and create your own definition of them.

CHAPTER

7A

ADDITIONAL DATA TYPES, CHARACTER STRINGS, AND OTHER FEATURES

This chapter explains two major elements of FORTRAN not previously described—additional data types and character string processing. This chapter also describes additional FORMAT specifiers, some additional statements and features having relatively little use, and some added instructions for subprograms. Some statements that exist but should normally not be used because they impair clear, well-understood programming are also summarized. The features described in the chapter tend not to be required for the most common uses of FORTRAN.

Additional Data Types

The concept of data type was presented in Chapter 2A where the difference between integer and real types was explained. The first letter convention (I-N for integer type data) has been used to identify the two types. The reason for the two types has become more apparent in the programming problems. The two types are based on a need for data having different characteristics. Internally, they are represented differently (although the machine representation is not usually of interest to the FORTRAN programmer). The internal representation of an integer number is exact, whereas the internal representation of a real data item is a processor-dependent approximation which may not be exact for some values of real data.

Four additional types of data are allowed in FORTRAN. The section will explain the four types, their representation, and the way a variable is specified as being of a given type. The four additional data types are character, double-precision, complex, and logical.

1 Character data items store alphabetic, numeric, and special characters in an internal representation which codes each character separately. For example, a street address must be stored as characters. The variable name or names which reference the character data are defined as character-type. Numeric data defined as character type is stored as individual characters and cannot be used directly in arithmetic operations.

2 Double precision data items are real data items which provide more precision (usually double) than the precision of the single precision real variables normally used. This requires two storage spaces for each double precision data item. A single variable name which is defined as double precision type is used to reference the double-length representation. A double precision constant is written in the same form as a constant with an exponent except it is written with a D instead of an E. For example, 0.317657695D-15 and 134565D+50. The reason for double precision is to improve the precision of computation and output. Some compilers use a high precision for single precision variables, and so double precision is rarely needed; but some compilers use fairly limited precision, thus making double precision useful for large numbers.

3 Complex data items are represented by an ordered pair of real data items: one representing the real part and one the imaginary part of a complex number. A complex data constant is written as an ordered pair inside parentheses; for example, (3.5,4.1) where 3.5 is the real part and 4.1 is the imaginary part.

4 Logical data variables assume only values for true or false. Values to input to a logical variable are T (or .TRUE.) or F (or .FALSE.); output of a logical variable is T or F. Logical constants consist of .TRUE. or .FALSE.. For example, if X is defined as a logical variable, X = .TRUE. will set X to the value for true.

The Type Declaration

Integer and real data types may be defined by the first-letter convention, but that convention may be overridden by a type declaration. The four additional data types (CHARACTER, DOUBLE PRECISION, COMPLEX, and LOGICAL) may use any symbolic name (up to six characters) with any first letter. The name chosen for these data types is designated as referring to a given type by a type declaration. The type declaration must appear prior to the first use of any variable it defines. We recommend that it be placed in the storage allocation block at the beginning of the program in which it is used.

TYPE DECLARATION

type $v_1, v_2, \ldots, v_n$

where *type* may be:

   INTEGER
   REAL
   CHARACTER
   DOUBLE PRECISION
   COMPLEX
   LOGICAL

v_i refers to a variable name, array name, array declarator, or function name to be defined as of the stated type

---

Note that the type declaration can be used for a single variable, an array, or a function name. The array can be dimensioned as part of the type statement. Some examples illustrate the type declaration (the CHARACTER declaration will be explained and illustrated later in the chapter):

COMPLEX ALPHA   makes ALPHA refer to a complex type variable

DOUBLE PRECISION X,Y,Z makes X, Y, and Z the names of double precision variables

INTEGER A,B,C   makes A, B, and C integer variable names

REAL INNER,KIX(100)   makes INNER a real variable name and KIX a real array with 100 positions

LOGICAL FLAG   makes FLAG refer to logical data

Some programmers use any data names they wish for real and integer data in the program and then explicitly declare all variables as being real or integer.

They feel that explicit definition is better than relying on the first-letter convention. Our feeling is that the first-letter convention for integer and real is so deeply imbedded in the language that it is confusing to declare an opposite convention and, therefore, type declarations to alter the first letter convention should be used with caution.

It is also possible to alter the first-letter convention by making all variables with a given first letter a declared type. This is the IMPLICIT declaration. It must appear before any other specification statements. When used to make all variable names integer, e.g., IMPLICIT INTEGER (A–Z), it can be useful, but otherwise, it may lead to errors.

IMPLICIT DECLARATION

IMPLICIT type $(C_1, C_2, \ldots, C_n)$ makes any variable name starting with the letter C_i of the declared type

IMPLICIT type $(C_m - C_n)$ makes all characters from C_m to C_n of the declared type

EXAMPLE

```
IMPLICIT INTEGER (A,B), REAL (L-N)
COMPLEX ABLE, BAKER
```

The first statement defines variables with names starting with A or B as integer and variable names starting with L, M, or N as real. Variable names ABLE and BAKER refer to COMPLEX variables even though they begin with A and B because the subsequent type declaration overrides the IMPLICIT declaration.

Additional Intrinsic Functions

There are intrinsic functions to handle arithmetic involving the double precision and complex data types. The generic name or the specific name may be used. In general, the specific name is the same one used for real variables but with a D prefixing double precision functions and a C prefixing complex functions (where complex functions make sense). For example, the SQRT real function is DSQRT for double precision and CSQRT for complex data types. The complete list of functions is given on the inside of the front cover.

Self-testing Exercise 7-1

1 Declare variables YEARS and PERIOD as integer variables and MONTH as a real variable.
2 Declare ALPHA, M, and Y as double precision variables.
3 If ALPHA is declared as a double precision variable, what does this mean in terms of (*a*) storage required and (*b*) precision (explain)?
4 Assume *X* is defined as the type specified and write statements to store the constant value in *X*.

Type	Constant to be stored
(a) COMPLEX	Real value of 4 and imaginary value of 2.1
(b) DOUBLE PRECISION	91.05676500007482
(c) LOGICAL	Value for false condition

5 Take the square root of a double precision variable DRATE. Store the result in DX.

Character Strings

Alphanumeric character strings can be input, manipulated, and output by FORTRAN statements. An implicit method of defining character variables by an A field input was described in Chapter 3. The 1977 FORTRAN drops the very restrictive implicit method (although it is allowed as an optional extension of the language). Many compilers (such as WATFIV) implement the older implicit method as well as the new explicit method. This section describes the 1977 standard FORTRAN features to explicitly define character variables and features to manipulate and output character data. The features remove many of the restrictions of the older implicit method.

Defining a Character String or Substring

The string of characters is assigned a variable name. Variable names assigned to character strings do not have any special first letter. A variable name is explicitly defined as character type by a CHARACTER statement. The CHARACTER statement can be used for individual variable names, for character arrays, and for functions that are to be declared as character type. Variables declared to be CHARACTER by a type statement can be any length because the length is specified by the type statement. Also, variables declared to be CHARACTER can be initialized in a DATA statement.

CHARACTER-TYPE DECLARATION

CHARACTER [*len[,]]name,name,...

where the names may be of the form:

v[*len]   where *v* is variable name or function name
a[*len]   where *a* is an array name
a(d)[*len]   where *a*(*d*) is an array name with a dimension declarator

*len defines the length in characters of the character variable. It must be used unless the length is 1. It is generally an integer constant, but can be an integer constant expression enclosed in parentheses, or an asterisk enclosed in parentheses (a special case for use with a character function).
If *len appears in front of the list of names, the same length applies to all the names which do not have a specified length.

[ ] enclose an optional element

EXAMPLES

CHARACTER * 10 , ANAME , BNAME , R	Defines all variables in list as length 10
CHARACTER A * 10 , B * 6	Defines A as character variable name with length 10; B is length 6
CHARACTER X , NAME * 5	Defines X as character variable of length 1 and NAME as length 5
DIMENSION ARRAY (10) CHARACTER ARRAY * 6 or CHARACTER ARRAY (10) * 6	Dimensions the array and then defines each element in ARRAY as holding a 6-position character string Dimensions 10-element character array of length 6 for each element

Character data can also be assigned by a character assignment statement in the program. The character string is enclosed in apostrophes. For example,

ANAME = 'G .   B .   DAVIS'

stores the name in 11 character positions assigned to the variable name ANAME (already declared to be CHARACTER type and length 11):

G	.		B	.		D	A	V	I	S

Any reference to ANAME will obtain the string of characters. In older FORTRANs, such constants were written using an H; for example,

ANAME = 11HG .   B .   DAVIS

Character data may be stored in character variable locations by the DATA statement explained in Chapter 4. For example:

CHARACTER NAME * 6 , TITLE * 4
DATA NAME / 'ALISON' / , TITLE / 'SOPH' /

In older versions of FORTRAN, the character data items are defined in the DATA statement by an nH followed by the characters. No character type is declared. For example,

DATA NAME / 6HALISON /

defines a value for NAME.

In general, any input or assignment of data into a character variable moves the data beginning at the left. Any unused positions are filled with blanks; any extra characters are truncated and lost. For example, X = Y will give the following results for different lengths of X (both X and Y are character type):

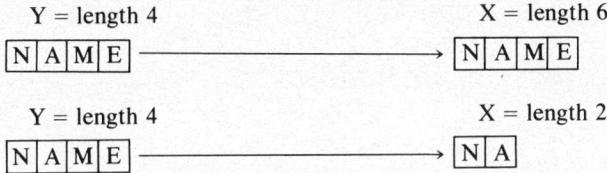

A new 1977 FORTRAN feature is the substring. A character substring is a continuous portion of a character string. It has a name and may be assigned values and referenced. The substring name is followed by the character identification for the first and last characters to be included, separated by a colon. For example, the characters stored in positions 8 to 10 of character variable ALPHA are assigned a substring name BETA by the following:

BETA (ALPHA (8 : 1 0))

Integer expressions can also be used to specify the limits of the substring. For example:

BETA (ALPHA (3 ∗ J I X : 2 0))

where the beginning of the substring is the integer value of 3∗JIX and the end is 20.

Manipulation and Output of Character Strings

Character strings may be compared by using the relational operators. For example, two names stored in NAME1 and NAME2 may be compared to see if they are identical. If so, processing should go to statement 500. NAME1 and NAME2 have been declared as character type.

I F (NAME 1 . EQ . NAME 2)GOTO 5 0 0

If the strings being compared are of unequal length, the logic assumes the shorter one has trailing blanks to make them equal in length.

A character constant may be used in the comparison. For example, a test to see if an input is the word END (and if so, GOTO 600) would read:

I F (WORD . EQ . `END`)GOTO 6 0 0

In older FORTRANs the Hollerith comparison statement might be

I F (WORD . EQ . 3HEND)GOTO 6 0 0

Character strings or substrings can be combined by the concatenation operator //. For example, if A, B, and X are defined as a character type and A and B contain 'NOW' and ' IS', the statement:

X = A / / B

will produce a string X with the value 'NOW IS'. Character constants may be used. For example:

X = 'NOW' / / B

will also yield a stored value in the character variable X of 'NOW IS'.

For output of character data, the program may use A edit specifications with a FORMAT statement, or output may be list-directed, in which case the output will be printed with no spaces, commas, or apostrophes between two successive character outputs. In A editing, an A field size greater than the character variable length will result in leading blanks in the output field; an A field too small for the string will truncate the rightmost characters for output.

Intrinsic Functions for Character Data

There are a number of intrinsic functions designed especially to process character data. Four functions are provided to locate position and length of character data.

Intrinsic function	Argument	Result
LEN (c)	Character variable name	Length of the character string stored in the character variable
INDEX (c_1, c_2)	Character variable names for a string c_1 and substring c_2	Integer giving starting position of first occurrence of substring in string

The n characters in the processor collating sequence are numbered from 0 to n − 1

CHAR (ie)	Integer or integer expression	The character in the integer position
ICHAR (c)	A character variable containing one character	An integer identifying position in collating sequence of the character defined by the argument

EXAMPLES
Assume collating sequence with A = 0, B = 1, etc.

IDL = ICHAR (UNKNON) will yield a value of 6 for IDL if UNKNON stores 'G'.

IDN = CHAR (NCARA) will provide a value of 'F' if NCARA contains 5.

ISTR = INDEX (STR1, STR2) will provide a value of 3 for ISTR if STR1 contains AWFUL and STR2 contains FU.

There are four intrinsic functions for comparing standard lexical relationships of two character strings.

Intrinsic function	Result returns value of true if
LGE (a_1,a_2)	The character string a_1 is equal to or follows a_2 in the collating sequence
LGT (a_1,a_2)	The character string a_1 follows a_2 in the collating sequence
LLE (a_1,a_2)	The character string a_1 is equal to or precedes a_2 in the collating sequence
LLT (a_1,a_2)	The character string a_1 precedes a_2 in the collating sequence

The collating sequence in all cases is defined as the American National Standard collating sequence. Programs using these functions will therefore produce identical results without regard to the collating sequence designed into the computer being used. As an example of the lexical intrinsic functions, assume two character strings named NAME1 and NAME2 containing JENNIFER and CLARK. The instruction

    IF (LGT (NAME1,NAME2)) GOTO 200

will transfer control to statement 200 because JENNIFER follows CLARK in the standard collating sequence.

Self-testing Exercise 7-2

1 Define ANAME and LNAME as character variable names of length 10.
2 Define a five-element character array BARRAY of length 6.
3 Compare a character variable LNAME with the constant CLARK. If equal, go to 600.
4 Define a substring ABREV as characters 1 to 3 of LNAME.
5 Concatenate the contents of ABREV and the constant 'ABC' to form CBREV.
6 Read 10 eight-character names in fields of 8 from a card and store in a 10-element array NAMES.
7 Initialize a character variable FNAME with AARON.
8 An 11-character field MISSISSIPPI is to be printed using a specification of A6. What will be printed?
9 Write statements to read an employee's name from a punched card (columns 1-15) and print it as the heading for an analysis of the employee's performance. The name should be printed starting at column 45.

Advanced FORMAT Features

The basic FORMAT features were explained in Chapter 3. However, the additional data types explained in this chapter require special FORMAT edit descriptors. Also, there are additional FORMAT descriptors that are not commonly used, but they may be useful in special situations. It is also possible to be more flexible in format specification use by storing and referencing them as character variables or character arrays or by writing them in the input or output statement.

Additional FORMAT Edit Descriptors

Before presenting the added edit descriptors, it may be helpful to review the basic edit descriptors already explained (w = field length in characters, d = number of positions to right of decimal, n = integer constant, and h = Hollerith character).

Descriptor	Meaning
Iw	Integer input/output
Fw.d	Real input/output
Ew.d	Exponent form of real input/output
Aw	Character input/output
'h . . .'	Apostrophe form of character output
nHhhh . . .	H form of character output
/	Terminate record
Tc	Tabulate to position c for next output or input
nX	Skip over n positions

These basic edit descriptors are all included in Subset FORTRAN except for Tc. Of the additional edit descriptors, only Lw, BN, BZ, and nP are included in Subset FORTRAN.

A useful alternative to F or E when data values have a wide range is:

Gw.d	Same as F editing for input; compiler chooses E or F editing on output based on data

The FORMAT edit descriptors for the double-precision and logical data types are:

Dw.d	To define input or output editing for double precision data. The output will be similar to F format, but a larger number of digits may be available for use.
Lw	Logical field containing a T (or .TRUE.) for true or F (or .FALSE.) on input and a T or F on output.

Complex data (in two parts) is read by two F, E, D, or G edit descriptors.

There are also added FORMAT edit descriptors to alter the normal editing for input or output.

FOR INPUT

BN	BN specifies blank characters are to be ignored
BZ	BZ specifies blanks are zeros (the normal case in FORTRAN)

Specifies all subsequent handling of blanks in editing of numeric data by the input or output unit

As an example of BN and BZ edit specifications, assume integer data called JCOUNT is defined as being in columns 1–5, but the data has not been right-justified. Using three cards to illustrate, the data will be misinterpreted by an I5 specification.

Card	Data					Interpreted by I5 as
1			3	7		00370
2		1	2			01200
3				1	3	00013

Using a BN specification causes the input system to ignore the blanks:

(B N , I 5 , B Z , . . .)

The BN refers to all subsequent data from the unit, so BZ is used to restore the normal case of blanks interpreted as zeros.

FOR INPUT AND/OR OUTPUT

nP Scale factor. Used with F, E, D, and G fields. The scale factor is an integer constant or an integer constant signed with a minus. The scale factor of n on an input field without an exponent or on an F field for output increases the size of the number by 10^n. On input with an exponent, there is no effect; on output, the decimal point is shifted n places and the exponent adjusted accordingly so that the value is unchanged. Once the scale factor is written, it applies to all succeeding real field descriptors in the FORMAT statement. If normal scaling is to be reinstated, a zero scale factor is written.

The scale factor is most commonly used with an E field to shift the decimal point in the output. For example, if E17.8 causes an answer to be printed out as 0.34769334E+05, then 2PE17.8 will cause an output of 34.76933425E+03.

TLc The next character is input or output c positions backward from (to the left of) the current position. Essentially, this is a backward positioning.

TRc The next character is input or output c positions forward (to the right) from the current position—a forward positioning.

Ew.dEe Used for an exponent form in which the exponent may be more than three digits. The e represents an integer which specifies the number of digits in the exponent. For example, a FORMAT of E22.12E5 allows a 12-digit fraction and a 5-digit exponent. An edited output might be: −0.371945673256E+19050.

: (colon) Terminates format control if there are no more items in the input/output list.

FOR OUTPUT

SP	Print + for positive data for all subsequent data
SS	Do not print + for positive data (The most common default conditions.)
S	Restore + convention used by compiler
Iw.m	m defines minimum number of digits for integer output. Leading zeros may be necessary. For example, at least a three-digit output may be desired even if result is less than three digits. The specification I5.3, if data is 7456, will print as 7456, but if data is 2, it will print three digits or 002.

FORMAT Specifications in Character Storage

Chapter 3 described the FORMAT statement in detail. In some situations, it is useful to store format specifications in a character variable or character array. This allows the program to alter the format specifications themselves as a function of program computations. As an example, suppose an array, IFORM, is initialized with a data statement to contain the following character string (including the parentheses):

```
( 1H 1 , T 9 , 6F 4 . 2 )
```

Assume each character is stored in a separate cell in IFORM, i.e., IFORM(6) = T and IFORM(14) =). It would then be possible to do the following:

```
IF    (LINE   .EQ. 1 ) THEN
      I FORM ( 4 )= ' 1 '
ELSE
      I FORM ( 4 )= ' 0 '
ENDIF
WRITE   ( 6 ,   I FORM )  list
```

IFORM would be used as the format specification and if LINE, a counter, equals 1, the page would be set to the top before printing by the 1H1 in the format. Otherwise double spacing would occur since IFORM would contain:

```
( 1H 0 , T 9 , 6F 4 . 2 )
```

Variable horizontal positioning could be achieved by altering IFORM(7).

Older FORTRAN versions may have similar character capabilities for referencing formats, but with slightly different rules. It is wise to check the implementor manual before attempting to use this feature.

Self-testing Exercise 7-3

1 Write FORMAT statements to print the variables X, Y, Z under each of the following specifications:
   (*a*) Make output as decimal numbers or as exponent form, depending on size of output (eight significant digits).

(b) The variable X is complex type data (field size of 12 with 6 fractional digits for each part of X); field size of 10 with 2 fractional digits for Y and Z.

(c) The output of Y is double precision (16 significant digits).

(d) The output of Z is a logical field (field size of 5).

(e) The plus sign is to be printed for X (field size of 10 with 2 fractional digits) but not Y or Z.

2   Write FORMAT statements for input of A and B when blank characters should not be treated as zeros but are to be ignored.

3   Print the value for X but make it exponent form with an exponent which can be six digits.

4   Summarize the edit descriptors that are included in Subset FORTRAN (and therefore will be generally available on all sizes of computers). Make a separate list of specifiers included only in full FORTRAN.

5   Define an 80-character array called FARRAY that will be used to hold a format specification. Write an output statement to write X and Y using the format specification in FARRAY.

Format Specifications in Input/Output Statement

In 1977 full FORTRAN (but not Subset), the format specifications may be included in the input or output statement as a character constant following the FMT = specifier. The format specifications in parentheses are enclosed in apostrophes. For example, the following are equivalent:

```
      WRITE  (5, 700)  A, B, C
700   FORMAT ('  THE  ANSWERS  ARE',   3F10.2)

      WRITE  (5,  FMT = '('  THE  ANSWERS  ARE',   3F10.2)')
```

Additional Statements and Features

There are a number of additional, useful features that will be described in this section. In general, they are either new with the 1977 FORTRAN or have not received substantial use.

The PARAMETER Statement

The PARAMETER statement is used in full 1977 FORTRAN to give a constant a symbolic name. For example:

```
PARAMETER  FIVE = 5.0,  RATE = 4.3,
HEADING = 'PAYROLL  REPORT'
```

The constant name can be used in any statement to refer to the constant. For example, IF (X .GT. FIVE). . . . But the value of the name cannot be altered by an assignment statement. The statement FIVE = FIVE + 1.0 is not allowed.

Upper and Lower Dimension Bounds

The basic form of the DIMENSION statement is:

```
DIMENSION  (k₁, k₂, . . . , kₙ)
```

The full FORTRAN allows the dimensions *k* to be expressed as an upper and lower bound:

$k_l : k_u$

The value of either bound may be positive, negative, or zero, but the value of the upper bound must be greater than that of the lower bound. This feature is useful in situations where the subscripts reference data but the data does not start at 1. For example, data (called D) for the years 1945 to 1959 can be referenced by subscript as D(1) to D(15) but it might be more meaningful to name it D(1945) to D(1959). By using lower and upper bounds, this can be done.

```
DIMENSION  D(1945:1959)
```

Other situations arise when the subscripts would be more meaningful starting at zero or starting with a negative number. An interest problem over ten periods might have data at time zero, after one period, two periods, etc. A scientific experiment might generate data to be identified as starting at −10 and going to +20.

```
DIMENSION  PERIOD  (0:10)
DIMENSION  EXPRNT  (−10:20)
```

When upper and lower bounds are used, the compiler calculates the space required as (upper bound − lower bound + 1). In the examples above, $10 - 0 + 1 = 11$ and $20 - (-10) + 1 = 31$ storage locations. The subscripts within the bounds are used in the program, and the computer converts them internally to suitable storage references.

One other dimension feature of full 1977 FORTRAN allows constant expressions (expressions using constants and + or − operators) and also exponentiation in dimensions. For example, $5 + 30$ and $10 ** 2$ are allowed.

Logical Equivalence or Nonequivalence

Two additional logical operators were added to the 1977 FORTRAN:

.EQV.   Logical equivalence (expression is true if both expressions connected by .EQV. have same truth value—both are true or both are false)

.NEQV.   Logical nonequivalence (opposite of .EQV.)

The precedence of EQV and NEQV is the lowest logical operator (performed last). For example,

```
   IF  (A.GT.B.EQV.C.LT.D)  GOTO  301
or IF  ((A.GT.B).EQV.(C.LT.D))  GOTO  301
```

In this example, for the IF to be true so control goes to statement 301, A must be greater than B and C must be greater than D (both are true) or A is not greater than B and C is not less than D (both are false).

Main PROGRAM Statement

FORTRAN does not need or require a main program to have a name, but it does allow it. Some operating systems make use of the name, so that it may be required by some computer centers. The naming is performed by a PROGRAM statement which is the first statement of the main program. It consists of the word PROGRAM followed by the symbolic name. For example, a program to be called DAVIS will use the statement PROGRAM DAVIS.

Self-testing Exercise 7-4

1 Write a statement to define SIXTY as always referring to the constant 60.0.
2 A statement in a FORTRAN program reads:

```
IF (A.EQ.100.0.EQV.A.EQ.1.0) GOTO 301
```

For what values of A will the program transfer to statement 301?
3 Data is being collected for women born in the years 1930 through 1945 who now have 0, 1, 2, 3, 4, . . . , up to 18 children. Dimension an array WOMEN with upper and lower bounds for this data analysis.

Additional Subprogram Features

As explained in Chapter 5, subprograms are a useful and versatile feature of FORTRAN. The fundamental features of subprograms were presented in that chapter; this section describes additional features. In general, these features receive less use than the basic features described in Chapter 5.

SAVE Variables for Subprograms

It was noted in Chapter 5 that variables in a subprogram that are not in blank COMMON or in the argument list are lost when control is returned to the calling program. It is possible to save all the data from the subprogram by the SAVE statement.

THE SAVE STATEMENT	
SAVE program unit name	Saves all variables in a unit such as a subroutine, e.g., SAVE SUBA
SAVE variable or array names or named COMMON block name (written within slashes)	Save named items, e.g., SAVE X, Y, /NBLOCK/

Alternate Entry to Subprogram and Alternate Return Points for the Calling Program

The ENTRY statement (in full FORTRAN but not Subset) allows a call to a function subprogram or subroutine subprogram to begin at a point other than the beginning. In essence, ENTRY defines a subprogram within a subprogram. There may be more than one such entry point in a subprogram. At each alternate entry point, the statement is written as ENTRY *en* or ENTRY *en* (dummy argument list) where *en* is the name assigned to the entry point. The call to the alternate entry point uses the name (and appropriate argument list) for the entry point. Program execution begins at the entry and proceeds until a RETURN or END statement is encountered.

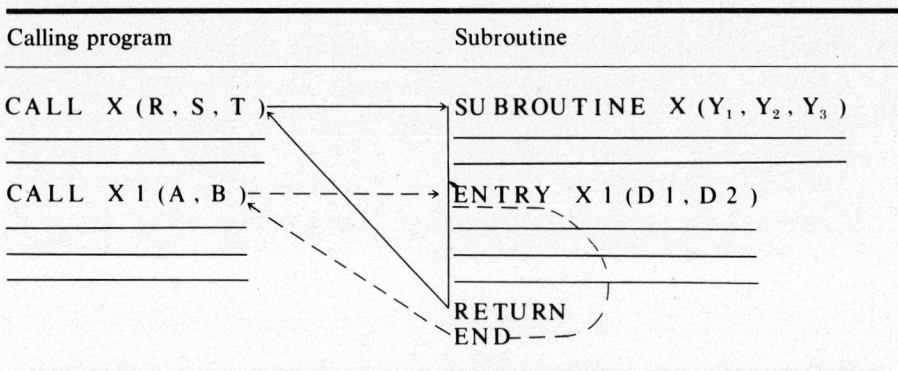

In Chapter 5, the subroutine return was always to the calling statement. In 1977 full FORTRAN facilities were added to allow alternate return points in the calling program. The several return statements are defined by n statement numbers in the argument list of the CALL statement, each preceded by an asterisk. For example:

CALL SUBX (X , Y , * 1 0 1 , * 2 1 0 , * 2 1 5)

This specifies that the first return point (the first in the list) is 101, the second is statement 210, and the third is 215. The RETURN statements in the subroutine must then be numbered 1, 2, and 3. The subroutine dummy argument list contains asterisks to mark the existence of arguments that are alternate returns. If the RETURN statement is not numbered, control returns to the statements following the CALL.

The subroutine is written so that the numbered RETURN statements will be executed only if the return is to be to the alternate return associated with that statement. This approach might be useful in cases where the results of processing by the subroutine should be followed by alternate main program processing.

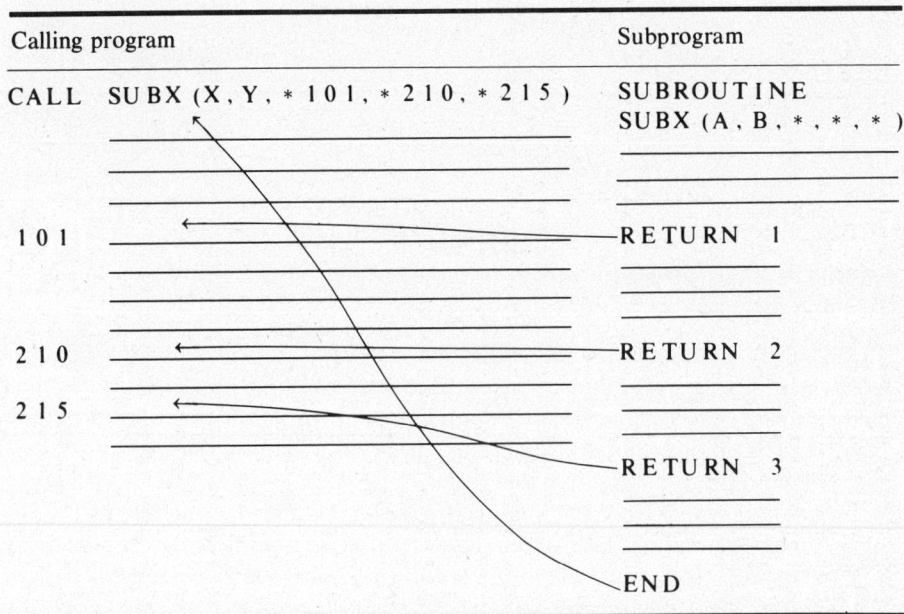

Variable Dimensions

DIMENSION has been previously defined as requiring an integer constant to define the maximum dimension requirements of an array. In a subprogram, DIMENSION statements can be written with an integer variable or an asterisk. The variable is called an adjustable array declarator; the asterisk is called an assumed size array declarator in which the subprogram array takes the size of the calling program array. The integer variable in an adjustable array declaration must have a value (in argument list or in common storage) before execution of the subprogram. This value determines the dimension size for the subprogram. For example:

Subprogram: SUBROUTINE SAMP (I)
              DIMENSION XDATA (I)   Adjustable array declarator
Main: CALL SAMP (100)   Value of I in argument list of CALL

Subprogram and Intrinsic Function Names in an Argument List

There may be programs in which an intrinsic function name, an external function name (i.e., name of function subprogram that is not intrinsic), or a subroutine needs to be used in an actual argument list of a function or subroutine call. The difficulty is that because of their similar form, the compiler cannot distinguish between variable names and function or subroutine names. In order to specify that an intrinsic function name in an actual argument list is to be interpreted as the name of an intrinsic function, the program must contain an INTRINSIC statement. An EXTERNAL statement is used in the same way for names of external procedures (functions or subroutines). The form is the word INTRINSIC or EXTERNAL followed by the name to be declared. As an example, a CALL statement may wish to specify which function (SIN or COS) the subroutine is to use (in place of a function called TRIG). The name SIN or COS is therefore part of the actual argument list. This requires an INTRINSIC statement in the main program to declare SIN and COS as intrinsic function names.

Main program	Subroutine
INTRINSIC SIN, COS	SUBROUTINE DOIT (A, B, TRIG)
CALL DOIT (X, Y, SIN)	
	X = TRIG (~~~~~~~~~)
	END

Self-testing Exercise 7-5

1   Write a subroutine subprogram called XD0 having dummy variables X and Y and I (with value of 0, 1, 2) with entry points at XD01 and XD02. Provide for alternate returns following XD01 and XD02. Code a single assignment statement for XD0, XD01, and XD02 setting X = Y**2 + 1.0 for XD0, + 2.0 for XD01 and + 3.0 for

XD02. Based on the value of I, a call to XD0 will execute the first, second, or third of these statements (value of I is 0 for first, 1 for second and 2 for third).
2 Code a call to XD0 with alternate return to 150 and 160 and actual variables A, B, and J.
3 Code a call to XD01 with actual variables A and B.
4 Save variables A, B, and J used locally in subroutine XDONE.
5 Write subroutine statements for an array ABX with variable dimension JIX. Show the main program statements required (array X in actual argument). Transfer dimension through common storage.

Statements and Features Recommended to Be Used with Care

There are some FORTRAN features that are part of the language, but experience has shown them to be error-prone or not consistent with a disciplined, clear programming style. The arithmetic IF (IF (condition) s_1, s_2, s_3) was explained in Chapter 2 with the recommendation that it not be used. Other features that generally should be avoided are the PAUSE statement, the assigned GOTO, and the statement function.

The PAUSE Statement

The PAUSE or PAUSE n statements are the same as the STOP and STOP n statements in that they cause the program to halt. In the case of PAUSE or PAUSE n, the halt is to be temporary; pressing RUN on the computer console or RETURN on a terminal allows the program to continue. PAUSE was useful in computing situations where results at a given point were to be examined before proceeding with the program. It is generally inconsistent with present computer center operations and will usually be treated the same as a STOP.

Assigned GOTO

Since it is part of the language, the assigned GOTO will be explained, but good programming practice suggests that it should not be used. The reason for advising against its use is that it makes the logic of a program difficult to follow. The assigned GOTO feature is essentially a variable GOTO. There are two statements: the ASSIGN and the assigned GOTO. The ASSIGN statement assigns a statement number to an integer variable.

ASSIGN s TO i

where s = a statement number
       i = an integer variable

EXAMPLE

ASSIGN 23 TO KIX

The assigned GOTO lists the possible statement numbers to which the program may go and specifies the variable which contains the value to be used to specify the current transfer of control.

$$GOTO \quad i(s_1, s_2, \ldots, s_n)$$

where s_i = statement numbers to which control can transfer
$\quad\quad\quad$ i = integer variable containing value of one of statement numbers to which control is to be transferred

As an example, suppose that the program might transfer to statements 13, 21, or 45 and that a variable KIX would specify which of these statements would be used, then the pair of statements to transfer control to 21 would be

```
ASSIGN 21 TO KIX
GOTO KIX (13, 21, 45)
```

The ASSIGN statement can also be used to assign a FORMAT statement number to a character variable which is used as the format reference in an input or output statement. For example, if there are three possible FORMAT statements labeled with statement numbers 360, 370, and 380 that can be selected by an output statement, the selection of 370 can be programmed by the ASSIGN statement as follows:

```
ASSIGN 370 TO FMAT
WRITE (6, FMAT) A, B, JIX
```

The Statement Function

If the same one-statement computation appears several times in a program, FORTRAN allows a statement function to be defined in the program itself instead of using a separate function subprogram. The statement function is used in a program in the same manner as an intrinsic function. The statement function is defined by writing a statement in which the name chosen for the function is set equal to an expression which uses the dummy variables in it. The list of dummy arguments are separated by commas and enclosed in parentheses. The name is formed in the same way as a variable name (begins with I-N for integer, etc.). This statement only defines the function; it is not executed. The definition statement must precede its first use as a function.

In order to use the function that has been defined, the name of the function is written in an expression with the actual variable names to be employed written in place of the dummy variables. The actual variables are listed in the same order and have the same type as the dummy variables. The program will make the computation defined by the function using the values of the actual variables in the argument list. The resulting value will be put into the statement being executed as the value of the function. For example:

Defining statement $DESCF (B, A, C) = (B**2 - 4.0*A*C)$

Using the function $X = BETA + DESCF (ALPHA, Y, Z)$

The effect of the function is the insertion of the function into the statement using the calling variables in place of the dummy variables. In the example, this means that the statement to be executed will perform the following computation:

$$X = BETA + (ALPHA**2 - 4.0*Y*Z)$$

If it is appropriate to use this feature, confusion can be avoided by placing the statement function definition in a separate block preceding any executable statements.

Order of Statements

The order of program statements is as follows:

1. PROGRAM (if used), FUNCTION, SUBROUTINE, or BLOCK DATA. In the block structure style in the text, this statement is the first in the program preceding the identification block.

2. PARAMETER

3. IMPLICIT

4. Type statements

5. Other specifications (DIMENSION, COMMON, EQUIVALENCE, EXTERNAL, INTRINSIC

6. DATA

    In the storage allocation block

7. Statement function definition statement. If used, place in separate block.

8. Executable statements

Comments may appear anywhere in the program. FORMAT statements may appear anywhere after the first group of statements listed above (PROGRAM, FUNCTION, etc.) but, as a matter of style, we have chosen to place them immediately after the first input or output statement in which they are used.

Summary

Three major items were explained in this chapter: additional data types, character and character string processing, and advanced format features. The chapter also summarized advanced features or features having limited use which were not explained in detail.

The additional data types—complex, double precision, and logical—were explained. The type statement is used to declare explicitly which variables are of these types. The first-letter conventions for integer and real can be changed for specific variables by a type declaration or for alternative first-letters by an IMPLICIT statement.

Although FORTRAN was not originally designed for handling characters, useful new features for manipulation of character strings are defined with the 1977 ANS FORTRAN. Character variables can be declared with a type statement. Putting together or concatenation of character strings is performed with a concatenation operator. Strings can also be compared.

There are a number of additional format edit descriptors present in the chapter. In addition, a method in FORTRAN for referencing the list of format descriptors stored as character data was explained. This stored character data reference approach allows more flexible formatting and input of format editing lists as variable data.

Additional statements and features presented were the PARAMETER statement for naming a constant, upper and lower dimension bounds, logical equivalence, and the main PROGRAM statement.

Additional features for subprograms were summarized. These provide for saving of subprogram variables, using intrinsic function and external procedure names in an actual argument list, alternate entry to subprograms, alternate return points, and variable dimensions for a subprogram.

Some statements were explained, but their general use is cautioned. These are PAUSE, assigned GOTO, and the statement function.

Answers to Self-testing Exercises

Exercise 7-1

1 INTEGER YEARS, PERIOD
   REAL MONTH
2 DOUBLE PRECISION ALPHA, M, Y
3 The computer uses a double storage area for a double precision variable. The precision is the number of significant digits that are represented; for double precision variables this is approximately double the precision of a single precision variable.
4 (a) X = (4.0, 2.1)
   (b) X = 91.0567650000784 2D + 00 or
       9.1056765000078 42D − 0 1
   (c) X = .FALSE.
5 DX = DSQRT (DRATE)

Exercise 7-2

1 CHARACTER ANAME * 10, LNAME * 10
2 CHARACTER BARRAY (5) * 6
3 IF (LNAME.EQ. 'CLARK') GO TO 600
   or for older compilers
   IF (LNAME.EQ. 5HCLARK) GO TO 600
4 ABREV = (LNAME (1 : 3))
5 CBREV = ABREV // 'ABC'
6   CHARACTER NAMES (10) * 8
       READ (5, 700) (NAMES (I), I = 1, 10)
   700 FORMAT (10A8)
7 DATA FNAME / 'AARON' /
8 MISSIS
9   CHARACTER EPMN * 15
       READ (5, 700) EMPNM
   700 FORMAT (A15)
       WRITE (6, 710) EMPNM
   710 FORMAT (T45, A15)

Exercise 7-3

1 (*a*) FORMAT (3G 1 6 . 8)
   (*b*) FORMAT (2F 1 2 . 6 , 2F 1 0 . 2)
      (The complex data item requires two FORMAT specifications for the real and imaginary parts.)
   (*c*) FORMAT (F 1 0 . 2 , D 2 3 . 1 6 , F 1 0 . 2)
   (*d*) FORMAT (2F 1 0 . 2 , L 5)
   (*e*) FORMAT (SPF 1 0 . 2 , S 2F 1 0 . 2)
2 FORMAT (BN , F 1 0 . 2 , F 1 0 . 2 , BZ)
3 FORMAT (E 1 9 . 8E 6)
4 See List of 1977 ANS standard FORTRAN statements (following the index).

In Subset FORTRAN	Only in full FORTRAN
Iw	Tc
Fw.d	Gw.d
Ew.d	Dw.d
Aw	Complex
'h...'	TLc
nHh	TRc
/	Ew.dEe
nX	Gw.dEe
Lw	SP
BN	SS
BZ	S
nP	Iw.m

5 CHARACTER FARRAY (8 0)
   WRITE (6 , FARRAY) X , Y

Exercise 7-4

1 PARAMETER SIXTY = 6 0 . 0
2 Both expressions can never be true. If A = 100, it cannot also equal 1.0. However, both expressions can be false and control goes to 301. Thus, control goes to 301 as long as A is neither 100 nor 1.0.
3 DIMENSION WOMAN (1 9 3 0 : 1 9 4 5 , 0 : 1 8)

Exercise 7-5

```
1       SUBROUTINE  XD 0 ( X , Y , I , * , * )
        GOTO  ( 5 0 , 1 0 0 , 2 0 0 ) ,  I + 1
        GOTO  2 5 0
  5 0   X = Y * * 2 + 1 . 0
        RETURN
        ENTRY  XD 0 1  ( X , Y )
1 0 0   X = Y * * 2 + 2 . 0
        RETURN  1
        ENTRY  XD 0 2 ( X , Y )
2 0 0   X = Y * * 2 + 3 . 0
        RETURN  2
2 5 0   PRINT  * ,  'ERROR WITH I' , I
        END
```

```
2  CALL  XD0  (A, B, J, *150, *160)
3  CALL  XD01(A, B)
4  SAVE  A, B, J
5  SUBROUTINE  EXAMPL (ABX)
   COMMON  JIX
   DIMENSION  ABX (JIX)
   _____

   _____

   Main program

   _____

   COMMON  JIX
   JIX=
   CALL  EXAMPL (X)
```

Questions and Problems

1 The programmer got confused. To fix the program, declare all integer variables in a program to be real and all real variables to be integer.

2 Code declaration and input/output to:

(*a*) Read a double-precision variable and print it.

(*b*) Read a complex variable and print it.

(*c*) Read a logical variable and print it.

3 Write a program segment to define the day names, SUNDAY, etc., for the first week in October 1978 and to compare a character input data item (say, MONDAY) to find out which day it is.

4 Write FORMAT statements to read and/or write to produce stated results.

Data		Output
(*a*) Input on cards as	45 13	45.13
(*b*)	0.1765E15	17.65E+13
(*c*)	347.0	+347.
(*d*)	78	0078
(*e*)	.TRUE.	T

5 Explain the use for:

(*a*) PARAMETER

(*b*) PROGRAM

(*c*) Upper and lower dimension bounds

(*d*) Logical equivalence

(*e*) Alternate entry for subprograms and return for subroutines

(*f*) SAVE statement

(*g*) ASSIGN statement (with FORMAT statements)

CHAPTER

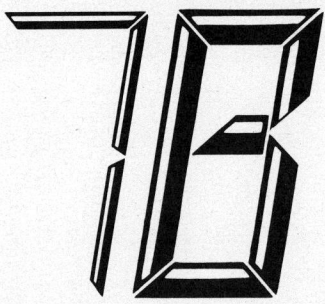

EXAMPLE PROGRAMS AND PROGRAMMING EXERCISES WHICH USE ADDITIONAL FEATURES

General Notes on Chapter 7 Examples

General Program Example 7—Manhattan Island
Problem Description for General Example 7
Program Documentation for General Example 7
Notes on General Example 7

Statistical Program Example 7—Geometric Series
Problem Description for Statistical Example 7
Program Documentation for Statistical Example 7
Notes on Statistical Example 7

Programming Exercises
Description of Assignment
Mathematics and Statistics
Business and Economics
Science and Engineering
Humanities and Social Sciences
General

The example programs illustrate the use of some of the additional data types and other features not frequently used in FORTRAN programs, but which may sometimes be useful or necessary.

General Notes on Chapter 7 Examples

Type declarations such as REAL and INTEGER allow the use of variable names which more clearly identify what they represent or how they are used without regard to the first letter. In some instances, in order to get sufficient accuracy, double precision variables may be required. Special intrinsic functions and data representations will be required for double precision computations. The P edit descriptor is used to move the decimal point in the output.

General Program Example 7—Manhattan Island

This program uses double precision computations in order to accurately find the value of an amount of money compounded over a long period of time. Depending upon the computer on which it is run, this may make a significant difference in the accuracy of the result.

Problem Description for General Example 7

The program is to compute the amount to which the original $24 paid for Manhattan Island in 1626 would have grown by a given year and assuming various interest rates. It is to compare the results obtained by both single and double precision computations. Input consists of a year and an interest rate.

Program Documentation for General Example 7

Full documentation is not given because of the simple nature of the program. The program listing is given in Figure 7-1. The sample input data has not been shown because it is printed as part of the output listing (Figure 7-2).

Notes on General Example 7

REAL, INTEGER, and DOUBLE PRECISION type statements are used to indicate the nature of several of the variable names (lines 1 to 3). Several other variables (e.g., DOLLAR) use the implicit type denoted by the first letter of their names. Double precision constants are found in line 14. Note that $0.4D+1$ is equivalent to $4.0D+0$; either could be used. The exponent (line 14) need not be double precision to achieve a double precision result. The intrinsic function DBLE is used in line 5 to obtain a double precision equivalent of a single precision variable.

Use of the format edit descriptor P is shown in the second and third lines of the FORMAT statement on line 16. In order to print out the decimal fraction percentage interest rate in the common form of a number greater than one, a '2P' is used to modify the F5.1 edit descriptor. In order to restore the multiplier to

```
********** PROGRAM IDENTIFICATION **********
*                                                                    *
*      MANHATTAN ISLAND PROGRAM CALCULATES THE AMOUNT TO WHICH        *
*      THE $24.00 INVESTED IN 1626 TO PURCHASE MANHATTAN ISLAND       *
*      WOULD HAVE GROWN BY A GIVEN YEAR, ASSUMING SOME INTEREST       *
*      RATE AND COMPOUNDING QUARTERLY.  INPUT YEARS LESS THAN         *
*      1626 OR RUNNING OUT OF DATA CAUSE PROGRAM TERMINATION.         *
*      BOTH SINGLE AND DOUBLE PRECISION COMPUTATIONS ARE MADE.        *
*      WRITTEN BY T. HOFFMANN 08/08/1977                              *
*                                                                    *
**********************************************************************
*                                                                    *
********** VARIABLE IDENTIFICATION **********
*                                                                    *
*      YEAR   = YEAR TO WHICH TO COMPOUND                             *
*      IRATE  = INTEREST RATE                                         *
*      DIRATE = INTEREST RATE (DOUBLE PRECISION)                      *
*      NYEARS = NUMBER OF YEARS TO COMPOUND                           *
*      AMOUNT = COMPOUND AMOUNT                                       *
*      AMTDBL = COMPOUND AMOUNT (DOUBLE PRECISION)                    *
*      DOLLAR = AMOUNT PAID FOR ISLAND = $24.00                       *
*      DBLDOL = DOLLAR EXPRESSED IN DOUBLE PRECISION                  *
*                                                                    *
**********************************************************************
*                                                                    *
********** STORAGE ALLOCATION **********
*                                                                    *
1.         REAL IRATE,NYEARS
2.         INTEGER YEAR
3.         DOUBLE PRECISION DIRATE,AMTDBL,DBLDOL
4.         DATA DOLLAR/24.0/
*                                                                    *
**********************************************************************
*                                                                    *
********** INITIALIZATION BLOCK                      BLOCK 0000
*                                                                    *
5.         DBLDOL = DBLE(DOLLAR)
6.         WRITE(6,3)
7.       3 FORMAT(1H1,6X,'MANAHATTAN ISLAND PROBLEM')
*                                                                    *
**********************************************************************
*                                                                    *
********** INPUT AND COMPUTATION                     BLOCK 0100
*                                                                    *
8.     101 READ(5,102,END=301) YEAR,IRATE
9.     102 FORMAT(I4,F3.2)
10.        IF(YEAR .LT. 1626) GOTO 301
11.        NYEARS = FLOAT(YEAR-1626)
12.        DIRATE = DBLE(IRATE)
13.        AMOUNT = DOLLAR*(1.0 + IRATE/4.0)**(4.0*NYEARS)
14.        AMTDBL = DBLDOL*(1.0D+0 + DIRATE/0.4D+1)**(4.0*NYEARS)
*                                                                    *
**********************************************************************
*                                                                    *
********** OUTPUT BLOCK                              BLOCK 0200
*                                                                    *
15.        WRITE(6,202) DOLLAR,YEAR,IRATE,AMOUNT,AMTDBL
16.    202 FORMAT(//5X,'$',F6.2,' INVESTED IN 1626, COMPOUNDED QUARTERLY ',
      1    'THROUGH',I5,', AND'/5X,'AT A RATE OF',
      2    2PF5.1,' PERCENT, WOULD AMOUNT TO'/
      3    1X,'$',0PE20.14,' OR, MORE PRECISELY, $',D30.24)
*                                                                    *
*      GO BACK TO READ ANOTHER DATA CARD                              *
*                                                                    *
17.        GOTO 101
*                                                                    *
**********************************************************************
*                                                                    *
********** TERMINATE                                 BLOCK 0300
*                                                                    *
18.    301 STOP
19.        END
```

FIGURE 7-1 Program listing for general example 7—Manhattan Island.

OUTPUT FROM CONTROL DATA CYBER—VERY HIGH PRECISION

```
        MANAHATTAN ISLAND PROBLEM


     $ 24.00 INVESTED IN 1626, COMPOUNDED QUARTERLY THROUGH 1976, AND
        AT A RATE OF  6.0 PERCENT, WOULD AMOUNT TO
    $ .27081355025273E+11 OR, MORE PRECISELY, $ .2708135502525549781470730+11


     $ 24.00 INVESTED IN 1626, COMPOUNDED QUARTERLY THROUGH 1976, AND
        AT A RATE OF  7.0 PERCENT, WOULD AMOUNT TO
    $ .84800087010391E+12 OR, MORE PRECISELY, $ .8480008701059226314847430+12
```

OUTPUT FROM IBM SYSTEM/370—MEDIUM PRECISION

```
     MANAHATTAN ISLAND PROBLEM

    $ 24.00 INVESTED IN 1626, COMPOUNDED QUARTERLY THROUGH 1976, AND
    AT A RATE OF  6.0 PERCENT, WOULD AMOUNT TO
    $ .27058163712000E 11 OR, MORE PRECISELY, $0.2708134250148970000000000D 11


    $ 24.00 INVESTED IN 1626, COMPOUNDED QUARTERLY THROUGH 1976, AND
    AT A RATE OF  7.0 PERCENT, WOULD AMOUNT TO
    $ .84790371942400E 12 OR, MORE PRECISELY, $0.8479987837387943000000000D 12
```

FIGURE 7-2 Output using two different computers for Manhattan Island problem with double precision processing.

normal for the rest of the values printed out, '0P' must be inserted before the next descriptor—E20.14 in the third continuation line.

Two sets of results from two different computers are given in Figure 7-2—the IBM System/370 and the Control Data Cyber computers. The results from double precision and single precision on the Control Data Cyber computer do not differ as much as the two results on the IBM System/370. These differences reflect the different precision built into the computer designs. The Cyber computer was designed for high-precision, scientific processing; the IBM computer was designed as a general-purpose computer without a need for high precision in most situations. In a problem of this type, the double precision is very important for the medium-precision IBM System/370 and less important for the high-precision CYBER.

It is not meaningful to print out as many digits as are shown. In a problem with figures in the billions, showing data beyond the nearest dollar (or perhaps hundreds of dollars) cannot be justified. The results, however, show the high precision of the CDC machine and show how the IBM computer handles output beyond the data available in the computer. The double precision results beyond 15 digits do not exist in the IBM computer, so they are replaced by zeros on output.

Statistical Program Example 7—Geometric Series

This program example shows the use of a LOGICAL type variable as well as the REAL, INTEGER, and DOUBLE PRECISION types shown in the previ-

```
         **********          PROGRAM IDENTIFICATION            **********
         *                                                              *
         *       TERMS AND SUMS OF GEOMETRIC SERIES WITH FIRST TERM     *
         *       EQUAL TO ONE AND THE RATIO OF SUCCESSIVE TERMS         *
         *       CHOSEN AS EITHER E OR THE RECIPROCAL OF E, DEPENDING   *
         *       UPON WHETHER THE INPUT NUMBER OF TERMS IS PLUS OR MINUS.*
         *       WRITTEN BY T. HOFFMANN 08/08/1977                      *
         *                                                              *
         ****************************************************************
         *                                                              *
         **********          VARIABLE IDENTIFICATION            **********
         *                                                              *
         *       FLAG    = SWITCH -- TRUE = E, FALSE = 1/E              *
         *       TERMS   = NUMBER OF TERMS IN SERIES                    *
         *       INFSUM  = SUM OF INFINITE SERIES OF TERMS              *
         *       RATIO   = RATIO OF SUCCESSIVE TERMS                    *
         *       SUM     = SUM OF FIRST 'TERMS' OF SERIES               *
         *                                                              *
         ****************************************************************
         *                                                              *
         **********          STORAGE ALLOCATION                 **********
         *                                                              *
 1.         LOGICAL FLAG
 2.         INTEGER TERMS
 3.         REAL INFSUM
 4.         DOUBLE PRECISION RATIO,SUM
         *                                                              *
         ****************************************************************
         *                                                              *
         **********          INITIALIZATION                  BLOCK 0000
         *                                                              *
 5.         WRITE(6,2)
 6.       2 FORMAT(1H1,10X,'GEOMETRIC SERIES PROBLEMS')
 7.       3 READ(5,7,END=301) TERMS
 8.       7 FORMAT(I5)
 9.         WRITE(6,4)
10.       4 FORMAT(//' FOR A GEOMETRIC SERIES WITH A RATIO OF')
         *                                                              *
         ****************************************************************
         *                                                              *
         **********          COMPUTATION                     BLOCK 0100
         *                                                              *
11.         IF(TERMS .LT. 0) THEN
12.              TERMS = -TERMS
13.              RATIO = DEXP(-1.0D+0)
14.              FLAG = .FALSE.
15.              INFSUM = SNGL(1.0D+0/(1.0D+0-RATIO))
16.         ELSE
17.              RATIO = DEXP(1.0D+0)
18.              FLAG = .TRUE.
19.         ENDIF
20.         SUM = (1.0D+0 - RATIO**TERMS)/(1.0D+0 - RATIO)
         *                                                              *
         ****************************************************************
         *                                                              *
         **********          OUTPUT                          BLOCK 0200
         *                                                              *
21.         WRITE(6,203) RATIO
22.     203 FORMAT(1H+,37X,D15.8)
23.         IF(FLAG) GOTO 210
24.         WRITE(6,204) INFSUM
25.     204 FORMAT(5X,'THE SUM OF AN INFINITE NUMBER OF TERMS IS',E15.8)
26.     210 WRITE(6,211) TERMS,SUM,RATIO**(TERMS-1)
27.     211 FORMAT(5X,'THE SUM OF THE FIRST',I5,' TERMS IS',D30.24/
        1     19X,'AND THE LAST TERM IS',D30.24)
         *                                                              *
         *       GO BACK TO READ ANOTHER DATA CARD                      *
         *                                                              *
28.         GOTO 3
         *                                                              *
         ****************************************************************
         *                                                              *
         **********          TERMINATE                       BLOCK 0300
         *                                                              *
29.     301 STOP
30.         END
```

FIGURE 7-3　Program listing for statistical example 7—geometric series.

ous example program. It also illustrates the use of an expression in the output list.

Problem Description for Statistical Example 7

Compute the sum of a particular geometric series as well as its last term, given the form of the series and the number of terms. The series is:

$$1 \quad r \quad r^2 \quad r^3 \ldots r^n$$

where r is either e or $1/e$. If it is the latter, then compute also the sum of the infinite series of terms. The number of terms is input; if it is negative, then use the ratio of $1/e$. Compute both single and double precision values for the finite sum and the last term.

Program Documentation for Statistical Example 7

Only the program listing (Figure 7-3) and the output (Figure 7-4) are given. Input data can be inferred from the output values.

Notes on Statistical Example 7

In reviewing the program listing, the following points are of interest:

1 The variable FLAG is declared to be a logical variable (line 1). It is set to .FALSE. in line 14 or .TRUE. in line 18. The logical variable FLAG is tested for the true condition in line 23 by the statement IF(FLAG) . . . .

```
            GEOMETRIC SERIES PROBLEMS


FOR A GEOMETRIC SERIES WITH A RATIO OF .27182818D+01
    THE SUM OF THE FIRST    2 TERMS IS .37182818284590452353 6029D+01
                AND THE LAST TERM IS .27182818284590452353 6029D+01


FOR A GEOMETRIC SERIES WITH A RATIO OF .27182818D+01
    THE SUM OF THE FIRST   20 TERMS IS .28235484213022628381 56030+09
                AND THE LAST TERM IS .17848230096318726084 49100+09


FOR A GEOMETRIC SERIES WITH A RATIO OF .36787944D+00
    THE SUM OF AN INFINITE NUMBER OF TERMS IS   .15819767E+01
    THE SUM OF THE FIRST   20 TERMS IS .15819767036086294044 0787D+01
                AND THE LAST TERM IS .56027964375372675400 1298D-08


FOR A GEOMETRIC SERIES WITH A RATIO OF .27182818D+01
    THE SUM OF THE FIRST   10 TERMS IS .12818308050524604210 0284D+05
                AND THE LAST TERM IS .81030839275753840077 1000D+04


FOR A GEOMETRIC SERIES WITH A RATIO OF .36787944D+00
    THE SUM OF AN INFINITE NUMBER OF TERMS IS   .15819767E+01
    THE SUM OF THE FIRST   10 TERMS IS .15819048852379486698 7859D+01
                AND THE LAST TERM IS .12340980408667954949 7637D-03
```

FIGURE 7-4 Sample output from geometric series problem with double precision results.

The flag is used as a program switch to determine whether the infinite sum line (lines 24 and 25) should be printed.

2 The variable TERMS which would normally be a real variable is declared as integer and INFSUM is declared to be real (lines 2 and 3). In line 4, RATIO and SUM are declared to be double precision.

3 When TERMS is read, the format specification is I5 (lines 7 and 8).

4 The expression with RATIO (line 13) uses a double precision exponential function DEXP and a double precision constant $-1.0D+0$.

5 INFSUM is a real, single precision variable, so double precision results are explicitly converted to single precision in line 15 by the SNGL conversion function.

6 The computation of the last term in the series is written in the output list as (RATIO**(TERMS-1)) in line 26.

Programming Exercises

Select one or more problems (or take the problem(s) assigned by your instructor). Write each of the programs so as to use features described in this chapter. Follow the style guidelines and prepare the following:

1 Pseudocode description
2 Program flowchart
3 Program listing
4 List of test data and expected results. Test for both valid and invalid data.
5 Output including testing for error conditions.

Mathematics and Statistics

1 Refer to problem 4-1. Make use of at least the PARAMETER statement.
2 Refer to problem 4-2. Make use of at least the INTEGER type statement and FORMAT specifications in character storage to print the output in the usual equilateral triangle shape.
3 Refer to problem 5-3. Make use of at least the Statement Function.

Business and Economics

4 Refer to problem 6-4. Make use of at least the LOGICAL and INTEGER type statements.
5 Refer to problem 4-5. Make use of at least the P format edit descriptor and the PNYRND function subprogram of general example 6 as a Statement Function.
6 Refer to problem 5-6. Make use of at least the Statement Function.

Science and Engineering

7 Refer to problem 4-7. Make use of at least the LOGICAL type statement.
8 Refer to problem 5-9. Make use of at least the PARAMETER statement and the Statement Function.
9 Refer to problem 6-9. Make use of at least the INTEGER and REAL type statements.

Humanities and Social Sciences

10 Refer to problem 4-12. Make use of at least the PARAMETER statement and INTEGER type statement.

11 Refer to problem 5-11. Make use of at least the DOUBLE PRECISION type statement and corresponding double precision intrinsic functions and the Statement Function.

12 Refer to problem 6-12. Make use of at least the LOGICAL and IMPLICIT statements.

General

13 Refer to problem 6-13. Make use of at least the LOGICAL and IMPLICIT statements.

14 Refer to problem 5-14. Make use of at least the IMPLICIT and REAL statements.

15 Refer to problem 6-15. Make use of at least the IMPLICIT statement and alternate entry feature.

APPENDIX

HOW TO USE
THE CARD PUNCH

Students of computer data processing frequently need to be able to operate the keydriven card punch, either to keypunch their programs or to make corrections in previously punched card decks. The purpose of this appendix is to aid in these activities; therefore, it covers only the basic elements of using the card punch. There are many features for facilitating its use which will not be explained. A person learning to be a keypunch operator needs additional training information not contained here.

The three most common card punches are the IBM Model 129, the IBM Model 29, and the IBM Model 26 printing card punches (Figure A-1). The Model 26 was the standard card punch until 1960; the Model 29 was introduced in 1960 in conjunction with IBM's System/360 computers; the Model 129 is similar to the 29 in keyboard but uses an internal buffer (memory) to hold the card contents as they are being keyed. In the Model 129 (and other buffered card punches), when the keying of data is complete for a card (and corrections have been made, if necessary), the card is punched from the data in the buffer. The punching occurs while the next card is being keyed, thus reducing the waiting time found on the nonbuffered 26 and 29 models. The features of the Model 129 buffered card punch are most significant for commercial keypunching. Occasional users are more likely to use a Model 29 (or a Model 26 because many of these older units are still in service). Other vendors supply keypunches with the same (and additional) features. The explanation to this appendix will concentrate on the Model 29 but with some attention to the IBM Model 26.

The alphabetic characters on the keypunch keyboard are identical to those on a typewriter. This means that a person who can type can keypunch alpha-

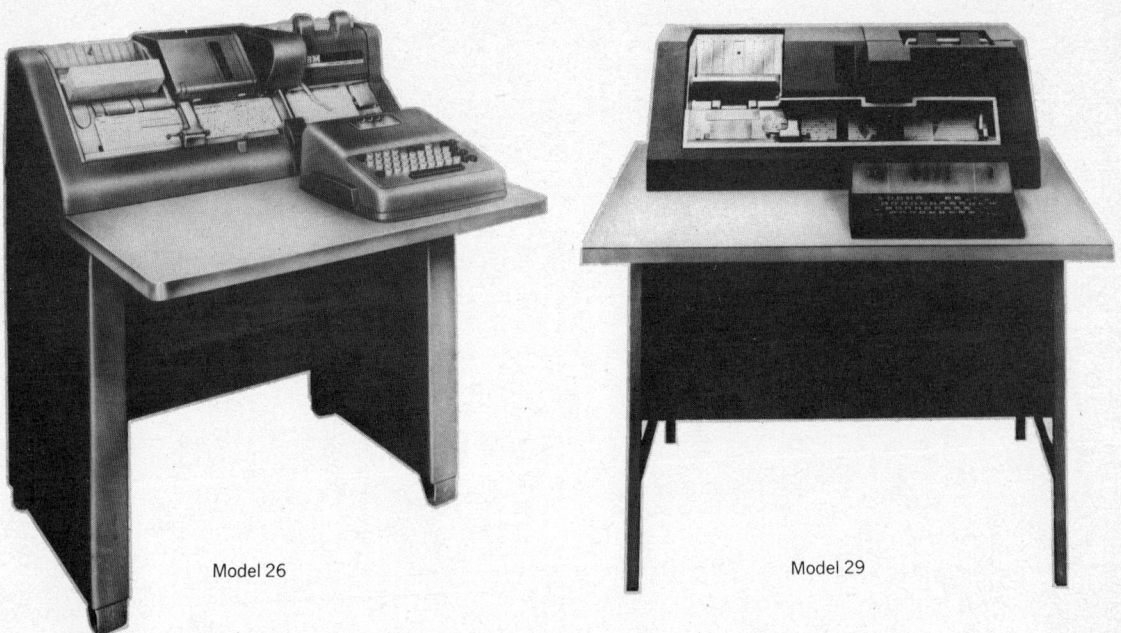

Model 26

Model 29

FIGURE A-1   IBM Model 26 and Model 29 card punches. *(Courtesy of International Business Machines Corporation.)*

Model 29

Model 26 with scientific keytops

FIGURE A-2 Keyboards of IBM Model 29 and Model 26 card punches.

betics without learning any new keying (Figure A-2). The numbers 1 to 9 are arranged so they can be punched with three fingers of the right hand.

There are differences between the Model 29 (and 129) and the older Model 26; these are differences in punching of the special characters. On Models 29 and 129 there are different punch patterns for each of 28 special characters, and each character has a unique position on the keyboard. The Model 26 has only 11 special characters with the same punch codes being used for five pairs of different characters—one set of characters termed *commercial* and the other set identified as *scientific*. The differences in the keyboards for Model 26 are as follows:

348 APPENDIX

MODEL 26 KEYBOARD AND
PRINTING CHARACTERS

Commercial	Scientific (FORTRAN)
#	=
&	+
%	(
⌼	)
@	' (apostrophe)

The punches are the same for either of each pair of characters; the only difference is the keytop character and in the printing character which is printed on top of the card when it is punched. This means that a user needing to punch the FORTRAN statement IF(X.GT.Y)X = 0 on a Model 26 commercial keyboard can get the correct punches by punching IF%X.GT.Y⌼X#0.

The use of the card punch is facilitated by features which perform functions that otherwise must be done manually. The beginner may wish to start out by doing punching without using these features and then, as more proficiency is developed, begin to use these aids to increase punching speed. The use of the card punch will therefore be described at three levels:

1 Punching without making use of the automatic features.

2 Punching with use of the automatic feed but not using a program card.

3 Punching with a program card.

Punching without Use of Automatic Features

The "on-off" switch for the card punch is on the inside of the right leg for the Model 29 and at the upper left in the card stacker for the Model 26.

On the panel directly above the keytops, there are six toggle switches on a Model 29 and three switches on a Model 26 (Figure A-3). Turn the AUTO SKIP DUP and AUTO FEED switches off (down). Turn the PRINT switch on. On a Model 29, the LZ print should be on; the PROG SEL and CLEAR are not used. In the upper part of the card punch, directly below the window showing a cylinder (program drum), there is a small program-control lever. Depress this lever to the right to deactivate the program-card mechanism.

Blank cards to be punched are placed in the card hopper at the upper right; cards which have been punched are moved by the card punch into a card stacker, at the upper left, from which they can be removed. The path of a card through the card punch is shown in Figure A-4.

Note, in Figure A-2, the three keys at the right-hand side of the keyboard labeled REL, FEED, and REG. These are the release, feed, and register keys. Using these keys, punching a card is performed as follows:

1 Press FEED key to move one card from the card hopper to the entrance to the punching station.

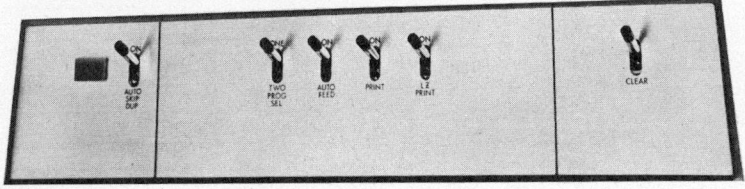

FIGURE A-3 Functional control switches for Model 29 and Model 26 card punches.

2 Press REG key to move the card into position for punching.

3 The card is punched serially (column by column) by striking the proper keys. The keyboard operates normally in alphabetic mode (the bottom character is punched if more than two are shown on a keytop). To obtain the upper character, which includes all the numerics, the numeric shift key at the lower left of the keyboard must be depressed while striking the keys. Columns may be skipped by depressing the space bar.

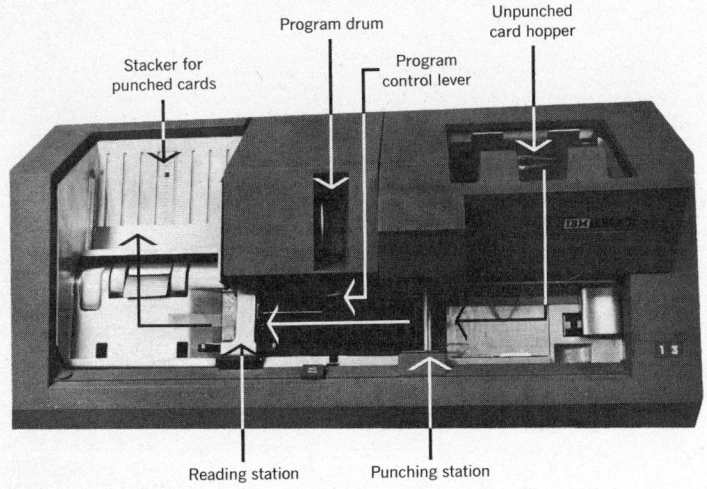

FIGURE A-4 Path of card through the card punch.

4   When all punching has been performed, the card is moved to the reading station by pressing REL.

5   If only one card is to be punched, immediately pressing REL and REG will move the card from the reading station to the card stacker where it can be removed.

If a card needs to be corrected, a damaged card needs to be replaced, or a card is to be duplicated, the card to be reproduced is manually inserted against the card hopper by depressing FEED (or a card is inserted manually at the punching station). Pressing the REG key will then register both cards. Depressing the DUP (duplicate) key will cause the punches in the card at the reading station to be punched into the card at the punching station. If one or more columns are to be omitted or altered from what is found in the card being reproduced, the operator depresses the space bar or keyboard characters instead of the duplicate key for the columns to be omitted or altered. The next column to be punched or duplicated is read from the column indicator in the opening which contains the program control drum.

Punching with AUTO FEED

If many cards are to be punched, the feeding of cards can be speeded up by using the AUTO FEED option. When this is on, it causes a new card to be

FIGURE A-5   *(a)* Program drum and *(b)* program drum in place. *(Courtesy of International Business Machines Corporation.)*

automatically fed and registered each time the card being punched is released. Since this provides a continuous supply of cards at both the punching and reading stations, it is turned off in order to insert a card to be duplicated or corrected.

Punching with a Program Card

In punching applications, there are repetitive operations—for example, the starting of the punching of a field at a certain column, the duplication of certain information from the prior card, or the switching to numeric or alphabetic for a group of columns. The program card allows these functions to be done automatically.

The program card is a regular punched card which is wrapped around the program drum. Control punches in the top five rows are read by program star wheels (Figure A-5) and cause certain functions to be automatically performed. On a Model 29 a second program may be punched lower in the same card. The second program is selected by the PROG SEL switch. This should be on ONE to use the control cards explained here. A small lever on the keypunch is depressed to the left to activate the program card and to the right to deactivate it. Some common control punches are:

Punch	Function
none	Beginning of numeric field to be manually punched.
1	Beginning of field and shifts keyboard to alphabetic mode with program control; the card places the keyboard in numeric mode unless this control punch is used. Used like a typewriter tab stop.
0	Starts automatic duplication (0 plus 1 starts automatic duplication of alphabetic field—punched as /) — AUTO SKIP DUP toggle switch must be "on" for duplication or skipping.
11 (minus punch)	Starts automatic skipping.
12 (& punch or + on Model 26 scientific)	Defines the columns for which the preceding punches apply. An & is used for a numeric field and A for alphabetic field (12 and 1 punches).

An example will illustrate the use of a control card. In punching a FORTRAN program, the first column is used to indicate a comment line, the next four columns are for a statement number (numeric). Column 6, indicating a continuation of a statement, is rarely used. Columns 7 to 72 are for alphanumeric punching, with alphabetics most common. Columns 73 to 80 are for identification (optional).

A control card for punching a FORTRAN program will illustrate the use of control cards and will make it easier to punch the FORTRAN programs assigned in this text using the suggested style.

Columns	
1	Used to indicate a comment line by a C or *
2–5	Used on some statements for a numeric statement label (except for comment cards)
6	Used very infrequently to indicate continuation. The control card will skip past it; if there is to be a punch in column 6, backspace one space
7	Start of punching for statements
11	Start of punching for indented statements and for imbedded comments
72	Last usable column for statement. If comment line is a comment block, an asterisk is punched (for style in this text)
73–80	Either duplicate an identification or skip. The sample control card duplicates an identification into each card (say programmer's initials and problem number or identification)

See Figure A-6 for an example control card. The FORTRAN control card causes the card to be in alphabetic mode for column 1 and in numeric mode for columns 2 to 6. Pressing the SKIP key repeatedly moves the card first to position 7, to 11, to 72, and finally to 73. When 73 is reached, the next 6 positions are automatically duplicated. When punching FORTRAN under program card control (and with the AUTO SKIP DUP switch on), there will be no need to manually skip the card to margins. The first column has either an * or c or a space. If punching is to start in column 7, pressing the SKIP once will position the card at that margin. If the FORTRAN statement is to be indented at column 11 or a comment is to be punched, pressing SKIP again will move the card to column 11. After punching the statement or comment, pressing SKIP again will move the card to column 72 (where, if it were a comment, an * would be punched). Pressing the space bar once moves the card to column 73, at which point the next eight columns are duplicated, the card is moved out, and a new card is brought into place.

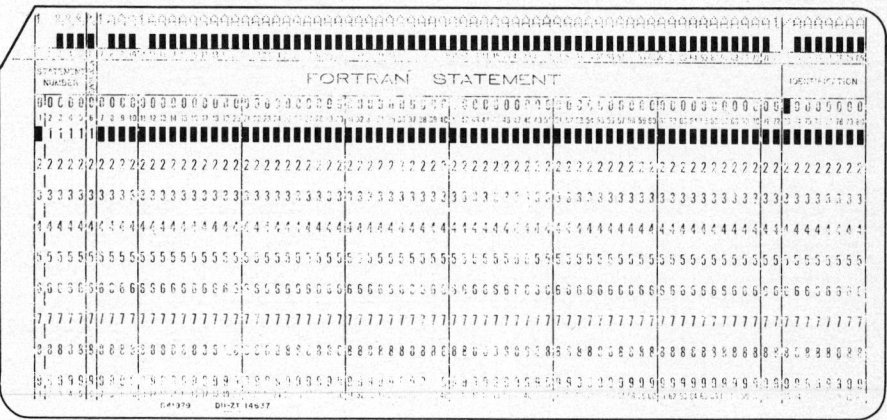

FIGURE A-6 Example of program card for punching FORTRAN programs.

Other Keys and Controls

The MULT PCH (multiple punch) key is for use when a punch combination not found for the machine is to be punched. If, for example, an 11, 5, 8 punch combination is to be punched on a Model 26, the MULT PCH key is depressed, and 11, 5, 8 are punched. The multiple punch key keeps the card from advancing in order to allow the three digits to be punched in one column.

The backspace control is a small rectangular button between the reading station and the punching station. Depressing the control backspaces one column.

On a Model 29 (but not on the 26) there are two additional switches not normally used by the student. If the LZ PRINT is OFF, it suppresses the printing of leading zeros in a field. The switch should usually be on for the student user. The CLEAR switch is a spring switch which causes all cards then in process to be moved through to the stacker without feeding any new cards.

APPENDIX

FORTRAN
PROGRAMMING
FROM A TERMINAL

The trend in programming is toward the use of terminals by both programmers and users. The terminal may be a teletypewriter or a visual display unit (often called a CRT). The terminal may be used for one or more of the following:

1 Original entry of program statements

2 Correction of a program already entered (through the terminal or by a separate input on cards)

3 Input of data

4 Instructions to execute (run) the program

5 Output of messages from program and operating system

6 Output of results from program

The advantages are reductions in elapsed time for programming, faster corrections and checkout cycles, etc. The disadvantages are a somewhat less efficient use of computer resources and a tendency to rely too heavily on the computer to do debugging.

The FORTRAN at a terminal is essentially the same as with cards; the major differences are the result of the difference in physical characteristics between terminals and line printers. Early terminals and those most common today are limited to a line width of 72 or 80 positions. They print at speeds of 10, 15, or 30 characters per second in contrast to line printer speeds of 1 to 4 lines per second where each line may be up to 120 or 132 characters wide. In addition, the terminal does not have vertical spacing control based upon the character $(0, +, 1)$ in column 1; hence column one is available for printing.

In an effort to overcome the limitations and capitalize on the advantages of interactive terminals, various compiler writers have modified the FORTRAN standards. There is no standard to cover these modifications, and hence the following remarks describe typical changes but anyone using FORTRAN from a terminal should refer to the local documentation for specific instructions.

Following are some major features of terminal (time-sharing) FORTRAN.

1 Each line of the FORTRAN program must be assigned a terminal identification and sequencing line number (different than the optional FORTRAN statement numbers) generally a five-digit number between 00001 and 99999. In other words, the terminal identification and sequencing line number precedes the FORTRAN coding on each line. These line numbers are usually not sequential (1, 2, 3, etc.) but rather spaced out (10, 20, 30, etc.) to allow for insertion of correction lines or additional code lines. FORTRAN statements are rearranged in numerical order by identification and sequencing number before compilation. This means that statements may be inserted between others or in place of others in a previously entered program merely by specifying a line number that is in the desired sequence:

Line No.   FORTRAN statement

| 00100 | 1 3 7 | X = Y + Z |
| 00110 | | R = 1.75 * SQRT(X) |

If a line coded X = X + 1.0 is to be inserted between these two lines, it can be coded later in the program as:

```
00105        X = X + 1.0
```

The operating system will arrange the statements, so line 105 will be inserted between 100 and 110.

2 The second major difference is that free-form input is allowed. That is, the convention of using particular columns for statement numbers and others for code are relaxed. If the column immediately following the line number contains a plus sign, it is considered a continuation of the previous line. If it contains anything else except a blank, it is interpreted as a comment line. If it is blank, then the balance of the line is considered a FORTRAN coding line. Immediately following the blank may be either a statement label number or a FORTRAN statement. For example, a short program might be entered as follows. Note comment lines, continuation (lines 110 and 120), and statement label (line 100).

```
00080* THESE COMMENT LINES DESCRIBE
00090* THE FOLLOWING CODE. NOTE THE
00095* FREE FORM INPUT.
00098 READ *, Y, Z
00100  105 X=Y+Z
00110 R=1.75*
00120+SQRT (X )
00130 PRINT*, Y, Z, R
00140 STOP
00150 END
```

3 The number of characters available in a line of FORTRAN coding may still be 72 characters (as with a standard manual coding form), but the characteristics of the terminal and compiler may make this smaller or larger.

4 Data to be entered from a terminal for program execution should generally use a list-directed input; it is difficult to format input data using a terminal, since it usually does not indicate at which column the print head is located. In addition, for each READ statement the system generates a question mark at the terminal to prompt the user for input data. To assist the user in responding to the READ a message should be printed by the program before the READ. To enter data in response to the request for input, the value is typed in followed by striking the ''carriage return'' key. No data, but just a carriage return may be interpreted the same as an end of file (or end of data) in a card (batch) system.

5 Output to a terminal may be formatted, but the area available for output is often limited to only 72 or perhaps 80 characters per line. However, some newer terminals do have full line-printer-width carriages. Using the terminal requires additional system-specific information which therefore cannot be included in this text. These procedures are to:
(a) Log onto the terminal. This includes user number, user password, etc.
(b) Specify that the statements to follow will be a FORTRAN program and give it an identifying name.
(c) Enter statements.
(d) Specify compilation and execution of the program.
(e) Specify correction of statements in a program.

(*f*) Specify corrected program execution.

(*g*) Input data as needed.

Figure B-1 shows a listing of a simple program as written at a terminal and Figure B-2 shows the dialog between a programmer at a terminal and the computer (command to run, input of data, and output).

Free-form entry of the FORTRAN coding lines at the terminal includes a relaxation of some of the style features associated with card input. In Figure B-1 note the reduced number of asterisks on comment headings and the location of the block number designation. The free form of the code lines is especially illustrated in lines 270, 280, 360, and 440. In line number 270 the FORTRAN

```
00100*****       PROGRAM IDENTIFICATION
00110*
00120*    THIS PROGRAM COMPUTES THE AMOUNT TO WHICH AN INITIAL
00130*    PRINCIPAL COMPOUNDS AT VARIOUS INTEREST RATES.
00135*    WRITTEN BY T. HOFFMANN  08/07/1977
00140*
00150*****       VARIABLE IDENTIFICATION
00160*
00170*    PRINCE = INITIAL PRINCIPAL
00180*    RATE   = INTEREST RATE
00190*    YEARS  = NUMBER OF YEARS TO COMPOUND
00200*    FREQ   = ANNUAL  FREQUENCY OF COMPOUNDING
00210*    AMOUNT = COMPOUND AMOUNT AFTER YEARS
00220*
00230*********
00240*
00250*****       BLOCK 0100      READ IN DATA
00260*
00270 101 PRINT *, 'WHAT IS YOUR PRINCIPAL AMOUNT'
00280 READ(5,*,END=401) PRINCE
00290 IF(PRINCE .LE. 0.0) GOTO 401
00300 102 PRINT *, 'WHAT IS THE INTEREST RATE'
00310 READ *, RATE
00320 IF(RATE .GE. 1.0) GOTO 901
00330 PRINT *, 'FOR HOW MANY YEARS, AND HOW OFTEN PER YEAR'
00340 READ *, YEARS,FREQ
00350*
00360*****       BLOCK 0200      COMPUTE COMPOUND AMOUNT
00370*
00380 AMOUNT = PRINCE*(1.0 + RATE/FREQ)**(YEARS*FREQ)
00390*
00400*****       BLOCK 0300      PRINT RESULTS
00410*
00420 WRITE(6,310) PRINCE,RATE,YEARS,FREQ,AMOUNT
00430 310 FORMAT('$',F8.2,' AT RATE OF',F6.4,' FOR',F4.0,
00440+    ' YEARS, COMPOUNDED',F3.0,' TIMES PER YEAR',/6X,
00450+    ' AMOUNTS TO $',F10.2//)
00460*
00470*    GO BACK TO READ MORE DATA
00480*
00490 GOTO 101
00500*
00510*****       BLOCK 0400      TERMINATION MESSAGE
00520*
00530 401 PRINT *, 'NORMAL STOP.'
00540 STOP
00550*
00560*****       BLOCK 0900      ERROR MESSAGE
00570*
00580 901 PRINT *, 'INTEREST RATES MUST BE LESS THAN 1.00'
00590*
00600*    GO BACK TO RE-READ INTEREST RATE
00610*
00620 GOTO 102
00630*
00640 END
```

FIGURE B-1   Listing of a FORTRAN program entered at a terminal.

```
User      { RUN
command

System    { 78/01/03. 14.47.08.
response  { MNF      PROGRAM    TSPROG


            WHAT IS YOUR PRINCIPAL AMOUNT
          ? 1000
            WHAT IS THE INTEREST RATE
Note      { ? 6
error       INTEREST RATES MUST BE LESS THAN 1.00
handling    WHAT IS THE INTEREST RATE
          { ? .06
            FOR HOW MANY YEARS, AND HOW OFTEN PER YEAR
          ? 5,4
          $ 1000.00 AT RATE OF .0600 FOR  5. YEARS, COMPOUNDED 4. TIMES PER YEAR
                  AMOUNTS TO $    1346.86


            WHAT IS YOUR PRINCIPAL AMOUNT
          ? 5000
            WHAT IS THE INTEREST RATE
          ? .055
            FOR HOW MANY YEARS, AND HOW OFTEN PER YEAR
          ? 3,4
          $ 5000.00 AT RATE OF .0550 FOR  3. YEARS, COMPOUNDED 4. TIMES PER YEAR
                  AMOUNTS TO $    5890.34

Note use
of value  { WHAT IS YOUR PRINCIPAL AMOUNT
to end    { ? -1
program     NORMAL STOP.

            CP      0.539 SECS.
System    { RUN COMPLETE.
message
```

FIGURE B-2 Dialog at execution of program from a terminal.

statement label starts in column 7; in line 280 the instruction itself starts in column 7. In line 360 the asterisk in column 6 (or it could have been a C) means that the entire line is a comment; in line 440 the + sign in column 6 indicates the continuation of the previous line.

When the program is run, the PRINT statement in line 270 is executed first to ask for the data to be input and the READ statement in line 280 causes a question mark to be printed. Since the user does not have control over the printing of the question mark, it is good style to write all the print statements preceding requests for input as questions rather than declarative sentences ("What is . . . ," rather than, "Enter data") so that the question mark makes grammatical sense to the user.

As suggested, list-directed input (lines 280, 310, 340) is used for input and a format-directed output statement is used for the printing of the results (line 420). The program terminates on either an END condition caused by a carriage return without data (line 280) or a negative input value for the principal (line 290). Line 135 was added at the end of the program but the compiler inserted it in the proper position for the listing and computation.

After typing in RUN, the system responds with the date, time, compiler, and program names before compiling and executing the program. This response is somewhat different for every time-sharing system. At the conclusion of the program, the system prints the message 'CP 0.539 SECS.' and 'RUN COMPLETE'. These system-dependent responses indicate how much central processor time was used to compile and execute the program and that the system considers the job run to be complete. If a program error were detected, an error message would print. A correction can be made immediately by typing the line number to be corrected and a corrected FORTRAN statement.

APPENDIX

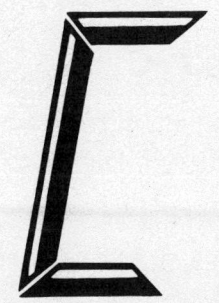

DIFFERENCES BETWEEN VERSIONS OF FORTRAN

Differences between 1977 Standard FORTRAN and 1966 Standard FORTRAN

Full 1977 FORTRAN Features not Included in 1977 Subset FORTRAN

Differences between WATFOR/WATFIV and 1977 Standard FORTRAN for Chapters 1 through 5

Differences between MNF and 1977 Standard FORTRAN for Chapters 1 through 5

Structured Instructions in WATFIV-S

The 1966 American National Standard FORTRAN was a landmark in the development of the FORTRAN language because the language, which began in the late 1950s, was codified into a standard version. During the period 1966 to 1977, many implementors of FORTRAN made enhancements to the language. Among the most significant developments were WATFOR and WATFIV, student-oriented FORTRAN compilers developed by the University of Waterloo in Ontario, Canada, for use on IBM System 360 and 370 computers. A student-oriented FORTRAN comparable to WATFIV, called MNF, was also developed at the University of Minnesota for use on large-scale Control Data computers. Another interesting development is WATFIV-S, a special version of WATFIV containing instructions for use in structured programming. The 1977 FORTRAN can be viewed as an enhancement of the 1966 standard FORTRAN, including most of the added features in WATFOR, WATFIV, MNF, and other compilers. The 1977 standard has a simplified version called Subset FORTRAN.

This appendix summarizes the language changes and enhancements from 1966 to 1977 standard FORTRAN, and compares the subset version with the full 1977 FORTRAN. It also compares both WATFOR/WATFIV and MNF with the fundamental features of 1977 FORTRAN presented in Chapters 1 through 5 of the text. The WATFOR/WATFIV and MNF comparison does not include the less commonly used file processing, character manipulation, etc., instructions described in Chapters 6 and 7. The features of WATFIV-S are described and compared with the standard. In general, a programmer is advised to check the reference manual for the compiler being used to learn the specific, current implementation of new features.

Differences between 1977 Standard FORTRAN and 1966 Standard FORTRAN

The newest 1977 American National Standard FORTRAN specifications are used in this text. The updated standard is generally compatible with the old 1966 standard, but there are a few conflicts. Also, new features have been added. These differences and additions will be listed in relationship to the text chapters.

Text chapter	Feature in 1977 FORTRAN	Conflict	New feature
1	List-directed input/output		X
2	Use of generic intrinsic function names		X
	Generic names MAX and MIN		X
	Block IF (IF...THEN...ELSE...ENDIF)		X
	Mixed-mode expressions		X
3	READ fs, list and PRINT fs, list		X
	Apostrophe edit descriptor		X
	T edit descriptor		X
	END for end of data and ERR for data error		X
	The + or − required before exponent in E field	X	X
	Dropping of restricted method for handling character (Hollerith) data	X	
	Expression in output list		X

Text chapter	Feature in 1977 FORTRAN	Conflict	New feature
4	Use of any integer arithmetic expression for subscript (limited to $i \pm k$, $k * i$, and $k * i \pm k$ in 1966 FORTRAN)		X
	DO loop index can be integer or real variable (instead of only integer variables)		X
	DO loop parameters may be negative, real variable, or integer or real expression (instead of only an integer or integer variable)		X
	If DO loop termination parameter value is greater than initial value, loop will not be executed (undefined previously)		X
	Comma in DO statement after statement number allowed but optional, e.g., DO s [,] $i = m_1, m_2, m_3$		X
	Transfer of control into range of a DO statement not allowed	X	
5	Comma optional before control variable in computed GOTO, e.g., GOTO(s_1,s_2)[,]i		X
	Any integer expression allowed as index for computed GOTO		X
6	OPEN, CLOSE, and INQUIRE statements		X
	UNIT = and FMT = control specifiers		X
7	Additional intrinsic functions—ACOS, ANINT, ASIN, CHAR, COSH, DACOS, DASIN, DCOSH, DDIM, DNINT, DPROD, DSINH, DTAN, DTANH, ICHAR, IDNINT, INDEX, LEN, LOG, LOG10, NINT, SINH, and TAN		X
	IMPLICIT declaration		X
	Dropping of Hollerith constant using H statement	X	
	Dropping of reading into Hollerith format descriptor	X	
	CHARACTER data type		X
	Concatenation operator		X
	Substrings		X
	Lexical relationship functions—LGE, LGT, LLE, and LLT		X
	Additional format edit specifications BN, BZ, Ew.dEe, Iw.m, Gw.dEe, TRc, TLc, S, SP, SS, and :		X
	FORMAT specifications in character storage		X
	FORMAT in input/output statement		X
	PARAMETER statement		X
	Upper and lower bounds for dimensions		X
	Exclusive OR (EQV and NEQV)		X
	PROGRAM statement		X
	SAVE statement		X
	Alternate entry and alternate return points for subroutines		X
	Variable dimensions		X
	INTRINSIC statement		X

Full 1977 FORTRAN Features Not Included
in 1977 Subset FORTRAN

The differences between the full FORTRAN and Subset FORTRAN will generally be significant for smaller computers. The differences are arranged by book chapter.

Chapter	Feature not included in Subset
1	List-directed input and output
2	Generic function name
3	ERR specifier READ *fs*, list and PRINT *fs*, list Tc format edit descriptor Expressions in output list
4	More than three subscripts (full FORTRAN allows seven subscripts) Array element reference or function reference in subscript DO variable can be real variable DO parameters can be integer or real expressions Implied DO loops in DATA statement (also, DATA statement must follow specification statement but precede executable statements in Subset) Real variables allowed in implied DO loop as index and parameters
5	Index expression of a computed GOTO may be an integer expression BLOCK DATA subprogram
6	Formatted direct-access records CLOSE statement INQUIRE statement OPEN (except for use with ACCESS = DIRECT and RECL = record length)
7	Double precision and complex types Double precision and complex expressions and intrinsic functions LEN, CHAR, and INDEX functions Unequal length for character variables Asterisk length specifier for character functions Character functions Substring Concatenation operator FORMAT edit descriptors—Iw.m, Dw.d, Gw.d, Gw.dEe, Ew.dEe, Tc, TLC, TRC, S, SP, and SS Format scan terminator (colon) UNIT = and FMT = control specifiers Use of character variables or array elements as format specification PARAMETER statement Lower bounds for array declarator SAVE statement without a list ENTRY statement Alternate return from subroutine

Differences between WATFOR/WATFIV and 1977 Standard FORTRAN for Chapters 1 through 5

WATFOR is a more restricted version of FORTRAN than WATFIV. The differences between these two versions and 1977 FORTRAN are summarized only for Chapters 1 through 5 of the text; most of the features in Chapters 6 and 7 are available (such as sequential file instructions and the explicit method of character variable definition, but for the new or advanced features, the user needs to have access to the specific installation specifications.

Chapter	Comments on WATFOR and WATFIV
1	List-directed input and output is written in WATFIV without an asterisk, e.g., READ,list. WATFIV allows multiple assignment statements of the form v1 = v2 . . . = expression on one line. This is not allowed by the 1977 standard.
2	The block IF is not supported by WATFIV.
3	WATFIV (but not WATFOR) allows list-directed I/O statements of the form READ(unit,*,ERR=s,END=s) list and WRITE(unit,*) list. These are the same as the 1977 standard. The WATFIV statements DUMPLIST and ON ERROR GOTO are not allowed in the standard. The implied method of defining character variables is permitted; the explicit method (Chapter 7) is also available.
4	Full FORTRAN allows real index variable in a DO loop and real or integer expressions as DO parameters; these are not allowed by WATFOR or WATFIV. It is possible to end a DO loop on a transfer of control in WATFOR/WATFIV, this is not allowed in 1977 FORTRAN. The WATFIV statement, NAMELIST//, is not allowed by the standard.
5	Variables in both blank and named (labeled) COMMON can be initialized by DATA statements; in the 1977 FORTRAN, only named COMMON can be initialized by DATA statements and only with a BLOCK DATA subprogram.

Differences between MNF and 1977 Standard FORTRAN for Chapters 1 through 5

MNF version 5, the version of MNF available in early 1978, allows all standard features described in Chapters 1 to 5. It also allows some nonstandard features such as multiple assignment statements and initialization of named COMMON with a DATA statement.

Structured Instructions in WATFIV-S

WATFIV-S is a structured programming version of WATFIV. It contains six sets of instructions to program the structured patterns described in Chapter 1 in FORTRAN without using GOTO instructions. Only one of these structured instructions, the block IF, has been incorporated in 1977 Standard FORTRAN (but slightly altered). The remaining instructions are therefore nonstandard, and our recommendation is not to use nonstandard instructions.

Structured instruction	Format of instruction

1 Block IF or IF DO instruction	IF (condition) THEN DO
	        statements
	ELSE DO
	        statements
	END IF

2 WHILE DO loop instruction	WHILE (condition) DO
	        statements
	END WHILE

3 The DO CASE statement	DO CASE 1
	        statements for case$_1$
	CASE
	        statements for case$_2$
	CASE
	        statements for case$_3$
	CASE
	        statements for case$_n$
	IF NONE DO
	        statements for case greater than n
	END CASE

4 EXECUTE A REMOTE BLOCK A block of code in a program is given a name by the REMOTE BLOCK statement and the end of the block is delineated by an END BLOCK statement The block is executed by an EXECUTE statement	REMOTE BLOCK name statements in block END BLOCK EXECUTE name-of-block
5 WHILE EXECUTE instruction	WHILE (condition) EXECUTE block name
6 AT END DO instruction When the end of file or end of input is detected, the program will execute the block of code between AT END DO and END AT END	READ( ) ⌇⌇⌇⌇⌇⌇⌇ AT END DO statements END AT END

INDEX

LIST OF
1977 AMERICAN
NATIONAL STANDARD
FORTRAN STATEMENTS
AND SPECIFICATIONS

SYMBOLS USED IN LIST OF STATEMENTS

Shaded	Not included in 1977 Subset of standard FORTRAN	n	An integer number of five digits or a character constant
A	Name of an array	s	Statement number label
d	Places to right of decimal in FORMAT	st	Statement
		u	Unit designator (integer constant or variable) for I/O statement
e	Expression		
f	Subprogram name or statement function name	v	Variable name (either real or integer)
		vk	Variable or constant (either real or integer)
fs	FORMAT statement number label	vek	Variable or expression or constant (either real or integer)
i	Integer variable		
ie	Integer variable or integer expression	w	Field width in FORMAT statement
ik	Integer variable or integer constant	[ ]	Optional item in statement
iek	Integer variable, integer expression, or integer constant		
k	Constant of any type		

EXECUTABLE STATEMENTS

Reference in text	Description of statement	Form	Example
	ASSIGNMENT		
	Assignment		
	v = e		
	Operators:		
	+ addition		
	− subtraction or negation		
	* multiplication		
	** exponentiation		
	// concatenation		
	where e =		
24–27, 56–59	arithmetic expression		$X = 5.0 + Y * Z ** 2$
318	character string		$NME = `NAME`$
319–320	character substring		$STRNG = SUB1 // SUB2$
315	logical variable		$SWITCH = .TRUE.$
330–331	Assignment of statement label	ASSIGN s TO i	ASSIGN 201 TO ILABEL
	TRANSFER OF CONTROL		
61–62	Unconditional GOTO	GOTO s (or GO TO s)	GOTO 910
233–236	Computed GOTO	GOTO $(s_1, s_2, \ldots, s_n)[,]i$	GOTO (210, 260, 320), INDX
		GOTO $(s_1, s_2, \ldots, s_n)[,]ie$	GOTO (210, 260, 320), I + (3 * J)
330–331	Assigned GOTO	GOTO $i(s_1, s_2, \ldots, s_n)$	GOTO ILABEL (320, 415, 210)
70	Arithmetic IF	IF (e) s_1, s_2, s_3	IF (SIN (X) + 0.3) 250, 350, 210
		(s_1 if e = negative, s_2 if zero, s_3 if positive)	
63–66	Logical IF	IF (e) st	IF (A.EQ.0.0) B = B + 1.0
		Where e is a relational expression or logical expression	IF (SWITCH) STOP
63–64		Relational operators:	
		.LT. Less than	
		.LE. Less than or equal	IF (X.GT.Y) GOTO 350
		.EQ. Equal	IF (X.LE.Y) Z = Z + 1.0
		.NE. Not equal	
		.GT. Greater than	
		.GE. Greater than or equal	

64–65		Logical operators: .NOT. Logical negation .AND. Logical conjunction .OR. Logical inclusive disjunction .EQV. Logical equivalence .NEQV. Logical nonequivalence	IF (X.GT.Y.AND.Y.EQ. 17.0) GOTO 260
326			

66–69	Block IF	IF (e) THEN
		  statement block
		ELSE
		  statement block
		ENDIF (or END IF)
			IF (IVAR.GE.JVAR) THEN
			  J2 = J2 + 1
			  K2 = J2 ** 2
			ELSE
			  KIX = JIX / 2
			ENDIF

66–69	Nested Block IF		IF (IVAR.GE.JVAR) THEN
			  J2 = J + 1
			  KJ = KJ ** 2
			ELSE
			  KIX = JIX / 2
			  IF (KIX.EQ.0) THEN
			    PRINT*, KJ
			  ELSE
			    PRINT*, J2
			  ENDIF
			ENDIF

66–69	ELSEIF	ELSEIF (e) THEN
		(or ELSE IF)
			IF (X.LT.3.5) THEN
			  KTR = KTR + 1
			  GOTO 260
			ELSEIF (X.GT.4.7) THEN
			  NTR = NTR + 1
			  GOTO 310
			ELSE
			  GOTO 710
			ENDIF

27	Stop with no restart	STOP [n]	STOP or STOP 3 or STOP 'ERROR'
320	Pause with restart	PAUSE [n]	PAUSE or PAUSE 2
27	End of program unit	END	END
	LOOP		
166–176	Establishing parameters	DO s[,]i = ik_1, ik_2, [ik_3] DO s[,]v = vek_1, vek_2, [vek_3]	DO 210 I = 1, N 3 DO 210 X = .01, 3.0*Y, .05
167	Define end of DO loop	s CONTINUE	210 CONTINUE

EXECUTABLE STATEMENTS *(continued)*

Reference in text	Description of statement	Form	Example
	INPUT AND OUTPUT		
21–22	Read, list-directed and predefined unit	READ *[,list]	READ *, X, I
112	Read, list-directed	READ (u, *)[list]	READ (5 , *) X , I
113	Read, format-directed and predefined unit	READ fs[,list]	READ 160, X, I
110–114	Read, with control list	READ (u,fs, control specifiers)[list] Control specifiers: END = s ERR = s For others, see text	READ (5 , 1 6 0 , END = 5 1 0 , ERR = 9 2 0)
129–130			
130			
278, 280	Read, unformatted (from files on external storage)	READ (u)[list]	READ (10) X , I
275			
22–24	Write, list-directed and predefined unit	PRINT*,[list]	PRINT , X , I , 'TOTAL'
112	Write, list-directed	WRITE (u, *)[list]	WRITE (6 , *) X , I , 'TOTAL'
110–114	Write, format-directed	WRITE (u,fs)[list]	WRITE (6 , 210) X , I
113	Write, format-directed and predefined unit	PRINT fs[,list]	PRINT 210, X , I
277–280	Write, with control list	WRITE (u,fs, control specifiers)[list] See text for control specifiers List (for any WRITE) may include constants and expressions	WRITE (6 , 210 , ERR = 910) X , I
130, 278,			
280, 325			WRITE (6 , 210) X , X ** 2 , 3 , 14
275	Write, unformatted (to files on external storage)	WRITE (u)[list]	WRITE (10) X , I
278–283	Files on external (auxiliary) storage (see text for details)	REWIND, BACKSPACE, ENDFILE, OPEN, CLOSE, and INQUIRE	REWIND 7 ENDFILE 8
	SUBPROGRAMS		
219–222	Transfer to function	Use function in statement	X = MYFNCT (Y , M) + 3 . 1 7 5
224–227	Transfer to subroutine	CALL subroutine CALL subroutine (argument list)	CALL DOIT CALL DONT (X , I , J)
328	Transfer to subroutine with alternate returns	CALL subroutine (argument list with *s for each alternate return statement number)	CALL STAT (A , Y , * 2 1 0 , * 3 4 0)
321	Return to calling program	RETURN	RETURN
328	Alternate returns	RETURN n	RETURN 2
327–328	Alternate entry points to subroutine	ENTRY name [argument list]	ENTRY ALT 3 (SAM)

FORMAT SPECIFICATIONS

Both Subset and Full FORTRAN

Reference in text	Specification symbol	Form	Specifies
115-121	F	Fw.d	Real data
115-121	E	Ew.d	Data in exponent form
115-121	I	Iw	Integer data
128-129	A	Aw	Character data, specified field width
128-129	A	A	Character data, field width based on data
123-124	X	wX	Skipping of field
131-133	/	///,...]	Skip to next unit record, or skip over n − 1 unit records
124-126	H	nH,...	Hollerith character (n = number of characters following H)
124-126	''	'characters'	Hollerith
322-324	L	Lw	Logical data
322-324	B	BN	Blanks on input ignored
322-324	B	BZ	Blanks are input as zero
322-324	P	nP	Scaling (nP precedes F, E, or D specification)

Full FORTRAN only

Reference in text	Specification symbol	Form	Specifies
115-121	E	Ew.dEe	Exponent of e digits
115-121	I	Iw.m	Integer data with at least m field length
322-324	G	Gw.d	Either E or F edit depending on data
322-324	G	Gw.dEe	Exponent of e digits depending on data
322-324	D	Dw.d	Double precision data
123-124	T	Tc	Tabulating to character location c
322-324	T	TLc	Tabulate backward c position from current position
322-324	T	TRc	Tabulate forward c positions from current position
322-324	S	S, SP, SS	S, SP, SS positions from current position. SP = print plus, SS = do not print +, S return to processor option
			Terminates FORMAT control if no more data items in list

CONTROL CHARACTERS FOR VERTICAL SPACING

Character in position 1 of output	Vertical spacing before output
Blank	One line (single space)
0 (zero)	Two lines (double space)
1	To first line of next page
+	No advance

NONEXECUTABLE SPECIFICATIONS OR DECLARATIONS

Reference in text	Description of specifications or declaration	Form	Example
114–124 131–134	FORMAT of data	fs FORMAT (specifications) (see separate specifications list on prior page.	210 FORMAT (F10.0, 2X, 'TOTAL')
178–179	Initialization	DATA $v_1, v_2, \ldots/c_1, c_2, \ldots/$ $k * c$ represents k values of c Implied DO loop in DATA statement	DATA X, Y, Z, A /1.0, 3.5, 2*0.0/ DATA (G(I), I=1, 10) /10*0.0/
160–162	Dimension of maximum size of array	DIMENSION $A_1(k_1), A_2(k_1, k_2),$ $A_3(k_1, k_2, k_3), \ldots$ Limited to 3 dimensions in Subset and 7 in full FORTRAN	DIMENSION A(100), B(5, 15, 3)
325–326		Upper and lower bound for a dimension In subprograms, the subscripts for dummy variable may be integer variables and asterisks	DIMENSION D(-3:12)
230–231	Define data-names in blank common storage	COMMON [//] $v_1, v_2, \ldots$ A(k) allowed where k is dimension as in DIMENSION	COMMON A, B, I or COMMON //A, B, I COMMON A(100), B, I
230–231	Define data names in named COMMON	COMMON/name/$v_1, v_2, \ldots$	COMMON /ABLOCK /X, M, O
231–232	Define data-names as using same storage	EQUIVALENCE $(v_1, v_2, \ldots)(v_3, v_4, \ldots)\ldots$	EQUIVALENCE (C, D), (I, N)

315–316	Define type of data	type $v_1, v_2, \ldots v_n$ A(k) allowed where A(k) is an array of dimension k. type may be: INTEGER REAL COMPLEX LOGICAL DOUBLE PRECISION	INTEGER G,ZED REAL IX,JON REAL IX(50),JON(2,3,5) LOGICAL SWITCH
317–318	Define type and length	CHARACTER [*length,] name	CHARACTER *10,LNAME
316	Define first letter as type	IMPLICIT type $(a_1, a_2, \ldots a_n)$ or $(a_1 - a_n)$	IMPLICIT INTEGER (A,B,R-T)
325	Equate constant and name	PARAMETER name = constant	PARAMETER FIVE=5.0
329	Define names as being function names	EXTERNAL list of routine names	EXTERNAL MYFUN
329	Define names as being intrinsic function names	INTRINSIC list of intrinsic functions	INTRINSIC SIN, COS
326–329	Main program (optional)	PROGRAM name	PROGRAM XAMPLE
331–332	Statement function declaration	$f(x_1, x_2, \ldots, x_n) = e$	CALC(A,B)=A**2+SIN(B)/4.0
219–227	Function subprogram	FUNCTION $f(x_1, x_2, \ldots, x_n)$	FUNCTION EOQ(S,C1,C2,CP)
224–227	Subroutine without arguments	SUBROUTINE f	SUBROUTINE X
224–227	Subroutine with arguments	SUBROUTINE $f(x_1, x_2, \ldots, x_n)$	SUBROUTINE X(A,I,M)
328	Subroutine with alternate returns	SUBROUTINE $f(x_1, x_2, \ldots, *, *, \ldots)$	SUBROUTINE XED(X,I,*,*)
230–231	Block data subprogram	BLOCK DATA [name]	BLOCK DATA A1
327–328	Optional entry into subprogram	ENTRY $f(x_1, x_2, \ldots, x_n)$	ENTRY N1(X,ALPHA)
327	Save data from subprogram	SAVE or SAVE list	SAVE X,L,M

JOB CONTROL CARDS FOR COMPILATION AND EXECUTION OF A FORTRAN PROGRAM ON YOUR COMPUTER

1

2

3

4

5 Program deck (last card is END statement) is placed here

6

7

8 Data cards (if any) are placed here

9

10

OTHER INSTRUCTIONS: